CW01082221

CHANGING PARADIGMS IN HISTORICAL AND SYSTEMATIC THEOLOGY

General Editors
SARAH COAKLEY RICHARD CROSS

CHANGING PARADIGMS IN HISTORICAL AND SYSTEMATIC THEOLOGY

General Editors: Sarah Coakley (Norris-Hulse Professor of Divinity, University of Cambridge) and Richard Cross (John A. O'Brien Professor of Philosophy, University of Notre Dame)

This series sets out to reconsider the modern distinction between 'historical' and 'systematic' theology. The scholarship represented in the series is marked by attention to the way in which historiographic and theological presumptions ('paradigms') necessarily inform the work of historians of Christian thought, and thus affect their application to contemporary concerns. At certain key junctures such paradigms are recast, causing a re-consideration of the methods, hermeneutics, geographical boundaries, or chronological caesuras which have previously guided the theological narrative. The beginning of the twenty-first century marks a period of such notable reassessment of the Christian doctrinal heritage, and involves a questioning of the paradigms that have sustained the classic 'history-of-ideas' textbook accounts of the modern era. Each of the volumes in this series brings such contemporary methodological and historiographical concerns to conscious consideration. Each tackles a period or key figure whose significance is ripe for reconsideration, and each analyses the implicit historiography that has sustained existing scholarship on the topic. A variety of fresh methodological concerns are considered, without reducing the theological to other categories. The emphasis is on an awareness of the history of 'reception': the possibilities for contemporary theology are bound up with a careful re-writing of the historical narrative. In this sense, 'historical' and 'systematic' theology are necessarily conjoined, yet also closely connected to a discerning interdisciplinary engagement.

This monograph series accompanies the project of *The Oxford Handbook of the Reception of Christian Theology* (OUP, in progress), also edited by Sarah Coakley and Richard Cross.

NOW AVAILABLE

Calvin, Participation, and the Gift
The Activity of Believers in Union with Christ
J. Todd Billings

FORTHCOMING

The Holy Spirit
Lewis Ayres

Newman
and the
Alexandrian Fathers

Shaping Doctrine in
Nineteenth-Century England

BENJAMIN JOHN KING

OXFORD
UNIVERSITY PRESS

OXFORD
UNIVERSITY PRESS

Great Clarendon Street, Oxford OX2 6DP

Oxford University Press is a department of the University of Oxford.
It furthers the University's objective of excellence in research, scholarship,
and education by publishing worldwide in

Oxford New York

Auckland Cape Town Dar es Salaam Hong Kong Karachi
Kuala Lumpur Madrid Melbourne Mexico City Nairobi
New Delhi Shanghai Taipei Toronto

With offices in

Argentina Austria Brazil Chile Czech Republic France Greece
Guatemala Hungary Italy Japan Poland Portugal Singapore
South Korea Switzerland Thailand Turkey Ukraine Vietnam

Oxford is a registered trade mark of Oxford University Press
in the UK and in certain other countries

Published in the United States
by Oxford University Press Inc., New York

British Library Cataloguing in Publication Data

Data available

Library of Congress Cataloging in Publication Data
Library of Congress Control Number: 2008942633

Typeset by SPI Publisher Services, Pondicherry, India
Printed in Great Britain
on acid-free paper by
the MPG Books Group

ISBN 978-0-19-954813-2

1 3 5 7 9 10 8 6 4 2

For Mum. For Dad.
Deo Gratias.

Preface and Acknowledgements

The British and Americans, it has been said, are predisposed to be Whigs with regard to the past. Because of their own political and economic history, they tend to see all history as ever changing and, in spite of setbacks, growing better. The only question is whether to be a 'fast Whig' or a 'slow Whig'.

John Henry Newman, a Tory in most of his attitudes, was a 'slow Whig' in his view of Christian doctrine. On the face of it, Newman was no believer in progress, for things were as likely to grow corrupt as to develop; yet Newman's frequent focus on change and renewal reflects a lifetime that spanned the nineteenth century and witnessed enormous religious, political, and economic change in Britain. Newman's first book showed that Christian doctrine was not static but had a history: the Council of Nicaea changed what had gone before, in some ways for the worse (moving from the days when no formula was needed to define the faith) and in other ways for the better (enabling the Church to confound heretics). Then, in the middle of his life, Newman became the most famous proponent of the development of doctrine in Britain and America. Finally, towards the end of his life, in the introduction to *The Via Media*, he wrote of the Catholic Church: 'it is her special duty... to keep up and to increase her various populations in this ever-dying, ever nascent world, in which to be stationary is to lose ground, and to repose is to fail' (*VM* i, pp. lxxx–lxxxi). Newman was, therefore, a slow Whig, who saw organic growth as inevitable, if not always an improvement. And at each stage—young Tractarian, middle-aged proponent of doctrinal development, elderly Cardinal—it was to the Alexandrian Fathers that Newman turned to make sure that contemporary growth was rooted in orthodox truth. Yet, he adapted his understanding of those Fathers to each stage of his life.

This book is Whiggish, too, as might be expected from something researched and written in Britain and America. It recognizes four important things about Newman's own growth and renewal: first, that his thinking about the Fathers changed, both in his writings and in his sermons; second, that consequently his understanding of what was and was not 'orthodox' changed; third, that these changes unfolded gradually in three major stages of his life and not cataclysmically at his conversion to Catholicism; fourth, that when writing a history of doctrine, Newman was both the recipient of a tradition of patristic interpretation and also someone who changed the way the Fathers were read after him. Newman is therefore a key figure in the growth and development of patristic scholarship, particularly in the Anglophone world.

There are so many ways in which this book would not have been possible without help on both sides of the Atlantic. The book's greatest debt is to Sarah Coakley, one of the series editors, who has given unceasing support and help to this research since it began. The other series editor, Richard Cross, has provided me with invaluable insights. My second greatest debt is to the encouragement of Andrew Louth, whom I am proud to call my Doktorvater. At the Birmingham Oratory, I would like to thank Francis McGrath FMS for his help in the Cardinal's Library; at Yale, I would like to thank Frank Turner both for conversation and for help with the microfilm version of the Oratory archive. I owe great thanks to those who have read versions of the whole manuscript: David Brown, Nicholas Lash, and Peter Nockles, whose suggestions have changed this book for the better. Those who read parts, and asked crucial questions of what they read, are John Behr, Todd Billings, Brian Daley SJ, Michael Himes, Fred Lawrence, and Mark McIntosh. Khaled Anatolios, Brigitte Hoegemann FSO, and Ian Ker responded generously to questions. David Cunningham showed me how to begin to write a book; Charles Hefling showed me how to finish one; and Kathleen Coleman showed me how to cope with the proofs. Joseph Chapman and Donald Larsen were kenotic with their time and the late Polly Warren was my 'other supervisor'.

My constant conversation partners, without whom I could not have written a book at all, are Dominic Doyle, Philip McCosker, Edmund Newey, and Matthew Treherne. Leyla, my fiancée, is the best editor a husband could want. Tom Perridge, Lizzy Robottom and all at Oxford University Press have been kindness itself. The students at Harvard have been endlessly encouraging; all errors are my own and, as Daniel Okobi among those students particularly knows, I make many!

Cambridge, Mass.
Feast of the Transfiguration, 2008

Contents

Abbreviations

Newman's Works

Apo	*Apologia Pro Vita Sua*, ed. Martin Svaglic (Oxford: Clarendon Press, 1967)
Apoll	'Apollinarianism', OM B.3.5 no. 1
Ari	*The Arians of the Fourth Century*, Birmingham Oratory Millennium Edition, ed. Rowan D. Williams (Leominster and Notre Dame, Ind.: Gracewing/University of Notre Dame Press, 2001)
Ath i, ii	*Select Treatises of Athanasius Against the Arians*, 2 vols. (5th edn.; London: Longmans, 1890)
AW	*Autobiographical Writings*, ed. Henry Tristram (New York: Sheed and Ward, 1957)
BI	*The Theological Papers of John Henry Newman on Biblical Inspiration and Infallibility*, ed. J. Derek Holmes (Oxford: Clarendon Press, 1979)
Cal	*Callista: A Sketch of the Third Century* (London: Burns and Oates, 1962)
CF	*The Church of the Fathers*, Birmingham Oratory Millennium Edition, ed. Francis McGrath (Leominster and Notre Dame, Ind.: Gracewing/University of Notre Dame Press, 2002)
Cons	*On Consulting the Faithful in Matters of Doctrine*, ed. John Coulson (London: Collins Flame Classics, 1986)
Critic	*British Critic, Quarterly Theological Review and Ecclesiastical Record*
DA	*Discussions and Arguments on Various Subjects*, Birmingham Oratory Millennium Edition, ed. Gerard Tracey and James Tolhurst (Leominster and Notre Dame, Ind.: Gracewing/University of Notre Dame Press, 2004)
Dev	*An Essay on the Development of Christian Doctrine* (2nd edn.; London: James Toovey, 1846)

Dev (1878)	*An Essay on the Development of Christian Doctrine* (uniform edn.; London: Longmans, 1909)
Diff i, ii	*Certain Difficulties Felt by Anglicans in Catholic Teaching*, new imp., 2 vols. (London: Longmans, 1920)
EH i, ii	*Essays Critical and Historical*, new imp., 2 vols. (London: Longmans, 1919)
Fleury i	*The Ecclesiastical History of M. L'Abbé Fleury, From the Second Ecumenical Council to the End of the Fourth Century*, with an 'Advertisement' and 'Essay on the Miracles Recorded in Ecclesiastical History' (Oxford: John Henry Parker, 1842)
GA	*An Essay in Aid of a Grammar of Assent* (London: Longmans, 1903)
HS i, ii, iii	*Historical Sketches*, 3 vols. (London: Longmans, 1908)
Idea	*The Idea of a University* (London: Longmans, 1907)
Jfc	*Lectures on the Doctrine of Justification* (3rd edn.; London: Rivingtons, 1874)
LD	*The Letters and Diaries of John Henry Newman*
LG	*Loss and Gain: The Story of a Convert* (London: Burns and Oats, 1962)
Lyra	*Lyra Apostolica*, ed. H. C. Beeching (London: Methuen, 1901)
Mon	'The Monophysite Heresy', OM B.2.5
Mir	*Two Essays on Biblical and on Ecclesiastical Miracles*, new imp. (London: Longmans, 1924)
Mix	*Discourses Addressed to Mixed Congregations*, Birmingham Oratory Millennium Edition, ed. James Tolhurst (Leominster and Notre Dame, Ind.: Gracewing/University of Notre Dame Press, 2002)
OM	Birmingham Oratory Manuscript
Ox Frs ii	*The Catechetical Lectures of S. Cyril*, A Library of the Fathers, ii (Oxford and London: John Henry Parker/ Rivingtons, 1839)
Ox Frs iii	*The Treatises of S. Cyprian*, A Library of the Fathers, iii (Oxford and London: John Henry Parker/Rivingtons, 1839)

Ox Frs viii	*Select Treatises of S. Athanasius in Controversy with the Arians*, A Library of the Fathers, viii (Oxford and London: John Henry Parker/Rivingtons, 1842)
Ox Frs xiii	*S. Athanasius Historical Treatises*, A Library of the Fathers, xiii (Oxford and London: John Henry Parker/ Rivingtons, 1843)
Ox Frs xix	*Select Treatises of S. Athanasius in Controversy with the Arians*, A Library of the Fathers, xix (Oxford and London: John Henry Parker/Rivingtons, 1844)
Perrone	[Newman–Perrone Paper on Development] trans. Carleton P. Jones, 'Three Latin Papers of John Henry Newman' (PhD thesis, Angelicum, 1995)
PN i, ii	*The Philosophical Notebook*, ed. Edward Sillem, 2 vols. (New York: Humanities Press, 1969–70)
Prepos	*Lectures on the Present Position of Catholics in England*, Birmingham Oratory Millennium Edition, ed. Andrew Nash (Leominster and Notre Dame, Ind.: Gracewing/ University of Notre Dame Press, 2000)
PS	*Parochial and Plain Sermons* (San Francisco, Calif.: Ignatius, 1997) (orig. 8 vols.; here cited by vol. and sermon no.)
SD	*Sermons Bearing on the Subjects of the Day*, new imp. (London: Longmans, 1898)
SN	*Sermon Notes of John Henry Newman*, ed. The Fathers of the Birmingham Oratory (London: Longmans, 1913)
Suff	'A Restoration of Suffragan Bishops Recommended . . . as Contemplated by His Majesty's Recent Ecclesiastical Commission', pamphlet (London: Rivingtons, 1835)
TT (1st edn)	*Tracts Theological and Ecclesiastical* (London: Basil Montague Pickering, 1874)
TT	*Tracts Theological and Ecclesiastical*, new imp. (London: Longmans, 1924)
US	*Fifteen Sermons Preached before the University of Oxford*, D. M. MacKinnon and J. D. Holmes (eds.), (London: SPCK, 1970)
VM i, ii	*The Via Media*, 2 vols. (3rd edn.; London: Longmans, 1877)

Other Works

ANF	Ante-Nicene Fathers
Apostolici	William Cave, *Apostolici, or, The history of the lives, acts, death, and martyrdoms of those who were contemporary with or immediately succeeding the Apostles* (London: Richard Chiswell, 1677)
de reb i, ii	[*De rebus Christianorum ante Constantinum Magnum commentarii*] Johann Lorenz von Mosheim, *Historical Commentaries on the State of Christianity during the First Three Hundred and Twenty-five Years from the Christian Era*, trans. Robert Studley Vidal and James Murdock, 2 vols. (New York: S. Converse, 1854)
de trin	Denys Petau [Dionysius Petavius], *De Trinitate* (Venice: apud Aloysium Pavinum, 1721), vol. ii of *De Theologicis Dogmatibus*
Defensio	[*Defensio Fidei Nicaenae*] George Bull, *A Defence of the Nicene Creed out of the extant writings of the Catholick Doctors, who flourished during the three first centuries of the Christian Church*, a new trans., 2 vols. (Oxford: John Henry Parker, 1851–2)
DNB	*Dictionary of National Biography*
Ecc Hist	Eusebius, *The History of the Church: From Christ to Constantine*, trans. G. A. Williamson (Harmondsworth: Dorset Press, 1965)
Ecclesiastici	[*Ecclesiastici*] William Cave, *Lives of the Most Eminent Fathers of the Church*, ed. Henry Cary (Oxford: J. Vincent, 1840)
Hist Lit	William Cave, *Scriptorum Ecclesiasticorum Historia Literaria* (London: Richard Chiswell, 1688)
NPNF	Nicene and Post-Nicene Fathers
OED	*Oxford English Dictionary*
PG	Patrologia Graeca
ST	Thomas Aquinas, *Summa Theologica*, in *Basic Writings of Saint Thomas Aquinas*, ed. Anton C. Pegis (Indianapolis, Ind.: Hackett, 1997)

TIS   Ralph Cudworth, *The True Intellectual System of the Universe: The First Part; Wherein All the Reason and Philosophy of Atheism is Confuted; and its Impossibility Demonstrated* (London: Richard Royston, 1678)

Latin abbreviations of patristic works appear in the footnotes. The titles have been translated when they first appear in the main body of this text.

Introduction

This book will trace the dynamism of the patristic scholarship of John Henry Newman (1801–1890) as he moved from young Evangelical, to scholar learning from Oxford's High Churchmen, to Tractarian leader alienated from the Church of England, to Catholic alienated from the Roman schools, and finally to cardinal. Throughout Newman's life, the early Church Fathers most important to his thought were those from Alexandria in Egypt. But how he read Clement and Origen, Athanasius and Cyril of Alexandria shifted at each stage of his life. Therefore something else must be traced in this book as well: how Newman shaped the tradition of patristic scholarship that he inherited into the quite different tradition that he bequeathed to those who followed him. Newman changed how the history of Alexandrian doctrine was understood and written about, so his work must be set in the broader context of Anglican and Catholic historiography of Christian doctrine.

The teachings of the Church Fathers, particularly on the doctrines of God's Trinity and Christ's incarnation, fascinated Newman from his teenage years until his death. He famously wrote that at the age of fifteen he was 'enamoured of the long extracts from St. Augustine, St. Ambrose, and the other Fathers' that he discovered in the second volume (1795) of Joseph Milner's *The History of the Church of Christ* (*Apo* 20). Although this recollection of his teenage years in the *Apologia Pro Vita Sua*, nearly fifty years later (1864), puts the stress on the Latin Fathers, that was Milner's own Evangelical stress, having little time for the theology and piety of the Greek Fathers. A Latin like Ambrose, Milner wrote, 'might have both preached and written better, had he always attended to the simple word of God, and exercised his own natural good sense in humble dependence on DIVINE GRACE, and paid less regard to the fanciful writings of Origen, which corrupted his understanding exceedingly'.[1] Yet Newman came to disagree. In 1833, Newman's first book regarded Origen's interpretation of scripture as something to be relished not regretted. Milner also found 'nothing important' in the writings of Athanasius, 'except what relates to the Arian controversy'; he held the patriarch to be a good judge of character 'except in the life of Anthony the monk . . . the superstitions and follies of which unhappy perversion of piety received but too liberal a support from his influence'.[2] Yet Newman would devote much of the 1840s and the late 1870s to Athanasius's theology, while Antony of Egypt provided the example for the ascetic disciplines of Newman's life. Albeit, due to Milner's influence, they were not Newman's first love, nevertheless the Greek Fathers, especially those from Egypt, became his lifelong companions.

Already the first theme of this book has become clear: Newman's alliances to various Fathers changed over the years. Although scholars have long been aware of the depth and breadth of Newman's patristic reading, there is a tendency to reduce all that he wrote on the Fathers to an expression of Athanasian orthodoxy. Attention has typically focused on Newman's handling of the fourth-century theological controversy, to which he returned time and again, because '[s]een Newman's way, contemporary civilization is a contest between the irreconcilable principles of Arius and Athanasius'.[3] To avoid such generalizations, this book will explore *which* Fathers interested Newman the most and *when*. Moreover, evidence from

---

[1] J. Milner, *The History of the Church of Christ*, ii (Boston, Mass.: Farrand, Mallory and Co, 1809), 228.

[2] Ibid. 165. For Milner's theological agenda, see J. D. Walsh, 'Joseph Milner's Evangelical Church History', *Journal of Ecclesiastical History*, 10 (1959), 174–87.

[3] Robert Pattison, *The Great Dissent: John Henry Newman and the Liberal Heresy* (New York: Oxford University Press, 1991), 116. The same trend can be seen among those more sympathetic to Newman, e.g., Denys Gorce, *Newman et les Pères* (2nd edn.; Bruges: Editions Charles Beyaert, 1946); George Dragas, 'Conscience and Tradition: Newman and Athanasios in the Orthodox Church', *Newman Studien*, 11 (1980), 73–84; and G. Tokarsik, 'John Henry Newman and the Church Fathers', *Eastern Churches Journal*, 7 (2000), esp. 102–3.

his patristic writings will replace mere speculation in discerning *what* Newman took from these Fathers.[4]

Such an exploration of Newman's patristic writing on the Fathers will reveal a second theme of this book: that his view of what was 'orthodox' doctrine changed. There was a period in Newman's life when his interest in doctrine depended less on the orthodoxy of Church Councils than was later the case. Clement and Origen predated conciliar 'orthodoxy', yet were central to Newman's understanding of doctrine in the 1830s. He would turn against Origen in the 1840s when, formulating his idea that doctrine develops, Newman promoted a version of orthodoxy that centred on Athanasius and judged those who predated Nicaea by the Creed of that Council which Athanasius promoted. In the 1870s, he began to rehabilitate Origen, reassessing the role he played leading up to the Council of Nicaea. In each of these periods, a causal connection will be revealed between the patristic theology Newman was reading and his own theology; but events in these periods will also be shown to change how he interpreted the Fathers. It is as if Newman tried on each of the Fathers for size, beginning with the pre-Nicene Greeks in the late 1820s, then the post-Nicene Greeks during his research into Christological controversies in the mid-1830s, and finding Athanasius the best fit in the 1840s—albeit this interpretation of Athanasius was made of a cloth that intertwined Latin threads with Greek. The patriarch of Alexandria whom Newman depicted was a composite figure. This was even more the case in the 1870s, when Athanasius was tailored to Catholic tastes. Moreover, measuring Origen up with the interpretations made by Aquinas and Suarez, in 1872 Newman found him a better fit than he had in the 1840s.

The multiple interpretations of the Alexandrian Fathers reveal multiple periods in Newman's life, which is the third theme of this book. Though taking a chronological approach to Newman's

---

[4] Others' speculations attribute to Newman's reading of the patristic sources some suspiciously modern ideas, e.g., G. Magill writes that Newman discerned a 'personal' rather than 'logical' style of reasoning from the Fathers, 'Newman's Personal Reasoning: The Inspiration of the Early Church', *Irish Theological Quarterly*, 52 (1992), 305–13; and V. F. Blehl discerns the 'The Patristic Humanism of John Henry Newman', *Thought*, 50 (1975), 274.

patristic writings, it will not divide Newman's life into Anglican and then Catholic periods as most studies do.[5] The account that Newman gave of his conversion to Catholicism governs such studies, an account that began in Lecture XII of 'Certain Difficulties Felt by Anglicans' (1850), was polished in the *Apologia Pro Vita Sua* (1864), and continued to be used against his Anglican critics.[6] Instead, this book depicts three periods (the 1830s, the 1840s and 50s, and the 1860s and 70s) rather than just two (Anglican and Catholic), in order to see the shaping of patristic teaching on the Trinity and Christology. Any way of dividing history up into periods is artificial, because of continuities across periods. Yet Newman's own history provides two clear divisions in his interpretation of the Alexandrian Fathers rather than just the one division of his conversion: the first came after the publication of Tract 90 in February 1841, which left him feeling increasingly alienated from the Anglican hierarchy, and the second came when the reaction to an article in the *Rambler* in July 1859, 'On Consulting the Faithful in Matters of Doctrine', left him feeling increasingly alienated from the Catholic hierarchy. In the periods of isolation that followed, Newman reassessed his own theology by turning to the Fathers, and in so doing reinterpreted the Alexandrians.

[5] This division is found from the beginning of Newman scholarship with John Oldcastle's pamphlet, *The Catholic Life and Letters of Cardinal Newman* (London: Burns and Oates, 1885) and Richard Church's 1891 study, *The Oxford Movement: Twelve Years 1833–1845* (London and New York: Macmillan, 1904). Some recent studies focus on the Anglican years only, notably Stephen Thomas, *Newman and Heresy: The Anglican Years* (Cambridge: Cambridge University Press, 1991) and Frank Turner, *John Henry Newman: The Challenge to Evangelical Religion* (New Haven, Conn.: Yale University Press, 2002). Even Ian Ker's thematic approach in *Newman on Being a Christian* (Leominster and Notre Dame, Ind.: Gracewing/University of Notre Dame Press, 1990) divides Newman's writings into 'Anglican' and 'Catholic' categories.

[6] In *A Letter Addressed to the Rev. E. B. Pusey* (1865), Newman says of his days as an Anglican: 'I recollect well what an outcast I seemed to myself, when I took down from the shelves of my library the volumes of St Athanasius or St Basil, and set myself to study them; and how, on the contrary, when at length I was brought into Catholic communion, I kissed them with delight, with a feeling that in them I had more than all that I had lost' (*Diff* ii. 3). In *A Letter Addressed to His Grace the Duke of Norfolk on Occasion of Mr. Gladstone's Recent Expostulation* (1874), he writes of the Tractarians that 'none of us could read the Fathers, and determine to be their disciples, without feeling that Rome, like a faithful steward, had kept in fulness and in vigour what our own communion had let drop' (*Diff* ii. 198).

The fourth and final theme of this book will set Newman's multiple interpretations of the Alexandrians in the wider context of the historiography of Christian doctrine. While Milner's *History* influenced his earliest interpretation of patristic doctrine, Oxford in the 1820s and early 1830s brought other influences to bear, especially from the High Churchmen. The High Church tradition of Anglican teaching was founded on two Testaments of scripture, three Creeds, and four Councils (only the Ecumenical Councils of Nicaea, Constantinople, Ephesus, and Chalcedon carried weight for Anglicans).[7] Greek theologians, rather than Latins, were since the seventeenth century the favourites of High Churchmen; indeed, it is noticeable in that era how few Latin Fathers were printed in England, compared to Greek Fathers.[8] Moreover, High Church historians like George Bull, the Bishop of St David's (1634–1710), and William Cave (1637–1713), Chaplain to Charles II, did not discriminate in praising both pre-Nicene and post-Nicene Greek theology, seeing continuity across the first five Christian centuries. Until his idea of doctrinal development, Newman likewise thought that pre- and post-Nicene Fathers taught the same doctrines as one another. But one difference from his Anglican predecessors in *The Arians of the Fourth Century* (1833), as Rowan Williams has observed, was Newman's view that 'doctrine, even if only in its outward expression, does have a *history*', an insight many High Churchmen found shocking.[9] While today many might find it equally shocking that Newman's own doctrinal writings also have a history, this book will trace that history as it is located in the events of his life. Those events led Newman to change his mind repeatedly about the Fathers and their doctrine.

The remainder of this introduction will begin where Newman's reading of the Greek Fathers did, with Oxford in the 1820s, before

[7] This tag was originally from the seventeenth-century bishop Lancelot Andrewes: 'Our faith is the ancient catholic faith contained in the two testaments, the three creeds, the four councils, only restored to its proper lustre', quoted in Robert L. Ottley, *Lancelot Andrewes* (London: Methuen, 1894), 164.

[8] Anglican scholars 'concentrated on ante-Nicene Fathers and on Greek Fathers and Byzantine writers,' and Augustine was usually read in Catholic editions, according to Jean-Louis Quantin, 'The Fathers in Seventeenth Century Roman Catholic Theology', in Irena Backus (ed.), *The Reception of the Church Fathers in the West: From the Carolingians to the Maurists*, 2 vols. (New York: E. J. Brill, 1997), ii. 999.

[9] Rowan Williams, 'Newman's *Arians* and the Question of Method in Doctrinal History', in Ian Ker and Alan G. Hill (eds.), *Newman after One Hundred Years* (Oxford: Clarendon Press, 1990), 276.

giving a brief overview of each chapter. The University of Oxford, like Cambridge, had gone through fifty years of vigorous intellectual activity when Newman went up. A. M. C. Waterman writes: 'During the 1770s the world changed', not only politically but also intellectually.

[Smith's] *Wealth of Nations* and Bentham's *Fragment on Government*, both of which were published in 1776, symbolically inaugurate a fundamentally new way of looking at human society and its ills. The first two volumes of [Gibbon's] *Decline and Fall*, which also appeared that year, marked the beginning of a frontal assault on Christianity; Hume's posthumous *Dialogues Concerning Natural Religion* was first printed three years later.[10]

With political and religious radicalism going together, scholars from the Universities tended to return to theological orthodoxy and a defence of the Thirty-nine Articles, as seen in the Cambridge-educated Joseph Milner and his brother Isaac (who became President of Queens' College) who went from being radical young Churchmen to vigorous opponents of heterodoxy. The Milners' orthodox generation taught the scholars who, in turn, helped shape Newman's Oxford and Hugh James Rose's Cambridge.

During his second summer as an Oxford undergraduate, Newman once again read Gibbon's *The Decline and Fall of the Roman Empire* and wrote that he relished '[his] happy choice of expressions, his vigorous compression of ideas, and the life and significance of his every word' (*LD* i. 67). Although 'disconcerted' by Gibbon's remark that 'Ambition is a weed which often flourishes in the vineyard of Christ', Newman was not as shocked as earlier readers because the intellectual world had changed since the 1770s, as intimated by the reference to Southey in the same letter (ibid.). The early years of the 1770s saw the births of Wordsworth, Southey, Coleridge, and Walter Scott—the group of English Romantics that would profoundly influence Newman's generation.[11] The Oxford undergraduate could

---

[10] A. M. C. Waterman, 'A Cambridge "Via Media" in Late Georgian Anglicanism', *Journal of Ecclesiastical History*, 42 (1991), 421–2.

[11] For a possible direct influence of the Romantics on Newman, see John Coulson, *Newman and the Common Tradition: A Study in the Language of Church and Society* (Oxford: Clarendon Press, 1970); Stephen Prickett, *Romanticism and Religion: The Tradition of Coleridge and Wordsworth in the Victorian Church* (Cambridge: Cambridge University Press, 1976); and David Goslee, *Romanticism and the Age of Newman* (Athens, Ohio: Ohio University Press, 1996).

relish Gibbon's storytelling because Newman had learned from the Romantics to value imagination.[12] The ancient world that Gibbon depicted continued to captivate Newman as a tutor at Oriel and curate of St Clement's, Oxford, when he began writing history himself. His first articles were on Cicero, in 1824,[13] and the first-century philosopher and wonderworker Apollonius of Tyana, in 1826, for the *Encyclopaedia Metropolitana*, the Church's rival to the godless *Britannica* (*HS* i. 239–331). Newman's imagination shaped the way he read the Fathers, a way that the older generation saw as dangerously 'enthusiastic'. While the English Romantics represented something new and radical for the generation of High Churchmen who were born or grew up in the 1770s and 1780s,[14] their ideas were constitutive of life in 1820s Oxford and Cambridge.[15] When Newman accused the older High Churchmen of being 'High and Dry', immune to feeling in their religion, overly rationalistic, and unwilling to appeal to the imagination, he was speaking the sentiments of a Romantic. In a series of three anonymous articles on Antony of Egypt in the *British*

---

[12] Appealing to the imagination in argument is typical of the English Romantics and not the Milners or William Paley (1743–1805). But where the Romantics spoke of imagination as co-creative with God, the Tractarians spoke of the imagination's grace-filled *recognition* of God's work. For Coleridge, imagination enables us to create the world we experience in order to know it, 'a repetition in the finite mind of the eternal act of creation in the infinite I AM' (*Biographia Literaria* 2 vols. (Princeton, NJ: Princeton University Press, 1983), i. 304). For Coleridge, this is a religious insight, but for the Tractarians 'the province of the true poet has been not to invent likenesses, but to trace out the analogies, which are actually impressed upon the creation', quoted from Pusey's unpublished 'Lectures on Types and Prophecies in the Old Testament' by A. M. Allchin, 'The Theological Vision of the Oxford Movement', in John Coulson and Allchin (eds.), *The Rediscovery of Newman* (London: SPCK, 1967), 64.

[13] While criticizing Gibbon's lack of belief, Newman's belief brought a different shape to his own history writing. Robert Pattison argues that 'Cicero's life was of little interest to [Newman] not for its lack of event but for its lack of application of belief to event', *Great Dissent*, 99.

[14] This generation of High Churchmen includes William Van Mildert (born 1765), William Howley (1766), John Watson (1767), H. H. Norris (1771), Joshua Watson (1771), Christopher Bethell (1773), John Jebb (1775), Henry Phillpotts (1778), Charles Le Bas (1779), John Kaye (1783), Charles Lloyd (1784), and William Lyall (1788). When introducing these older High Churchmen in my text, their birthdate has been mentioned to stress the generational difference from Newman's friends.

[15] Newman (born 1801) had as close contemporaries among High Churchmen: W. F. Hook (1798), R. W. Jelf (1798), A. P. Perceval (1799), E. B. Pusey (1800), Edward Churton (1800), William Gresley (1801), Isaac Williams (1802), Robert Wilberforce (1802), George Moberly (1803), William Palmer of Worcester (1803),

8 *Introduction*

Magazine, between July and September 1835, Newman did not argue for Evangelical sentiment but rather that 'enthusiasm is sobered and refined by being submitted to the discipline of the Church, instead of being allowed to run wild and external to it' (*HS* ii. 103). When the older generation thought of Antony, they were suspicious of his life as a hermit and his fights with demons. By contrast, Newman not only praised Antony's virtues but espoused the excitement of the English Romantics for a disciplined and holy way of life.[16]

In addition, Newman's three articles acted as a defence of Athanasius, who wrote the *Life of Antony*. Newman felt that the doctrine for which Athanasius was a spokesman, and which the High Churchmen revered, went together with the sort of asceticism embodied by Antony. Therefore, Newman criticized those who 'make it their boast that they are more *comfortable* than that ancient creed which, together with joy, leads men to continual smiting on the breast, and prayers for pardon' (*HS* ii. 125). Both morbid and emotional, both self-denying and fervent, the Tractarian ethos scared the older High Churchmen, whom Newman judged as too 'comfortable'. Judging by its ability to shock the older generation, this ethos represented something more Romantic than the ethics of Aristotle or Bishop Butler (1692–1752).[17] Newman and his friend Hurrell Froude insisted upon withdrawal from worldly affairs, looking to the Fathers for their example of holiness and reserve, but also to John Keble, himself a Romantic poet and the embodiment of self-denial, who exchanged reputation at Oxford for the role of a country parson. But the older High Churchmen were the generation who had lived through the fears of the French Revolution and whose nation had

Richard Hurrell Froude (1803), William Copeland (1804), Samuel Wilberforce (1805), and Henry Wilberforce (1807). Newman looked on Keble (1792) and Rose (1795), both slightly older, as his guides.

[16] For the way Coleridge also used enthusiasm to encourage moral development, see J. Robert Barth and John L. Mahoney (eds.), *Coleridge, Keats, and the Imagination* (Columbia, Mo.: University of Missouri Press, 1990), esp. 139.

[17] Nevertheless, for the importance of Butler and Aristotle, see James Pereiro, *'Ethos' and the Oxford Movement: At the Heart of Tractarianism* (Oxford: Clarendon Press, 2008). See also D. Newsome, *Two Classes of Men: Platonism and English Romantic Thought* (London: John Murray, 1974), ch. 4, who argues that Newman was more an Aristotelian and Coleridge more a Platonist.

defended their rights and liberties in the wars against Napoleon. Such men grew up worrying about national politics—seeing the stability of the State constantly threatened—whereas the younger generation named such politics 'Erastian', after the Swiss theologian who upheld the civil authority's jurisdiction over ecclesiastical affairs.

Two older High Churchmen became Newman's teachers in the Greek Fathers: first, in the 1820s, Charles Lloyd (b. 1784) and then, in the 1830s, Martin Routh (b. 1755). In 1823–4, alongside Edward Pusey and six others, Newman 'attended some private lectures in Divinity by the Regius Professor, Dr Charles Lloyd' (*LD* i. 167). Although Newman later reported that Lloyd kept his opinions to himself about the books of apologetics and biblical history which they read in class, nevertheless something of the Professor's High Church affinity for the Fathers must have rubbed off (*AW* 70–1). And although Newman later felt ashamed of 'some flippant language against the Fathers in the *Encyclopaedia Metropolitana*... on the Scripture Miracles in 1825–6'—the result of reading 'Middleton on the Miracles of the early Church'[18]—nevertheless he retained an interest in the Fathers (*Apo* 26). In January 1826, he asked Edward Smedley, editor of the *Encyclopaedia*, 'May I venture to inquire whether it would fall in with your arrangements, were I to undertake the Fathers of the 2nd and 3rd centuries in one paper... engaging to send it to you in two years[?]' (*LD* i. 274). In line with this timeframe, Newman told Lloyd in February 1827, by which stage he was Bishop of Oxford, of a plan to read the Fathers. He recorded in his journal that Lloyd said in response to the plan that 'our theological systems do not agree', although Newman thought they 'agree[d] more than when I was in class with him, but I do not tell him so' (*AW* 210).

---

[18] His article cited Conyers Middleton on the Fathers, whose book was entitled: *A Free Inquiry into the miraculous powers which are supposed to have subsisted in the Christian Church from the earliest ages* (1748). (*Mir* 79 n.r) By September 1831, Newman thought that Middleton was too liberal, Gibbon was too pagan, and Milner was too Protestant: 'of the historians I have met with I have a very low opinion— Mosheim, Gibbon, Middleton, Milner, etc.' (*LD* ii. 371). Newman's opinion did not change in 1842: 'What we meet in Fleury's work is a minute and exact narrative of the course of ecclesiastical events, as they occurred; and this, from the plan of their histories, is not found in Mosheim, Milner, Gibbon, Neander, Milman or Dollinger [*sic*], great as are the merits of these authors in various ways' (*Fleury* i, p. v). These other historians will be introduced below.

Grounds for further agreement came later in 1827, when Newman read the High Churchman William Wall (1647–1728) and 'drew up a defence of Infant Baptism from the patristical testimonies' that he found in *The History of Infant Baptism* (*AW* 83).

Indeed, from the humble beginnings of the class with Lloyd grew a fascination for the 'period between the Apostolical Fathers and the Nicene Council' (*LD* i. 274). The *Apologia Pro Vita Sua* recounts that another teacher, Richard Whately (b. 1787),[19] accused him of 'Arianizing' in a sermon preached in Oriel chapel in 1827, a term Newman interprets to mean being 'very strong for that ante-Nicene view of the Trinitarian doctrine' which made the Son of God subordinate to God the Father (*Apo* 25). Perhaps Newman imbibed this doctrine from what little he read of the pre-Nicene Greeks through the High Churchmen who, as this book will show, judged that some degree of 'subordinationism' could not be heretical because the Alexandrians had taught it. Newman only became aware of problems with the Alexandrian doctrine of the Trinity when drawn to the Latin doctrine from the 1840s onwards. Thus, it is with the hindsight of a conception of the Trinity learned later that Newman looks back on that Oriel sermon, writing elsewhere that he 'took, without knowing it, [George] Bull's doctrine of the "Subordinatio Filii"' (*AW* 142). At the time of writing *Arians of the Fourth Century*, however, he thought that neither he nor Bull's *Defensio Fidei Nicaenae* 'which at this time I read' (*Apo* 36), nor Origen, whom both were defending, had committed the heresy of subordinationism.

In the late 1820s, Newman's growing sympathy for Lloyd and growing opposition to Whately brought him closer to the Greek Fathers.[20] It was Lloyd who suggested that Pusey go to Germany to study Hebrew (Pusey would become Professor of Hebrew at Oxford).

---

[19] Newman worked on an article on logic with Whately, who wrote: 'I cannot avoid particularizing the Rev. J. Newman, Fellow of Oriel College, who actually composed a considerable portion of the work as it now stands' (*Elements of Logic, Comprising the Substance of the Article in the Encyclopaedia Metropolitana* (4th edn.; London: B. Fellowes, 1831), p. ix). At this stage of his life (though not later on), Newman agreed with Whately about the Schoolmen's 'waste of ingenuity and frivolous subtilty of disputation' (p. 8).

[20] An *Autobiographical Memoir*, written in the third-person for Newman's friend Ambrose St John in 1874, compared Lloyd with Whately: 'Lloyd professed to hold to theology, and laid great stress on a doctrinal standard, authoritative and traditional

By the time Newman told Lloyd of his patristic reading plans, he had already 'commission[ed]' Pusey, while there, to buy him some editions of the Fathers, and the first to be acquired were volumes of Chrysostom and Theodoret in November 1826 (*LD* i. 309). Newman told his mother when other volumes arrived from Germany in October 1827: 'huge fellows they are, but very cheap', probably referring to the *Bibliotheca Patrum*, large compilations in Latin of Fathers whose works were too small to be sold individually (*LD* ii. 30). In the summer of 1828, Newman finally started a chronological reading of the Fathers with Ignatius of Antioch and Justin Martyr (*Apo* 35). By July 1831, he had become proficient enough in the Fathers to begin writing *Arians of the Fourth Century* (*LD* ii. 340); work that was helped when, that October, his friends and pupils bought him another thirty-six volumes, described as 'so fine in their outsides as to put my former ones to shame' (*LD* ii. 369). These editions were mainly by the Benedictines of St Maur (the Maurists) and included the works of Origen and Athanasius.[21]

After Lloyd's early death in 1829, a second High Churchman greatly influenced Newman's patristic scholarship.[22] Martin Routh was the President of Magdalen College, who had collected together

teaching, and ecclesiastical history; Whately called the Fathers "certain old divines", and, after Swift or some other wit, called orthodoxy "one's own doxy", and heterodoxy "another's doxy"' (*AW* 70).

[21] The two most famous members of the order are Jean Mabillon (1632–1707), who worked mostly on Latin Fathers and whose book *De re diplomatica* invented the word 'diplomatic', and Bernard de Montfaucon (1655–1731), who from 1687 was 'working on the edition of the Greek Fathers, and particularly on Athanasius. In the year after Mabillon's death he produced *Paleographia graeca*, and in this case too the title of his book invented a word that has been the standard ever since' (L. D. Reynolds and N. G. Wilson, *Scribes and Scholars: A Guide to the Transmission of Greek and Latin Literature* (2nd edn.; Oxford: Clarendon Press, 1974), 171).

[22] T. M. Parker contends that, while Newman's 'work on the Arians led him inevitably to Bishop Bull... I would suspect that it was Martin Joseph Routh who encouraged him to read further in the seventeenth-century divines. In the beginning of February 1834, we are told by J. B. Mozley, in a letter to his sister Maria, 'Newman was closeted the other day two hours with Dr. Routh of Magdalen, receiving his opinions as to his work [*The Arians of the Fourth Century*], which were very complimentary'... Did Routh direct him to them [Laud, Bramhall, Stillingfleet]?' ('The Rediscovery of the Fathers in the Seventeenth-century Anglican Tradition', in John Coulson and A. M. Allchin (eds.), *The Rediscovery of Newman: An Oxford Symposium* (London: SPCK, 1967), 45, quoting *Letters of Rev J. B. Mozley, DD* (London: Rivingtons, 1885), 39).

various fragments of patristic writing in *Reliquiae Sacrae* (1814–18), a work to which Newman frequently turned. Routh taught history in the High Anglican tradition, as described in a letter from Newman in 1837 asking him to be the dedicatee of the 'Lectures on the Prophetical Office'. 'I have tried', Newman wrote, 'as far as may be, to follow the line of doctrine marked out by our great divines, of whom perhaps I have chiefly followed Bramhall, then Laud, Hammond, Field, Stillingfleet, Beveridge and others of the same school' (*LD* vi. 7). Newman and his followers came to propagate the view that, apart from Routh and Lloyd, other High Churchmen at the time were largely forgetful of the Fathers. Newman suggested this himself when, in his dedication to Routh, he thanked a scholar 'who has been reserved'—a word of highest praise—'to report to a forgetful generation what was the Theology of their Fathers' (*VM* i, p. i). In fact, the generations between Routh and Newman were fluent in the Fathers.[23] The difference was that Routh remained a constant friend of the Oxford Movement, whereas other High Churchmen criticized Newman. Routh received the praise of Richard Church fifty years later for having 'stood alone among his brother Heads [of Oxford Houses] in his knowledge of what English theology was'; which is to say, Routh stood alone in not criticizing Newman for Tract 90.[24]

Charles Lloyd's death before the Tracts meant that, in the historiography of the Movement, he could be safely idealized by Newman and friends.[25] Lloyd became a yardstick with which to measure other

[23] As so much Oxford Movement scholarship does these days, I depend here upon Peter Nockles, *The Oxford Movement in Context: Anglican High Churchmanship 1760–1857* (Cambridge: Cambridge University Press, 1994). Nockles has shown the exaggerated distance that Tractarian leaders, and subsequent historians of the Movement, put between themselves and the High Churchmen of the late eighteenth and early nineteenth centuries.

[24] Church, *The Oxford Movement: Twelve Years 1833–1845*, 304. For Church's animus against the heads of Oxford colleges, see Owen Chadwick, *The Spirit of the Oxford Movement: Tractarian Essays* (Cambridge: Cambridge University Press, 1990), 150–1. Routh's renowned sense of humour probably helped in his dealings with Newman's friend, William Palmer of Magdalen (not of Worcester College), as recounted in Robin Wheeler, *Palmer's Progress: The Life of William Palmer of Magdalen* (Berne: Peter Lang, 2006).

[25] Newman later wrote that he 'retained to old age an affectionate and grateful memory of Lloyd (an excellent man). Many of his pupils rose to eminence, some through his helping hand. Mr Jelf was soon made preceptor to Prince

theologians, not least Renn Dickson Hampden (b. 1793) in his 1832 Bampton lectures, against whose appointment as Regius Professor of Divinity, in 1836, Newman led a fierce campaign. That chair became open upon the unexpected death of Lloyd's successor as Regius Professor, Edward Burton (b. 1794). In the *British Critic* of July 1836, writing about a work by Burton, Newman lamented 'the sagacity of Bishop Lloyd [who] discerned the renewal of hostilities with the Romanists in prospect, and began, in this very Review [in 1825], to prepare for defence' (*Critic* 20: 210). Lloyd was the High Church ideal of a scholar, compared with whom Burton fell short: 'At this moment especially, when the orthodox doctrines of the Trinity, Incarnation, or Atonement, are so lightly treated in quarters where one might have hoped for better things, we regret the *accident*, which makes Dr Burton appear to put those divine truths in the second place in the Christian scheme.' Such a statement was animated more by Hampden, whose lectures Newman held to be heterodox, than it was by Burton—at least the latter had been 'zealous' for doctrine 'in former publications' (ibid. 229). But Burton takes the blame, along with other High Church scholars of the day, for not presenting doctrinal history in a way that it might oppose, on the one hand, 'Romanists' and, on the other, liberal Protestants like Hampden.

Another High Churchman, Hugh James Rose (b. 1795), was essential in encouraging Newman's earliest work on the Greek Fathers. A notable scholar and well-connected clergyman, Rose was Professor of Divinity at the new University at Durham in 1834, and then Principal of King's College London in 1836, where he remained until his early death in 1838. Rose commissioned *Arians of the Fourth Century*; moreover, throughout their correspondence in the early and middle 1830s, Rose was an important interlocutor in all of Newman's schemes, even sometimes acting as a brake. Newman shared with Rose a belief that scholarship was useless if it did not lead to action; its purpose was to make readers grow in holiness not just in

George...Mr Churton, who died prematurely, became chaplain to Howley, [then] Bishop of London...Mr Pusey he recommended to the Minister for the Hebrew Professorship, first sending him to Germany to study that language in the Universities there' (*AW* 71–2). Ibid. 70 mentions that 'Oakeley...testified to [Lloyd's] influence...having acted in a Catholic direction; but such men attended his lectures some years later', referring to *Historical Notes on the Tractarian Movement* (1865).

knowledge.[26] Newman tried to live such a life in his ministry as a priest. He wrote to Rose in September 1834 of his decision not to allow a parishioner to marry: 'The Primitive Church would never have sanctioned such a marriage. How could I allow a man calling himself a Churchman to commit himself to the peril of having a wife and then children (probably) who were without the Covenant?' (*LD* iv. 327). For Newman, the history of the early Church was the example for holy living in the present and that recognition should shape the way such history was written.

While some High Churchmen, like Rose, remained true to those who had been their teachers and priests, and who, as patrons, controlled ecclesiastical appointments, Newman persuaded other contemporaries to accompany him in his attempt to retrieve the holiness of the early Church for the present day.[27] Indeed, Rose became increasingly concerned about Newman's powers of persuasion among those training at Oxford to be clergymen. One article that Rose delayed publishing in the *British Magazine*, much to the frustration of Newman and Froude, was the two-part piece entitled, 'Home Thoughts Abroad.'[28] Subsequent commentators have rightly seen the letters between Rose and Newman, dating from the time of the article's publication in March and April 1836, as a parting of the ways. J. W. Burgon included the correspondence in his character sketch of Rose in *Lives of Twelve Good Men*, in order to suggest the Tractarians departed from the authentically High Church ways of Rose. Reginald Fuller has argued that, in these letters, Rose was 'protesting at the altered tone manifested in Newman's Tract 71 and in his "Home Thoughts from [*sic*] Abroad."' Newman had

[26] Rose wrote in his Durham Divinity lectures: 'In a word, in Milner there is no love of the cause, or, if the man had a heart, the writer thought it his duty to overlay his feelings with dry details of barren facts, without the record of a single moral lesson to which they can lead or a feeling which they can inspire'; quoted by Newman (*Fleury* i, p. iv).

[27] Among them, William Copeland found it 'a relief to contrast' antiquity with 'the cold-heartedness and semi-infidel conservatism of many of the maintainers of our so-called happy establishment' (to M. A. Copeland, 3 May 1836, Copeland MSS (Pusey House), quoted by Nockles, *The Oxford Movement in Context*, 28).

[28] It was republished in 1872 as 'How to Accomplish it' in *DA*. For Froude's frustration, see, e.g., *LD* v. 192.

spoken of the Church of England as "safe" and nothing more'.[29] In the letter quoted above, from May 1836, Rose addressed the question of Newman's passion for the early Church. Rose thought it dangerous for Newman to be

turning the readers [among the clergy], such as they are, out to grass in the spacious pastures of Antiquity without very strict tether. *All* that is in Antiquity is not good; and much that was good for Antiquity would not be good for us... Antiquity should be studied by them only with full, clear and explicit directions how to derive from it that good which is to be derived from it; and to avoid the sort of quackery of *affecting* Antiquity.[30]

Rose worried that Newman's disciples, in reading the Fathers, were not getting them right, to which Newman replied: '*Where* have I bid people to search into Antiquity without guide?' (*LD* v. 304). Pusey attempted to reassure Rose, saying that 'we do take care not to build on one or other Father, but on Catholic Antiquity... This is what I meant by saying that we must spread our sails, not knowing whither we should be carried'.[31]

Meanwhile, in the *British Critic* in July 1836, Newman portrayed the Tractarians as the rudder to steer High Church scholarship, discounting his various rivals. The article already cited took the death earlier that year of both the Regius Professor of Divinity, Edward Burton, and the former Regius Professor of Divinity at Oxford and Bishop of Durham, William Van Mildert, to indicate the end of an era. But he does not lament its passing, writing:

The highly to be revered school of divinity, commonly called high Church, has lately been bereaved of its brightest ornament, in the admirable Prelate who filled the See of Durham [Van Mildert]; while it is fast losing ground in the Christian Knowledge Society. As to the party who seem to be succeeding to their power, and are full of hope of triumph in consequence, they have no internal consistency, clearness of principle, strength of mind, or weight of ability sufficient to keep the place they may perhaps have to win. (*Critic* 20: 212–13)

---

[29] Reginald Fuller, 'The Classical High Church Reaction to the Tractarians', in Geoffrey Rowell (ed.), *Tradition Renewed* (London: Darton, Longman and Todd, 1986), 52.
[30] Burgon, *Lives of Twelve Good Men*, 2 vols. (5th edn.; London: John Murray, 1889), i. 210.
[31] Quoted ibid. i. 220 n.

According to Newman, it was Froude who originally 'said Waterland was the first, and Van Mildert the last of the school' (*LD* v. 363). While Van Mildert was to be revered, Newman found his school as lacking in passion as their High Church forebears: 'Bull, Waterland, Petavius, Baronius and the rest', Newman wrote in October 1831 to his friend at the time, Samuel Rickards (b. 1796), 'are magnificent fellows, but they are Antiquarians or Doctrinists, not Ecclesiastical Historians' (*LD* ii. 371).[32] What Newman regrets about 'Doctrinists', from Bull and Waterland to Van Mildert, is that detail overwhelms plot: they are 'Antiquarians' who are interested in the past for its own sake, not 'Ecclesiastical Historians' who tell the story of the past in order to change lives in the present. In the same letter, Cave and Tillemont[33] are called 'highly respectable, but biographers', suggesting that, already in 1831, Newman thought he offered something new to the writing of Church history. In the *British Critic* in 1836, Newman proclaims what he has to offer: history written with an eye to current events, not like Burton's history writing, which had 'too little of moral or lesson'. Burton was at least 'a very considerable advance upon Mosheim's history; which is as dry and sapless as if the Church were some fossil remains of an antediluvian era', Newman taking his view of the German historian straight from Rose (*Critic* 20: 214).

With the death of Van Mildert and Burton, this school had been left directionless—not that either of them offered much direction. Of those High Churchmen who could replace them, Bishop John Kaye of Lincoln 'has apparently been led by an accurate taste, critical

---

[32] Newman must have read portions of the Anglican Daniel Waterland's *A Critical History of the Athanasian Creed* (1723) and *Review of the Doctrine of the Eucharist* (1737), the Jesuit Denys Petaus's *De Theologicis Dogmatibus*, 4 vols. (1644–50), and the Oratorian Cesare Baronius's *Annales Ecclesiastici*, 12 vols. (1588–1607). Similar criticism of George Bull came in his article from Oct. 1838: 'Bull, again, is beyond his other traits, remarkable for discursiveness. He is full of digressions, which can only be excused because they are so instructive and beautiful. If he is often rhetorical, he is never dry; and never tires, except from the abundance of his matter. This same remark applies *mutatis mutandis* to Pearson's Vindiciae [*Epistolarum S. Ignatii* (1672)] and Wall's Infant Baptism [2 vols. (1705)]' (*Critic* 24: 348/*EH* i. 180).

[33] See Louis-Sébastien le Nain de Tillemont, *Mémoires pour servir à l'histoire ecclésiastique des six premiers siècles*, 16 vols. (2nd edn.; Paris: Charles Robustel, 1701–12). Upon receiving a gift of the *Mémoires* from his former student, Frederic Rogers (b. 1811), Newman wrote in Aug. 1833: 'The 'Church of the Fathers' [in the *British Magazine*] is in great measure drawn up from it' (*LD* iv. 36).

exactness, and dislike of theory or paradox, into an over-estimation of facts, as such, separated from their meaning and consequences'; too many facts with too little interpretation was no way to write history (*Critic* 20: 214). What about younger men in the tradition of Van Mildert, like William Lyall? These he describes as having 'no internal consistency [or] clearness of principle'. Hugh James Rose himself? According to Newman in a letter to Froude in January 1836, at this stage Rose's editorship of the *British Magazine* was making him 'jealous of the Critic', and 'I think he wished the Oxford Tracts to stop, as ticklish things, which might go he knew not where' (*LD* v. 223–4). Newman thought the various High Church leaders, like Rose and the proprietor of the *British Critic*, Joshua Watson (b. 1771), were divided among themselves. Watson was an influential layman and sometime treasurer of SPCK, the brother of John James Watson (b. 1767), rector of Hackney. Together with Henry Handley Norris (b. 1771), perpetual curate and then rector of South Hackney, the brothers led the so-called Hackney Phalanx of influential London High Churchmen. With Rose divided from the Phalanx, Newman felt confident to demand, here in Joshua's own *British Critic*, that new leadership was needed among the High Churchmen to bring about a return to the Fathers. By January 1838, Newman had manoeuvred into such a position of leadership as editor of the *Critic*.[34]

Rose's concern in 1836 was for the Oxford students whom Newman influenced. Two of those students provide a commentary on the shape of that influence in the 1830s. S. F. Wood (b. 1809), whom Newman taught and who went on to become a London lawyer, expressed similar concerns to Rose's after a meeting with Newman in January 1836. The subject of Wood's disagreement was how to get from the tenets of the early Church to what came after, thinking Newman too mired in the Fathers. Ironically, to get him out of the mire, Wood proposed doctrinal development as an alternative, an idea like the one Newman would propound in the following decade. But, at the meeting, Newman rejected the idea, leading Wood to write to his Oxford contemporary, Henry Manning (b. 1808):

---

[34] For the publishing battles of Tractarians and High Churchmen in London, see Pereiro, *'Ethos' and the Oxford Movement*, 14–25.

[Newman] says that before the Reformation the Church never deduced any doctrine from Scripture, and by inference blames our Reformers for doing so. Moreover he objects to their doctrine in itself as to Justification by Faith, and complains of their attempt to prove it from the Fathers... Generally, his result is, not merely to refer us to antiquity but to *shut us up* in it, and to deprive, not only individuals but the Church, of all those doctrines of Scripture not fully commented on by the Fathers.[35]

James Pereiro's research into Wood supports Louis Allen's findings that Newman did not sympathize with Rome's teachings in the middle 1830s.[36] Thus, Rune Imberg, finding evidence for a Catholic drift in the corrections Newman made to the early Tracts that were republished in 1836–8, is too hasty to see a move towards *Development of Christian Doctrine* (1845) and thence to Rome.[37]

F. W. Faber (b. 1814) was an Evangelical undergraduate at Balliol when he wrote to a friend in 1835, expressing suspicion of Newman's love of antiquity. Initially drawn to Newman because they shared an antipathy to 'the rationalities of Whately', Faber nevertheless thought that

a very serious blow may be given to the Church by bodies of young men going out to be parish priests, believing that there are inner doctrines, which it is well not to reveal to the vulgar—mysteries—I am using Newman's own words, which are his peculiar treasure—'thoughts which it is scarcely right to enlarge upon in a mixed congregation'.[38]

Faber continued that, given 'the accidents of depth of thought, peculiar line of study, and a somewhat monastic seclusion, I do not wonder that Newman's mind has been deeply tinctured by that mystical allegorizing spirit of Origen and the school of Alexandria.

[35] To Manning, 29 Jan. 1836, Manning Papers (Bodleian), printed ibid. 248–9 (App. I).
[36] Pereiro, 'S. F. Wood and an Early Theory of Development in the Oxford Movement', *Recusant History*, 20 (1991), 540–1. Allen remarks that where development 'is referred to in Newman's early work it is usually an attribute of "Romanism", in other words it is a case against which he argues' (Allen (ed.), *John Henry Newman and the Abbé Jager: A Controversy on Scripture and Tradition 1834–1836* (Oxford: Oxford University Press, 1975), 12).
[37] Rune Imberg, *In Quest of Authority: The 'Tracts for the Times' and the Development of the Tractarian Leaders 1833–41* (Lund: Lund University Press, 1987), 124–5.
[38] John Edward Bowden, *The Life and Letters of Frederick William Faber, D. D.* (London: Thomas Richardson & Son, 1869), 21.

I can answer from personal experience for the manner in which it captivates a mind which is in the least imaginative'.[39] In the 1830s, Newman was so 'shut up' in pre-Nicene doctrine that many feared he would be stuck there.[40]

The later chapters of this book will argue that, in the 1840s, Newman changed his focus. His paradigm for conceiving of the Fathers shifted from the pre-Nicenes to Athanasius. In doing so, Newman also changed the paradigm by which Athanasius was understood by many subsequent scholars, through the annotations to his translation for A Library of the Fathers. In the wake of Tract 90, Newman abandoned his aim of making the ancient Church live once more in England. Instead, he sought an authority who would guarantee that developments in doctrine were legitimate, and in his reading of Athanasius he found such a guarantor. Throughout his life, though, Newman retained his High Church formation. Etienne Gilson finds it still present in the 1870s,[41] which explains why in 1879, the year Newman became a cardinal, he was hard at work on a translation of Athanasius. This was a retranslation of the *Select Treatises of S. Athanasius in Controversy with the Arians* of 1842–4. By the later date, however, he was reading the Greek Father through the lens of scholasticism, which led Athanasius's theology to be translated in very different terms in the version published in 1881. Here, the patriarch is introduced as the one 'in whose name and history years ago I began to write, and with whom I end' (*Ath* i, p. ix); but was it the same Athanasius? Newman contributed to the history of doctrine by bequeathing to those who read him different views of the Fathers at different stages of his life.

In what follows, Chapter 1 gives an overview of the way that the three different stages of Newman's life shaped his writing on the Alexandrians. The first period (broadly covering the 1830s) came

[39] Ibid. 20.

[40] Ironically, by Apr. 1837, Faber was translating for A Library of the Fathers the work of 'Optatus, Bishop of Milevis, on the schism of the Donatists' (ibid. 70).

[41] Gilson wrote: 'while it would be wrong to imagine Newman as unacquainted with scholasticism when he wrote the *Grammar of Assent*, it must not be forgotten that, born and educated in the Anglican Church, his first theological formation owed little to the scholastics...[rather,] owing to him, the great theological style of the Fathers has been worthily revived in the nineteenth century' (introduction, *An Essay Towards a Grammar of Assent* (New York: Image Books, 1955), 17–18).

to an end with Newman's alienation from the Anglican Church after Tract 90. Seeking seclusion at Littlemore, in the quasi-monastic community he set up in his parish, he could work hard on translating Athanasius and perhaps see himself as an exile making the journey to Rome with the saint. In Rome to study, he then rejected scholastic theology in favour of a Latin dissertation on Athanasius. The second period (the 1840s and 50s) ended with alienation from the Catholic Church after 'On Consulting the Faithful', which, as John Coulson pointed out, 'provides the reasons for his silence as a Catholic writer between the publication of the *Lectures and Essays on University Subjects* in 1858 and the writing of the *Apologia* in 1864, as well as helping to explain why Kingsley's attack produced such a volcanic reply'.[42] The third period (the 1860s and 70s) saw Newman return to scholastic theology. Thus, Note II in the appendix to the 1871 republication of *Arians of the Fourth Century* refers to 'the received Catholic teaching *de Deo* and *de SS. Trinitate*', which reflects the sort of division of the doctrine of God into two parts, *de Deo uno* and *de Deo trino*, found in his Catholic contemporary, Johannes Baptist (later Cardinal) Franzelin (*Ari* 417). This reconceiving of patristic doctrine was a change first of all from the 1833 *Arians of the Fourth Century*, but also his retranslation of *Select Treatises* presented a neo-Thomist Athanasius compared with the 1842–4 version, justifying the claim that Newman read the Fathers differently in the three stages.

Chapters 2 and 3 focus on the first stage. In the 1830s, Newman dealt separately with the doctrines of the Trinity (in *Arians of the Fourth Century*) and the incarnation (in three subsequent summers of research). Taking the doctrine of the Trinity as its theme, Chapter 2 examines in detail Newman's first book, written in 1831–2, looking at the ways in which the previous two centuries of Anglican debate on the Alexandrian Fathers helped form his opinions. *Arians of the Fourth Century* set the stage for all subsequent discussion of the early Alexandrians, both in Newman's and in Anglophone scholarship.

Chapter 3 examines what Newman had to say between 1834 and 1840 about the person and work of Christ. Covering the period from the publication of *Arians of the Fourth Century* to his first insights into doctrinal development, its focus will be three summer vacations

---

[42] Coulson, introduction, *Cons* (p. 1).

which Newman spent researching different Greek patristic views of Christ and the sermons which resulted. In the summer of 1839, examining various Fathers before and after the Council of Chalcedon, he began to see doctrine no longer as something static but as in development. Newman became aware of the need for an idea whereby pre-Nicenes like Origen and Dionysius of Alexandria could 'develop' into the fuller doctrinal positions of Athanasius and Cyril. But even Athanasius and Cyril needed some later interpreters to clarify their positions, particularly the trio of Leontius of Byzantium, Maximus, and John of Damascus.

By the 1840s, Newman understood Christology and the incarnation as an integral part of the doctrine of the Trinity, so that Chapters 4 and 5 consider these themes together, through the lens of Newman's changing opinions on the theology of Origen and Athanasius. Chapter 4 shows that Newman's opinion of Origen and Athanasius changed in the 1840s and 50s, as a consequence of the very different conception of the Trinity from that he held in the 1830s—one that was different again from that he held in the 1870s, discussed in Chapter 5. Comparing Newman's earlier translation of the anti-Arian works in A Library of the Fathers (1842–4) with his later version of *Select Treatises* (1881), the increasingly 'Latin' ways in which Newman came to read Alexandrian theology will be charted. Notice that this Latin reading begins before his conversion. Subsequently, in Rome, in 1846–7, he was challenged to make his reading of the Fathers accord specifically with the theology of the Roman Schools. His views on the Fathers continued to get him into trouble, leading to his being investigated for heresy after 'On Consulting the Faithful' appeared in the *Rambler* in 1859. Therefore, not only did his reading of the Alexandrian Fathers change before he went to Rome, but it changed even more in the 1860s and 70s when he began to engage fully with scholastic theology. In his freer translation of Athanasius, discussed in Chapter 5, it is not so much Thomas Aquinas but the neo-Thomism of the teachers of Leo XIII that he read back into Athanasius. Origen, too, in 'Causes of Arianism' (1872) is seen through Aquinas's interpretation of him.

The general reader might like to know that each chapter begins with Newman's biography and gets more theological towards the end of the chapter. The theological reader might like to know what I mean by Newman's 'Latin' reading of the 'Greek' Fathers. This book is not concerned with the oversimplified accounts of the differences between Greek and Latin notions of the divine Trinity found in twentieth-century historical theology; in fact, it attempts to locate Newman's writing in a period *before* such categories came to dominate doctrine. The arguments about what French scholar Theodore de Régnon said, or might not have said, about Greeks approaching God from the Three and Latins from the One, in the last years of the nineteenth century, are not relevant to discussions of doctrine taking place before.[43] My suggestion, following others, is that readers of the Fathers today find it difficult to see past the doctrinal terminology of the late nineteenth and twentieth centuries.[44] Yet Newman's viewpoint is not ours: he could read the Fathers without inflicting on them notions of East–West difference that have arisen since him. Newman's own ideas of what are distinctively Greek or Latin conceptions of God's Trinity begin with his critique of Gibbon in the 1840s. Newman's categories for how the three divine persons can be one are those of Latin 'numerical' and Greek 'generical' unity, which he claims are ways of saying the same thing.[45]

The description in Chapters 4 and 5 of Newman's changing interpretation of Origen and Athanasius avoids the categories which beset a certain type of historical theology, doing so in order to reveal the mistakes in the historiography of doctrine that Newman himself introduced. The conclusion will suggest what influence these mistakes had on subsequent scholarship of Athanasius's view of the Trinity and on the importance of Origen. Labels used

---

[43] Theodore de Régnon, *Études de théologie positive sur la sainte trinité*, i (Paris: Retaux, 1892). See also Michel René Barnes, 'De Régnon Reconsidered', *Augustinian Studies*, 26 (1995) and Kristin Hennessy, 'An Answer to De Régnon's Accusers: Why We Should Not Speak of his Paradigm', *Harvard Theological Review*, 100 (2007), 179–97.

[44] For an example of this sort of historiography of doctrine, see Sarah Coakley (ed.), 'Introduction: Disputed Questions in Patristic Trinitarianism', *Harvard Theological Review*, 100 (2007), 125–38.

[45] 'Gibbon remarks that the doctrine of "a numerical rather than a generical unity", which has been explicitly put forth by the Latin Church, is "favoured by the Latin language; τριάς [lit: three] seems to excite the idea of substance, *trinitas* of qualities"; ch. 21, n. 74' (*Ox Frs* viii. 46, n. k). Quoting Gibbon, *Rise and Fall of the Roman Empire*, ed. J. B. Bury (2nd edn.; London: Methuen, 1909), 374 n. 74.

below—Anglican, Catholic, Latin, or neo-Thomist—are not intended to be pejorative but heuristic, attempting to name the changes going on in Newman's brilliant but generally unsystematic mind. Only once these changes have been described can we judge 'in whose name' Newman really wrote.

1

Three Views of Doctrine: Three Phases of Newman's Life

Newman's writings on doctrine, specifically the doctrine of the Fathers, fall into three periods. Here the general differences between the periods will be shown, as the basis for a more detailed discussion of his writings on the Trinity and incarnation in subsequent chapters. Newman shifted from the twofold system of doctrine in the 1830s, to the idea of the development of doctrine in the 1840s and 50s, to viewing doctrine as a theological science in the 1860s and 70s. Each of these can be called a 'system' of doctrine that he claimed was grounded in the Fathers, but only the last was an attempt at systematic theology.

What did Newman mean by 'system' as opposed to systematic theology? A brief examination of his usage of the word shows that in the first period he differentiated the 'Catholic system', which he understood to come from the Fathers, from both the systematic theology of Protestants based on the doctrine of Atonement and 'the Roman Catholic system' seen at first hand in Rome in 1833 (*LD* iii. 273). His 'Lectures on the Prophetical Office' were delivered in the Adam de Brome Chapel of St Mary's, Oxford, in 1836, and published the following year. In Lecture V, discussing on the one hand a popular Protestantism that looks only to 'private judgement' for guidance in what scripture teaches, and on the other a Romanism that disallows private judgement, Newman proposes a '*Via Media*' between the two that follows the scriptural interpretation offered by the Fathers of Antiquity. 'Little of systematic knowledge as Scripture may impart to ordinary readers,' he ventures, 'still what it does convey may surely tend in one direction and not in another. What it imparts may look towards the system of the Church and of Antiquity, not oppose it' (*VM* i. 139). Scripture, though it does not offer a system of doctrine itself, nevertheless points in the direction of the system that the Church Fathers discerned when interpreting scripture. That system, he wrote in January 1839, is present in the writings of the 'Apostolical Fathers'—the immediate successors of the apostles—in which '[i]t is hardly too much to say that almost the whole system of Catholic doctrine may be discovered, at least in outline' (*Critic* 25: 72/*EH* i. 261). In this article, and for the final time before Newman's thought turned to development, the later Fathers merely reiterated the system which the earlier Fathers taught (*Critic* 25: 66/*EH* i. 247).[1] In July 1838, he praised *A Treatise on the Church of Christ*, by William Palmer of Worcester College (b. 1803), for presenting a 'system . . . which shall at once be conformable to ancient doctrine . . . and to the necessities of the modern English Church; an attempt to place us in a position in which we can defend ourselves against both Romanists and sectaries' (*Critic* 24: 353/*EH* i. 189). Historically speaking, this was the system that Anglicanism lacked and which, at one stage in 1833, Newman sought with Palmer of Worcester to provide.

Yet this was not 'systematic' scholarship of the sort Newman encountered in the Roman schools in 1846–7, but a system that told a story—and which had a moral attached. In his introduction to *The Ecclesiastical History of M. L'Abbé Fleury*, published in 1842, Newman preferred a 'system or philosophical view' of truth to a particular 'theory' put forward by Protestant historians (*Fleury* i, pp. v–vi). This system or philosophy took a 'view' of history, rather than presenting it as a series of facts.[2] The *Essay on the Development of*

---

[1] The danger, as Isaac Williams wrote in the controversial Tract 87, published in 1840, was 'substituting a system of man's own creating for that which GOD has given. Instead of the Sacraments and ordinances, it [the Protestant system] has put forth prominently a supposed sense of the Atonement, as the badge of a profession' (pt v, sect. 8). Instead, as the title of pt vi has it, 'The System of the Church [is] One of Reserve'.

[2] 'View' is a rightly topographical image. 'When we have lost our way, we mount up to some eminence to look about us . . . [not] into the nearest thicket to find out [our] bearings', Newman wrote to Mrs Anstice in Dec. 1845 (*LD* xi. 69). Nicholas Lash points out the overtones of the word 'view' make it especially pertinent to Newman as a historian rather than a systematic theologian (*Newman on Development: The Search for an Explanation in History* (London: Sheed and Ward, 1975), 37–8).

Christian Doctrine was Newman's attempt in the 1840s to give such a system of ecclesiastical history. But this was not systematic theology. As Nicholas Lash observes, 'One of the reasons for Newman's insistence that he was "no theologian" and that the *Essay* was not a work of theology, was that, for much of his life, he accepted the view that deduction was the only appropriate method of proof and argument in theology'.[3] Lash shows that Newman went on thinking in a way that separated scientific theologians from historians like himself until a third period of his life: 'By 1870, he could group together "experimental science, historical research, or theology" as classes of "concrete reasoning" (*GA* 359)...By the time he came to revise the *Essay* [1878], the shift in his conception of the theological method allowed him to use the term "theology" in contexts where he had previously been unwilling to do so.'[4] This chapter will argue that Newman only came to engage with scientific theology after 1859, during a long struggle to understand the scholastics and to relate them to the Fathers; but when he did it changed the way he wrote patristic history in this last period.

THE HIGH CHURCH CONTEXT:
(1) THE CHURCH FACES PERSECUTION

Images of the recent revolutions in Europe were in the minds of the handful of High Churchmen who gathered at Hugh James Rose's Rectory in Hadleigh, Suffolk between 25 and 29 July 1833. Images of the English Revolution, the last time the established status of the Church of England had been threatened, were also in their minds. But so, crucially, were images of the early Church. The sermon preached in Hadleigh that Sunday by A. P. Perceval, a chaplain to the king, invoked Jesus's warnings to his earliest followers in Matthew 24:

---

[3] 'View' is a rightly topographical image. 'When we have lost our way, we mount up to some eminence to look about us...[not] into the nearest thicket to find out [our] bearings', Newman wrote to Mrs Anstice in Dec. 1845 (*LD* xi. 69). Nicholas Lash points out the overtones of the word 'view' make it especially pertinent to Newman as a historian rather than a systematic theologian (*Newman on Development: The Search for an Explanation in History* (London: Sheed and Ward, 1975), 23.
[4] Ibid. 24.

All the signs and the tokens of evil which marked the days when good King Charles was put to death, are gathering around, and showing themselves again... Already, indeed, as far as words go, the persecution has begun: and, as in all times of trouble, the first mark at which evil men aim, has always been the ministers of religion, so it is now. The ministers of religion are openly reviled and abused... Too soon, I fear, many of us may be called upon to put in practice those lessons which the Scriptures teach, of how to suffer persecution.[5]

Although John Henry Newman was not at the gathering, he, like Perceval, saw the courage of the early Church, when faced with persecution, as an example for worried clergymen to follow. It was in the context of a Church under siege that Newman began to shape his interpretation of the Fathers in the early 1830s.

The repeal of the Test and Corporation Acts in 1828, the emancipation of Catholics in 1829, and the Reform Act in 1832 had, in the minds of High Churchmen, brought the unwelcome influence of non-Anglicans in national life and presaged an end of the privileged status of the Church of England. Worse was to follow, when the government introduced the Irish Church Temporalities Bill to parliament, for now the Whigs were involving themselves in the established Church of Ireland. Although John Keble's sermon against 'National Apostasy' at St Mary's in Oxford on 9 July 1833 has become famous, neither Keble nor Newman were at Hadleigh two weeks later to discuss ways to involve High Church clergy in the defence of the establishment. (The Bill was passed into law by the House of Lords the day after the Hadleigh gathering.) As William Palmer of Worcester put it in his account of events a decade later: 'The first sound of the tocsin of revolution at Paris in 1830, ought to have re-united the scattered friends of established order in England: it left them engaged in dissensions.'[6] Dissension arose among those at Hadleigh and their friends, too—dissensions that would grow throughout the 1830s. Perceval and Palmer, whom Richard Hurrell Froude came to label 'the Orthodox' or 'Zs', found themselves at odds at Hadleigh with Froude, and

[5] This attribution to Perceval comes from the sermon appearing in his *Collection of Papers Connected with the Theological Movement of 1833* (London: Rivingtons, 1842), 42.

[6] William Palmer, *A Narrative of Events Connected with Publication of the Tracts* (rev. edn.; London: Rivingtons, 1883), 97.

afterwards with Keble and Newman, whom Froude labelled 'the Apos-
tolicals' or 'Ys'. Perceval and Palmer, along with Rose, honoured
the Reformers more than Newman, Keble, and Froude. But in honour-
ing the early Church Fathers, in finding in them ammunition for
the fight against reform, all were in full agreement.

Where the Zs and Ys did agree, as the first half of this book will
argue, was to focus on 'doctrine and discipline' as they originated in
the Church Fathers. Perceval and Palmer drafted 'Suggestions for the
Formation of an Association of Friends of the Church', a document
coming out of the discussions at Hadleigh, which diagnosed what
was happening in the nation:

> Every one who has become acquainted with the literature of the day, must
> have observed the sedulous attempts made in various quarters, to reconcile
> Members of the Church to alterations in its Doctrines and Discipline.
> Projects of change, which include the annihilation of our Creeds and the
> removal of doctrinal statements incidentally contained in our worship, have
> been boldly and assiduously put forth... Our Apostolical polity has been
> ridiculed and denied.[7]

Concern for historic doctrine and apostolic polity were at the front of
High Church minds in the summer and autumn of 1833. But there was
disagreement over how to disseminate High Church ideas. As Palmer
looked back on those days, he wrote: 'The difficulties which were felt in
regard to the publication of Tracts by an association, led to the designed
omission of any mention of Tracts in the "Suggestions" which formed
the original basis of our Association.'[8] Palmer portrayed Froude as an
opponent of his plan for regional associations of clergy to be addressed
by travelling speakers, and added Newman's name in a parenthesis
when he revised his thoughts in 1883.[9] It seems Froude and Newman
were focused on their own plan to disseminate opposition to reform in
a series of bold and short publications coming from Oxford. By
November 1833, Palmer wanted the Tracts controlled by a committee
and even called for a halt to their publication (*LD* iv. 97).

.   There were certainly divisions among these High Churchmen,
Palmer 'muster[ing] the zs in great force against the Tracts, and

---

[7] William Palmer, *A Narrative of Events Connected with Publication of the Tracts*
(rev. edn.; London: Rivingtons, 1883), 104.
[8] Ibid. 119 n. 1.   [9] Ibid. 105.

some Evangelicals' (*LD* iv. 100–1).[10] But there was much in common too. How near Newman was to other High Churchmen can be judged by the similar use of the language of persecution and sense of foreboding in his anonymous Tract 1 and in Perceval's sermon at Hadleigh. In Tract 1, Newman reminded his fellow Anglican priests of their relation to bishops, 'THE SUCCESSORS OF THE APOSTLES':

surely we may be their shield-bearers in the battle without offence; and by our voice and deeds be to them what Luke and Timothy were to St Paul. Now let me come at once to the subject which leads me to address you. Should the Government and the Country so far forget their God as to cast off the Church, to deprive it of its temporal honours and substance, *on what* will you rest the claim of respect and attention which you make upon your flocks?[11]

For Newman as for Perceval, a sense of persecution was the impetus for action.

Newman, Froude, and Keble, three Fellows of Oriel College who had first united in their opposition to Sir Robert Peel's bid for re-election as Oxford's MP after he had introduced a parliamentary bill to emancipate Catholics, were now more certain of impending persecution of Anglican clergy than they had been in 1828. The rapid succession of publications before the year's end suggests frantic energy. By 9 September 1833, Newman had written and published the first three Tracts.[12] Keble's Tract 4 was printed about 21 September. Newman's friend from his undergraduate days, John Bowden, wrote Tract 5, which was printed on 24 October. Two more of Newman's were printed on 29 October (numbers 6 and 7). Another of Newman's, number 8, of which Froude might have shared in the

---

[10] A 'Z' like Palmer was more open than Newman or Froude to Evangelicals—the 'Xs' or 'Peculiars' as Froude labelled them. Palmer wrote: 'Mr. Rose, in establishing the *British Magazine*, had resolved to keep clear of questions which had divided the Church, and in this we cheerfully concurred. I *know* the kind and charitable feelings which existed in others towards the party called "Evangelical", and am sure that no different sentiment ever existed in my own mind' (ibid. 116).

[11] *Tracts for the Times*, i (London: Rivingtons, 1834). Herein parts and sections of longer Tracts are cited, but not pages, because of the diversity of pagination in available editions.

[12] See *LD* iv. 48, in which Newman tells Froude he had written four Tracts, leading Imberg to argue that Newman must have originally considered the long Tract 3 as two separate works (Rune Imberg, *In Quest of Authority: The 'Tracts for the Times' and the Development of the Tractarian Leaders 1833–41* (Lund: Lund University Press, 1987), 22).

authorship, was printed on 31 October together with Froude's number 9. Newman's Tracts 10 and 11 were published on 5 and 11 November respectively, and his numbers 19 and 20 on 27 December. Palmer joined with Newman for Tract 15, printed on 16 December. Perceval joined with the Oriel group to contribute Tract 23, which was printed before 17 January 1834.[13]

It should be noted that most of the Tracts were anonymous, although Pusey added his initials at the end of number 18 and Newman added his to number 21, a defence of Pusey's Tract. Pusey brought a change to the later Tracts too, which after his sprawling essay on baptism (numbers 67–9) became fewer, longer, and more serious in tone from 1836 to 1841. The Fathers continued to be mined for their resources, as was most controversially seen in Isaac Williams' two Tracts on reserve in preaching (numbers 80 in 1837 and 87 in 1840).

Between December 1832 and July 1833, Newman travelled to the Mediterranean, and was inspired by his surroundings to compose a number of poems on the early Church. His imagination, joining with his fear of persecution, led him to pen:

> When shall our Northern Church her champion see,
> Raised by Divine decree,
> To shield the ancient Truth at his own harm?

> (*Lyra* 96–7)

Similar feelings led Newman to begin the Records of the Church, translations of early Church documents that fuelled the High Church imagination with examples of how to defend the truth even at the risk of harm to oneself. Publishing such poems upon his return and starting the Records were part of the same strategy, Newman admitted to John Bowden in November 1833, of '*indirect* inculcation of the Apostolical doctrines . . . to familiarize the imagination of the reader to the *Apostolical state* of the Church' (*LD* iv. 109).

Complementing the Tracts, the Records appeared at a rapid rate. Rune Imberg notes that the first Record was published on 11 November and by 17 December a dozen had been printed.[14] Among

---

[13] See Imberg, *Quest*, 196–210, for the attribution of authors and dates of the Tracts.
[14] Ibid. 23 n. 12.

these twelve, seven were the letters of Ignatius of Antioch, dating from the early years of the second century. Another was the account of Ignatius's martyrdom, to which Newman appended this conclusion: 'We are always on our trial, always have duties, always can be promoting GOD's glory. Ignatius wrote his letters when he was a prisoner, travelling a weary way across a whole continent to his death.'[15] The theme of persecution was present in the other Records too: number 11 was an 'Account of the Martyrdom of St James the Apostle' and 12 was 'The Martyrdom of Polycarp'. Record 6 was an 'Account of the Martyrs of Lyons and Vienne', from which Newman drew this conclusion: 'we learn beside, how blessed it is to suffer boldly in a good cause, for we encourage others to do the same.' After the first twelve Records, there was a shift in theme made possible by the fact the early martyr Justin also left an 'account of Baptism, the Lord's Supper, and the Public Worship of God'. Likewise, the prominence of baptism and eucharist in the early Church, and the question of who was granted the 'secrets' of these sacraments, was a theme of *Arians of the Fourth Century,* published on 5 November 1833 but completed at the end of June 1832 (*LD* iii. 60). In the Records and in *Arians of the Fourth Century,* Newman was publishing exactly the sort of history that he liked best—a presentation of the past that gave a clear moral for the present.

Along with the activities in Oxford, Hugh James Rose had responded to the reform crisis by beginning the *British Magazine* in 1832, as an ecclesiastical voice of opposition to the Whigs. Rose worried about those who had joined in the opposition to the Whigs only out of 'a negative recoil from "French principles"', as Nockles puts it, and wanted instead a commitment to 'philosophical depth' and 'ethical insight', goals which the introduction above showed that Newman shared.[16] Under Rose's editorship, the *British*

---

[15] Records 1–18 were bound with the Tracts for 1833–4 in *Tracts for the Times,* i (1834) and Records 19–25 with the Tracts for 1834–5 in vol. ii (1836). Although Newman did not translate the Records ('Ch[rist] Ch[urch] men have been translating Ignatius' (*LD* iv. 141)), he probably wrote the short introductions, notes, and conclusions.

[16] Peter Nockles, *The Oxford Movement in Context: Anglican High Churchmanship 1760–1857* (Cambridge: Cambridge University Press, 1994), 323–4. Here Nockles points out the lack of the latter two was '[w]hat most dismayed Victorian High Churchmen about their Georgian forebears'.

Magazine aimed to instil these characteristics in its readership, so in August 1833 Newman sent Rose a set of letters about the fourth century for publication in the magazine: three on the way Ambrose of Milan (*c.*339–97) withstood imperial pressure and a fourth on the opposition of Basil of Caesarea (*c.*330–79) to the Emperor Valens's incursions into the Church. The tone of impending persecution of the English Church was there from the beginning of the first Ambrose article, for political reform 'makes it a practical concern for every churchman to prepare himself for a change, and a practical question for the clergy, by what instruments the authority of Religion is to be supported, should the protection and patronage of the Government be withdrawn' (*HS* i. 339).

Newman's tone was stronger than anything Rose himself wrote, whose aim was to avoid splits within the Church.[17] Therefore what Newman sent him was published in the correspondence section, under the comment: 'The Editor begs to remind his readers that he is not in any way responsible for the opinions of his Correspondents.'[18] But the difference between editor and author should not be exaggerated. Rose continued to print Newman's anonymous articles, writing in December 1835 that 'your *Church of the Fathers* series has done more good than almost anything which has come forth of late' (*LD* v. 178 n. 1). He also stood up for the fiery rhetoric of the Tracts when Palmer tried to take them over by committee; Newman reported in December 1833 that Rose 'had *remonstrated with him* [Palmer] *for thwarting the Tracts*' (*LD* iv. 141). In September 1834, it was to Rose that Newman wrote for guidance in his controversy with Abbé Jager, a French Catholic admirer of the early Tracts. Newman asked Rose to 'name which of our divines treats the Popish question best' (*LD* iv. 326). The resulting system, put forward in the debate with Jager, polished in what was called 'The Brothers' Controversy', and presented in the Lectures on the Prophetical Office, was a fusion of the Anglican divines and Newman's interpretation of the Fathers.

---

[17] According to Palmer, Rose was cautious about his 'Address to the Archbishop of Canterbury', sending 'letters expressing very serious apprehension that this Address would cause schism in the Church', *Narrative*, 108. This came to be signed by 7,000 clergymen before it was presented at Lambeth Palace in Feb. 1834.

[18] Quoted McGrath, introduction, *CF* (p. xxi).

A TWOFOLD SYSTEM OF DOCTRINE (1830s)

Compared with the exposition of pre-Nicene tradition in *Arians of the Fourth Century*, Hurrell Froude thought that a resort to Anglican 'fundamentals' in opposing Abbé Jager's Catholicism left Newman too dependent on 'Bible-Christianity' (*LD* v. 98).[19] Froude opposed the idea that scripture contained 'all things necessary to salvation', as the sixth of the Thirty-nine Articles put it, and preferred to put his faith in tradition. Yet in this section it will be argued that Newman saw continuity between the twofold sense of scripture in *Arians* and the twofold pattern of doctrine of his debates with Jager; to imply that Newman was mortgaging tradition to scripture was to miss how rich the interpretation of scripture by tradition could be. Moreover, in response to Froude, it will be seen that Newman interpreted Vincent of Lérins's *Commonitorium* as confirming that the traditions of the Church were in any case merely shorthand for scripture. Tradition followed the direction of scripture, rather than developed over time, at this stage of Newman's thought.[20]

In his correspondence with Jager, Newman distinguished two categories of orthodox doctrine in the early Church. First, Newman put the 'fundamentals' of doctrine into a category he called 'Apostolical' or 'Episcopal Tradition'. He claimed that these teachings are necessary to salvation, unchanging, and all found in scripture. Secondary, but extremely important none the less, are the teachings that supplement 'Episcopal Tradition', which he called 'Prophetical Tradition', although he was not always clear which doctrines belonged here. Whether or not such an account can be discerned in the history of the early Church—and Jager thought it could not—Newman's

---

[19] The idea of 'fundamentals' in Anglicanism came especially from Daniel Waterland's *A Discourse of Fundamentals* (1735). See S. W. Sykes, 'Newman, Anglicanism, and the Fundamentals', in Ian Ker and Alan G. Hill (eds.), *Newman after One Hundred Years* (Oxford: Clarendon Press, 1990), 353–74.

[20] Ian Ker suggests of the '*Via Media*' Tracts, 38 and 41, that the second 'shows how even at this point Newman took the principle of doctrinal development for granted' (*John Henry Newman: A Biography* (Oxford: Clarendon Press, 1988), 105). However, based on the letters of S. F. Wood, Pereiro thinks it 'unlikely that [Newman] would have professed in 1834 what he would deny so emphatically some months later' to Wood ('*Ethos*' and the Oxford Movement, 165).

theory aimed to seal up the essentials in one category, while allowing room in the second category for dynamism and enrichment of the faith. Questions to do with how this twofold division actually works, and to which category various doctrines belong, were less important to Newman than the observation that the pre-Nicenes recognized that some dimensions of doctrine are unchanging, and others are dynamic. A doctrine as unchanging as the unity of the three divine persons, for instance, was nevertheless taught by the pre-Nicenes with ever-shifting terminology. The secondary teaching or doctrine was expansive, sometimes speculative, although the primary teaching—the three persons in one God—remained unchanged.

The *Lectures on the Prophetical Office of the Church, Viewed Relatively to Romanism and Popular Protestantism* were published in 1837. Within the twofold pattern of doctrine, as laid out here, 'Prophetical Tradition' was

> partly written, partly unwritten, partly the interpretation, partly the supplement of Scripture, partly preserved in intellectual expressions, partly latent in the spirit and temper of Christians; poured to and fro in closets and upon the housetops, in liturgies, in controversial works, in obscure fragments, in sermons, in popular prejudices, in local customs. (*VM* i. 250)

What is clear is that, while he considers the essentials of doctrine found in scripture and the creeds to be written and fairly fixed in content, secondary teachings (levels of interpretation, secrets, customs) are mainly oral and embodied.[21] An interpretation of the relation of Father to Son, such as the Nicene Creed's definition that they are consubstantial (*homoousios*), is thus a secondary 'explanation' of the primary tradition that God is three persons in one. That is why, in the Lectures, Newman classed *homoousios* as secondary tradition, rather than as 'Episcopal Tradition' like the rest of the Creed. This word was introduced at Nicaea 'merely in explanation of a great article of faith', he writes (*VM* i. 228).

This account of doctrine was far richer than the accounts offered by many of his contemporaries. His twofold systematizing of tradition was offering a critique on two fronts. First, contra the rationalists of his day

---

[21] Günter Biemer shows how radical these claims were, given the Anglican context, in *Newman and Tradition*, trans. K. Smyth (New York: Herder and Herder, 1967), 17.

like Whately, Newman wanted the faith to be fixed in essentials, but also rich and creative rather than dry and logical. This was what the Prophetical *should* be all about, had the rationalists not 'reduced [prophecy] to "prediction" that could be verified; and so men lost sight of the way in which prophecy was a means of declaring God's works and words'.[22] Then, contra the Evangelicals of his day, with whom he agreed on essentials, he promoted the importance of secondary tradition as a way to delve far deeper into scripture than they allowed, in order to discern expansive images with which to teach doctrine.

There is a third dimension that Newman adds to this twofold system in these Lectures, a dimension that guided both 'Episcopal Tradition' and 'Prophetic Tradition' in the early Church. It is the Rule of Faith (*regula fidei*). There are two important points to Newman's understanding of the Rule. First, being identical with the creeds of the early Church, the Rule was also part of the primary 'Episcopal Tradition'. But it also had a role independent of 'Episcopal Tradition' because it governed the secondary teachings of the Church that were discerned in scripture and found in custom. Moreover, as an *unwritten* Rule in the pre-Nicene Church, it shared the major characteristic of the 'partly unwritten' 'Prophetical Tradition'. Only the initiated knew the creed, which was learnt gradually over the course of a convert's catechumenate, memorized not written down, and kept secret from anyone outside the Church.[23]

The Rule of Faith had practical consequences for the way early Christians lived, which is why it was called a 'rule'. In the *Lectures on Justification* (1838), Newman gave a clear differentiation between practical 'rules' and propositional 'principles'. Here he argues that

22 Andrew Louth, 'The Oxford Movement, the Fathers and the Bible', *Sobornost*, 6 (1984), 32.

23 Edward Burton argued for a secrecy that guaranteed credal unity until the end of the second century. Burton wrote in *The History of the Christian Church, from the Ascension of Jesus Christ to the Conversion of Constantine* (1836): 'any person who was a bearer of a letter from his bishop, was admitted to communion with the church in any country which he visited ... It may be supposed that these precautions were very effectual in preserving the unity of the Church, and in preventing diversity of doctrine. The result was ... that up to the end of the second century no schism had taken place among the great body of believers' (quoted by Newman, *Critic* 20: 220).

one misses the fullness of Christian life if one focuses on *principles* to the exclusion of *rules*. 'Principles are great truths or laws which embody in them the character of a system, enable us to estimate it, and indirectly guide us in practice. For instance, "all is of grace", is a great principle of the Gospel.' Rules 'are adapted for immediate practice... and are directed and moulded according to the end proposed, not by correctness of reasoning or analysis' (*Jfc* 333– 4).[24] Rules are immediately embodied, bringing about action in the Christian community, and so it is with the Rule of Faith. The pre-Nicene creeds did more than provide the principles of the faith; as the Rule of Faith, the creeds entered into the arena of the unwritten 'Prophetical Tradition'. They formed the ethos by which Christians lived.[25]

It was the living out of the Rule of Faith by the pre-Nicenes that was most important for Newman. The primary doctrines they taught were embodied in this secondary tradition, becoming the authority to which later Christians turned; so by simply referring to the tradition of the Fathers one testified to the veracity of any particular doctrine. Newman traced this understanding of the Rule to various Fathers. From Irenaeus (*c*.130–*c*.200) came the idea that even if

----

[24] Polemically this statement is to the detriment of 'Protestants', whose principles have become detached from a holy way of life. Reverting to principles alone, which do not directly guide practice, caused some of the mistakes of the Reformation: 'justification by faith only is a principle, not a rule of conduct... This is where men go wrong. They think that the long and the short of religion is to have faith; that is the whole, faith independent of every other duty; a something which can exist in the mind by itself, and from which all other holy exercises follow' (*Jfc* 334–5). Justification was an important topic for Newman in this period; in Aug. 1836, Newman cited Origen's *Commentary on Romans* to interpret Rom. 3: 26 (*LD* v. 338).

[25] Isaac Williams said this most clearly in Tract 87: 'The Fathers seem always to imply that the secrets of CHRIST'S kingdom are obtained only by a consistent course of self-denying obedience; that a knowledge of these things is not conveyed by mere words, nor is a matter of excited emotion, but is a *practical knowledge of the heart*, obtained more and more by self-renouncing duties like prayer and the like; and thus it is, that, by the Cross of CHRIST, we are brought to Him, and led on to the knowledge of GOD. So that this higher degree of faith "goeth not forth but by prayer and fasting." This is often explicitly stated, or incidentally implied by Origen and the others. St Augustine sets it forth' (pt iv, sect. 13, my italics).

the Apostles left us no Scriptures, doubtless it had been a duty to follow the course of Tradition, which they gave to those whom they put in trust with the Churches. This procedure is observed in many barbarous nations, such as believe in Christ, without written memorial, having salvation impressed through the Spirit on their hearts, and diligently preserving the Old Tradition. (*VM* i. 244)[26]

From 'Athanasius, Theodoret, etc.' came other thoughts on the nature of creeds, responding in August 1835 to Froude's criticism (*LD* v. 126). In the *Lectures on the Prophetical Office*, Newman aims to show that precisely these two Fathers, Athanasius (*c.*296–373) and Theodoret (*c.*393–*c.*460), shared but one Rule of Faith, together with Vincent of Lérins (d. before 450) whom Anglicans had historically considered the standard-bearer of what counts as right doctrine.[27] Moreover, all three inherited the Rule from the pre-Nicene Fathers. Newman argues in Lecture XIII on the early Church that *scripture* requires the Rule of Faith in order to be interpreted rightly and *tradition* requires the Rule to insure that the doctrines taught are those found in scripture. Scripture must take priority over tradition here; 'There is no other way of accounting for [Vincent's] saying, "*first* the authority of the Divine Law, *next* the Tradition of the Church Catholic"... The very *need* of Tradition arises only from the obscurity of Scripture, and is terminated with the interpretation of it' (*VM* i: 322–3). In this quotation, Newman thinks, Vincent is saying the same thing as Athanasius and Theodoret.[28] Athanasius is confident that tradition should be enough to silence heresy, because tradition is the embodiment in earlier Fathers of the Rule of Faith, the rule by which they discerned doctrine from scripture. If tradition

---

[26] *Adversus Haereses*, 3.4.1–2.

[27] Jean Stern says the same is true of seventeenth-century Anglicans and Catholics (apart from Petavius): 'Comme son contemporain Bossuet, Bull entend que le canon de Lérins, "quod ubique, quod semper, quod ad omnibus", soit pris à la lettre' (*Bible et tradition chez Newman: aux origines de la théorie du développement* (Paris: Aubier, 1967), 81).

[28] Vincent is quoted from *Commonitorium* 2. Athanasius is quoted extensively at *VM* i. 323–6 including from *Contra Apollinarem*, which Newman did not doubt (as most scholars do today) was by Athanasius (see Ch. 3 n. 62, below). Theodoret is quoted at *VM* i. 326–7, closing with the pithy statement, 'Here is the doctrine of the Gallic Vincentius in the mouth of a Syrian bishop'.

does not convince heretics, then they must be taken to the relevant passages of scripture itself. And in those passages, if interpreted rightly, will be found nothing other than the truth already taught by tradition.

Although the twofold system of 'Episcopal Tradition' and 'Prophetical Tradition' was not completed until the *Lectures on the Prophetical Office* (1837), nevertheless Newman had seen a similar twofold pattern in the patristic method of interpreting scripture in *Arians of the Fourth Century* (1833).[29] Among the early Alexandrians, like Clement (*c.*150–*c.*215) and Origen (*c.*186–*c.*254), it was known that '(as a general rule) every passage has some one definite and sufficient sense, which was prominently before the mind of the writer, or in the intention of the Blessed Spirit, and to which all other ideas, though they might arise, or be implied, still were subordinate'—an Episcopal sense, as it were (*Ari* 60). But through allegory and typology a text will also admit of 'the secondary and distinct meaning of the prophecy'—what might be called a Prophetical sense—which 'is commonly hidden from view by the veil of the literal text, lest its immediate scope should be overlooked; when that is once fulfilled, the recesses of the sacred language seem to open, and give up the further truths deposited in them' (*Ari* 61). The two levels of interpretation represented a pre-Nicene distinction between a primary or 'literal' sense of scripture and various secondary or 'figurative' senses.[30]

Many nineteenth-century Churchmen saw Origen's use of allegory in interpreting the Bible as an 'abuse' of scriptural meaning. Newman came to his defence: 'So far then as the Alexandrian Fathers partook of such a singular gift of grace (and Origen surely bears on him the

[29] Lash discerns in *Arians of the Fourth Century* a twofold treatment of 'Apostolic Tradition' as 'both the process of oral transmission, and the content of that process, the creed (p. 135), in so far as the latter term is understood to refer, formally, to "the great doctrines of the faith" (p. 134).' The dynamic and oral are thus separated from the fixed and credal, although Lash continues by clarifying that at this stage Newman does *not* mean by 'creed' the 'explicit crystallisation in authoritative conciliar formulae' (*Newman on Development,* 125).

[30] 'Now the Old Testament, as we know, is full of figures and types of the Gospel; types various, and, in their literal wording, contrary to each other, but all meeting and harmoniously fulfilled in Christ and His Church' (*PS* vii.12: 1512); 'The Gospel Feast', May 1838.

tokens of some exalted moral dignity)...in the same degree they stand not merely excused, but are placed immeasurably above the multitude of those who find it easy to censure them' (*Ari* 63–4). Although aware that Origen could sometimes over-allegorize a text to defend the patriarchs from charges of immorality, 'spiritualiz[ing] the account of Abraham's denying his wife, the polygamy of the Patriarchs, and Noah's intoxication', yet Newman is the Alexandrian's champion (*Ari* 64). Besides, governing both levels was the 'general rule' which prevented abuse, first by discerning the primary sense of a passage and then by making sure the secondary senses run in line with the 'immediate scope' (Newman's translation of *skopos*).

This rule or scope of a passage is a third thing in addition to the twofold pattern of the literal and figurative senses of scripture; it is different from both senses but intimately connected. It is what Origen called the *skopos*, perhaps better translated as 'aim', of any particular scriptural passage. It sets the framework in which the passage should be interpreted. For instance, Newman says, the Alexandrians held that the aim of John 5: 26, 'As the Father hath life in Himself, so hath He given to the Son to have life in Himself', was to teach that the Father begot the Son (*Ari* 159).[31] Put in Newman's terms, the 'general rule' by which the pre-Nicenes interpreted this text enabled them to discern within these words the primary (fixed) doctrine of the Son's eternal generation from the Father. Secondary (dynamic) levels of teaching were also discernable from this text, which understood in line with the *skopos* would enrich the Fathers' understanding of that doctrine.

There are two things to point out about this rule. Firstly, it was usually taken from the primary, or literal, level of the scripture. However, the Alexandrian Fathers were prepared to flip the priority of the two senses of scripture depending upon what they discerned as the *skopos*, on occasion making a figurative reading become the primary sense of a text. Newman writes, 'sometimes the secondary

---

[31] It is not surprising that Newman chose a text from John to show the pre-Nicenes' Christological doctrine. As Ronald Heine notes, Origen 'referred to the *skopos* of the Gospel of John when he says, in the introduction to his commentary on that Gospel, that none of the other evangelists has shown Jesus' "divinity as perfectly as John"' (*Gregory of Nyssa's Treatise on the Inscriptions of the Psalms* (Oxford: Clarendon Press, 1995), 41).

sense may be more important in after ages than the original, as in the instance of Jewish ritual; still in all cases (to speak generally) there is but one main primary sense, whether literal or figurative' (*Ari* 61). As 'The words of Scripture were appropriated to their respective senses by their *writers*; they had a meaning before we approached them, and they will have that same meaning, whether we find it out or not' (*Jfc* 119). Here Newman is establishing a primary level—or sense—of scripture, one that is sealed up and protected, even to the extent we might miss it. However, in addition to the primary sense are a number of secondary senses that allow further richness in the inter- pretation of scripture. Put succinctly, the two levels of interpretation of scripture are guided by one rule or *skopos*, just as in doctrine the two levels of Tradition—'Episcopal' and 'Prophetical'—were guided by one Rule of Faith.

Secondly, just as the Rule of Faith was the embodiment of doc- trine, the 'rule' in scriptural interpretation had practical connota- tions. The rule of any particular passage was not written down but embodied, shared by word of mouth, probably secretly, and through hortatory preaching could be lived out. For the way that the early Christians interpreted scripture carried consequences for the way they lived; hence in 1835 Newman wrote of fourth-century Egyptian 'traditionary practice' that came from 'principles of interpretation' (*HS* ii. 106).[32] The fruit of the Alexandrians' reading of scripture was a life of devotion to God, lived with the sort of 'enthusiasm ... sub- mitted to the discipline of the Church' seen in the holy life of Antony of Egypt (*HS* ii. 103). Scripture, properly interpreted, led to the proper ethos, which in turn led to a richer understanding of the secondary teachings of scripture. The movement was circular. Two years after *Arians of the Fourth Century*, Newman was preaching the same view as the Alexandrians held: 'to understand [the scriptures] we must feed upon them, and live in them, as if by little and little growing into their meaning' (*PS* iii. 10: 566). Newman's own horta- tory sermons, admittedly written for publication, tried to embody

---

[32] Scripture commandments were 'acted upon as [rules and admonitions] by the primitive Christians, whether from their received principles of interpretation or the traditionary practice of the Church' (*HS* ii. 106). 'Traditionary' means 'to be obser- vant of a tradition', as used in Tillotson's *Rule of Faith* (1666), iii, p. x: 'Himself and his Traditionary Brethren' (*OED*).

the ethos for holy living that came from a rich understanding of scripture.[33]

Such a view embraced the difficulties of scripture, as had Origen's view described by Pierre Daniel Huet in the *Origeniana* (1668) that Newman read for *Arians of the Fourth Century*.[34] So that these difficulties would not lead to the destruction of a person's faith, however, Origen, like Clement before him, taught scripture 'economically'. To Newman, this meant being economical with the truth in the sense of taking a gradual approach to expounding scripture to new converts, as opposed to 'loading or formalizing the mind' (*Ari* 49)—that is, as opposed to the teachings of his rationalist contemporaries or the easy formulas of Protestant Evangelicalism.[35] In *Arians of the Fourth Century*, Newman portrayed Alexandrian scriptural pedagogy as a method that reflected God's own pedagogy:

> What, for instance, is the revelation of general moral laws, their infringement, their tedious victory, the endurance of the wicked, and the 'winking at the times of ignorance', (Acts 17: 24) but an '*Economia*' of greater truths untold, the best practical communication of them which our minds in their present state will admit? What are the phenomena of the external world, but a divine mode of conveying the realities of existence . . . ? And our blessed Lord's conduct on earth abounds with the like gracious and considerate condescension to the weakness of His creatures, who would have been driven either to a terrified inaction or to presumption, had they known then as afterwards the secret of His Divine Nature. (*Ari* 75–7)[36]

---

[33] In 1840, S. F. Wood wrote: 'In 1834 appeared the first volume of Mr. Newman's Sermons . . . This volume hardly contains a directly theological sermon. The scope of the whole of it appears to be the production of a certain moral temper—a temper, for the most part, in strong contrast with the prevalent one of the day' ('Revival of Primitive Doctrine', printed in App. II of Pereiro, '*Ethos' and the Oxford Movement* (pp. 255–6)).

[34] Huet wrote that Origen's phrase '*Non historiae narrantur* (it is not histories that are recounted)' meant 'that histories are indeed recounted but that the point is not to tell the story but to devise mysteries' (*Origeniana* 2.2.14.5, quoted Henri de Lubac, *History and Spirit: The Understanding of Scripture According to Origen*, trans. A. E. Nash and J. Merriell (San Francisco, Calif.: Ignatius, 2007), 133).

[35] 'There are, doubtless, difficulties in Scripture in proportion to its depth; but I am speaking of a mode of interpretation [i.e. the Protestant one] which does not feel depth nor suspect difficulty' (*Jfc* 124).

[36] Here Newman makes the Fathers sound like Joseph Butler (1692–1752). In pt ii, ch. 4 of the *Analogy of Religion* (1737), Butler wrote: 'God makes use of a variety of

The Alexandrians taught Newman that God's revelation occurs through the conscience and morality, through the external world, and through the scriptures, all pointing towards the God who gave them—an 'economy' also in the sense of a gradual revealing of God to, and through, the world.[37] Alexandrians interpreted God's economy so well, Newman thought, because they recognized that God was present in every person's conscience.

Moreover, Newman writes, the Alexandrian 'Fathers considered they had the pattern as well as the recommendation of this sort of teaching in Scripture itself' (Ari 49). After all, obscurity and gradual unveiling were employed in the scriptures, which were full of parables and 'dark sayings' (cf. Ps. 49: 4, Ps. 78: 2 and Matt. 13: 35 quoting the prophet Ezekiel). Clement and his Latin contemporary Tertullian both invoked the text (Matt 7: 6) against casting pearls before swine 'in justification of their cautious distribution of sacred truth' (Ari 47). Newman's curate, Isaac Williams, showed that Origen's Commentary on St Matthew interpreted Jesus's discussions with his disciples 'in the house' as indicating that God's wisdom is revealed in secret.[38] Newman thought the privacy and reserve of the pedagogy of pre-Nicene Christians testified to their ability to preserve doctrinal and scriptural truth better than post-Nicenes could. And this is where Newman's claims became particularly controversial among High Church Anglicans. As will be seen at the start of Chapter 3, the

means, what we often think tedious ones, in the natural course of providence, for the accomplishment of all his ends' (my italics). James Pereiro has shown how important the Analogy was to the Oxford curriculum ('Ethos' and the Oxford Movement, esp. 89–92). Francis McGrath thinks that in the late 1820s Newman's 'remarks on personal conscience run parallel to Bishop Butler's own remarks in three "Sermons Upon Human Nature"' (John Henry Newman: Universal Revelation (Tunbridge Wells: Burns and Oates, 1997), 48).

[37] Robin Selby writes that Origen's 'idea that an economy is the nearest approach we can make to truth, compatible with our condition, is found frequently in Newman's writings, and we may conjecture that when he expressed his notorious maxim that it is no more than a hyperbole to say that a lie is the nearest thing to truth [in University Sermon XV], he may have had in mind this sentence of Origen's: "Do you not say, Celsus, that it is allowable to use deceit and lying as a medicine? Why, then, is it unthinkable that something of this sort occurred with the purpose of bringing salvation?"' (The Principle of Reserve in the Writings of John Henry Cardinal Newman (Oxford: Clarendon Press, 1975), 11).

[38] Tract 80, pt i, sect. 4.

historians among them found no evidence for a 'secret tradition' (*disciplina arcani*) of teaching the faith in the first three centuries of Christianity.[39]

Newman's response to this criticism is found in a letter he wrote to Thomas Falconer in 1834. There he uses a distinction we have already encountered, writing that the secret tradition originated as a 'principle' in the first century, but had become a 'rule' by the fourth (*LD* iv. 180). That is why the best evidence for the secret tradition dates from the fourth century, by which stage it had become a practical rule, exemplified in lectures by which Cyril of Jerusalem (*c*.315–86) gradually taught his catechumens, rather than a principle to guide teaching. Moreover, as evidence for the existence of a secret tradition before the fourth century, Newman pointed to the agreement of most of the Fathers who came to Nicaea in AD 325 upon what the content of the faith was. Guaranteed in the faith by the secrecy in which the Rule of Faith was held before then, those at the Nicene Council agreed upon *most* of the Creed. Their only difference was in secondary matters—in the explanations that comprised 'Prophetical Tradition'—such as finding the right word for the relation of Father to Son. In a preface he wrote for Cyril of Jerusalem's lectures in 1838, Newman saw his heroes in 'the Athanasian School' sharing with 'S. Cyril, with Eusebius of Caesarea, Meletius, and others' a view of the relation of Father and Son that was not reducible to one word alone. Although the latter group 'shrunk from' seeing the Son as 'consubstantial' with the Father (*homoousios*), they nevertheless held to the 'traditionary doctrine' of the divine relation, by which Newman means the teachings of 'Episcopal Tradition' (*Ox Frs* ii, p. x). 'Their judgment [about *homoousios*], which was erroneous, was their own; their faith was not theirs only, but shared with them by the whole Christian world' (*Ox Frs* ii, p. x). In the 1830s, Newman's preface to Cyril is representative of the twofold system of doctrine in which

[39] Although Newman had cited Joseph Bingham as evidence in notes at *Ari* 45 and 46, apart from the reference to casting pearls before swine in Clement and Tertullian, Bingham's references to *disciplina arcani* were post-Nicene: the 'testimonies of Theodoret, St. Austin, St. Ambrose [t]o which we may add that of St. Cyril of Jerusalem' (*The Antiquities of the Christian Church: Reprinted from the Original edn.*, 2 vols. (London: Henry G. Bohn, 1845), 470).

primary teaching is fixed but flexibility is allowed at secondary levels.[40]

Why, in the 1830s, did Newman believe the creeds of various Christian communities agreed? Not simply because they were nearer the Apostles and not only because they preserved the secret traditions—although both were part of the answer.[41] Above all, he believed that pre-Nicenes had an access to God that Christians in subsequent ages, beginning with the Arian heretics, lost. He believed their ethos was purer, preserved by their rules, and their 'spiritual senses' sharper than in those who came after. Newman alludes to the spiritual senses in a sermon from 1839: 'As *hunger and thirst, as taste, sound, and smell*, are the channels through which this bodily frame receives pleasure, so the affections are the instruments by which the soul has pleasure ... Our real and true bliss lies in the possession of those objects on which our hearts may rest and be satisfied' (*PS* v. 22: 1158–9, my italics). One recent commentator has written, 'sometimes Origen will talk of the spiritual senses as the 'faculties of the heart', for with them love—properly purged—finds its integration with mind in the Logos (Christ)'.[42] Newman says something similar about faculties of the heart, for while most people try to satisfy their affections with 'love of home and family'—objects which in themselves are not wrong to desire—the soul remains restless until it finds 'what is more stable', the divine Object (*PS* v. 22: 1159).[43] Desire for

---

[40] Newman rehearsed a version of this argument in his Sept. 1836 article for the 'Letters on the Church Fathers' in the *British Magazine*: 'If, then, we see that in all points, as regards the sacraments and sacramentals, the Church and its ministers, the form of worship, and other religious duties of Christians, Eusebius and Cyril agree entirely with the most orthodox of their contemporaries ... we have proof that that system, whatever it turns out to be, was received before their time' (*HS* i. 406–7).

[41] 'State of Religious Parties' in Apr. 1839 argued that the Fathers 'might have traditionary information of the general drift of the inspired text which we have not. We argue from what alone remains to us; they were able to move more freely. Moreover, a certain high moral state of mind, which times of persecution alone create, may be necessary for a due exercise of mystical interpretation' (*Critic* 25: 412). The later Newman no longer included himself in the collective 'we', changing the second sentence to: 'Moderns argue from what alone remains to them; they are able to move more freely' (*EH* i. 286).

[42] Coakley, *Powers and Submissions: Spirituality, Philosophy and Gender* (Oxford: Blackwell, 2002), 137.

[43] Augustine's *Confessions* might have been another influence on this sermon, entitled 'The Thought of God, the Stay of the Soul'.

what is missing leads to a feeling of peace once that Object is received. This is why, for Newman, intellectual clarity is always accompanied by a 'feeling' of peace, for we have received the missing Object, God's gift of Christ in the Spirit (*PS* v.22: 1162). It was this religious feeling that Newman claimed for the pre-Nicenes and found lacking in Christians from later ages.

But how can a thought be *felt*? It can be felt in a spiritual sense within the soul. For Newman, as well as for the Romantics, the physical and psychic were intertwined in moments of peace.[44] The early Fathers had this feeling more keenly than those who came later. Here, I think, is the reason for what Stephen Thomas regards as the '*tension*' Newman sees 'between the preciser Trinitarian language of the era of the ecumenical councils ("Creeds"), and the looser language of pre-Nicene Christianity, where words are organically related with the worshipping life of a community ("doxologies")'.[45] In *Arians of the Fourth Century* Newman writes, 'We count the words of the Fathers, and measure their sentences; and so convert doxologies into creeds' (*Ari* 180). The early Fathers did not reduce their feelings about God to single words, whether *homoousios* or *homoiosios*. Words were used, instead, to express feelings; they were poetry.[46] This required a multiplicity of secondary language, most of it unwritten and subsequently lost, to express their experience of this Object.

Newman's twofold system would be replaced in the 1840s by the idea of doctrinal development. But to get an impression of what was to change, another piece from the 1830s will be examined. In 1836, in the *British Critic* article known as 'The Brothers' Controversy',

---

[44] Likewise Newman wonders how is music *felt*? Perhaps music is an 'electric current passing from the strings through the fingers into the brain and down the spinal marrow. Perhaps thought is music' (*LD* xxii. 9). Thomas Vargish compares Newman's 1865 letter and Wordsworth's *The Prelude* (1805–6): 'The mind of man is fram'd even like the breath / And harmony of music.' (*Newman: The Contemplation of Mind* (Oxford: Clarendon Press, 1970), 51 n. 2). In the same year as this letter Newman endowed the soul of Gerontius with spiritual senses in sect. 4 of the poem 'The Dream of Gerontius'.

[45] Thomas, *Newman and Heresy*, 178.

[46] 'The Protestant sense [of scripture] is more close upon the word, the ancient use is more close upon the thing. A man, for instance, who described bread as "the staff of life", need not disagree with another who defined it only chemically or logically, but he would be his inferior in philosophy and his superior in real knowledge' (*Jfc* 99).

Newman distinguishes written (primary) 'creeds' from the unwritten (secondary) category here called 'Apostolic Tradition' (*Critic* 20: 170). Nicholas Lash says of this article: 'it is important to notice that the process by which "Bishop compares notes with bishop", enabling them to recognise in each other's local credal formulae the profession of a common faith, "implied time and accurate thought, freedom of discussion, questioning, reviewing".'[47] Lash is attempting to add dynamism to the category that in 1837 would be called 'Episcopal Tradition', but it has been shown why Newman would refuse Lash's attempt. Newman argues that the Rule of Faith

was from the first *fixed* in a set form of words called the Creed... These articles varied somewhat in the different branches of the Church; but inasmuch as they were but heads and tokens of the Catholic doctrine, and when developed and commented on implied each other, this argued no difference in the tradition of which they were the formal record. (*Critic* 20: 187)

While Newman does use the word 'developed', it carries the sense of 'explanation' used in 1837 of secondary tradition. The bishops are interpreters only, representatives of 'Prophetical Tradition', basing their interpretations on a rule—the Rule of Faith of their respective creeds. At the point of acknowledging their agreement, the bishops recognized that 'Episcopal Tradition' was fixed; in fact, Newman thought there had been agreement all along due to the one divine author. As will now be seen, Newman conceived of doctrinal development taking place within 'Episcopal Tradition' only in the 1840s.

DOCTRINE DEVELOPS (1840–59)

Newman was a Catholic in Rome in 1847 when he wrote his first novel, *Loss and Gain*. The novel's hero, Charles Reding, is an undergraduate at Oxford who begins to feel inexorably drawn towards the Catholic Church. In the novel William Sheffield, another

---

[47] Lash, *Newman on Development*, 127.

undergraduate who is more aware of the theological controversies raging inside the university, tells Reding of

an Oxford man, some ten years since, [who] was going to publish a history of the Nicene Council, and the bookseller proposed to him to prefix an engraving of St. Athanasius, which he had found in some old volume. He was strongly dissuaded from doing so by a brother clergyman, not from any feeling of his own, but because 'Athanasius was a very unpopular name among us'. (*LG* 118–19)

Newman the novelist suggests the unpopularity of Athanasius was part of the Anglican Church's problem—enough of a problem to encourage some to leave its fold. *Loss and Gain* was published in 1848. Just three years before, when still an Anglican, Newman had written in the *Essay on the Development of Christian Doctrine* that, '[d]id St. Athanasius or St. Ambrose come suddenly to life, it cannot be doubted what communion they would mistake for their own', given the choice between Anglican and Catholic Churches (*Dev* 138). Newman was received into the Catholic Church on 8 October 1845.

In this section it will be seen that, between a review of H. H. Milman in the *British Critic* of January 1841 and University Sermon XV of 1843, Newman found the time to put patristic flesh on the bones of his new system: doctrinal development. He was given this time because, after the publication of Tract 90 in February 1841, Newman was alienated from many in the Church of England. Therefore, from September 1841, he could spend eight to twelve hours a day with Athanasius (*LD* viii. 380)—a Father who Newman claimed was as unpopular among Anglicans as himself. In Tract 90, Newman took the method of scriptural interpretation he had learned from Origen and, applying it to non-biblical material, argued for a secondary ('catholic') sense of the primary ('uncatholic') doctrine in the Thirty-nine Articles.[48] Having used this interpretive model in Tract 90, it reappeared in *Development of Christian Doctrine*. In a way, therefore, Origen's senses of scripture provided the tools for the

---

[48] This is Lash's observation (ibid. 93). The introduction to Tract 90 says it aims 'to show that, while our Prayer Book is acknowledged on all hands to be of Catholic origin, our Articles also, the offspring of an uncatholic age, are, through GOD's good providence, to say the least, not uncatholic, and may be subscribed by those who aim at being catholic in heart and doctrine'.

downfall of the pre-Nicenes that will follow, as Newman begins to require that non-biblical texts be interpreted in senses other than the literal. Newman now sees a deeper meaning expressed in pre-Nicene writings than the plain sense suggests; for example, 'the Creeds of that early day make no mention in their letter of the Catholic doctrine [of the Trinity] at all.... To give a deeper meaning to their letter, we must interpret them by the times which came after' (*Dev* 12–13). Post-Nicene interpretation stopped them looking heretical.

The need for later Fathers 'to give a deeper meaning' to what had gone before explains why Newman later credited only post-Nicenes with leading him to the Catholic Church. *Loss and Gain*, with its emphasis on Athanasius, was the first of Newman's own conversion narratives to invoke post-Nicene Fathers. In 'Lectures on Certain Difficulties Felt by Anglicans in Submitting to the Catholic Church' in 1850, Newman wrote that he had realized eight years earlier, while translating *Select Treatises of S. Athanasius in Controversy with the Arians*, that, by upholding Anglicanism, he was 'turning devil's advocate against the much-enduring Athanasius' (*Diff* i. 388). Here, too, Newman credited the arguments of Augustine (354–430) against the Donatists, presented by Nicholas Wiseman in the *Dublin Review*, with having pulled him Romewards (ibid. 373). In August 1839, when rector of the English College in Rome, Wiseman had challenged the Oxford Movement to admit its inheritance among the North African schismatics led by Donatus, against whom Augustine said the rest of the Christian world judged ('securus judicat orbis terrarum'). Newman may have asked himself whether the Christian world likewise judged against the Church of England?[49] However, it is just as likely that Newman's alienation from the Anglican bishops in the wake of Tract 90 *pushed* him out of the Church as that Wiseman's analogy pulled him to Rome. In a review of High Churchman A. P. Perceval's book on the Apostolic Succession in January 1840, Newman responded to the Catholics that 'might we not bring against them the great maxims of the Fathers about standing in the old ways

---

[49] In Sept. 1839, Newman wrote: 'I have had the first real hit from Romanism which has happened to me...[from] Dr. Wiseman's article in the new Dublin [Review]' (*LD* vii. 154). He confirmed this opinion in Nov. 1845 (*LD* xi. 27).

with equal cogency, to say the least, as they urge us with St. Austin's maxim about the authority of the orbis terrarum' (*Critic* 27: 68/*EH* ii. 41). The arguments made against Wiseman and the Church of Rome in the *Critic* article were reiterated in Newman's *Letter to the Bishop of Oxford* in March 1841, explaining that Tract 90 was not a Romanizing work. Ultimately, as Frank Turner writes, 'Conversion for Newman was a confession of failure both to secure latitude for Catholics in the English Church and to define a Catholic faith that could hold a congregation'—specifically the small group that, from 1842, gathered around him at Littlemore.[50] In the seclusion of Littlemore, Newman was more like Donatus—alienated from all of Christendom—than he was like Augustine.

Newman also claimed in *Certain Difficulties Felt by Anglicans* that his conversion was motivated by another post-Nicene analogy, between Anglicanism and the Monophysite heretics who believed that Christ had one nature (*physis*) and therefore rejected the Council of Chalcedon's teaching that Christ has two natures in one person. The hero of the so-called Chalcedonian Definition was Pope Leo the Great (d. 461), who made with Athanasius and Augustine the three exemplary 'holy Fathers' of *Development of Christian Doctrine* (*Dev* 353). The Pope upheld the truth and the Monophysites rejected it. Researching the Monophysites in 1839, Newman claimed later, he began to think the same was true of the Anglican relation to the Pope today. As Newman restated the parallel in the *Apologia Pro Vita Sua*, twenty-five years after the event: 'I saw my face in that mirror, and I was a Monophysite' (*Apo* 108). It is, however, difficult to demonstrate that this vision had much effect on what he wrote at the time. Indeed, while Newman's research in the summer of 1839 made him aware that later Fathers were needed to make sense of earlier ones, he discovered that Leontius of Byzantium (c.490–c.545) was one such Father who was needed to clarify the confusion caused by Leo's terminology at Chalcedon.

After his summer researching the Monophysites, Newman also began work on a proposed Theological Dictionary.[51] Yet in this

[50] Turner, *John Henry Newman*, 546.
[51] Stern writes: 'Newman a dû écrire ce passage entre les années 1839–1845' (*Bible et tradition chez Newman*, 125 n. 108).

work he no more than hints that the Monophysites may hold an analogous position to Jeremy Taylor's '*Dissuasive [against Popery]* part ii. 1. § 4' cited in the *Lectures on the Prophetical Office* (*VM* i. 228 n. 4):

I am in doubt whether my quotations from Jeremy Taylor of what was done at Ephesus and Chalcedon about there being no fresh additions to the Creed (Romanism, lecture 9) is fair... Eulogius [bishop of Alexandria at the end of the sixth century] argues a[gain]st the Monophysites, who said that there might be no additions, that there might, only not contrary to Nicaea.[52]

Newman thinks, contrary to Taylor, that 'Other additions, i.e. developments, are of course what we sh[oul]d allow', as long as they are in line with conciliar orthodoxy.[53] The 'we' here appears to be his fellow Tractarians, who should face up to the fact that their darling, Jeremy Taylor, and the *Lectures on the Prophetical Office*, were wrong. His work on Monophysitism in 1839, therefore, caused him to question his earlier certainty that doctrine did not grow, but cannot be seen to provide a reason to separate from fellow Tractarians. While the role of post-Nicene theological controversies in Newman's conversion is uncertain, the controversies definitely played a part in his theory of doctrinal development.

The theory of development pointed to something constant at the centre of doctrinal growth: a revealed body of doctrine.[54] Although the content of revelation was no different at the Council of Nicaea than it had been just after Christ's death, in the earliest times Catholic fullness had yet to be comprehended. Privately, he first wrote this in a

---

[52] OM D.18.4 (quoted ibid.).   [53] Ibid.

[54] Peterburs shows that for Newman in late 1840 revelation was constant: 'Newman had come to reject entirely the view that there was once an age of pristine Christianity, and had arrived at the opinion that Christianity, as it is now known, had developed by "fits and starts", in a rather haphazard manner; though perhaps the one constant underlying the change in his views is expressed in a letter to [his brother] Francis on 22 October 1840, namely that "if the fact of a revelation be granted, it is most extravagant and revolting to our reason to suppose that after all its message is not ascertainable and that the divine interposition reveals nothing"', a statement opposed to Francis's Unitarianism ('Scripture, Tradition and Development towards Rome: Some Aspects of the Thought of John Henry Newman', in Philip McCosker (ed.), *What is it that the Scripture Says? Essays in Biblical Interpretation, Translation, and Reception in Honour of Henry Wansbrough OSB* (Edinburgh: T. & T. Clark, 2006), 187, quoting *LD* vii. 412).

letter to his brother Francis in November 1840, admitting that 'tracing backwards, the evidences of this [fourth- and fifth-century] religion are fainter, but still they exist in their degree' (*LD* vii. 440). Publicly, Newman wrote in the *British Critic* in January 1841 that liberals, like H. H. Milman, 'are ever hunting for a fabulous primitive simplicity' while 'we repose in Catholic fulness [*sic*]' (*Critic* 29: 103/ *EH* ii. 233).[55] Golden ages were make-believe, Newman now thought, not something to be sought in the pre-Nicene Church by Tractarians.

The epistemology that made sense of a growing awareness of already present truth awaited elaboration in Newman's University Sermon XV, 'The Theory of Developments', in 1843. As James Pereiro puts it, this was the culmination of a series of sermons recognizing 'the progress from "implicit" to "explicit" knowledge ... The Church's progressive "realizing" of revealed truths grows in "intenseness", and manifests itself in verbal expression, theological treatment, dogmatic definition, and the like. As a result of this process revealed doctrines are more or less present to the consciousness of the Church'.[56] Compared with the categories of the 1830s, the movement from unwritten to written tradition (which Newman then regarded as a loss) was now the development from implicit to explicit knowledge (which he now regarded as a gain). Research into Athanasius had proved to Newman that the implicit knowledge of God possessed by the pre-Nicenes was nothing without the explicit knowledge of later Fathers.

The same year as Newman's University Sermon XV, William Palmer of Worcester brought out his *Narrative of Events Connected with the Publication of the Tracts for the Times*. Here Palmer exhibited the fury of the High Church reaction to Isaac Williams's Tract 87, Newman's Tract 90, and W. G. Ward's writings on development in the *British Critic*. Palmer argued that Newman and his friends had

---

[55] H. H. Milman's *The History of Christianity: From the Birth of Christ to the Abolition of Paganism in the Roman Empire*, 3 vols. (London: John Murray, 1840) claimed that 'in her first ages the Church separately *encountered* Judaism, Paganism, and Orientalism; and again, that her system *resembles* all three' (*Critic* 29: 103; cf. *EH* ii. 234). There are overtones of Origen in Newman's response, 'We prefer to say, and we think that Scripture bears us out in saying, that from the beginning the Moral Governor of the world has scattered the seeds of truth far and wide over its extent' (*Critic* 29: 101; *EH* ii. 232).

[56] Pereiro, '*Ethos*' and the Oxford Movement, 178.

been wrong in the 1830s to cherish the unwritten tradition (*disciplina arcani*) of Christian Antiquity: 'The weakness of this system having been demonstrated, the modern defenders of Romanism have adopted a new theory'.[57] In a way, Palmer was right. Newman had stopped valorizing the 'secrets' of the pre-Nicenes and started upholding a new theory of development that valorized explicit doctrine instead. But Palmer was wrong to think that Newman altogether rejected the unwritten tradition. In 1845, Newman wrote: 'that [the *disciplina arcani*] existed as a rule, as regard the Sacraments, seems to be confessed on all hands', and 'goes some way to account for that apparent variation and growth in doctrine, which embarrasses us when we would consult history for the true idea of Christianity; yet it is no key to the whole difficulty' (*Dev* 25–6). The 'whole difficulty' of why doctrine is different today from what it was in the past, Newman thought, was better explained by his theory of development than by putting too much emphasis on a secret tradition; but the latter existed nevertheless. Indeed, Newman's second novel, *Callista* (1855), depicts Cyprian's North African Christians protecting themselves from persecution in the third century by means of various secrets.[58]

Researching Athanasius from the summer of 1840, Newman found that, for all their secret traditions, the pre-Nicenes lacked the certainty that the Son of God was coequal with God the Father. Newman no longer believed what he had read in George Bull's *Defensio Fidei Nicaenae* in the early 1830s, which he had still espoused to his brother Francis in November 1840.[59] Bull had been Newman's

---

[57] Palmer, *Narrative*, 166.

[58] Cyprian (d. 258), whose resistance to Pope Stephen had given him a prominent role in Anglican polemics against Rome, was fitted into Newman's theory of development. By May 1844, Newman was convinced that 'the doctrine of the Papacy was a primitive one' and thus Cyprian's resistance showed no more than that 'when a doctrine or ordinance has to be developed, collision or disturbances seem previous conditions of its final adjustments' (*LD* x. 243).

[59] 'There are sufficient doctrines developed from a very early date both to remove the difficulty of the notion of a dogmatic system'—i.e. the difficulty for which *Dev* was to account in 1845—'and actually to furnish portions and indices of the whole system afterwards confessedly existing. Ignatius has unfolded the episcopal and sanctioned the mystical principle; from Justin downwards we have an uninterrupted testimony to the Homoüsion (as I consider it will be felt that Bull has shown)' (*LD* vii. 441).

introduction to the High Church Anglican view, expressed in *Arians of the Fourth Century,* that the pre- and post-Nicene Fathers have 'parallel language' in which to express doctrine (*Ari* 198). The exact words of doctrine might shift before and after the Nicene Council, but there remained parallels in the language used to describe the relation of Father and Son. Translating *Against the Arians,* however, Newman learned that Athanasius 'expressly denies Bull's statement that "first-born" means "à Deo natus", "born of God"' (*Ox Frs* viii. 279, quoting *Defensio* ii. 484). Newman no longer holds that Athanasius, nor his later Alexandrian successor Cyril (also quoted), shared parallel language with pre-Nicene writers. Moreover, he charges some of the pre-Nicenes with thinking the Son a creature born of God. In *Arians of the Fourth Century,* Theophilus and Hippolytus had been quoted in order to declare all pre-Nicenes innocent of such a charge (*Ari* 198). In 1842, the latter two are judged guilty; Athenagorus and Tatian are found innocent; while the jury is out on Novatian (*Ox Frs* viii. 280). And in 1846 he put it more strongly still: 'I really do not think you can deny, that the [early] Fathers, not merely did not contemplate true propositions, (afterwards established) but actually contemplated false' (*LD* xi. 183).[60] Against Bull and the High Churchmen, then, Newman in the 1840s thinks the Christian understanding of God was better developed by the time of Nicaea than it had been before.

But the idea that doctrine develops was no more appealing to the Catholic Church than to the Church of England he was leaving behind. Thus Newman found himself, in the 1840s and 50s, in the awkward position of presenting a *new* idea for the *antiquity* of the Church he was entering—an idea, moreover, unattractive to Catholics themselves. The nearest thing to a theory of development within the Catholic Church came from the Tübingen School in the 1820s and early 1830s, but even J. A. Möhler called his 1825 book *Unity in the Church* 'youthful folly' in 1834.[61] Rather than driving Newman

---

[60] Newman also wrote in this letter to Henry Wilberforce in June 1846: 'The fact I believe to be this—the early Fathers made incorrect intellectual developments of portions or aspects of that whole Catholic doctrine which they held, and so far were inconsistent with themselves.'

[61] Quoted at Owen Chadwick, *From Bossuet to Newman* (2nd edn.; Cambridge: Cambridge University Press, 1987), 110. Chadwick (p. 111) argues that Möhler had

towards Rome, as Wulfstan Peterburs argues, development played an ambiguous role in his conversion, finding supporters in neither Anglican nor Catholic Churches.[62]

This explains why, from his arrival in Rome in the autumn of 1846 onwards, Newman saw himself as a historian of doctrine rather than a theologian.[63] Scholastic theology confused him and he reverted to the Fathers as the subject for his Roman dissertation.[64] But, persuaded by his fellow Oratorians to accept the position of rector of the Catholic University in Dublin, at the invitation of Cardinal Cullen in July 1851, Newman was forced to engage with scholastic theology. As a result, most of his publications in the 1850s pondered the nature of scholasticism, beginning with *Discourses on the Scope and Nature of University Education* in 1852.[65] Unsurprisingly, Newman soon took an historical approach. In a series of articles for the *Catholic*

no influence on Newman in spite of the reference to him at *Dev* 27. Newman's views intersected with neither the controversy over Möhler in England between W. G. Ward and William Palmer of Worcester in 1842–3 nor in Rome, where Newman's future friend Giovanni Perrone cited Möhler's *Symbolik* in his textbook *Praelectiones Theologicae* (1843 edn.) against charges that the Catholic Church both ignored history and changed historic doctrines.

[62] Against the thrust of Peterburs's 'Scripture, Tradition and Development towards Rome' (pp. 183–96), Newman learned that the Catholic Church was more interested in his conversion than in his theology when, in 1845, 'Dr. Wiseman judged that it would be more effective if [*Dev*] received no theological revision' (according to Wilfrid Ward, *The Life of John Henry Cardinal Newman*, 2 vols. (London: Longmans, 1912), i. 99).

[63] In 1851, Newman wrote: 'Theologians proceed in the way of reasoning; they view Catholic truth as a whole, as one great system of which part grows out of part, and doctrine corresponds to doctrine... The other means of attaining religious truth is the way of history; when, namely, from the review of past times and foreign countries, the student determines what was really taught by the Apostles in the beginning' (*Prepos* 57).

[64] Wilfrid Ward suggested: 'It was perhaps Newman's keen sensitiveness to his surroundings, and his instinctive craving to persuade and desire to be understood, which made him write at this time [1847] his Latin treatises on St Athanasius, as he found his English writings so imperfectly comprehended. They included a dry historical exhibition of the variations in the use of the terms finally employed in the definitions which fixed the doctrines of the Incarnation and Trinity—a point of great importance to some of his arguments in the "Development" Essay' (*Life of John Henry Cardinal Newman*, i. 172). Ward does not mention that they were a translation into Latin of extended notes on Athanasius from *Ox Frs* (pub. as ch. 1 of *TT*).

[65] These *Discourses on the Scope and Nature of University Education*, published by James Duffy in Dublin in 1852, were adapted for *The Idea of a University* (1873). See

University Gazette from June to October 1854, he traced the European university from its origins in the ancient schools in Athens, Macedonia, and Rome, to medieval Paris, Oxford, and, of course, Dublin—a university was founded in the last by means of the letter Pope Clement V sent to the Archbishop of Dublin in 1311 or 1312 (*HS* iii. 207). What is surprising in all of these writings, however, is Newman's neglect of the early Fathers. There is hardly any discussion of the theological schools of Antioch and Alexandria, which were the focus of *Arians of the Fourth Century*. Newman mentions the decline of the centres of early Christian learning, Antioch and Alexandria,[66] but hardly ever their glories,[67] and looks instead to Charlemagne for the 'principles of which a University is the result, in that he aimed at educating all classes, and undertook all subjects of teaching'. Moreover, the fact that Charlemagne 'betook himself to the two Islands of the North for a tradition' of scholarship under Alcuin, enables Newman to give a teleological account of the 'the new civilization of Europe' appropriate to his position in Dublin (*HS* iii. 152). Newman was replacing a former fascination for the ancient Alexandrian school with a medieval scholasticism that had strong Anglo–Irish connections. While the schools of the early Church 'lectured from Scripture with the comments of the Fathers', he wrote, 'the medieval schools created the science of theology' (*HS* iii. 203).

In 1855, a lecture on 'Christianity and Scientific Investigation' argued for the 'science' of theology—from the medieval understanding of the Latin *scientia* or knowledge—to be open to the work of natural science. After all, 'if there be any one science which, from its sovereign and unassailable position, can calmly bear such unintentional collisions on the part of the children of earth, it is Theology' (*Idea* 466). His biographer, Wilfrid Ward, sums up the effect on an Irish Catholic audience:

Louis McRedmond, *Thrown among Strangers: John Henry Newman in Ireland* (Dublin: Veritas, 1990), 58–67.

[66] *HS* iii. 112 and 123.

[67] There is brief praise for the Cappadocian 'school' as well as the Benedictines: 'I do not mean that there are no traces in Christian antiquity of a higher pattern of education, in which religion and learning were brought together—as in the method of teaching which St Basil and St Gregory brought into Asia Minor from Alexandria, and in the Benedictine Schools of Italy' (*HS* iii. 151).

[Newman] observed that even when the Church was at the height of her temporal power—in the thirteenth century—it was not by intolerant opposition but by freedom of discussion, among her theologians, of the new theories of the time, by their adopting what was good even in the hitherto detested philosophy of Aristotle, that the pantheistic and rationalistic movement of the neo-Aristotelians was effectually checked. He could urge the example of the 'Angelic Doctor' [Thomas Aquinas] even on the most conservative Irish divines with effect.[68]

This was an argument from history for theology's openness to other sciences. The argument in 'On Consulting the Faithful in Matters of Doctrine' tried for the same effect on conservative divines. Written for the *Rambler* in July 1859, soon after his retirement as rector of the Catholic University in November 1858, this article argued that the lessons of the fourth-century Arian controversy were that theology should be open—this time open to consulting the faithful. When the Church sets out to discern its mind, the faithful (including priests and religious)[69] contribute as much as bishops. The outcry over 'On Consulting the Faithful' demonstrated how little the conservative divines wanted Newman's history; theologians in Rome opposed his article as they had opposed his theory of doctrinal development twelve years before. Roman theology wanted doctrine expressed scientifically not historically.

DOCTRINE AS SCIENCE (1860–81)

The end of the 1850s saw Newman holding together a historical view of doctrine, based on his theory of development, with his argument that scientific theology should remain open to those outside. The

[68] Ward, *Life of John Henry Cardinal Newman*, i. 405.

[69] Ian Ker reminds us 'the "faithful" turn out to include both priests and religious', in response to Coulson's tendency to align the priests with the bishops rather than the people ('Newman on the Consensus Fidelium as "The Voice of the Infallible Church"', in Terrence Merrigan and Ker (eds.), *Newman and the Word* (Louvain: Peeters Press, 2000), 77). Coulson is right, however, that one of the references Newman removed for the version in *Arians of the Fourth Century* (1871) was 'St Hilary's charge that the ears of the laity were holier than the hearts of the priests' (*Common Tradition*, 126).

result was what Cardinal Manning would dismissively call 'English Catholicism'. This section will show that, in the 1860s and 70s, Newman retained much of 'the old Anglican, patristic, literary, Oxford tone' that Manning disliked, even as he tried to throw off his reputation of English Catholicism.[70] Yet from 'On Consulting the Faithful' until *An Essay in Aid of a Grammar of Assent* (1870), it will be shown that Newman examined scientific theology more closely than before and that this had an impact on his interpretation of doctrine.

Newman was the editor of the *Rambler* at the time that 'On Consulting the Faithful' was published. He resigned his editorship after the fateful article and, although he continued to contribute to the *Rambler* until July 1860, he began to distance himself from the new editor and the owner over whether or not a chemical analysis should be carried out on the phials purportedly containing the blood of early Roman martyrs. Wendel Meyer explains:

> The battle which followed pitted the proponents of Ultramontanism, led by Wiseman, Manning and now Northcote [Newman's friend from Oxford and a fellow convert], against the last bastion of Liberal Catholicism, the *Rambler*, held by its editor and its owner, Simpson and Acton. For some time Newman attempted to sit on the fence, trying hard to develop a compromise which would enable the two factions to co-exist. Gradually, however, he realised that he too differed from Acton and Simpson on matters relating to the Church's authority and the search for truth.[71]

Newman's shift to a fuller engagement with theological science came at the expense of his former openness to natural science.

[70] In Feb. 1866, Archbishop Manning described Newman as the chief source of 'an English Catholicism. It is the old Anglican, patristic, literary, Oxford tone transplanted into the Church' (quoted from a letter to Talbot at Coulson, *Common Tradition*, 148).

[71] Meyer, 'The Phial of Blood Controversy and the Decline of the Liberal Catholic Movement', *Journal of Ecclesiastical History*, 46 (1995), 88. Meyer explains that Acton and Simpson gave the *Rambler* the new guise of *Home and Foreign Review* before that too was closed down as a result of the events of 1864: 'In September of [the previous] year, the Bavarian church historian J. J. I. Döllinger [Acton's teacher] had argued for an academic freedom in scientific investigations at the international congress in Munich. He had also pointed to the correlative need to recognise the independence of scientific and historical investigations from the authority of the Church. Rome responded to these appeals by sending a papal brief to the archbishop of Munich, which implicitly condemned Döllinger's notion of academic freedom . . . The *Munich Brief* paved the way for the publication of the *Syllabus of Errors* which appeared in December of 1864' (ibid. 90).

The timing of this shift must have had to do with the bishops' reaction to 'On Consulting the Faithful'. As Lord Acton himself later wrote: 'After sixteen years spent in the Church of Rome, Newman was inclined to guard and narrow his theory of development.'[72] In the late 1850s, Newman had struggled to combine his theory of development with scientific theology. In the Catholic University's journal *Atlantis*, 'On St Cyril's Formula' (1858) began with what appeared to be a retreat from his initial views on development, taking the position that Giovanni Perrone taught him in Rome in 1847:

> Every Catholic holds that the Christian dogmas were in the Church from the time of the Apostles; that they were ever in their substance what they are now; that they existed before the formulas were publicly adopted, in which, as time went on, they were defined and recorded, and that such formulas, when sanctioned by the due ecclesiastical acts, are binding on the faith of Catholics, and have a dogmatic authority. (*TT* 333)

Yet, after this nod to the teaching at Rome, he went on: after 'this profession once for all, I put the strictly theological question aside; for I am concerned in a purely historical investigation into the use and fortunes of certain scientific terms' (ibid. 334). History was still Newman's way to understand doctrine in the late 1850s, as Nicholas Lash points out, rather than the 'deductive method employed by theologians'.[73] After 'On Consulting the Faithful', however, Newman sought to improve his theological method when writing on the Fathers.

[72] John Acton, 'Doellinger's Historical Work', *English Historical Review*, 5 (1890), 723. Writing that Acton 'based his conclusions on two letters he received from Newman in 1862', Hugh MacDougall concludes, after a discussion of the relevant passages, 'There seems to be absolutely no grounds for Acton's assumption that the delation to Rome of his 1859 article...prompted Newman to narrow his theory' (*The Acton–Newman Relations: The Dilemma of Christian Liberalism* (New York: Fordham University Press, 1962), 161–4). Yet the earlier view of development, which Acton rightly saw change after 1859, argued that when certain 'Ante-Nicene Fathers...seemed to hold that the Word was not always the Son...they wrongly developed, for the time being, what the Church had not yet clearly developed' (Perrone 96). This view, expressed to Giovanni Perrone in 1847, led Perrone to correct Newman's historiography of doctrine with a scientific formula that Newman would recount from time to time. MacDougall has taken this formula to be Newman's true view in the 1850s; but, if it were, why did Perrone need to correct Newman again in the 1860s for the content of 'On Consulting the Faithful'? See Ch. 5, below.

[73] Lash, *Newman on Development*, 25.

When Newman again made a nod to Rome, writing a note in 1861 for 'The Teaching of the Fathers', it was more pronounced. He remarked, with a slight tone of self-justification:

I have been told to speak in private to such persons as are in perplexity... I wished two years ago to begin a course of Explanations, when I undertook the R., [i.e. editorship of the *Rambler*] but this was not liked.
Two things must be observed, 1. it is very inexpedient for oneself to go as near the wind as possible in faith but 2. it is very wrong not to open the necessary faith as wide as possible for others.
I begin by declaring my belief in the H[oly] C[atholic] Church as the oracle of Heaven. (*BI* 97)

Here Newman commits himself to further study of Catholic theology, writing that 'a man may take Caietan' (ibid.) as representative of the scholastic view of biblical inspiration (suggesting Newman was reading Cardinal Cajetan (1469–1534) at the time). This course of study continued, as is shown in another unpublished set of notes called 'Discursive Enquiries', where in March 1866 Newman quoted from Thomas Aquinas (*c.*1225–74), citing together with the *Summa Theologica* Ia.1.8 the commentary of Cajetan and an 1859 introduction to dogmatic theology by the Franciscan Bernard Van Loo (*PN* ii. 104).[74] Returning to the same article of the *Summa* in 1874, but still unconfident in his gifts as a theologian, Newman begins not with a nod to Rome but with a caveat:

if I might speak when I do not know enough of him to speak at all, and should be obliged, did I know him ever so well, to speak under correction... St Thomas seems to me, to take this as an instance, to think it incumbent on our reason to show that the propositions in which the dogma of the Holy Trinity is conveyed are not in collision with each other. (*PN* ii. 177)

Patristic categories did not necessarily accord with scholastic categories, but in this period Newman sought to bring them closer together. In the midst of an exposition of patristic views for 'Preliminary Remarks on the Problem of Inspiration', from 1861, Newman

[74] *PN* ii intersperses *Discursive Enquiries*, which Newman never finished, with 'Sundries', which became *Grammar of Assent*. See *PN* i. 241–50.

ponders the complex scholastic debate about the relation of grace and merit in God's providential order. His argument is that modern liberals are nothing like those who took the liberal view of scripture (that it was not verbally inspired) or providence in earlier generations. Thus he contrasts both 'rigid' (*rigidior*) and 'liberal' (*latior* or *liberior*) views in this debate with the liberals of his own day on the subject of biblical inspiration. His complex argument runs:

> the words rigidior and liberior may be used respectively of the doctrine of St Thomas and St Alfonso [of Ligouri], Francis of Sales as to the question of the praevisa merita. The theologians of the four first centuries took the liberior view; St Augustine the rigidior; and it was transmitted through St Gregory, St Anselm, St Thomas, and their schools down to the 16th century... When the Jesuits, St Francis of Sales, St Alfonso and Fr Morin took [their position] ... at least they could appeal to the age of the Apostles as agreeing with them. They appealed emphatically to 'Apostolic Tradition'. But can the 'laitor' doctrine received on the question of inspiration now make a similar appeal? Certainly not. (*BI* 15–16)

The truth, Newman wrote, was that the Fathers believed that scripture was 'inspired' even if that did not mean it was inerrant; this was far nearer the medieval and baroque 'liberals' than the moderns. But notice how this argument against modern liberalism depends upon a digression into abstruse scholastic theology. Notice also that the legitimacy of Augustine is proved by the transmission of his doctrine by the scholastics. (Reading Augustine through the theologians who came after him became the pattern for much of Newman's writing in the 1870s.) Perhaps Newman was proving to himself that he could enter into the debates of Catholic theology. Even though these papers went unpublished, the side he took in such debates was the *rigidior* rather than the *liberior* one that Catholic theologians might have expected him to take based upon the *Rambler* article.

The editor of these papers on biblical inspiration, Derek Holmes, has suggested that one impetus for Newman's writing on this subject was 'the controversy over the nature and extent of inspiration [that] was occasioned by the publication of *Essays and Reviews* in 1860'.[75]

---

[75] Holmes, introduction, *BI* (p. vii).

Typical of Newman's response to controversy in the present, his first thought was to learn a lesson from history, particularly early Church history. *Essays and Reviews* raised questions about the historical accuracy of the biblical narrative and the inerrant status of scripture. Concerning the accuracy of events portrayed in the Bible, Newman thought that because the post-Nicene Fathers tended to interpret the Old Testament figuratively, they were more helpful in the face of historical-critical challenges than the pre-Nicene interpreters who were trying to defend the literalism of the Old Testament against Marcion (d. *c.*160). 'The Post-Nicenes on the contrary were not so much controversialists with Pagans . . . and again they were spiritualists—hence *they* speak of Scripture, not so much as a history, but as a mystery—(Origen, by the bye, must be taken with them, and *Clement* for his *organa* as well as mysteries)' (*BI* 83).

The Bible, by this account (the same account as is found in *Arians of the Fourth Century*, although now Clement and Origen are an afterthought), was not a document to teach history. Concerning the inerrancy of scripture, therefore, the Fathers had no such concept:

So it seems, that a work may be written under the plenary inspiration of the Holy Ghost, in the judgment of the Fathers, yet at the same time may be so far human still, as not to be guaranteed against errors short of serious ones . . . The strong language in which the Fathers speak of [the scriptures'] inspiration, is no obstacle to their also holding, whether in fact they hold it or not, that the inspiration does [no] more than secure them from any faults except errors against faith and morals. (*BI* 91)

Newman admits that the modern question of whether the agency at work in the scripture is divine, to the point of excluding human error, is not asked by patristic authors; rather the Fathers will say, 'God *speaks* in Scripture', 'The power of God played upon the scriptural writers', 'The Holy Ghost *wrote* Scripture', or 'The Holy Ghost *inspired* the sacred writers' (*BI* 84–5). 'Is any part of Scripture the work of that individual person whom the Holy Ghost moved to write it?' asks Newman: 'I conceive the Fathers hardly ask themselves this definite question, as it might be asked in the Schools subsequently' (*BI* 88). There is a gap, Newman recognizes, between the patristic understanding of scripture as God's Word and the scholastic understanding. But, as the neo-Thomists would come to argue, a larger gap exists for Newman between the patristic-scholastic authors and the historical-critical methods of modern authors.[76]

An Essay in Aid of a Grammar of Assent (1870) is Newman's attempt to align patristic and scholastic theology. He begins, as a good scholastic should, with a series of propositions and definitions. Yet, as the work continues, Newman interweaves with these propositions the difference he discerned from the Fathers in the 1830s between principles and rules or, as he now calls them, that to which people give 'notional assent' and 'real assent'. While Newman by 1870 has come to conceive theology scientifically, as 'a system of truth', he recognizes that people only ever give notional assent to such systems, which is not the sort of assent that changes lives (*GA* 140). Real assent is what people give to 'religion'.[77] Given what Newman wrote in the 1830s, it makes sense for the rules of the Creeds to be part of religion in the *Grammar of Assent*, for, 'As to the proper Nicene formula itself, excepting the one term "Consubstantial", it has not a word which does not relate to the rudimental facts of Christianity' (*GA* 144). The 'rudimental facts' of religion are those that can be lived out through the real assent of Christians, whereas with regard to *homoousios* Newman repeats what he wrote in his first book about a word 'adopted to meet the evasion of the Arians' (ibid.). Likewise, the *Quicunque*, or Athanasian Creed, is not 'a mere collection of notions, however momentous' but 'a psalm or hymn of praise, of confession,

---

[76] The neo-Thomist, Josef Kleutgen, began the first volume of his *La Philosophie scholastique exposée et défendue* arguing that although most Fathers into the first half of the middle ages were inspired by Plato and scholastics attached to Aristotle, 'on ne peut nier, cependant, ce qui du reste est généralement admis, que la philosophie des saints Pères est, au fond, la même que celle des scholastiques. Cette unité ressort surtout, lorsqu'on les considère dans leur contraste avec la nouvelle philosophie' (meaning philosophy since Descartes) ((Paris: Gaume frères et J. Duprey, 1868), 1–2). Ch. 5, below has more on Kleutgen.

[77] 'Religion has to do with the real, and the real is the particular; theology has to do with what is notional, and the notional is the general and the systematic. Hence theology has to do with the dogma of the Holy Trinity as a whole made up of many propositions; but religion has to do with each of those separate propositions which compose it, and lives and thrives in the composition of them. In them it finds the motives for devotions and faithful obedience; while theology on the other hand forms and protects them by virtue of its function of regarding them, not merely one by one, but as a system of truth' (*GA* 140).

and of profound, self-prostrating homage... It appeals to the imagination quite as much as to the intellect' (ibid. 153).[78]

The trouble is that while the 'declarations' of the Creed can be broken down into three parts and a *real* assent made separately to Father, Son, and Spirit, yet God the Three-in-One can receive only *notional* assent. Why? Two scholars have recently disagreed about what Newman says on this question. Terrence Merrigan opposes Colin Gunton's

> assertion that Newman holds that 'it is *not* possible to assent rationally to the whole [of Trinitarian] doctrine'... Newman's view is that this is the only assent which it is possible to give to the doctrine as a whole! If it were not susceptible of rational—i.e., notional assent—it could not be accepted at all, since Newman's whole argument is that it cannot be the object of imaginative or real assent.[79]

Merrigan highlights the tension between Newman's former patristic style of theology, which appealed to the imagination, and theology now understood in scientific terms. Inability to give real assent to the Trinity suggests that Newman has, by 1870, begun to espouse the scholastic difference between the doctrines of *de Deo uno* (on God's unity) and *de Deo trino* (on God's Trinity). Newman had probably read manuals on Aquinas arguing for a 'natural knowledge' of God's unity that came prior to God's self-revelation as Trinity (*ST* Ia.2.2).[80] Theologians in

---

[78] The scriptures appeal to imagination too: 'And if the New Testament be, as it confessedly is, so real in its teaching, so luminous, so impressive, so constraining, so full of images, so sparing in mere notions, whence is this but because, in its references to the Object of our supreme worship, it is ever ringing the changes (so to say) on... propositions [of the faith]...?' (*GA* 138).

[79] Terrence Merrigan, 'Newman on Faith in the Trinity', in Merrigan and Ian Ker (eds.), *Newman and the Word* (Louvain: Peeters Press, 2000), 115 (quoting Colin Gunton, *Theology through the Theologians: Selected Essays* (Edinburgh: T. & T. Clark, 1996), 29 (Merrigan's emphasis)).

[80] Edward Sillem lists the 'works from [Newman's] library by earlier nineteenth century Scholastic authors' J. Dmowski, G. C. Urbaghs, A. Bonelli, Cardinal Gerdil, M. Liberatore, B. Fushias, J. Balmes, and J. Kleutgen (*PN* i. 239–40). Their view of natural and revealed religion is different from that Newman encountered in Butler's *Analogy*, in which God the Father (not God's unity) is discerned by natural religion. Butler wrote in pt ii, ch. 1: 'the essence of natural religion may be said to consist in religious regards to *God the Father Almighty*; and the essence of revealed religion, as distinguished from natural, to consist in religious regards to *the Son* and to *the Holy Ghost*' (Butler's emphasis). For more on Newman's considerations of who is the One God, see Chs. 4 and 5, below.

Newman's time thought that Aquinas treated as different doctrinal loci the God discerned from natural knowledge (*de Deo uno*) and the God revealed to the Church (*de Deo trino*).[81] This interpretation of Aquinas may have shaped the argument of the *Grammar of Assent*, for no theologian would have been shocked to hear that God as Trinity could receive only notional assent. Certainly, when the new Pope Leo XIII made Aquinas the papal theologian of choice in 1878, Newman had no misgivings about what he had written in the *Grammar of Assent*.[82] Although with some grounds[83] Thomas Harper challenged the *Grammar of Assent* in 1870 for its 'seeming dissidence' from what 'is commonly taught at present in our catholic schools', nevertheless, more recently Gillian Evans has shown Newman's view of assent was based upon Aquinas's *Commentary on the Sentences*.[84] Moreover, the culmination of Newman's Catholic theology would be his application of this more scholastic theology to his revisions to the Athanasius translation, published in 1881.

What was new in the *Grammar of Assent* was fused with what was old. Newman retained some of his earliest arguments when he wrote

[81] J. B. Franzelin's *Tractatus de Deo Trino secundum personas*, published in 1869, is a good example of this division, beginning with *de Deo uno*, because it is the 'foundation' for reflection on the Trinity ((4th edn.; Rome: Typographia Polyglotta, 1895), 3). However, the assumption that Aquinas's *Summa* started with God's unity before moving to God's Trinity has been shown to be false by Fergus Kerr (*After Aquinas: Versions of Thomism* (Oxford: Blackwell, 2002), e.g., pp. 181–3, on twentieth-century interpretations of Aquinas).

[82] Newman wrote to Robert Whitty SJ, on 22 Dec. 1878, regarding the *Grammar of Assent*, with his usual deference about Catholic theology: 'If anyone is obliged to say "speak under correction" it is I; for I am no theologian and am too old, and ever have been, to become one. All I can say is I have no suspicion, and do not anticipate, that I shall be found in substance to disagree with St Thomas' (*LD* xxviii. 431).

[83] In 1869, Newman was still holding that: 'In physical matters, it is the senses which gives [*sic*] us the first start...In like manner we have to ascertain the starting points for arriving at religious truth. The intellect will be useful in gaining them and after gaining them—but to attempt to *see* them by means of the intellect is...a method of proceeding which was the very mistake of the Aristotelians of the middle ages, who, instead of what Bacon calls "interrogating nature" for facts, reasoned out everything by syllogisms' (*LD* xxiv. 275–6).

[84] T. Harper, 'Dr. Newman's Essay in Aid of a Grammar of Assent', *Month* (Aug. 1870), 159 (quoted at G. R. Evans, 'Newman and Aquinas on Assent', *Journal of Theological Studies*, 30 (1979), 210). Connections between Newman and Aquinas are more clearly drawn by Evans than by H. Francis Davis's 'Newman and Thomism', *Newman Studien*, 3 (1957), 157–69.

about the 'illative sense', nicely described by Sheridan Gilley as the 'power to pass straight from facts to conclusions'.[85] Yet while Gilley notices the similarities and differences between Newman's illative sense and the thought of Locke and Keble, he does not make the connection with Newman's work on the Fathers. This is the same illative sense the *Grammar of Assent* describes in terms of Aristotle's doctrine of *phronesis*:

the rule of conduct for one man is not always the rule for another, though the rule is always one and the same in the abstract, and in its principle and scope. To learn his own duty in his own case, each individual must have recourse to his own rule; and if that rule is not sufficiently developed in his intellect for his need, then he goes to some other living, present authority, to supply it for him, not to the dead letter of a treatise or a code (*GA* 356).

The vital importance of moral conduct, of duty and authority, and of a living rule rather than a dead letter, all reflect Newman's earliest thinking on patristic doctrine together with his teaching, as an Oxford tutor, of Aristotle's *Nicomachean Ethics*. Christians inherit normative truths from their forebears, which become the presumptions upon which they build up good habits.[86] The secondary tradition of the 1830s is evoked once more: the secret ways of living together as the Church. On 17 June 1846, Newman was delighted to discover that Aquinas thought the same as he had in the University Sermons: 'Protestants are wrong to hold that "reason comes first, and *then* comes the will and faith". "*Presumption* supported by the *will*" is "the proof"; *cogitatio* and *assensus* go together.'[87] This insight is the 'starting point' for the *Grammar of Assent*.[88] While in 1870 it is only the intellect that can assent to God's Trinity, nevertheless presumptions learned through worship and custom join with our reason to make a real assent to God.

---

[85] Sheridan Gilley, *Newman and his Age* (London: Darton, Longman and Todd, 1990), 360.

[86] While Dean Inge said (following F. D. Maurice) that it is 'Locke whom Newman resembles in his theory of knowledge', he also offered this Lockean critique: 'To most people... the fact that opinions *are* so manufactured is no proof that they *ought* to be so' (W. R. Inge, *Outspoken Essays*, First Series (2nd edn.; London: Longmans, 1921), 193).

[87] Evans, 'Newman and Aquinas on Assent', 205, quoting OM B.9.11.

[88] Ibid. 209.

CONCLUSION:
THREE VIEWS OF 'CONSUBSTANTIAL'

Having ended up surprisingly near to where Newman began, with talk of rules and secondary tradition, it is worth recalling what has changed. His view of doctrine in the 1830s can be seen in a series of four sermons from November and December 1835 called 'The Patristical Idea of Antichrist', published in 1838 as Tract 83, which employ the Alexandrian method of reading scripture. Newman writes that if the Fathers were to 'say, "These are our opinions: we deduced them from Scripture, and they are true", we might well doubt about receiving them at their hands. We might fairly say, that we had as much right to deduce from Scripture as they had' (*DA* 45). Rather than offering a private judgement on scripture *deduced* from the context of particular texts—the method he attributes to Protestants—patristic interpretations are based upon a *skopos* or goal, commonly agreed upon since apostolic times. The Fathers 'are witnesses to the fact of those doctrines having been received, not here or there, but everywhere' (ibid.). Implicit here in Newman's suspicion of deduction is his praise for Church tradition, the truth of which depends, at this stage in his life, on a Platonic sort of intuition that he seems to find in what Origen called the spiritual senses. But in matters 'prophetical', such as scriptures about the Antichrist, the interpretation of scripture was far more flexible than in matters 'doctrinal'. This is another way of viewing the division between a primary and a secondary interpretation elaborated in the first section above. Yet the Fathers remain the best guides to interpreting prophecy about Antichrist. It is mainly to the interpretations of Irenaeus and Hippolytus that Newman turns, for

> though the Fathers do not convey to us the interpretation of prophecy with the same certainty as they convey doctrine, yet, in proportion to their agreement, their personal weight, and the prevalence, or again the authoritative character of the opinions they are stating, they are to be read with deference. (*DA* 47)

The difficulty for Newman's contemporaries in interpreting prophecy has mainly to do with the form of expression used. He is convinced prophecies were given in oral rather than in written form, and that their obscurity was a deliberate part of God's own pedagogy in the scriptures and the justification for the Church's *disciplina arcani*.[89]

By the 1840s and 50s, much had changed. With doctrine no longer seen as fixed by tradition but as developing, pre-Nicenes like Hippolytus came under suspicion for their view of the Trinity. No longer thinking Rome home to the Antichrist, 'the fourth beast of Daniel's vision and persecutor of the infant Church', as he had the first time that he visited in 1833, Rome became his home in 1846–7 (*LD* iii. 253). No longer able to be suspicious of the deductive method in theology, he was introduced to it at the Propaganda Fide where he stayed. To the more Platonic mode of a theology shaped by the early Alexandrians[90] was added what he called the more Aristotelian mode.[91] But this theology did not interest him at first, with 'lecture after lecture to drawl through a few tedious pages' (*LD* xii. 48). Replacing these lectures with personal study, he felt rejected by the theologians at the Roman College whose disputations he attended.[92] As rector of the Catholic University he grew more aware of this theology, and felt more influential at Rome when he visited next in 1856 to sort out a dispute between the London and Birmingham Oratories, recognizing in a memorandum he now had 'an entrée to the ecclesiastical authorities at Rome' (*LD* xvii. 151). To feel comfortable in the Roman schools, however, would require a fourth visit to Rome, when he was

[89] 'What the Apostles disclosed concerning the future, was for the most part disclosed by them in private, to individuals—not committed to writing, not intended for the edifying of the body of Christ—and was soon lost. Thus, in a few verses after the passage I have quoted, St Paul says, "Remember ye not, that when I was yet with you, I told you these things?" (2 Thess 2: 5) and he writes by hints and allusions, not speaking out' (*DA* 46).

[90] In Dec. 1835, Oxford undergraduate F. W. Faber described his 'recoil from Newman's theology and Platonism' (recorded in Bowden, *The Life and Letters of Frederick William Faber*, 42).

[91] Newman's own analysis in 1847 of the Church he had entered was that 'Ancient heretics wanted to marry theology to Aristotle—with what unfortunate results! However, in time, after twelve centuries, the Church was divinely led to do just that, to the great benefit of Catholics' (Perrone 102).

[92] See Ch. 5, below. Although Newman became friends with Perrone, Carlo Passaglia lectured against *Dev* in 1847, and Johannes Baptist Franzelin, also from the Roman College, lectured against 'On Consulting the Faithful' in 1867.

made cardinal in 1879, by which time he was attuned to neo-Thomist theology.[93]

It has been shown that the years of Newman's shift away from the pre-Nicenes were those from 1840 which he spent working on Athanasius. He now viewed Trinitarian doctrine from the vantage point of later conciliar definitions, and found heresy where he had not before. Therefore, in a preface in 1838, Newman could claim that those who did not agree with the Nicene formula—the so-called 'Semi-Arians', Cyril of Jerusalem, Eusebius of Caesarea, Meletius of Antioch—nevertheless remained faithful to the divine Trinity, because the doctrine was not reducible to a single word (*Ox Frs* ii, p. x). In January 1840, Newman still acknowledged that the life of Meletius of Antioch can 'prove that saints may be matured in a state which Romanists of this day would fain call schism' (*Critic* 27: 84/*EH* ii. 65)—a polemic against Nicholas Wiseman's accusation that the 'schismatic' Church of England was not recognized as legitimate by the rest of Catholic Christendom. But, in 1850, the polemic is against the Church of England, using Eusebius of Caesarea as a weapon in *Certain Difficulties Felt by Anglicans*. Newman points out that the seventeenth-century Anglican, Jeremy Taylor, 'not only calls Eusebius, whom it is hard to acquit of heresy, "the wisest of them all", but actually praises the letter of Constantine [to Alexander and Arius] . . . as most true in its view and most pertinent to the occasion' (*Diff* i. 390). In the eyes of Newman, the Emperor Constantine, an unbaptized layman, had interfered in the secrets of the faith, urged to do so by Eusebius.[94] Newman is not surprised that 'Erastian' Anglican divines would prefer the Emperor's words to Catholic truth. That the turning point in his view of the Semi-Arians was the translation of Athanasius is shown by Newman's claim, in 1842, that it is 'remarkable that . . . the word "One in substance"' does not 'occur in S. Cyril's Catecheses, of whom, as being suspected of

[93] For detail on Newman's four visits to Rome, see Brigitte Maria Hoegemann, 'Newman and Rome', in Philippe Lefebvre and Colin Mason (eds.), *John Henry Newman in his Time* (Oxford: Family Publications, 2007), 61–81.

[94] Although the same argument was used in *Ari* 249, in 1850 Newman writes that 'The author has now still less favourable views of Eusebius' theology than he had when he wrote [*Arians of the Fourth Century*] in 1832' (*Diff* i. 381 n. 1). The argument appears again in *GA* 132.

Semi-Arianism, it might have been required, before his writings were received as of authority' (*Ox Frs* viii. 157 n. i). By 1842, Newman thought *homoousios* should be required as a test of orthodoxy of Fathers whom previously he thought had kept the faith, if not accepted the word.

Throughout his life, then, Newman took differing views of the role that *homoousios* played in the Church's teaching. He always recognized that one way of guaranteeing orthodoxy was to come up with a formula—a word to guard against heresy; but, in the 1830s, he also recognized that to do so limits the richness of doctrinal language. In *Arians of the Fourth Century*, he had argued that the doctrine of God's Trinity was constant from the time of the Apostles; yet, with the introduction of *homoousios* at Nicaea, the formulization and promulgation of the Creed somehow inhibited the richer truths about God that had previously been secretly preserved. A formula like *homoousios* was, at best, a necessary evil that came with Christianity being the public religion of the Empire. In the 1840s, by contrast, he felt *homoousios* was the only word to guarantee a true understanding of the relation of Father and Son and thus a 'duty to be received on account of its Catholic sense' (*Ox Frs* viii. 157 n. i). As *Development of Christian Doctrine* put it: 'Christians were bound to defend and to transmit the faith which they had received, and they received it from the rulers of the Church; and, on the other hand, it was the duty of the rulers to watch over and *define* this Traditionary faith' (*Dev* 341, my italics). Definitions became necessary for Newman in the 1840s and he looked to the rulers of the Church to provide them. With the *Grammar of Assent* in 1870, he appears to move back to his position of the *Lectures on the Prophetical Office* (1837), in which *homoousios* was likewise seen as 'the one instance of a scientific word having been introduced into the Creed from that day to this' (*GA* 144). Yet, in describing the doctrinal word as 'scientific', Newman shows his new awareness of a scientific theology that will come to dominate his second translation of Athanasius later in the decade.

2

The Sources of *The Arians of the Fourth Century* (1831–3)

Before ascertaining the contribution that Newman made to scholarship on the teachings of the Alexandrians, it is necessary to see what he inherited from earlier scholars. This chapter will show that Newman's first book drew from the seventeenth-century High Church scholars George Bull and William Cave, in spite of dismissively calling them respectively a 'doctrinist' and a 'biographer' when he began work on *Arians of the Fourth Century* in the second half of 1831 (*LD* ii. 371). He also drew from the Cambridge Platonist Ralph Cudworth (1617–88), sharing an affinity for early Alexandrian allegory in which the world's history could be interpreted for signs of God's revelation.[1] This is what in the *Apologia Pro Vita Sua* Newman called: 'The broad philosophy of Clement and Origen... drawn out... in my volume, with the zeal and freshness, but [also] with the partiality, of a neophyte' (*Apo* 36).[2] In 1864, Newman implies that this (broadly Platonic) philosophy prevented his own theology at the time from being orthodox; *Arians of the Fourth Century* espoused early Alexandrian 'philosophy, not the theological doctrine' of Athanasius, 'the champion of truth' (*Apo* 36). But these are the

---

[1] For a concise account of Newman's sharing an interest in the Alexandrians with earlier Anglicans, see Charles F. Harrold, 'John Henry Newman and the Alexandrian Platonists', *Modern Philology*, 37 (1940), 279–91.

[2] Some have been misled by this sentence in *Apo* to portray Newman as interested in early Alexandrian philosophy and not theology (e.g., Robin C. Selby, *The Principle of Reserve in the Writings of John Henry Cardinal Newman* (Oxford: Clarendon Press, 1975), 4–5 and J. Stern, *Bible et tradition chez Newman: aux origines de la théorie du développement* (Paris: Aubier, 1967), 24).

reminiscences of one who increasingly interprets 'theological doctrine' in Latin terms, which opposed Platonism.

In fact, it will be shown that Newman inherited his view of pre-Nicene *theology* from his Anglican forebears, especially in Trinitarian doctrine (the subject of the second half of this chapter). Moreover, he learned from these forebears that the *philosophy* of Alexandria was the precursor to Arian heresy, adding that this philosophy actually flourished in Antioch (the subject of the first half of this chapter). In each section it will be seen that, as for Origen and Cudworth, the changing events of history took their significance not from the world but from the unchanging God who infused it. Changing events revealed unchanging doctrines for Newman as he wrote *Arians of the Fourth Century* in 1831–2. Ten years later, at Littlemore, although now believing that doctrines develop, he still thought that to ignore the divine when writing 'sacred history' is 'to write the events of a reign, yet to be silent about the monarch' (*Fleury* i, p. xii). In both periods, he felt let down by the changeableness of Anglican bishops.

THE HIGH CHURCH CONTEXT: (2) THE ROLE OF BISHOPS

In spite of the pre-eminent role in doctrine and discipline he envisaged for bishops, Newman was highly critical of the part they played in the 1829–32 reforms of religious and political life in England. Newman had invoked the English bishops as successors of the apostles in Tract 1. The Records of the Church that accompanied the Tracts began with the letters of Ignatius of Antioch because, he wrote, 'They are especially important to us at the present day, as shewing us how important it is, in the judgment of this blessed Martyr, to honour and obey our Bishops'. But, in many of Newman's writings at this time, the bishops also received blame for the way the State seemed to be taking over the Church, including in *Arians of the Fourth Century*, the subject of this chapter.[3] In August 1833, three

[3] As Nockles says, 'Tractarian anti-erastianism entailed a repudiation not of the role of the state *per se* in matters ecclesiastical, but true to the Caroline model, repudiated only a secular or infidel and indifferent state enslaving the Church'

months before the book's publication, Newman used an unflattering comparison of contemporary bishops with their fourth-century predecessors in a letter to his friend John Bowden:

As to the state of the Church. I suppose it was in a far worse condition in Arian times, except in one point you mention, that there was the possibility of true-minded men becoming Bishops, which is now almost out of the question. If we had one Athanasius, or Basil, we could bear with 20 Eusebiuses—though Eusebius was not at all the worst of the bad...I wish the Archbishop had somewhat of the boldness of the old Catholic Prelates; no one can doubt he is a man of the highest principle, and would willingly die a Martyr; but, if he had but the little finger of Athanasius, he would do us all the good in the world. (*LD* iv. 33)

Archbishop Howley and other High Church bishops were nothing like their early Church predecessors, who had stood up to the secular authorities;[4] and Eusebius of Caesarea, whom Newman disliked, was nevertheless more 'true-minded' than contemporary bad bishops.

The reason for Newman's lack of confidence in bishops was revealed in the *British Critic* in July 1836. In his review of Edward Burton, Newman demanded dogma from bishops, not dandyism. He wrote of the Oxford-educated bishops:

from the latter part of last century almost down to the recent passing of the Emancipation Bills, elegant scholarship and literature have been the main road to distinction, and an abstinence from subjects purely ecclesiastical. Some of the most eminent members of the Episcopal Bench at this moment are instances of the truth of this remark, at the time they were promoted. (*Critic* 20: 209–10)

('"Church and King": Tractarian Politics Reappraised', in Paul Vais (ed.), *From Oxford to the People: Reconsidering Newman and the Oxford Movement* (Leominster: Gracewing, 1996), 95).

[4] See James Garrard, 'Archbishop Howley and the Oxford Movement', ibid. 269–85. Garrard traces the ambiguities of the Tractarians' relationship with Howley, assuming that Newman wanted to 'athanasize' Howley, influenced by the reference to Athanasius in University Sermon V on 22 Jan. 1832: 'A few highly-endowed men will rescue the world for centuries to come. Before now, even one man has impressed an image on the Church, which...shall not be effaced while time lasts' (*US* 97). But Athanasius is not the only one who 'transmits the sacred flame' (ibid.); it should not be forgotten that Basil is mentioned with Athanasius at *LD* iv. 33 and in the last paragraph of *Ari* 394.

Similarly, Richard Church, who translated Cyril of Jerusalem for *A Library of the Fathers*, wrote of the 1830s bishops: 'Three or four of them might be considered theologians—Archbishop Howley, Phill-potts of Exeter, Kaye of Lincoln, Marsh of Peterborough.'[5]

The judgement of Newman and Richard Church is harsh, especially because these four were distinguished scholars—the first three of them in the High Church tradition of Cave and Bull. William Howley (b. 1766) had been Regius Professor of Divinity at Oxford. Henry Phillpotts (b. 1778) was a Fellow of Magdalen College, Oxford, who, in his book, *A Letter to an English Layman on the Coronation Oath* (1828), defended the sacred responsibilities of the monarchy. John Kaye (b. 1783) had been Regius Professor of Divinity at Cambridge and, in 1826, when Bishop of Bristol, had written *Ecclesiastical History of the Second and Third Century* to show the continuities between Tertullian's theology and the Thirty-nine Articles of Religion. Herbert Marsh (b. 1757) had been Margaret Professor of Divinity at Cambridge;[6] although no High Churchman, 'Marsh's correspondence with Norris and Joshua Watson', Nockles writes, 'points to his links and alliance of interest with the Hackney circle'.[7] Other scholars on the Episcopal Bench included the Bishop of Salisbury, Thomas Burgess (b. 1756), author of *Primary Principles of Christianity* (1829), and the Bishop of Bangor, Christopher Bethell (b. 1773), a Fellow of King's College, Cambridge. Add to their number William Van Mildert (b. 1765), the High Church Bishop of Durham and founder of Durham University, and these were the men best placed to discuss doctrine at the time of the reform crisis. According to Newman, they utterly failed.

Rose did not agree with Newman's view of the Episcopal Bench. The parallels of the Episcopal Bench to bishops during the Arian controversy in *Arians of the Fourth Century* may have been one reason why Rose and Archdeacon Lyall rejected the book from

[5] Church, *The Oxford Movement: Twelve Years 1833–1845* (London and New York: Macmillan, 1891), 249.

[6] Marsh introduced German methods of theology to Cambridge in *A Course of Lectures Containing a Description and Systematic Arrangement of the Several Branches of Divinity* (1812).

[7] Peter Nockles, *The Oxford Movement in Context: Anglican High Churchmanship 1760–1857* (Cambridge: Cambridge University Press, 1994), 29 n. 115.

inclusion in the Theological Library series for which it had been commissioned. However, it should be borne in mind that, in 1834, Rose was given a Professorship at Durham by Van Mildert and was serving as a chaplain to Archbishop Howley, upon whose patronage Lyall also depended.[8] Rose owed his preferment to High Church bishops. In October 1834, Rose used his editorial powers on a letter Newman submitted to the *British Magazine* on 'Centralization', explaining to Newman in personal correspondence: 'you will not, I hope, be angry at my having—not altered the sentiments of course, but—softened the expressions in the conclusion... Your remarks on the Bishops were not only rules for our Rulers—but very severe reflexions on their past conduct... I think the Clergy are more to blame than the Bishops on the points to which you refer' (*LD* iv. 343 n. 1).

Newman's reply to Rose expressed a willingness to be guided by someone wiser, claiming that '[i]f I have ever seemed to write against the Bishops, I meant to be writing against the Clergy more, though indirectly' (ibid. 344). There is evidence that Tract 3 in September 1833 was written to clergy as 'we'; for given the letters of Clement of Rome and Ignatius 'and other such strong passages from the Apostolical Fathers, how can we permit ourselves in our present *practical* disregard of the Episcopal authority?... Do we support the Bishop, and strive to move all together with him...?' Yet, in Newman's other writings in this period, the bishops bore the brunt of his criticism. In 1833–5, he thought bishops should know their responsibilities to the clergy, who in turn should know their responsibilities to parishioners, so that the Church could once more be a force for action throughout the nation.[9]

[8] For these chains of patronage, see Clive Dewey, *The Passing of Barchester* (London and Rio Grande, Ohio: Hambledon Press, 1991), 31, who suggests that Howley moved from opposition to the reform in Church and State to accommodation because of his change of advisers: 'two of his more intransigent counselors—Hugh Rose (his most assertive domestic chaplain) and William van Mildert (the most forceful bishop) were in the grip of terminal illnesses. Their place was filled by reformers like Blomfield (Howley's first choice as Archdeacon of Colchester) and Lyall (Blomfield's successor).'

[9] It was to this end that Newman proposed 'some dioceses must be divided or must be provided with a number of suffragans' (*LD* iv. 342). He also wrote an article for the *Edinburgh Review*, later published in pamphlet form as 'A Restoration of Suffragan Bishops', advocating suffragan bishops (or 'Chorepiscopi') based on

Rowan Williams shows that, in *Arians of the Fourth Century*, Newman feared the Confessional State was being *lost* by bishops, just as in the fourth century, when, in the face of the Arian onslaught, 'The orthodox majority of Bishops and divines... timorously or indolently, kept in the background' (*Ari* 294).[10] By contrast, Stephen Thomas argues that Newman thought the reforms were *won* by 'modern liberal churchmen such as Thomas Arnold of Rugby', who, like 'the party centred around the courtly ecclesiastic Eusebius of Nicomedia' were 'scheming, power-seeking and dishonest'.[11] Those who gained most from the fracturing of the Confessional State, according to this view of Newman's polemic, were those he dismissed as mere 'Protestants'. Thomas argues that 'the Arian prelate Acacius', who criticized the Nicene Creed for containing non-biblical language, is likened to a present-day 'wily church-politician invoking vague assent to Scripture in order to weaken the authority of a test which could be used to exclude him from power and influence'.[12] The Protestant cry of *sola scriptura*, Newman warned, was a diversionary tactic in the liberals' power grab.[13] In Williams's interpretation of *Arians of the Fourth Century*, the Council of Nicaea represented a decline like that in Newman's own time, which resulted from the Bishops' refusal to stop the State interfering in the Church. Once 'the *Homoüsion*', as Newman called it in *Arians of the Fourth Century*, was introduced into the Creed as a test, the golden age of the Church

primitive practice, which ended: 'As to our country, situated at the furthest extremity of the West, it but slowly received that ecclesiastical organization, which sprang up in Asia almost under the feet of those who first "preached the good tidings" there' (*Suff* 31–6). Newman thus exerts pressure on biblical Protestants to look to the early Church, for 'to such as turn their minds ever so little to its history and antiquities, it is evident that the Church "is like a man that is a householder, which bringeth forth out of his treasure things new and old"' (ibid. 2–3).

[10] Williams comments: 'The overwhelming majority of the bishops during these years had supported the extension of the rights of Protestant Dissenters and had been at best ineffectual and lukewarm in their resistance to Catholic Emancipation; a substantial minority had backed the Reform Bill of 1832' (introduction, *Ari* (p. xxiv)).

[11] Stephen Thomas, *Newman and Heresy: The Anglican Years* (Cambridge: Cambridge University Press, 1991), 37.

[12] Ibid.

[13] Boyd Hilton shows the interaction of liberal political economy and Christian rhetoric in *The Age of Atonement: The Influence of Evangelicalism on Social and Economic Thought 1795–1865* (Oxford: Clarendon Press, 1988).

was at an end. 'We move towards a "technical" language', in Williams's paraphrase, 'superseding the innocent variety of earlier days'.[14] Williams rightly stresses that this is a radical version of High Churchmanship, for Newman is arguing that the pre-Nicene Fathers did a better job of conserving the faith than did subsequent conciliar orthodoxy through fixing the faith in a technical formula. *Arians of the Fourth Century* was a theological, not just a historical work, then, and Newman was aware of some unhistorical aspects of what he wrote. Maybe he tried to pre-empt criticism by writing: 'it is not the actual practice of the Primitive Church, which I am concerned with, so much as its principle. Men often break through the rules, which they set out for themselves for the conduct of life, with or without good reason' (*Ari* 52). In the 1830s, Newman recognized in the *rules* (grounded as Chapter 1 showed in the principles) of the pre-Nicenes, a richness and dynamism of doctrine that subsequent eras, including his own, had forgotten.

Therefore, *Arians of the Fourth Century*'s representation of pre-Nicene history is a play of mirrors. Newman was writing history within an Anglican tradition that sought to return to the primary sources. Yet, just as those primary sources did not accurately reflect what was happening in the pre-Nicene Church, so the seventeenth- and eighteenth-century commentators, in whose train Newman was following, gave their own interpretive gloss. When Newman came to the sources, he had a breadth of interpretations from which to choose, including scholars from outside his own tradition, such as the French Jesuit Denys Petau or Petavius (1583–1652) and the Lutheran Johann Lorenz von Mosheim (1694–1755). As the rays of truth bounced off these various mirrors, it was for Newman to try to work out where those rays intersected with his own purposes, such as awakening the bishops of his own day. In his turn, Newman made changes to these prior interpretations of events, recording history in a way that would be paradigmatic for those in the English tradition who followed him.

---

[14] Rowan Williams, 'Newman's *Arians* and the Question of Method in Doctrinal History', in Ian Ker and Alan G. Hill (eds.), *Newman after One Hundred Years* (Oxford: Clarendon Press, 1990), 270.

Newman took many arguments directly from the primary sources. This can be seen most clearly in a quotation from Alexander of Alexandria, preserved in Theodoret's *Ecclesiastical History*, Book I, Chapter III, which sums up Newman's account of the origins of Arius's heresy:

'Ye are not ignorant', [Alexander] writes to the Constantinopolitan Church concerning Arianism, 'that this rebellious doctrine belongs to Ebion and Artemas, and is in imitation of Paulus of Samosata, Bishop of Antioch, who was excommunicated by the sentence of the Bishops assembled in Council from all quarters. Paulus was succeeded by Lucian, who remained in separation for many years'. (*Ari* 24)

Newman starts with the early Church historians Theodoret, Epiphanius, Eusebius, Sozomen, and Socrates, not only because they contain much of what remains extant of the pre-Nicene period, but also because the writings which these early historians chose to preserve share Newman's prejudices. For instance, in this quotation, the main pre-Nicene villains of *Arians of the Fourth Century* (particularly Paul of Samosata) are introduced, connected together, and focused on Antioch, the basis for Newman's own thesis. He treats his primary sources less critically than his Oxford contemporary, Edward Burton.[15] Newman also drew heavily upon early-modern commentators for his sources. 'Rough notes preparatory to writing History of the Arians', extant among Newman's papers in the Birmingham Oratory, show that even references to Athanasius were taken mostly from Bull and Petavius.[16] As for pre-Nicenes, a page entitled 'On the Patristical view' contains references to Bull for Origen, to Petavius for Clement of Alexandria, and to both later commentators for Athenagoras,[17] under the subheading '$\pi\epsilon\rho\iota\chi\acute\omega\rho\eta\sigma\iota\varsigma$' (*perichoresis*).

---

[15] Edward Burton weighs the trustworthiness of his various sources in the introduction to his 1829 Bampton Lectures—e.g., 'Wherever Epiphanius and Theodoret differ, few persons would hesitate to follow the latter' (*An Inquiry into the Heresies of the Apostolic Age* (Oxford: Rivingtons, 1829), p. xiii). An introduction to the sources seems to have been conventional, but Newman has no such introduction. Cave named his sources for information on the fourth century: 'the chief whereof (setting aside Eusebius, of whom elsewhere, and a small part of whose history relates to this period) are four, all writing much about the same time, viz. Socrates, Sozomen, Theodoret, and Philostorgius' (*Ecclesiastici*, p. ix).

[16] OM A.12.11. In the book he quotes the anti-Arian Discourses from Petavius (*de trin* e.g., p. 341 nn at *Ari* 208).

[17] Ibid. He cites neither in the book when quoting Athenagoras: 'Let no one ridicule the notion that God has a Son...the Father and the Son being one. The

Among early-moderns, Petavius was especially critical of the early Alexandrians. In order to refute him Newman employed the Gallican scholars who reacted against Petavius and the Socinian Christoph Sand, or Sandius (1644–80), who appropriated the Jesuit's arguments. These Gallicans—Pierre Daniel Huet (1630–1721), Louis Ellies Du Pin (1657–1719), Jean-François Baltus (1667–1743), and Rémy Ceillier (1688–1763)—were all favourable in their judgement of Clement and Origen, Du Pin claiming that the last 'provided material for all the Greek and Latin Fathers who followed him, who nearly did no more than copy him'.[18] Louis-Sébastien Le Nain de Tillemont (1637–98), though suspicious to French Catholics because of his Jansenism, was an important source for Newman.[19] A page of the 'Rough notes' reminds Newman to 'consult Tillemont' on fifteen of the book's themes (citing volumes ii to vi); in volume iii he would have found a list of Origen's work.[20]

What of Origen himself did Newman read? Probably very little, given that most of his knowledge of Origen appears to be second hand. Page twelve of the 'Rough notes', headed 'On Origen &c in particular', shows that Newman knew 'Hom[ily] 25' and the 'Philocalia' from Huet's *Origeniana*.[21] (Here, Newman also refers to Origen's 'mode of arguing with the infidel & the disciplina secreta [*sic*]'.) Although the quotations in *Arians of the Fourth Century* reveal that Newman read sections of *On First Principles* and *Against Celsus*, it seems that most of his insights into the controversial passages of

---

Son being in the Father, and the Father in the Son, in the unity and power of the Spirit, the Son of God is the Mind and Word of the Father' (*Ari* 172).

[18] Louis Ellies Du Pin, *Nouvelle bibliothèque des auteurs ecclésiastique* (1731 edn.), i. 142 (quoted at Henri de Lubac, *History and Spirit: The Understanding of Scripture According to Origen*, trans. A. E. Nash and J. Merriell (San Francisco, Calif.: Ignatius, 2007), 39).

[19] For Tillemont's method, see Jean-Louis Quantin, 'The Fathers in Seventeenth Century Roman Catholic Theology', in Irena Backus (ed.), *The Reception of the Church Fathers in the West: From the Carolingians to the Maurists*, 2 vols. (New York: E. J. Brill, 1997), ii. 976–7.

[20] Tillemont, *Mémoires pour servir à l'histoire ecclésiastique des six premiers siècles*, 16 vols. (2nd edn.; Paris: Charles Robustel, 1701–12), iii. 551–83.

[21] Cave and Bull also cite Huet, who was Bossuet's tutor—e.g., Bull debates with Petavius (and Sand) using Huet to defend textual variations that are charitable to Origen (*Defensio* i. 231).

Origen came from Bull.[22] When these notes became a book, however, in spite of how little Newman had read of him, Origen was one of its greatest heroes.

MIRROR OPPOSITES: (I) ANTIOCHENE HERESY

Newman considered the primary difference between the Alexandrians and Antiochenes to have been a dispute about how to read scripture. Of the two ways of reading biblical texts, the materialistic and literal way was the preserve of the school of Antioch, while the spiritual and allegorical way was that of the school of Alexandria. But this difference in scriptural interpretation resulted in two views of episcopal authority, and consequently in two views of the Christian ethos. The triad that was interacting in Newman's life in Oxford—scripture, authority, and ethos—was interacting in *Arians of the Fourth Century* too. For instance, the following quotation on (i) the interpretation of scripture combines (ii) the authority of 'orthodox' belief in Christ's divinity with (iii) right religious feeling. By implication, (i) an improper exegesis of scripture will result in (ii) a false teaching about the Son and (iii) a materialist rather than a spiritual ethic:

since a belief in our Lord's Divinity is closely connected (how, it matters not) with deep religious feeling generally,—involving a sense both of our need and of the blessings which He has procured for us, and an emancipation from the tyranny of the visible world,—it is not wonderful, that those, who would confine our knowledge of God to things seen, should dislike to hear of His true and only Image. (*Ari* 273)

This is suggestive of Origen's desire to penetrate the veil of the world and of Christ's human nature to see the glory of God beneath. Moreover, it will become clear that Newman saw Church order as related to proper exegesis of scripture and to living a good life. The

[22] Although neither text is cited, *Ari* 170 quotes *de Principiis* 1.2.6 and *Ari* 165 quotes *Contra Celsum* 8.15.

problem of Arianism, Newman thinks, lies not so much with Arius declaring the Son 'subordinate' to the Father (Newman admits Origen also subordinated the Father to the Son) but with Arius's exegetical method, his opposition to bishop Alexander, and his unethical living.

For Newman, the dispute between Antioch and Alexandria was about the way scripture doctrines came to be embodied—in ecclesiastical order and ethos. The Arian sophists challenged ecclesiastical order, which included the teachings of the Fathers before them, and all the while acted unethically. The force of Newman's argument lies in his ability to link all these factors together in his portrayal of Arianism, but it is worth looking at each factor in turn.

Exegesis

In Newman's argument, the Antiochene method of exegesis represents the mirror opposite method of reading scripture to that of the Alexandrian school. Paul of Samosata, for instance, expressed 'contempt for the received expositors of Scripture at Antioch', and thus set the pattern for subsequent Antiochene exegesis in the way he argued against the doctrine of the Father's equality with the Son (*Ari* 36). Instead of producing a *skopos* that might elevate the allegorical sense of scripture over the literal sense, Newman laments that the Antiochene rule elevates the literal to the exclusion of the allegorical, infamously resulting in a Son who is a mere creature. Newman writes:

The Catholics (not to speak of their guidance from tradition in determining it) had taken '*Son*' in its most obvious meaning; as interpreted moreover by the title '*Only-begotten*', and as confirmed by the general tenor of Revelation. But the Arians selected as the sense of the figure, that part of the original import of the word, which . . . is at best what logicians call *a property* deduced from the essence or nature (*Ari* 206).

It is important to recognize that Newman conceives the Arians as those who deal in the arguments of 'logicians'; in this use of logic over tradition, the Arians show themselves to be the inheritors of an Antiochene mode of exegesis begun by Paul of Samosata which prizes 'abstract logical process' over allegory and typology (ibid. 220). The

rule of the school of Antioch was based on small portions of scripture, and not sufficiently open to the breadth and depth of interpretation of both Testaments.[23] Unlike for the Alexandrian school,
Antiochene teaching is seen only from the point of view of the heresy
it produced—Arianism. Newman's argument will be seen to invert
his predecessors' view that it was the Alexandrians who brought
philosophy to Christian doctrine. The connection of Antioch and
heresy was as unquestioned for Newman as Alexandria and Arianism
had been for his predecessors.

Church order

Crucial, for Newman, is not simply that Arius's exegesis threatened
Trinitarian doctrine, but that he both rejected 'a traditional system of
theology, consistent with, but independent of, Scripture' and challenged Church order by disputing with his bishop, Alexander of
Alexandria (*Ari* 220). Newman does not make much of the fact
that Arius was an Alexandrian clergyman; his apparent schooling
under Lucian seems to Newman enough to distance him from the
orthodoxy of the Alexandrian Church where he served. Again, the
Antiochenes are mirror opposites of the Alexandrians for Newman,
with one school breeding heresy by opposing the Fathers' tradition
and the other breeding orthodoxy by maintaining it. Those receiving
a sophistical education at Antioch challenged 'received opinions'
merely 'for the sake of exercise or amusement' (ibid. 31).

Ethics

The full force of Newman's thesis comes only with the argument that
the Arians' literal interpretation of scripture, and their disregard for

[23] There is a grain of truth in Newman's account of Alexandrian–Antiochene
differences in reading scripture, but no more than a grain. As Henri de Lubac has
shown, the Antiochenes 'did not cut themselves off from the Church in any of their
activities. And they were fully aware of the "ecclesiastical canon" of the harmony of
the two Testaments, even though they understood it more modestly, and they
certainly did not reject all typology. But it is beginning with them that the exegesis
of the Bible starts to lead a life of its own. Their attitude of mind and their form of
work entitle them to be considered as the real founders of biblical exegesis' (*Scripture
in the Tradition*, trans. Luke O'Neill (New York: Herder and Herder, 2000), 47).

ecclesiastical authority, failed to bring holiness of life. This thesis is outlined in the opening section of Chapter I, 'The Church of Antioch', where he establishes the 'latent connection between a judaizing discipline and heresy in doctrine' (*Ari* 21). The final section of Chapter II, called 'The Arian Heresy', is followed by Chapters III–V on the historical outcome of Arianism—a depiction of the bloody repression of holy men and women by the 'arianizing' or 'judaizing' emperors and bishops of the fourth century. This is largely the thesis of Athanasius too—that holiness of life is the result of right reading of scripture guided by sound ecclesiastical authority; the supporting evidence for this argument is his *History of the Arians*.[24] But in this respect, of course, both Newman's and Athanasius's thesis depended wholly on Origen's earlier connection between literalism in scriptural exegesis and a failure to penetrate the veil of the flesh of Christ. As Origen said in the preface to *On First Principles*, those who refuse to acknowledge that the Son, who for us dwelt in the flesh, is the Word of God do not 'derive the knowledge which calls men to lead a good and blessed life'.

As a pupil of the Antiochene school, not of the Alexandrian, Arius's unethical behaviour makes sense to Newman: 'Arius followed in the track thus marked out by his predecessor [Paul]. Turbulent by character, he is known in history as an offender against ecclesiastical order, before his agitation assumed the shape which has made his name familiar to posterity' (*Ari* 28). Newman wants to trace a lineage from the bloodshed resulting from Arius's heresy and Eusebius of Nicomedia's influence at court, back through Lucian, to Paul of Samosata—all supposedly members of the Antiochene school—and discerns in all of them characteristics of self-importance and disobedience. In what follows, each of Newman's suggested causes of

[24] Newman's account of post-Nicene Alexandria follows Athanasius: the people were far more holy when he was bishop than when Arians were in charge. Upon his return from exile, 'How many unmarried women, who were before ready to enter upon marriage, now remained virgins to Christ! How many young men, seeing the examples of others, embraced the monastic life! How many wives persuaded their husbands, and how many were persuaded by their husbands, to give themselves to prayer, as the apostle has spoken! How many widows and how many orphans, who were before hungry and naked, now through the great zeal of the people, were no longer hungry, and went forth clothed!' (*Historia Arianorum* 25 (trans.: NPNF ser. 2 iv)).

Arianism will be discussed, before turning to Newman's depiction of
the orthodox alternative.

The causes of Arianism: confusion of philosophy
and theology in Alexandria?

Newman recognizes two causes of Arius's heresy that the Son was not
one with God but created: sophistical methods of argument and a
literal exegesis of scripture. Both causes represent, for Newman, a
confusion of philosophy and theology. But there was nothing new in
interpreting early heresies in this way. Many of his predecessors
perceived Arianism to result from an interaction of heretical theology
with the wrong philosophy—and the lesson drawn, therefore, was
that in any account of Arianism one must consider which theology
and which philosophy were involved. In the seventeenth century,
Cudworth considered this interaction, and Cave followed him
closely. Cave, like Mosheim, who followed in the eighteenth century,
accepted Cudworth's account that Alexandrian Neoplatonic philosophy bred the subordinationist doctrine of the Trinity that was central
to Arian theology.

These three did not agree on all points, however. While editing a
version of Cudworth's *True Intellectual System,* Mosheim found
much to criticize in its analysis of philosophy and theology in the
early Church.[25] Cudworth was favourable to the Christian appropriation of Platonic philosophy in the pre-Nicene era, whereas Mosheim
argued that, in appropriating Plato, 'the Alexandrian doctors... conceded to philosophy some authority in matters of religion' (*de reb*
ii. 143). But, generally speaking, Cudworth, Cave, and Mosheim
portrayed the catechetical schools of Alexandria as closely linked to
the city's philosophical schools. Neoplatonism was suited alike to
Alexandrian theologians or 'doctors' and philosophers.[26] While

[25] Mosheim translated *TIS* into Latin—published in two volumes in Leyden
(1773).
[26] Mosheim writes: 'All things that exist, whether corporeal or void of gross matter,
emanated eternally from God, the source of all things. This first principle of the new
Platonic school, derived from Egyptian wisdom, was the basis or foundation of
Origen's philosophy' (*de reb* ii. 150). Today, Mark Edwards argues that Origen was
no Neoplatonist, in terms similar to Cudworth's. For Origen, the 'substance' of 'God

Mosheim attacks theologians for imbibing it, Cave simply accepts that Alexandria is the first place to look for the rise of Arianism.

All of the commentators under examination considered academic centres like Alexandria to have had 'schools' understood more or less in the terms of their own day, with a formal structure and curriculum, a headmaster (or 'rector' as Mosheim's translator puts it, *de reb* ii. 150), and often assistant masters. More recently, this view of the catechetical school has been questioned.[27] It is Cave's opinion that Origen 'took in Heraclas, who had been his scholar... to be his partner, dividing the work between them, the younger and more untutored catechumens he committed to [Heraclas]' (*Apostolici* 220, citing *Ecc Hist* 6. 15)—thus implying a structured school at Alexandria, which received sponsorship from the bishop, for whose benefit the tutors taught. In fact, the bishop was attempting to bring the school under the greater control of the church in that city, uniting the church and school for a generation to come.[28] But Cave (using Origen's letter ibid. 6.19) conceived a school that was already sponsored by the church, a relationship begun a generation before by Pantaenus.

The problem Cave and Mosheim perceived in the Neoplatonism of the third and fourth centuries in Alexandria is that some teachers were more interested in questions of philosophy than theology. This seems to have been a pattern, earlier in the third century, in Rome. Here the philosophical school of Artemas, according to Eusebius, had taught his disciples to use their philosophy to misinterpret scripture (*Ecc Hist* 5. 28). Later in the century Rome was also host to Plotinus, whose Neoplatonism followed the fashion of his Alexandrian teacher, Ammonius. This same Ammonius sought to be the reconciler of 'the Schools of Plato and Aristotle', hence Cave's claim that the Eclectics took what was best from each philosopher

is Mind, [while] the Logos as his demiurgic instrument may be styled his soul ([*de Principiis*] 2. 85) and the Spirit is his matter when he makes himself present in us (*Com John* 2. 62)' 'Christ or Plato?', in L. Ayres and G. Jones (eds.), *Christian Origins: Theology, Rhetoric and Community* (London: Routledge, 1998), 17.

[27] See G. Bardy, 'Aux origines de l'école d'Alexandrie', *Recherches de science religieuse*, 27 (1937), 65–90.

[28] John Behr suggests a power struggle over teaching, concluding 'that [Bishop] Demetrius was more directly involved' in Heraclas's appointment 'and that Origen was ousted from his previous role' (*The Way to Nicaea* (New York: SVS Press, 2001), 166).

(*Apostolici* 216). Above all, though, the Eclectics were Neoplatonists, and their philosophy brought flaws to theology. Mosheim writes of even Origen's discontent of Heraclas, that 'upon placing himself under the tuition of Ammonius, he assumed the philosopher's mantle, and continued ever after to wear it', both as head of the catechetical school and as presbyter (*de reb* i. 340, reading Origen's letter in *Ecc Hist* 6. 19 as critical of Heraclas). Mosheim here reveals the naivety of Cave's account of the happy interaction of Origen and Heraclas as co-heads of the school. In other respects, however, Mosheim agreed with Cave's argument that the Alexandrian catechetical school swallowed too large a dose of Neoplatonism; the result was Arianism.

Newman sees the opposite to be the case. It was the catechetical school under Paul in Antioch that swallowed too large a dose of that city's philosophy, while, in Alexandria, theologians like Origen took only what they wanted from the philosophical schools.[29] When it comes to the rise of Arianism, Newman's focus is on a different city— and thus on a different philosophy. In all that follows, it is important to see that where Newman conflates the two types of school (catechetical and philosophical) in Antioch, Cudworth, Cave, and Mosheim conflate philosophy and theology in Alexandria under Pantaenus and his successors.

While Newman rejects Mosheim and Cave's suggestion that Clement was a member of the Eclectic 'sect', he does accept that the philosophical school in Alexandria bred this form of Neoplatonism.[30] Following Cave, who used the terms 'Junior Platonism' and 'Electivism' almost interchangeably, Newman refers to 'infant Platonism' and 'Eclecticism' at Alexandria. But Newman wants to end

---

[29] Newman followed Tillemont, holding that Origen 'studied philosophy only after having become famous in the school of Catechesis' (*Mémoires*, iii. 516, at de Lubac, *History and Spirit*, 31).

[30] Clement is given membership of the 'Elective sect' by Cave in virtue of being one of those thinkers 'who obliged not themselves to the dictates and sentiments of any one philosopher, but freely made choice of the most excellent principles out of all' (*Apostolici* 195). Equally eclectically, 'Origen made himself perfect master of the Platonic notions, being daily conversant in the writings of Plato, Numenius, Cronius, Apollophanes, Longinus, Moderatus, Nichomachus, and the most principal among the Pythagoreans, as also of Chaeremon and Cornutus, stoics' (ibid. 217, using Porphyry's words quoted in *Ecc Hist* 6. 19).

the notion that the catechetical schools of Alexandria taught Neoplatonic philosophy—largely, it seems, in order to remove all suspicion of taint from Origen. Mosheim, for instance, thought Origen's
theology was corrupted by 'his preceptor *Ammonius Saccas*, the
celebrated founder of the new Platonic school', and that Origen
never more than 'slightly modified' what he learned there (*de reb*
ii. 150).[31] While following Mosheim in portraying Ammonius as
'virtually the founder of the Eclectic sect', Newman nevertheless
rejects the claim of Mosheim and Cave that Ammonius remained a
Christian throughout his life (*Ari* 101). The more Ammonius moved
towards philosophy, for Newman, the more corrupt his theology
became. Eventually, according to Newman, Ammonius renounced
what he had learned in the catechetical school and lapsed from
orthodoxy. But Newman has to show—in spite of the confusion in
the primary sources—that it was not until after he taught Origen that
Ammonius 'gradually disclosed the systematic infidelity on which
[his teaching] was grounded' (ibid. 102). After all, Newman argues,
Origen would not truck with a philosophy that attacked Christian
doctrine (as shown when Origen refused to hear Paul of Samosata,
with whom he shared a patron (ibid. 98)). He is sure Origen would
have nothing to do with the philosophy of a lapsed Christian.
Although it will be seen that his English predecessors defended
Origen from many of his critics, they did not work as hard as Newman to retell the story of pre-Nicene Alexandria.

The causes of Arianism: confusion of philosophy and theology in Antioch?

Cave says it was not just the philosophical doctrine of Alexandrian
Neoplatonists that became the source of Arian heresy, but also the
theology of Lucian of Antioch. Lucian's catechetical school in

---

[31] For Mosheim, Origen was not only a philosopher: although the 'philosophical
light, which shone in Origen and others, *was not great,* yet it was sufficient to dissipate
and entirely overthrow the absurd fictions of [Gnostic] sects' (*de reb* ii. 243, my
italics). But philosophy is also where Origen is at his weakest, says Mosheim, for his
'timidity and changeableness are apparent, when he offers *philosophical explanations*
of those Christian doctrines which theologians call revealed truths' (ibid. 147).

Antioch has long been a highly debated subject of fourth-century theology, in spite of the little that is known about it. Cave saw Lucian teaching Arius a theology to match the philosophy Arius had learned in Alexandria. Quoting Arius's admission, in a letter to Eusebius of Nicomedia, that they were 'Fellow-Lucianists', Cave nevertheless remains ambiguous about quite how close Arius was to Lucian's school. Cave thinks Arius was admitted to this fraternity, but he will not say whether Arius learned his heresy from Lucian himself. For, whether Arius learned Lucian's doctrines 'at the first or second hand', he writes, 'it is hard to say' (*Ecclesiastici* 155). Such refusal to speculate leaves Arius located in Alexandria in Cave's account, whereas Newman situates him in Antioch. Newman will, by contrast, quote Arius's letter to Eusebius of Nicomedia in full, as evidence in his case that Arius was a member of Lucian's school, for Newman wants to portray an Arius who took both his theology and his philosophy from Antioch.

Newman seems to have been the first to argue that the sources show a school of theology in Antioch dating from roughly the same era as that in Alexandria. Cave cannot have doubted that schools to teach catechumens existed, but their formal status is not recognized in the sources. All Cave mentions are the 'Sophistical' schools—which had no church affiliation beyond that one of these schools of philosophy had the presbyter, Malchion, as 'head' (*Hist Lit* 99). Not until Cave's account reaches the fourth century will he find a catechetical school in Antioch in which Lucian was 'master' of Eusebius of Nicomedia (*Ecclesiastici* 160). Newman, by contrast, considers Paul 'the founder of a school rather than of a sect, as encouraging in the Church the use of those disputations and sceptical inquiries, which belonged to the Academy and other heathen philosophies' (*Ari* 6). His consideration of the role this 'school' played in the Church suggests Newman has in mind a parallel with Alexandria's catechetical school. But he thinks Paul's school in Antioch is really only masquerading as a catechetical school. Newman knows he is setting himself against two of his predecessors here. On one hand, Newman turned around Mosheim's argument regarding the Alexandrian catechetical school and used it regarding this purported Antiochene school. Mosheim thought it was the Alexandrians who had a philosophical school that masqueraded as a catechetical school. On the other hand, Cave had already shown that the methods Newman called 'disputations and sceptical inquiries' were typical of Antiochene sophism, and even implied that Paul used these methods at the first gathering of the council of Antioch to avoid 'the severe censure of the Synod by sly pretences' (*Hist Lit* 98).[32] But Cave did not suggest there was any official Antiochene catechetical school in the third century.

Although Cave and Newman agree that Antioch was home to 'Aristotelian' sophism, beyond this Newman tells a very different tale. In contrast to Cave, who says that Neoplatonism continued in Alexandria after Ammonius, Newman argues that when Ammonius stopped teaching 'the infant philosophy languished' in Alexandria, switching its focus to Rome, where Plotinus 'began his public lectures A.D. 244' (*Ari* 107). Neoplatonism was also taught in Antioch. And who in Antioch took over this philosophy, corrupted as it has become by (what Newman mistakenly thought was) Ammonius's renunciation of Christianity? In Newman's eyes, the obvious candidate was the heretical Paul of Samosata. The elements that Newman discerns in Arius's heresy are coming into conjunction in Antioch, 'Paulus of Samosata, the judaizing Sophist, being the favourite of a court which patronized Eclecticism, when it was neglected at Alexandria' (ibid. 132). Newman turns Queen Zenobia into the matrix of heretical cross-fertilization of 'carnal' Judaism, Paul's sophism, and the Eclectics' faulty Trinitarianism.[33]

At times, Newman struggles to convince even himself of this new thesis, as Williams puts it, showing 'signs of strain as he attempts to fit into one pattern the diversity of theologies he deals with'.[34] Newman plays with his mirrors far more than Cave, for instance, who will

---

[32] The charge of 'sophistry' is frequently found in patristic texts. In antiquity, as Paul Kolbet writes, 'the person who learned doctrines without going to the trouble to live them was dismissed as a mere "sophist"' ('Athanasius, the Psalms, and the Reformation of the Self', *Harvard Theological Review*, 99 (2006), 87).

[33] Newman does not really explain how this cross-fertilization worked. He describes great differences between the various schools of thought: 'The Eclectics . . . had followed the Alexandrians in adopting the allegorical rule . . . Judaism, on the contrary, being carnal in its views, was essentially literal in its interpretations; and, in consequence, as hostile from its grossness, as the Sophists from their dryness, to the fanciful fastidiousness of the Eclectics' (*Ari* 110).

[34] Williams, introduction, *Ari* (p. xxxviii).

say no more of Paul and Lucian's relationship than that they flourished in the same city, and that the latter altered and (from the orthodox perspective) improved the earlier man's heretical doctrines. Newman goes much further, claiming that Paul introduced the Aristotelian philosophy found among the sophists to the theology of the East, bequeathing to the whole Church a heritage of heresy. But he dare not explore too closely the interaction of Paul and Lucian, seeing as, '[t]hough a friend, as it appears, of Paulus', Lucian had an opposing view on the pre-existence of the Son (*Ari* 7 n. 3).[35] Newman also faces the question that, if all 'Lucian's pupils were brought together from so many different places, and were promoted to posts of influence in so many parts of the Church', then where was the commonality among them (ibid. 25–6)? Newman is consistent, however, with what he writes elsewhere at this time: that unity of schooling, rather than the diversity of location, is what is important.[36] But Newman dare not throw too much light on the exact relationship of people to places, lest his view of the East as heretical, and Alexandria as orthodox, begins to look doubtful.

The causes of Arianism: Judaism?

Newman's genealogy of Arianism is at its least accurate in the role he gives to Judaism. Newman wrote of Arius's predecessor in Antioch, 'Ancient writers inform us that [Paul's] heresy was a kind of Judaism in doctrine, adopted to please his Jewish patroness' (*Ari* 5). The list of sources, Athanasius, Chrysostom, Theodoret, and Philaster, is similar to Mosheim's list for the same claim, although Nicephorus replaces the less trustworthy Philaster (*de reb* ii. 231). Imputed Judaism is an ancient slur that the later commentators pick up, and it seems Newman is just as keen as his predecessors to discredit Paul based on scant evidence for his Judaism.

---

[35] Paul seems to have denied the pre-existence of the Son as the Word, whereas this footnote continues: 'Epiphanius (Ancor. 33) tells us, that [Lucian] considered the Word in the Person of Christ as the substitute for a human soul.'

[36] The unity of schooling was what made Basil and Gregory of Nazianzus brothers-in-arms, even though they lived in different places (*HS* ii. 52); and, in Newman's own experience, Keble lived out the Oxford ethos in his Gloucestershire parish.

Yet, while it is true that the sources say Zenobia was Jewish, there was also a long heritage to the belief that, if there was a natural home for Jewish thought in the ancient world, it was Alexandria. Mosheim most clearly makes the connection between Jewish thought and the teachers of the Alexandrian catechetical school. 'Notwithstanding all the desire which these good men evince to persuade us that they entertained a partiality for no particular [philosophical] sect, they were certainly attached to the *Eclectics*, a sect that flourished formerly in Egypt'; for instance, continues Mosheim, 'compare Clement and Origen with Philo Judeaus, one equally a disciple of the Eclectic school' (*de reb* i. 343). Newman, who wants to portray Antioch as the home of a philosophy infected with Judaism, therefore faces a problem: what to do with Philo of Alexandria? Cudworth had defended the Middle Platonism of Philo.[37] Newman, by contrast, criticizes Philo in spite of his being from Alexandria—but does so not from the perspective of his philosophy so much as his Judaism. Newman suggests Philo's religion led him to misunderstand the Platonic Trinity in a way that is seen 'perhaps to prepare the way for Arianism' (*Ari* 93).

Materialism and literalism were, in the view Newman took from Origen, the same problem: one could not penetrate the veil of the flesh, the other the veil of words. Newman, in fact, attributed literalism to Jewish materialism, in perhaps the most fascinating play Newman makes with his predecessors' mirrors. Mosheim, for whom allegory (in the form of parables) is an archetype of Jewish exegesis, claims 'this practice of annexing to the words of Scripture several different senses, [derived] from the Jews', reached its nadir 'in Egypt' among the Alexandrians (*de reb* i. 358–9).[38] Newman claims the very opposite—that the Jews taught the Antiochenes how to read the Bible too literally. Newman saw such literalism in many early heresies. The materialism of Judaism appealed to Cerinthus and

[37] For instance, Cudworth writes: 'Platonick and Pythagorick doctrine exactly agreeth [with] Philo the Jew also, That God which is before the Word or Reason; is better and more excellent than all the rational nature; neither is it fit that anything which is generated, should be perfectly like, to that which is originally from itself, and above all' (*TIS* 585).

[38] Cave thought that Origen 'learned that allegorical and mystical way of interpretation, which he introduced to the Christian doctrine', from the stoics Chaeremon and Cornatus 'as Porphyry truly enough observes' (*Apostolici* 217).

Ebion, Newman says, who, compared to other first-century Gnostics, thought the Jewish Law more helpful (although, as Mosheim states, 'it was *a part* only of the law of Moses which appeared to Cerinthus worthy of being retained' (*de reb* i. 256)). Newman treats Cerinthus and Ebion as Jews who failed to penetrate the veil of the Law and thereby failed to recognize the reality of the Son of God about whom it spoke. The results for their Christology were heretical: 'the Cerinthians and the Ebionites... though more or less infected with Gnosticism, were of Jewish origin, and observed the Mosaic Law; and whatever might be the minute peculiarities of their doctrinal views, they also agreed in entertaining Jewish rather than Gnostic conceptions of the Person of Christ' (*Ari* 20). Albeit this 'Jewish' Christ was not a Gnostic emanation of God (Aeon) but a fully human Messiah, still Jewish materialism did not give the full picture of Christ as Son of God. Thus it was no surprise that, as Burton put it, some early heretics 'believed with Cerinthus that [Christ] was a mere man, born of human parents'.[39]

With the materialism and literalism of the first-century heretics came a 'carnal' ethic, which Newman in line with Englishmen like Burton, described as typically Jewish. Mosheim, it should be noted, did not accept this connection. Employing the historical-critical methods of German historiography, Mosheim argued that the account Cerinthus purportedly gave, of deeds of 'the grossest sensuality' that would be licit during the Millennium at the end of time, was really only a later slur on this sect. He explained that this account of the Millennium was not taught by Cerinthus but attributed to him at a later date; in fact, the account 'originated with Caius, the presbyter and Dionysius Alexandrinus, two writers of the third century, as it appears from Eusebius... To prior ages it was utterly unknown' (*de reb* i. 254, citing *Ecc Hist* 3. 28). Burton calls this 'conjectural criticism'.[40] While Mosheim was critical of his sources, the English were more in their thrall. Burton is so sure of the Ebionites' Judaism that he doubts that they can 'be entitled to the name of Christians'.[41]

---

[39] Burton, *Inquiry into the Heresies of the Apostolic Age*, 184.

[40] Ibid. 483.

[41] Ibid. 499. This is based on the testimony of Epiphanius, a source Burton usually treats with suspicion.

Burton upholds 'ancient testimony' when it alleges a connection between a heretic and Judaism, and Newman is no different.

The sensuality of Ebion and Cerinthus inform the Jewish practices and doctrines that, for Newman, find a home in Antioch. When Burton claimed of Ebion's teachings, 'that he disseminated them in Asia, and in the neighbourhood of Ephesus, can hardly admit of dispute',[42] the older historian provided Newman with a way to bridge the 'parallel' doctrines 'of the Ebionites' and 'followers of Paulus of Samosata' (*Ari* 120). With the help of such analysis, Newman constructed a bridge from Judaism on one side to Antiochene sophism, literalism, and sensuality on the other, rather than to Alexandrian philosophy (as for Cudworth) or exegesis (as for Mosheim). As has already been seen, sophism, literalism, and sensuality find their matrix in Queen Zenobia; indeed, this Antiochene/Jewish heresy has powerful gender symbolism. Williams carefully maps together Newman's anti-Eastern, anti-Jewish, and anti-female stance. As exemplified by Queen Zenobia, Williams says of Newman: 'The false theology of Syria is "female"—sensual, preoccupied with appearance rather than reality (hence the literalism in interpreting Scripture), incapable of rational detachment from the self-interested deliverances of unaided human intellect . . . Spiritually speaking, men are from Alexandria, women from Antioch.'[43] However, Williams overemphasizes Newman's originality by failing to remark that Cave's account of Arius has a similar gender division with roots in the primary sources on Paul of Samosata.[44] For instance, the Synodal Letter asked: 'How could [Paul] reprove another man, or advise him not to associate any longer with a "bride", for fear of a slip—as Scripture warns us [Eccles. 9: 8–9]—when he has dismissed one

    [42] Burton, 183.

    [43] Williams, introduction, *Ari* (p. xl). Newman used Gibbon and the French Protestant Jacques Basnage (1653–1723) for information on Zenobia; see OM A.12.11, 'General References', 2 (dated 10 Jan. 1832).

    [44] Newman's younger contemporary, John Mason Neale (1818-66), in a posthumously published work, expressed similar views on Paul's 'effeminacy', based upon the Synodal Letter's depiction of the Bishop of Samosata: 'On a certain Easter-day he filled his church with a choir of women, who desecrated the festival by odes in praise of the many virtues of their bishop' (*A History of the Holy Eastern Church: The Patriarchate of Antioch (A Posthumous Fragment)* (Piscataway, NJ: Gorgias Press, 2003), 46).

already and now has two in his house, both young and pretty, whom he takes round with him whenever he leaves home, living, I may add, in luxury and surfeiting?' (*Ecc Hist* 7. 30). Cave noted the affinity between Arius and women, especially in using women 'to solicit the justice of the public tribunals, to take cognizance of [Arius's] case, and to rescind the sentence of his diocesan...bishop' (*Ecclesiastici* 157). Many of Newman's observations about the heretics come from primary sources mediated through an English tradition, such as when he records that '[Alexander] speaks especially of younger females as zealous in [Arius's] cause, and as traversing Alexandria in their eagerness to promote it' (*Ari* 139).

Judaism, both in Newman and the sources he follows, furnishes a particular view of male sexuality too. This is shown in the way both primary sources and secondary commentators treat circumcision. Epiphanius, for instance, writes that Ebionites 'boast also of having circumcision, and they pride themselves in considering this as the seal and mark of the patriarchs', as do the Cerinthians.[45] In the early Church, as well as in the work of later commentators, attention is drawn to the relation of circumcision, first, to sensuality and, secondly, to effeminacy. Heretics seem to associate with women rather than with men, and women seem especially prone to falling under their influence; the result is a confusion of gender roles—the heretic is either oversexed or de-manned. Origen is an example of the confusion in gender caused by mutilation of male genitalia. Origen is said by the early historians to have castrated himself in order to prove his chastity while he lived and taught among women. Cave gives three sources for the story: Epiphanius says that Origen's chastity was due to 'Medicinal applications'; Jerome claims that 'it was done with the knife'; and Eusebius (whose explanation Cave, sympathetic to Eusebius and Origen, makes his own) explains it was 'partly out of a perverse interpretation of our Saviour's meaning, when he says, "There be some which make themselves eunuchs for the Kingdom of Heaven's sake"' (*Apostolici* 219). Newman, by

[45] The quotation continues of the Cerinthians, 'according to their absurd argument, *It is enough for the disciple to be as the master*: now Christ was circumcised; do thou therefore be circumcised' (*Panarion* 30.16, trans. Burton, *Inquiry into the Heresies of the Apostolic Age*, 500). Attention is drawn to Burton here in *Ari* 20.

contrast, does not mention Origen's self-mutilation at all. Maybe he recognizes the allegation as a piece of malicious gossip to discredit Origen. However, Newman's treatment of his hero provides an instructive contrast to his treatment of 'Judaizing' heretics like Paul of Samosata. The latter is accused of insisting that his followers be circumcised based upon one particularly dubious source. In spite of the doubts he expresses elsewhere about the accuracy of Philaster, Newman quotes this source to claim that Paul was circumcised (*Ari* 22).[46] As will now be seen, without knowing much of Paul's theology, Newman slurred him with whatever he could find.

The causes of Arianism: Paul of Samosata?

For Newman, as has now been sufficiently shown, the 'sophistical' trajectory of Antiochene Christian thought began with Paul of Samosata and led, via Lucian, to Arianism. Newman describes as 'a wretched sophism' Paul's view that, were there to be a common substance between Father and Son, logically that substance must be prior to both persons (*Ari* 192). Since nothing can be prior to the Father, Paul considered this argument as sufficient for rejecting *homoousios* in favour of viewing the Son as a human being only. In Newman's opinion, Paul, even at his most theological, is no more than a sophist philosopher.

Newman is less concerned with what Paul said than how he said it, admitting that 'The arguments of Paulus (which it is not our purpose here to detail) seem fairly to have overpowered the first of the Councils summoned against him (A.D. 264), which dissolved without coming to a decision' (*Ari* 27). Two points stand out from this sentence. Firstly, Newman seems fascinated by Paul's sophistical method of argument, fascinated by the skill of any rhetor, himself included, to win disputes. Secondly, Newman closely reflects his sources when suggesting it is 'not our purpose' to examine in detail Paul's theology. In commenting upon Paul's argumentative

---

[46] *Liber de Haeresibus* 64. At *Ari* 5 n. 9, Newman hints with his use of 'but' that Philaster (d. *c*.397), the Bishop of Brescia and an opponent of Arianism, was incorrect to say that Paul was so much a Jew that he persuaded his patroness 'to judaize' ('docuit Zenobiam judaizare').

character, Newman seems to be replicating his source, Eusebius, who was in turn replicating the Synodal Letter condemning Paul—indeed, the only extracts of the Letter preserved by Eusebius are those to do with ethical and political concerns, not with doctrine.[47] The letter itself sustains the prurient interest of Eusebius and Newman by focusing on Paul's flaws. It decries Paul's character before following up with a disclaimer that 'as we said before, a man could be called to account for these things, if only he had a catholic mind and was one of our number'; but since (as the Council judged) neither of these applied to Paul, he could not be expected to behave in any way other than immorally (*Ecc Hist* 7. 30). The letter continues, 'But when he burlesqued the mystery and paraded with the filthy sect of Artemas (it is our unpleasant duty to name his father), we do not feel called upon to ask for an explanation of all this'. Paul, because of his consorting with heretics like Artemas, is judged a heretic—by the Council, by Eusebius, and by Newman—but never has the chance to give his theological explanation.

Before a little more is said about Artemas, it is worth noting the sources Newman used for Paul. The 'Rough notes preparatory to writing History of the Arians', on a page headed 'Lucian', report Athanasius's claim that 'Paul S. was literally a sophist'.[48] A page on 'Paulus of Samosata' also cites Athanasius, as well as Sozomen, Petavius, and Tillemont, while 'General References' cites 'Mosheim, Tillemont, Euseb[ius]', revealing the play of mirrors between primary and secondary texts in Newman's depiction of Paul.[49] Newman does not seem to have followed up on Cave's entry in the *Historia Literaria* on Paul's accuser at the Council of Antioch, Malchion, for 'From th[eir] *disputatio* or *Dialogus*, Leontius drew selections for the book *contra Nestorium*' (*Hist Lit* 99). A full examination of Leontius of Byzantium awaited the summers of 1835 and 1839, as Chapter 3 will show. In the meantime, he refers to a letter in his friend Martin Routh's *Reliquiae Sacrae*, that six bishops sent to Paul, probably

---

[47] A point made by Behr, *Way to Nicaea*, 207.

[48] OM A.12.11, 'Rough notes preparatory to writing History of the Arians', 5. Newman's original plan for the book, as he wrote to Hugh Rose in Aug. 1831, was 'to add a series of notes or discussions under various heads—"On Sabellianism", "On the tenets and character of Lucian", "on the word οὐσία" etc.' (*LD* ii. 353).

[49] OM A.12.11; 'General References', 2.

before the last of the three sessions of the Council of Antioch, which
Newman mistakenly calls the 'Synodal Letter' (*Ari* 128).[50] This
source suggests that Paul taught that the Son had no pre-existence
before the birth of Jesus Christ, to which the bishops make the
counter-argument that scripture shows 'His ministrative office
under the Jewish law, such as His appearance to Abraham and
Jacob, and to Moses in the burning bush' (ibid. 129). Newman
describes Paul's 'doctrinal opinions' as 'grossly humanitarian' (ibid. 22),
sharing Burton's view of Samosatene heresy: 'that a person called
Jesus was conceived by the Holy Ghost and born of the Virgin Mary,
but that in every other respect he was a mere human being, and
nothing which was born in him had any preexistence.'[51]

Yet, in *Arians of the Fourth Century*, Newman was not investigating
Paul's theology but his method of argument. Even Paul's chief accuser at the Council, Malchion, is mentioned primarily for the fact
that he was trained as a sophist like Paul. It made sense to Newman
that only one Antiochene sophist could triumph over another in
argument: 'Malchion, a presbyter of Antioch, who, *having been* by
profession a Sophist, encountered his adversary with his own arms'
(*Ari* 27, my italics). Newman's use of the past tense implies that
Malchion turned his back on philosophy when he embraced Christian theology, or at least made it the handmaid of theology. Malchion
had raided the Egyptian stores for the most convincing rhetoric he
could find and then used it to teach Christian truth—just as Origen
did in Alexandria. By contrast to Malchion, Newman says that Paul
remained a sophist and never became a theologian, which prevented
him from seeing the fullness of Christian truth. It should be noted,
however, that Eusebius shows Malchion as head of the school of

[50] Tillemont distinguishes the Synodal 'circular letter' and 'This letter, which as far
as we know is contested by no-one, [and] was written at the beginning of the final
Council, according to Mr. Valois, which is more probable than Baronius who
attributes it to the first. It is only from six bishops, Hymenaeus, Theophilus, Theo-
tecnus, Maximus, Proclus and Bolanus, of whom the two last are named along with
the four others at the head of the circular letter of the Council' (*Mémoires*, iii. 298).
Arians of the Fourth Century cites Henri de Valois or Valensius (1603–76) and Cesare
Baronius (1538–1607); in addition, Newman knew that Jacques Basnage, who wrote
after Tillemont, thought that the letter of six bishops was 'spurious' (*Ari* 128).
[51] Burton, *Inquiry into the Heresies of the Apostolic Age*, 582.

sophists in Antioch at the time of his dispute with Paul—a fact that Newman's account omits.[52]

Both Cave and Newman refer to Paul's heresy as the reincarnation of Artemas (or Artemon). In this they follow Eusebius, who writes: 'Artemon's heresy, which again in my own day Paul of Samosata has tried to revive . . . [held] that the Saviour was merely man' (*Ecc Hist* 5. 28).[53] Eusebius does not explain the consequences of this Christology,[54] but considers this doctrine to be reflected in the Synodal Letter's remark that '[Paul] will not admit that the Son of God came down from heaven . . . especially where he says that Jesus Christ is "from below"' (ibid. 7. 30). While Eusebius does not give his readers much more on which to base a depiction of Paul's/Artemas's Christology, Mosheim supplements this with Epiphanius's claim that, for Paul, '*The divine Reason came* (to the man Christ, long after his birth, and when in mature life) *and solely* (without any community of action with the human nature) *operated in him, and afterwards returned to God*' (*de reb* ii. 239).[55] Based on this same source, Cave argues that Paul '(as Epiphanius says) . . . revived the Artemonian heresy, denying that Christ the Word of God had an hypostasis [subsistentia] distinct from the Father, and that on earth he was a mere fallen man; before Mary he did not exist, and the Name of the Son of God merited nothing but good works' (*Hist Lit* 98). Newman's interest in Artemas's heresy takes the perspective not of what

[52] Eusebius describes Malchion as 'principal of a school of rhetoric, one of the centres of Hellenic education at Antioch' (*Ecc Hist* 7. 29).

[53] Burton was less sure of the connection: 'Eusebius, Theodoret, the bishops at the Council of Antioch, and others, agree in connecting the heresies of Artemon and Paul with each other, so that the accordance of their opinions cannot be doubted: but there is reason to think that Artemon and Theodotus went beyond not only their predecessors, but also their immediate followers, in denying the divinity of Christ' (*Inquiry into the Heresies of the Apostolic Age*, 580).

[54] Eusebius does, however, quote a writer who sees Paul's view as a rejection of 'the books of Irenaeus, Mileto, and the rest, which proclaim Christ as God and man, and all the psalms and hymns written from the beginning by faithful brethren, which sing of Christ as the Word of God and address Him as God' (*Ecc Hist* 5. 28).

[55] *Panarion* 65.1.5. Behr comments: 'Epiphanius also claims that Paul held the Word to be a nonsubstantial, nonpersonal utterance of God, or thought existing in God like "reason in the heart of man", perhaps echoing the distinction between an "immanent" and an "uttered" logos taught in Antioch a century earlier by Theophilus' (*Way to Nicaea*, 217).

he said but, once again, of his philosophical argumentation. Newman writes:

the argument by which Paulus of Samosata baffled the Antiochene Council was drawn from a sophistical use of the very word *substance*, which the orthodox had employed in expressing the scriptural notion of the unity subsisting between the Father and the Son. Such too was the mode of reasoning adopted at Rome by the Artemas or Artemon, already mentioned, and his followers, at the end of the second century. (*Ari* 34)

Although resident at Rome, and not in Antioch, Artemas ran a school of sophists in the vein followed by Paul. Newman has gone beyond Cave's *Historia Literaria* by connecting a sophistical philosophy to the 'very word substance' as it referred to the unity of Father and Son. Paul's sophistry allowed him to trick the bishops at the Council of Antioch, making the abandonment of *homoousios* less a result of theological doctrine than a result of sophistical argument. This, Newman thinks, was the basis for the Arians' sophistical rejection of *homoousios* at the Council of Nicaea too.

MIRROR OPPOSITES: (II) ALEXANDRIAN ORTHODOXY

In the remarkable Chapter II of *Arians of the Fourth Century*, the young Newman shows that what are regarded as 'traditional statements of the Catholic doctrine, which were more explicit than Scripture, had not as yet, when the [Arian] controversy began, taken the shape of formulae' (*Ari* 233). The words that Newman uses to describe the Nicene Creed— the 'imposition of the "*consubstantial*"' (*Ari* 234), the faith 'consigned to arbitrary formulas' (ibid. 181)—suggest that doctrine becomes frozen rather than living in order to test against heresy. Newman sees an inevitable decline in the way that doctrine was taught after Nicaea, brought on by the Arian controversy; and that view was not quite compatible with his Anglican forebears.

Early-modern and modern writers on patristic doctrine were in one way or another commenting on the great Catholic scholar Petavius. In recognizing a gulf between pre- and post-Nicene teaching on the

Trinity, Petavius's *On the Trinity* set the scene for succeeding generations to explain early Trinitarian doctrine. Petavius challenged the idea
that the faith of the pre-Nicene Church resembled the categories
employed at the Council of Nicaea. Indeed, in many instances, the
pre-Nicene Fathers had more in common with the Arians than with the
Council that condemned Arius's teaching. Petavius regarded Origen as
a particularly dangerous example of the inherently heretical teaching of
the pre-Nicenes on the Trinity. Petavius argued that the source of
the early Fathers' heresy was Platonism, and this can be seen in three
loci of Trinitarian doctrine. The first locus centres on the pre-Nicene
conception of the relation of creation to the creator God. The second
and third loci discuss 'subordinationism' of Son to Father in the
pre-Nicene conception of God with reference to two different perspectives on Trinitarian doctrine, in turn the theological and the economic.
Newman discerned the distinction between the theological and
economic view of the Son's relation to the Father in the writings of
Clement and Origen: 'Thus ["*economia*"] is applied by the Fathers, to
the history of Christ's humiliation, as exhibited in the doctrines of
His incarnation, ministry, atonement, exaltation, and mediatorial
sovereignty, and, as such distinguished from the '*theologia*' or the
collection of truths relative to His personal indwelling in the bosom
of God' (*Ari* 74).

The difference between the 'economic' and the 'theological' Trinity
is that between God's self-revelation to us and God's inner-relations
to the extent that these can be discerned by us. The 'theological'
Trinity is thus protected by a veil of unknowability. In all these loci,
Newman saw Clement and Origen as the originators of a doctrinal
language that was shared by the later Alexandrians; but the earlier
Fathers were able to use the language more richly because they were
not constrained by conciliar formulae.

The question of the divide between Father and Son

By the time of Nicaea, theologians drew a clear divide between God
on the one hand, and the things God had created *ex nihilo* on the
other. But the foundational question of Nicene theology—whether to

set the divide between God and the Son or between the Father/Son/ Spirit triad and creation—was far from decided in the pre-Nicene era. A failure to recognize the subtleties of this debate about division explains some of the confusion among later commentators on this early period. So here the subtleties will be discussed briefly.

'Up to about A.D. 200', Williams writes, 'the consensus among philosophers was that God and matter were co-eternal (that is, matter was *agenētos*)'.[56] Origen (d. 253) was writing around the time that the philosophical consensus was shifting, and some of his arguments played a part in the rejection of the idea of two 'unoriginates' by Methodius of Olympus (d. *c*.311), who was successful in radically dissociating the Creator from creation.[57] This philosophical shift had an obvious impact among Christian theologians, and provides a good historical reason both why Arius thought only the Father was unoriginate ($\dot{a}\gamma\epsilon\nu\eta\tau\acute{o}s$) and why Athanasius depicted Arius as saying the Son was merely a creature ($\kappa\tau\acute{\iota}\sigma\mu a$). Either the Son was God, or he was created by God: Nicene orthodoxy put the Son on the divine side, while the Arians were seen to put him on the side of the creatures (Discourse I. 12). When judged by the standards of this later theology, the terms of which had not been set in Origen's day, many of Origen's writings seem to place the Son on the side of creatures. Indeed, Petavius wrote: 'Origen, as he preceded Arius in time, so was he his equal in impiety; nay, he taught him his impious doctrine' (*de trin* i. 12.9).[58]

For Petavius, then, it was Origen who handed on to the Arians the idea that the Son of God was to be classed with creatures, rather than with God. For example, Origen described the Son as 'made' by the Father, rather than 'begotten'.[59] In *On First Principles* (4. 4), Origen calls the Son 'a thing created, wisdom' using the Greek word for 'creature' ($\kappa\tau\acute{\iota}\sigma\mu a$) rather than the word used by the Nicene Fathers

[56] Williams, *Arius* (2nd edn.; London: Student Christian Movement, 2001), 184.

[57] In fact, Methodius 'takes the Origenian assumption that God cannot "begin" to be the creator of a world of ordered matter . . . and turns it against Origen by pointing out that an eternally passive material principle cannot but be an *agenētos* substance' (ibid. 186).

[58] Trans. *Defensio* i. 220.

[59] Origen's translator notes: 'Jerome, *Ep. ad Avitum* 2, says that in the beginning of the first book of the *De Principiis* Origen declared that "Christ was not begotten the Son of God, but made such" (Latin *factum* = Gr. $\gamma\epsilon\nu\eta\tau\acute{o}\nu$). Rufinus has modified this

for a 'thing begotten' (γέννημα).[60] Petavius also discusses (at *de trin* i. 4.7) Origen's description of the Son as 'a generated God' (γενητὸν Θεόν) in the missing commentary on Psalm 1, as recorded by Epiphanius in *On the Heresy of Origen*. To Petavius, Origen appeared as the source of the Arian arguments that the Son was a creature rather than, as the Nicene Creed held, *homoousios* with the Father. Petavius did not take into account the rapid development in terminology between the year 200 and the Council of 325; indeed, it will become clear that few later churchmen did consider the pre-Nicenes on their own terms, even the ones who defended them from Petavius's charges. Rather, the standard by which to judge theologians like Origen was whether they placed the divide between the God and creation, as the Nicenes did, or between the hypostases, as the Arians did. Were the Son and Spirit one with the Father or with creation?

Cudworth was aware of the need to avoid using the language of *homoousios* when it did not apply. The Neoplatonists of Origen's day had no conception of 'one and the same numerical substance or essence', yet even they 'acknowledg[ed] none of those hypostases to be creatures, but all God' (*TIS* 592). The Neoplatonists were not, then, the source of the heresy that saw the Son as merely a creature. Or were they? Cudworth, though more sympathetic to the Neoplatonists than Petavius, nevertheless shows how perilously close they came to leaving the third hypostasis on the side of creatures. Lydia Gysi notes that, for Cudworth, 'it is obviously but a small step towards considering the third "hypostasis" ψυχή as World-Soul, which is immersed in matter and directs the universe in vital union from within'.[61] Cudworth recognized within the Neoplatonists a tendency towards 'dividing out' the hypostases, the third hypostasis

statement. It is probable, however, that γενητόν and γεννητόν were not very clearly distinguished in Origen's time. Origen certainly taught that the Son and Holy Spirit were created, but he thought that the alternative to this was to assert that they were unbegotten, which was true of the Father alone' (Origen, *On First Principles*, trans. G. W. Butterworth (Gloucester, Mass.: Peter Smith, 1973), 3 n. 1).

[60] Ibid. 314 n. 6. Moreover, Origen is using the image of created wisdom from Prov. (8: 22 is quoted) and equating it to the 'first born of every creature' in Col. 1: 15.

[61] Lydia Gysi, *Platonism and Cartesianism in the Philosophy of Ralph Cudworth* (Berne: Herbert Lang, 1962), 107, citing *TIS* 552.

in particular descending, as it were, far below. This is similar to what Arius is recorded as writing in the *Thalia*: 'You should understand that the Monad [always] was, but the Dyad was not before it came to be... and he [lit.: this one—the Holy Spirit?] is different from both.'[62] As Cave argues, the Arians interpreted Neoplatonic philosophy to mean that the second and third hypostases are detached from the One (*Ecclesiastici* 155).

Conditioned by the later Church to speak in the doctrinal terms taken only from the Councils, the later commentators discussed the pre-Nicenes in terms of whether they considered the divine hypostases to be *homoousios*. Origen and Justin Martyr (*c*.100–*c*.165) will function as the exemplary pre-Nicenes of these later discussions of consubstantiality. Bull is sure Justin spells out the doctrine of consubstantiality when Justin 'says that the Son is begotten of the Father, just as fire is kindled of fire. But who will refuse to allow that the fire which is kindled of another fire is of the self-same nature and substance as it? as Justin himself [says] elsewhere in the same Dialogue' (*Defensio* i. 138).[63] Newman, however, does not perceive the language of *homoousios* here. Rather, it was a word chosen *later* to make clearer the sorts of argument Justin was making: 'For this purpose the word *homoüsion* or *consubstantial* was brought into use among Christian writers' (*Ari* 186). Newman recognizes that only after a good deal of thought did the Fathers fix upon consubstantiality as the best way to describe the relation of the three hypostases. This is at the heart of what separates Newman from early moderns like Bull. These less historical thinkers are more ready to read the later terminology of Nicaea into the language of the pre-Nicenes. Newman has no need to do so; and to understand why he has no need, the difference in context between himself and the earlier English scholars should be explained.

Arians of the Fourth Century holds that the pre-Nicene Church stayed robustly 'orthodox' precisely because it refused to formulate what orthodoxy was. Williams interprets Newman as saying:

Yes, belief had been there from the start, but the language of Christians had taken time to catch up with the fullness of what was believed; in an era

---

[62] Translation (including square brackets) Williams, *Arius*, 102.
[63] Referring to Justin Martyr's *Dialogue with Trypho* 61.

when Christian commitment was radical and deep, and there was a proper spiritual formation for members of the Church, it was simply the case that those who needed to understand *did* understand. Furthermore, theological language, though unsystematic in this early age, had had its own ways of correcting misunderstanding by its variety and fluidity; it was never mortgaged to one set of images, even though it dealt with images rather than formulae.[64]

By resisting 'mortgaging' themselves to a single formulation of doctrine, the language of the earliest Fathers (unlike the post-Nicenes) was rich and fluid. One practical example of this is Origen's description of the Son as *homoousios* with the Father.[65] Only at Nicaea was the looser language of 'doxologies' replaced by credal orthodoxy (*Ari* 180). *Arians of the Fourth Century,* then, was a manifesto on behalf of a movement that sought to reclaim the robustness and richness of the pre-Nicene Fathers. This movement was fighting a different set of battles from those of the seventeenth-century divines. In the seventeenth century, High Churchmen like Bull and Cave responded to puritans, who claimed an ordered Church was unbiblical, by arguing that little had changed between the 'primitive' era and Nicaea. They also had to reply to Petavius's idea that the pre-Nicenes erred without a Magisterium, by showing that the Church had always taught the same thing. Rather than needing to justify the orthodoxy of the Fathers in response to these challenges from left and right, as Bull and Cave had done, Newman sought to regroup the Church of England around patristic teachings in all their richness, holiness, and emotion.

However, none of this is to say Newman rejected the idea of a pre-Nicene 'orthodoxy' in line with later Fathers. Newman agreed with Bull that Justin was opposing heresy with some early understanding of orthodoxy.[66] Orthodoxy is, for Bull and Newman, the Church's

[64] Williams, introduction, *Ari* (p. xxxiii).

[65] 'In Origen's comment on the Hebrews, the *homoüsion* of the Son is deduced from the figurative title ... *radiance,* there given to Him ... But at this era, the middle of the third century, a change took place in the use of it and other similar words' (*Ari* 188–9).

[66] Bull sees Justin opposing 'the heresy of those who were at that time teaching very nearly the same as was afterwards maintained by Sabellius' (*Defensio* i. 138).

truth as it is taught in response to the heresies of the day. While Newman does not accept that the pre-Nicenes had fixed the truth in terms of *homoousios*, nevertheless they were already talking about the unity of God's *ousia*, which

was from the earliest date used to express the reality and subsistence of the Son ... Justin Martyr, for instance, speaks of heretics, who considered that God put forth and withdrew His Logos when it pleased Him, as if He were an influence, not a Person, somewhat in the sense afterwards adopted by Paulus of Samosata and others. To meet this error, [Justin] speaks of Him as inseparable from the substance or being, *usia*, of the Father. (*Ari* 186)

Newman here cites the *Dialogue with Trypho* 128, a complicated piece of early 'orthodoxy'. Although, in respect of the Father, the Son is 'something numerically distinct', it is not 'as if the essence [*ousia*] of the Father were divided'.[67] Justin is working hard with language to depict within God a distinction (from the verb ἀπομερίζω) that is not a division (from the verb μερίζω).[68] What Newman means in using Justin, however, is to prove that the pre-Nicenes conceived *ousia*-language as having to do first of all with divine personality.[69]

Newman took the passage from Justin to be proof that the pre-Nicenes had a language of *ousia* that was unlike the Neoplatonists'. Before him, Cudworth had shown that the Neoplatonists spoke of God as *hyperousios* precisely to keep the divine One transcendent and divided from the hypostases that were closer to creation.[70] Newman,

[67] ANF trans.

[68] Interestingly, Petavius took this distinction that is not a division within God to be what the Nicene Creed meant by 'Light from Light'. Petavius asks rhetorically, 'What can be added to this profession of the faith and of the Trinity? or what has been set forth more express, more significant, more effectual, in the assembly of the fathers at Nice[a] itself, or after it? For the formula which was there settled, God of God, Light of Light, very God of very God, was anticipated so long before by this sentiment of Justin' (preface 3.1 to *de trin*, trans. *Defensio* i. 138).

[69] Personality here does not have 'psychological' connotations. Newman rejects what Rowan Williams rejects: 'the assumption that hypostasis means (or includes in its meaning) "personality", the assumption, that is, that it is a psychological category. Any historical survey—indeed, even a moment's sober reflection—should make it plain that this is not and could not be the case' ('Person and Personality in Christology', *Downside Review*, 94 (1976), 254. See also Paul McPartlan's entry on 'Person' in Jean-Yves Lacoste (ed.), *Encyclopedia of Christian Theology*, 3 vols. (New York: Routledge, 2005), iii. 1227–31.

[70] In fact, Newman cites both Cudworth and Petavius for this term (*Ari* 195 n. 8).

however, argues that the pre-Nicenes were not primarily Platonic when they referred to God's *ousia*. Instead, they used the notion of *ousia* on biblical grounds, he says, especially the Septuagint's translation of the divine name as Being (ὁ ὤν), while the Platonists 'from an affectation of reverence refused to speak of God except as *hyperusios* [beyond being]' (*Ari* 186). Put simply, the pre-Nicenes referred to the divine *ousia* as a way of thinking about God's personality, which is to say God's revelation through the person/*ousia* of the Son—first as a voice in the burning bush, then in the flesh.[71] The Neoplatonists, on the other hand, wanted to use *ousia* language as a protection against trying to think of God as *ousia* in precisely this personal sense, which is to say a protection against making the Logos equal to God. Heretics, Newman writes, tried to employ this Platonic argument to attack the use of *homoousios* among the early 'orthodox'. But, not least to confute the heretics, the Alexandrian Fathers held on to the word *homoousios* in the sense of *ousia* used by Justin, with its personal and not material meaning:

It is worth observing that, when the Asiatic Churches had given up the *consubstantial*, they [the Alexandrians], on the contrary, had preserved it. Not only Dionysius willingly accepts the challenge of his namesake of Rome, who reminded him of the value of the symbol; but Theognostus also, who presided at the Catechetical School at the end of the third century. (*Ari* 193)

Newman sees a dynamic continuity between the thought of the Greek-educated Justin, Clement, and Origen, and those who followed in the Alexandrian school. But in this the later Newman realized *Arians of the Fourth Century* was mistaken. For in using *ousia* of the Logos and Spirit both Origen and the Neoplatonists sought to express a division between God and the lower hypostases in terms of *ousia*. Some time later in the 1830s, Newman annotated his own copy of *Arians of the Fourth Century* with '*Contra Celsum* iv. 64',[72]

[71] Newman writes that the Word and Spirit each have a personality, rather than the 'apparent Personality ascribed to Them in the Old Testament', but it is a personality derived from the Father's (*Ari* 154).
[72] OM B.3.5, Newman's copy of the first edition of *Ari* (p. 212). The date of this annotation must precede Apr. 1839, when he was still considering 'That the Arians is coming to a second edition, and I must rewrite it' (*LD* vii. 65 and n. 2). A second edition did not appear, in fact, and a third edition awaited 1871, when this annotation was added in square brackets at p. 186 n. 2.

where he learned that Origen described God as 'beyond being'. Just as much as the Neoplatonists, though Newman did not realize it in the early 1830s, Origen drew a distinction between the being of the Logos and the God beyond being.

The question of subordination in the 'theological' Trinity

Petavius presented the scholars who followed him with two arguments. Firstly, as seen above, he regarded certain pre-Nicene Fathers to be the source of the Arian heresy. Secondly, Petavius opposed the subordinationist language of the pre-Nicenes not just because it resulted in heresy, but because the special influence of Platonism on the pre-Nicenes made them inherently heretical. Cudworth accepts this second argument only in part: he is willing to admit that doctrine in the early Church was not 'pure' (at least in the sense which Petavius means—that is, doctrine free from Platonism).[73] But Cudworth challenges Petavius's view that the pre-Nicene Fathers erred owing to their Platonism. For Cudworth, Platonism is part of Christian discourse, and his aim is to distinguish a good type of 'Refined Platonism' in Christian doctrine from the 'Junior Platonism' of certain Neoplatonists.[74] He argues that the pre-Nicene use of Plato was acceptable—indeed, given the similarities of Platonic and Christian notions of the Trinity, it was inevitable. Petavius was right, Cudworth says, to see Trinitarian doctrine before Nicaea to be different from that which came later, but he was wrong to claim that pre-Nicene doctrine tended towards Arianism simply because it was Platonic. Cudworth argues for a distinction between the type of Neoplatonism that tended towards subordination of the hypostases outside of God ('*ad extra*') and the type of Neoplatonism that recognized subordination within God ('*ad intra*'). The first type

[73] Cudworth affirms that the pre-Nicene Fathers are by Petavius' 'taxed for Platonism, and having by that means corrupted the purity of the Christian faith, in this article of the Trinity. Which how it can be reconciled with those other opinions, of Ecclesiastick Tradition being a Rule of Faith, and the impossibility of the visible Churches erring in any fundamental point, cannot easily be understood' (*TIS* 595).

[74] e.g., *TIS* 601. Cave also wrote of the Neoplatonists as 'junior Platonists' (*Ecclesiastici* 155).

resulted in the heresy of Arius, Cudworth writes, while the second type resulted in the 'orthodox Fathers' of the Nicene Council.

Cudworth, then, accepts the charge that subordination was part of the pre-Nicene account of the 'theological Trinity'. Petavius accuses the early Fathers of error on the grounds of their subordination. But, to Cudworth, it is unjust for Petavius to criticize the pre-Nicenes when Petavius himself praises the Fathers after Nicaea for something approaching subordination:

> [W]hen Athanasius, and the other orthodox Fathers, writing against Arius, do so frequently assert the inequality of all the Three Persons, this is to be understood in way of opposition to Arius only, who made the Son to be unequal to the Father, as ἑτεροούσιον, of different essence from him, one being God, and the other a creature; they affirming on the contrary, that he was equal to the Father, as ὁμοούσιος, of the same essence with him; that is, as God and not a creature. Notwithstanding which equality, there may be some subordination in them, as Hic Deus and Haec Persona (to use Petavius's language) This God and that Person. (*TIS* 599–600)

Cudworth thinks the Nicene Fathers accepted *homoousios* precisely because it allowed room for some sort of subordination, unlike two other options: *tautoousios* and *monoousios*. Epiphanius spoke of *tautoousios* as 'a generical or specifical, and not of a singular or individual sameness', the three hypostases each having the same kind of substance, something like a universal (*TIS* 611)—an important concept in Chapter 4, below. Sabellians, who considered the hypostases to be individually all the same, or *monoousios*, did not allow for difference between the hypostases. As Gysi puts it, 'Cudworth comes to the conclusion that the Trinity cannot be comprehended at all, without the assumption of a certain subordination "*ad intra*".'[75]

Even if they disagree about the extent of subordination in the pre-Nicenes, the early moderns agree that subordination was part of Neoplatonism, and that this has consequences for Arianism. Cudworth and Cave suggest, following Petavius, that the Neoplatonists' 'gradual subordination' led to the idea of divided hypostases.

[75] Gysi, *Platonism and Cartesianism*, 107.

Cudworth's argument about the Neoplatonists is by far the most subtle. He even complains that many 'late writers' (Petavius?), who are unwilling to accept the terms of Platonism, have latched on to the idea of 'gradual subordination' as inherently Arian without understanding it in the context of a philosophical framework with no notion of consubstantiality:

And this is the true reason, why so many late writers, have affirmed Platonism to symbolize with Arianism, and the latter to have been indeed nothing else than the spawn of the former, meerly [*sic*] because the Platonists did not acknowledge one and the same numerical essence or substance of all their three hypostases; and asserted a gradual subordination of them; but chiefly for this latter ground. Upon which account some of the ancients also, have done the like, as particularly S. Cyril [of Jerusalem]. (*TIS* 592)

The use of 'merely' here is interesting, suggesting that the arguments for a direct link between Platonism and Arianism are minimal. Without an idea of one divine substance, how can the Neoplatonists be blamed for subordinating the hypostases? There was no substance in which they found their unity. But, in spite of this, they conceived not of multiple gods, but of a One with two subordinate hypostases.[76] Still, Cudworth admits 'manifest disagreements' between himself and the Neoplatonists, disagreements which can 'by no means be dissembled, palliated, or excused' (*TIS* 592). The trouble with a 'gradual subordination' within the Trinity is the hypostases become divided out or graduated according to the relation to the earth, as discussed in the first doctrinal locus above, leading to subordination '*ad extra*'.

Cave took up Cudworth's argument and inserted an element of paranoia. The Neoplatonists, 'out of spite to Christianity, (to which the old scheme [of the Platonic Trinity] did too near approach) began to depart from the ancient doctrine of Plato in this matter, stretching the differences, and gradual subordination, which the elder Platonists had made among the hypostases into too wide

[76] For Cudworth, three hypostases—if they were identical and undifferentiated— spoke of tritheism. Rather, 'the Platonick Christian would further apologize for these pagan Platonists after this manner. That their intention in thus subordinating the hypostases of their Trinity, was plainly no other, than to exclude thereby a plurality of co-ordinate and independent Gods, which they supposed an absolute co-equality of them would infer' (*TIS* 596).

a distance' (*Ecclesiastici* 155). It is important to note that, as for Cudworth, a degree of subordination among the hypostases is acceptable, as long as it does not go to 'too wide a distance', which it did with the Neoplatonists and—crucial for Cave—with Arius whom they taught in Alexandria. Bull also recognized that the pre- and post-Nicene Fathers found some degree of subordination required by the doctrine of the Trinity.

For Newman, following the three earlier Anglicans, the pre-Nicenes' subordinationism was not responsible for the Arian misunderstanding of the Trinity. Newman rejects Petavius's first argument, that pre-Nicenes are to blame for Arianism, and seeks to defend the Fathers against Petavius's second argument, that to be subordinationist was inherently heretical.[77] *Arians of the Fourth Century* draws particularly on Bull for help in this second argument: 'The Catholic doctors, says Bishop Bull, "both before and after the Nicene Council, are unanimous in declaring that the Father is greater than the Son, even as to divinity; i.e. not in any nature or essential perfection . . . but alone in what may be called authority, that is in point of origin" ' (*Ari* 164–5, quoting *Defensio* ii. 571). Put simply, Bull says that the pre-Nicenes conceived the Father as different from the Son only as origin, or author; the two are not divided in substance or perfection. Bull affirms the so-called doctrine of the monarchy (*monarchia*), in which the Father is the source of the other two persons and thus 'greater than the Son, even as to divinity'. Bishop Bull shares Cudworth's recognition that the Fathers unanimously held to some degree of subordinationism within the Trinity. Newman agrees with the earlier Anglicans in their interpretation of the Alexandrians, for whom some degree of subordination '*ad intra*' of the Son to his point of origin was required by Trinitarian doctrine.

[77] Newman begins by showing the irony of Petavius's position towards the Alexandrians: 'Athenagoras is charged with Sabellianism by the very writer (Petau), whose general theory is that he was one of those Platonizing Fathers who anticipated Arius.' Newman lists the contradictions inherent in criticizing the early Fathers from the perspectives of two different heresies: 'Gregory of Neo-Caesarea was called a Sabellian, because he spoke of one substance in the Divine Nature; he was called a forerunner of Arius, because he said that Christ was a creature. Origen, so frequently accused of Arianism, seemed to be a Sabellian, when he said that the Son was Auto-aletheia, the Archetypal Truth' (*Ari* 224). Newman takes this criticism of Petavius straight from Bull (*Defensio* ii. 438).

Newman will admit, however, unlike Bull, that the pre-Nicenes had a real problem finding the right language to differentiate properly the divine persons. 'Contrasted with all created beings, the Son and the Spirit are of necessity Unoriginate in the Unity of the Father. Clement, for instance, calls the Son, "the everlasting, unoriginate, origin and commencement of all things." It was not till [the Fathers] became alive to the seeming ditheism of such phrases, which the Sabellian controversy was sure to charge upon them, that they learned the accurate discrimination observed by Alexander [when writing against Arius]' (*Ari* 183). Clement appeared to divide the hypostases, but also to diminish their differences, suggesting an emanation of the Son from the Father as a ray emanates from the sun. Newman defends Clement from potential heresy in his customary way, acknowledging the dynamic quality of doctrinal language in this period. For this reason, though, he will not accept Bull's easy statement that 'Origen himself manifestly teaches, in more than one place, that the Son is equal to and on a par with the Father' (*Defensio* ii. 583). Cudworth, of course, has already noted that while Athanasius, in *Defence of the Nicene Definition* 27, 'amongst others cites Origen's testimony too; yet was this only for the eternity and divinity of the Son of God, but not at all for such an absolute co-equality with the Father, as would exclude all dependence, subordination and inferiority' (*TIS* 595). That the language Origen used was subordinationist cannot be escaped, a fact Newman conceded.

In a footnote to the quotation of what Bishop Bull 'says', Newman also quoted Cudworth and Petavius (*Ari* 164–5 n. 7). It has been shown that these three—Petavius, Cudworth, and Bull—do not hold the same view on the 'orthodoxy' of the pre-Nicenes, and Newman wants to correct them all. Notwithstanding that many of the early Fathers accepted the language of subordination,

orthodox theology has since [Arius's] time worn a different aspect; first, inasmuch as divines have measured what they said themselves; secondly, inasmuch as they have measured the Ante-Nicene language, which by its authors was spoken from the heart, by the necessities of controversies of a later date. And thus those early teachers have been made appear technical, when in fact they have only been reduced to system; just as in literature what is composed freely, is afterwards subjected to the rules of grammarians and critics. (*Ari* 164)

Newman argues, contra Petavius, that the pre-Nicenes should not be 'afterwards subjected' to the standards of a later council; contra Cudworth, that what is 'spoken from the heart' is not the same thing as a systematic argument; and, contra Bull, that there is now a 'difference' in 'theology... since [Arius's] time'. The pre-Nicenes freely spoke of the Son's subordination because, for them, this did not contradict divine unity. Here Newman agreed with Cave, that philosophical systems were not always suited to theological arguments. Only once Arius had forced the Church into a choice between seeing the Son as God or as a creature, did the notion of subordination begin to imply division within the divine *ousia*. Only after Arianism, Newman thinks, do doubts arise in our mind about pre-Nicene theology, forcing Christian writers to become more 'measured [in] what they said'.

The question of subordination in the 'economic' Trinity

The Athanasian arguments for confuting Arianism are the ones accepted among these later commentators. But this does not mean that Newman, even when he followed his predecessors, necessarily thought of himself as 'Athanasian'. By the time of writing *Arians of the Fourth Century*, the standard for orthodoxy in English theology was Athanasius. The argument being made here, however, is that in spite of the Athanasian air which he breathed, Newman was strikingly open to pre-Nicene theology, particularly that of Origen. There were some English precursors to this praise for Origen, not least Cave and Bull. Cudworth was the most plainly Athanasian of the English commentators, his arguments resembling the man whose theology he seemed to value above all others.

Athanasius, in pointing out the mistakes of the Arians, put this question to them: If you are suggesting that the act of creation is beneath God's dignity, then why is it not also beneath God's dignity to create a Son who in turn will enact the creation of the world? Athanasius saw the Arian argument as one with infinite regress, for

if some being as a medium be found for Him [i.e. God the Father], then again a fresh mediator is needed for this second [i.e. the Son], and thus tracing back and following out, we shall invent a vast crowd of accumulating mediators.[78]

Cudworth made this same argument against the Neoplatonists, again summed up succinctly by Gysi:

> In a gradual descent the transcendent One sends itself out into the Many; the divine is conceived as a divine sphere, which can be symbolised as a continuum, upon which any number of points can, ad libidum, be fixed; the result is the interpolation of intermediary hypostases; thus ἑνάδες ('Ones') were interpolated between the ἕν and the νοῦς; νόες between the νοῦς and the ψυχή; and ψυχαί from the ψυχή down to animal souls. They represent a continuous descent from the transcendent One down to animal souls. The fixation of three main hypostases on this continuum appears as arbitrary and unjustified.[79]

Cudworth argued this to be a mistake, for in trying to solve the derivation of the Many from the One, the Neoplatonists lost the particularity of the hypostases within a great chain of being. The Neoplatonists attempted not just to subordinate the Platonic hypostases *ad intra*, as seen above, but also *ad extra*—divided them, in other words, according to their activities in the divine economy.

The question that is relevant in this section, of course, is whether the pre-Nicenes had a similar subordination within the Godhead based on a division of activities? Arius conceived an interval (διάστημα) in time between God's existence and the coming into being of the Father-Son dyad, during which time the Son is made in order to do the work of creating the cosmos. The Father and Son divide their labour, as it were. But this also leaves the Son divided from the creation by another διάστημα. For communication to occur between God and humans, a being *other than* the Father must make the unknowable God known; thus, if the incarnation is to occur at all, it must be undertaken by a being who is not of the same substance as the Father.[80] The Son takes flesh, in the Arian view of the economy, to

---

[78] Discourse II. 26.

[79] Gysi, *Platonism and Cartesianism*, 108, citing *TIS* 555–6.

[80] According to Williams, 'What is most *distinctive* about the *Thalia*', as far as it can be reconstructed from the writings of Athanasius, is 'the absolute unknowability of the Father' (*Arius*, 105).

mediate better the Father to creation, which is the second of the Logos's 'two phases of existence'.[81] The incarnation, for an Arian, further underscores the division in action and in will of the Son from the Father.

By the standards of Nicene orthodoxy, the Arians considered the Son as only quasi-divine, yet also the creator who fulfils the Father's will. The pre-Nicenes seemed to come close to this description of the Son too. Petavius paraphrases Tertullian as having said that the Father 'put forth out of Himself [à Patre genitum], and, as it were, embodied the Word, that is to say, gave unto Him a substance and a Person of His own, at the time when He framed all created things out of nothing, and employed the Word for that purpose' (*de trin* i. 5.3).[82] Petavius railed against Origen too, who seemed to mean something similar when he wrote, 'the immediate Creator, and, as it were, very Maker of the world was the Word, the Son of God; while the Father of the Word, by commanding His own Son—the Word— to create the world, is *primarily* Creator' (ibid. i. 4.5).[83] Petavius regards these as misunderstandings of the true relation of God to creation, and uses Athanasius as his standard of orthodoxy by which to judge the early Fathers.

Neither Cave nor Bull accepts that the early Alexandrians made mistakes akin to those of the Arians. Among those accused of mistakes, Origen was perhaps most in need of defence, and it is to his aid that they come above all—Cave's apology for Origen's purported heresies is far longer than that for Clement of Alexandria or Gregory of Neocaesarea, just as his 'Life' is longer than theirs. Such apologies for the heretical-sounding doctrines of the Alexandrians seem to follow a convention begun by Basil of Caesarea. Cave's 'Life' of Gregory of Neocaesarea quotes the defence Basil made of the Wonderworker: 'spoken in the heat of disputation', Gregory's language was not as careful as became necessary in a later age, so that later heretics 'strained to another sense' his meaning (*Apostolici* 280–1). Yet, even in spite of these patristic conventions, the extent of the Anglican defence of Origen is somewhat surprising. Origen

---

[81] Ibid. 117.
[82] Trans. *Defensio* ii. 534.
[83] *Contra Celsum* 6.60 (trans. ANF).

was anathematized at the Second Council of Constantinople (553)—
albeit not for his exegetical methods[84]—and thus required more
defending than others. But, for that very reason, it is all the more
surprising that Newman and Cave go to such lengths to find excuses,
and mitigating circumstances, for the passages in Origen that later
councils of the Church found 'heretical'.[85]

In a way that provides a model for Newman, Cave wrote that 'the
disallowed opinions that [Origen] maintains are many of them such
as were not the Catholic and determined doctrines of the Church, not
defined by Synods, nor disputed by divines, but either philosophical,
or speculations which had not been thought on before' (*Apostolici*
236). Even Bull agrees, in respect at least to Origen, that orthodoxy is a
work in progress, for some of his writings were 'revised when
his genius was somewhat tempered by age; others he poured out
with the profusion [of] . . . the heat of youth' (*Defensio* i. 220). Newman seems to follow them closely in arguing that Origen's 'speculations, extravagant as they often were, related to points not yet
determined by the Church' (*Ari* 98).[86] Newman's sixfold defence of
Origen from the charge of heresy (ibid. 98–9) is almost identical to the
defence of him found in Cave and in Bull. Newman's first line of
defence is Cave's last—the vanguard and rearguard position in their
respective arguments that Origen was no heretic. Newman recalls
Origen's 'habitual hatred of heresy', which Cave in his account describes as 'refusing so much as to communicate in prayer with Paul

[84] One of Origen's errors was the doctrine that all would be saved at the final
'Apocatastasis', found problematic by Richard Hooker (*c.*1554–1600): 'What way is
there for sinners to escape the judgment of God, but only by appealing to the seat of
his saving mercy? Which mercy we do not with Origen extend to devils and damned
spirits' ('A Learned Discourse on Justification', in *Of the Laws of Ecclesiastical Polity;
and other Works by and about Richard Hooker*, ed. John Keble, R. W. Church, and F.
Paget, 3 vols. (Ellicott City, Md.: Via Media, 1994), iii. 500.

[85] In Sept. 1836, Newman would use Origen's heretical status as part of the
argument for 'Episcopal Tradition': 'He surely was not in the episcopal conspiracy,
at least; . . . [yet] he is as high and as keen, as removed from softness and as reverential,
as any bishop among [the Fathers]. He is as superstitious (as men now talk), as
fanatical, as formal, as Athanasius or Augustine. Certainly, there seems something
providential in the place Origen holds in the early Church' (*HS* i. 406).

[86] Tillemont also thought that Origen sought the truth without attaching himself
to a particular party and 'seems to have had a very humble mind, very submissive to
the Church, very respectful of her doctrines and her decisions, very attached to her
unity' (*Mémoires*, iii. 495, quoted at de Lubac, *History and Spirit*, 39).

the Heretic of Antioch' who was a favourite of Origen's patroness (*Apostolici* 237). Newman's second point has already been discussed—that Origen's 'speculations...related to points not yet determined by the Church'. Thirdly, in Newman's words, '[Origen's] opinions...were imprudently made public by his friends'; as Cave explains, they 'were written privately, and with no intention of being made public' (ibid. 236). Newman's fourth point is also made by Cave, that the texts have become corrupt. Bull expands on this, saying that within his lifetime Origen complained that his 'works were corrupted and interpolated' (*Defensio* i. 218).[87] Fifthly (and more positively), Newman says, 'the doctrine of the Trinity is clearly avowed [by Origen], and in particular our Lord's Divinity energetically and variously enforced'. Cave says the same thing, albeit indirectly, when he notes that 'Athanasius, in all the heat of the Arrian [*sic*] controversies...particularly quotes [Origen] to prove our Lord's coeternity and coessentiality with the Father exactly according to the decisions of the Nicene Synod' (*Apostolici* 237). This becomes Newman's sixth argument.

In two additional ways, Bull defended Origen from the claim that he made the Son a creature of the Father. In respect of perceiving the Son as the creative 'Power' of God, Origen had called the Son the 'second God', which is to say, derived of the Father.[88] Bull's first argument is one he uses often for other pre-Nicenes—that, in spite of a difference of words, Origen meant the same thing as the post-Nicenes. He claims in this case that 'Origen called the Son second God, in no other sense than that in which Basil... called Him second in order from the Father' (*Defensio* ii. 585). Cudworth, however, had already recognized how selectively the post-Nicenes quoted from the earlier Fathers, for they did not necessarily mean the same things at all (Athanasius used Origen's arguments 'only for the eternity and divinity of the Son of God, but not at all for such an absolute co-equality

---

[87] See the letter recorded in Rufinus, *On the Adulteration of the Works of Origen* (trans.: NPNF ser. 2 iii. 423–4). Here Origen gives another instance from the ancient world of a writer dissociating himself from a work attributed to him, the Apostle Paul in 2 Thess. 2: 2.

[88] *Contra Celsum* 5. 35. Bull also quotes Jerome saying that this meant, for Origen, 'that the Son in comparison with the Father is a very small Light' (*Defensio* ii. 585), albeit that Bull has 'God' instead of Jerome's word 'Light'.

of him with the Father' (*TIS* 595)). Bull also had a second, more subtle, argument to show that Origen perceived the Father and Son as equal in their works. Earlier in his two-volume work he wrote about Origen's use of the 'adverb ὡσπερεί, "as it were"': '"The Son", his words are, "is the immediate Creator of the world, since He was, *as it were*, Himself the actual framer of it"; by which caution [Origen] meant, without doubt, to meet the error of those who refused to admit the undivided operation of the Father and the Son in the same work of creation' (*Defensio* i. 234). This suggests that Origen thought the Son 'secondary' to the Father only as a manner of speaking. After all, Bull holds Origen's doctrine to be that the Father is prior to the Son in no other respect than as source.[89]

Newman adapted Bull's way of defending the economic Trinity of the early Fathers by seeing them in continuity with the post-Nicenes. An example of this—and perhaps one of Newman's more slippery moments—is his reading of the later Fathers' notion of the Son as a 'connatural instrument' of the Father into the pre-Nicene writings. Alexander of Alexandria and his secretary Athanasius reported that the Arians held that the Son was created as an 'instrument' (ὄργανον), in order to do the work that the Father gave him.[90] Instead, Athanasius argued that to be called the 'Son' properly means he shares his nature (hence, 'connatural') with the Father. Newman imports this idea back into the pre-Nicenes, in place of what appeared to be something similar to the Arians. For instance, Irenaeus wrote that the Father 'is ministered to in all things by His own Offspring and Likeness, the Word and Wisdom', evidence that 'a ministry is commonly ascribed to the Son and Spirit, and a bidding and willing to the Father, by Justin, Irenaeus, Clement, Origen and Methodius'—a division of divine labour that seems to subordinate *ad extra* the second and third hypostases (*Ari* 166; quoting Irenaeus from

---

[89] Origen subordinated the Spirit even more (e.g., *Com John* 2.10): 'while all things were created through the Word, the Holy Spirit is of more honour than all others and first in rank of all who have been created by the Father through Christ' (quoted Butterworth, *On First Principles*, 3 n. 4).

[90] Newman believed Alexander of Alexandria's letter reporting the Arians' view of the Word: '"He was made for our sakes, in order that God might create us by Him as by an instrument; and He would not have had subsistence, had not God willed our making." Some one asked them, if the Word of God could change, as the devil changed? They scrupled not to answer, "Certainly, He can"' (*Ari* 218).

Petavius, *de trin* i. 3.7). Newman insists we can read these Fathers as 'altogether in the spirit of the Post-Nicene authorities . . . as soon as the second and third Persons are understood to be internal to the Divine Mind, *connaturalia instrumenta*' (*Ari* 166). The pre-Nicenes thought of the second and third hypostases not as instruments of God, as the Arians did, but as internal to the divine nature; the Latin phrase probably coming from Bull in response to Petavius (e.g. *Defensio* ii. 573). To make this claim, Newman has to invoke the 'spirit' of what the post-Nicenes said, rather than what they actually said.

However, Newman is not—in spite of first impressions—simply following Bull's practice of claiming that the pre-Nicenes used different words but meant the same things as the post-Nicenes. Instead, something new is going on, the implications of which Newman had not fully recognized. He makes the convincing argument that, since Origen had no conception of a creaturely Son, therefore, when he used subordinationist language, he must have meant by it something very different from what the Arians meant later. He reports:

> Having mentioned the absurd idea, which had prevailed, of parts or extensions in the Divine Nature, [Origen] proceeds: 'Rather, as will proceeds out of the mind, and neither tears the mind nor is itself separated or divided from it, in some such manner must we conceive that the Father has begotten the Son, who is His Image'. (*Ari* 170, quoting *de Principiis* 1.2.6)

Although meaning something different from the fourth-century heretics, Newman will not admit that Origen could also have meant something different from Athanasius or Basil, even though the logic of his position pushes him in that direction. Newman therefore says that Basil made a very similar argument to Origen, even though the exact content of this quotation from Origen reveals something else. Origen is drawing an analogy between, on the one hand, the relation of mind to will, and, on the other, the relation of Father to Son; thus, the Son equates to the will of God. (Origen does not call him specifically the divine 'Will' in the way Athanasius does.) In taking this to be an argument for *connaturalia instrumenta*, Newman retroactively forces Origen into a post-Nicene mould, in suggesting the Son can only be the will of God if he is connatural (or *homoousios*) with the Father. Newman need not regard the pre-Nicenes through the lens of 'connatural' language; he has, after all, shown the importance of regarding *homoousios* as a concept which came after the earliest patristic writings—a word, moreover, which was at the time of Origin the subject of debate with Paul of Samosata. Newman's (mistaken) leap from Origen's analogy to a post-Nicene defence of *homoousios* is completed a few pages later, when he tells us, 'it was one of the first and principal interrogations put to the Catholics by their Arian opponents, whether the generation of the Son was voluntary or not on the part of the Father; their dilemma being, that Almighty God was subject to laws external to Himself, if it were not voluntary, and that, if on the other hand it was voluntary, the Son was in the number of things created' (*Ari* 196). The Catholic retort, typical of Athanasius, is whose nature did the Son share—that of Almighty God or of things created?[91] Yet, framed thus, the question of the divine will was very different at Nicaea from the way Origen himself framed it.

Like those he followed, Newman sees Origen as a step along the way to Nicaea. But, in so viewing him, Newman is not measuring Origen with an Athanasian yardstick, as did Petavius, nor, like Cudworth, arguing that Origen and Athanasius said two different things. Rather, he conceives an 'Alexandrian' style of language, which Origen shares as much with Athanasius as with Cyril of Alexandria, who followed them both. In fact (a rather strange fact, unless he conceived these Fathers as sharing one language), in explaining the counter-arguments put to the Arians, Newman quotes Cyril before he quotes Athanasius:

Cyril of Alexandria [asks], 'Whether He is good, compassionate, merciful, and holy, with or against His choice? For, if He is so in consequence of choosing it, and choice ever precedes what is chosen, these attributes once did not exist in God.' Athanasius gives substantially the same answer, solving, however, rather than confuting, the objection. 'The Arians', he says, 'direct their view to the *contradictory* of willing, instead of considering the more important and the *previous* question; for, as *unwillingness* is opposed to willing, so is nature prior to willing, and leads the way to it'. (*Ari* 208; quoting the Fathers from Petavius's footnotes at *de trin* ii. 5.9, vi. 8.14)

---

[91] R. C. Gregg and D. E. Groh compare the substantialist logic of Athanasius with the voluntarist logic of the Arians, each of which is coherent but incompatible with the other (*Early Arianism: A View of Salvation* (Philadelphia, Pa.: Fortress, 1981), 161–83).

This Alexandrian style of language—which was also used by the Cappadocians—had its roots, for Newman, in Origen and Clement. Here, I would like to borrow the insight of Rowan Williams, who talks about pre-Nicene doctrine as 'what has been called an "ecology" of doctrinal language: within the whole system of Christian speech, words receive their proper sense, balanced by others, qualified and nuanced by their neighbours'.[92] Williams elegantly sums up here what *Arians of the Fourth Century* brought to the investigation of pre-Nicene doctrine, for unlike his predecessors Newman thought of orthodox doctrine in terms of a language. By referring to 'Christian speech', Williams recalls Newman's emphasis on the 'doxologies' in which the Church spoke before a fixed Creed was adopted in 325. I would emphasize within Williams's ecological metaphor that orthodox doctrine was, for Newman, a language that evolved. The Newman of *Arians of the Fourth Century* revelled in the dynamism of doctrine more, as will be seen in Chapter 4, than the Newman of *Development of Christian Doctrine.*

CONCLUSION: WHAT HAS OXFORD TO DO WITH ALEXANDRIA?

On the primary sources and their commentators

Petavius followed the early historians of the Church, especially Eusebius of Caesarea, in describing a 'catechetical school' at Alexandria. Cave liked Eusebius as a theologian, and as a historian followed him almost word for word.[93] Newman did not like Eusebius, finding him the exemplar of the Neoplatonism that Petavius saw in the pre-Nicenes: 'there is no sufficient evidence in history

---

[92] Williams, introduction, *Ari* (p. xlii).

[93] Cave's hagiography of Eusebius set him apart from contemporaries. 'He was charged, perhaps with a little more reason, by Le Clerc, who was then writing his "Bibliothèque Universelle", with "writing panegyrics rather than lives", and also with "having forcibly drawn Eusebius, who was plainly enough Arian, over to the side of the orthodox, and made a Trinitarian of him"; this produced a paper warfare between the two great writers' (*DNB* (1963), iii. 262).

that the Arians did make this use of Neo-Platonism, considered as a party. I believe they did not, and from the facts of history should conclude Eusebius of Caesarea alone to be favourable to that philosophy' (*Ari* 114–15). But Newman takes many arguments straight from Eusebius, especially to praise Origen and to demonize Paul of Samosata.

Yet more important than the primary sources at this stage in Newman's life is the High Church tradition of Bull and Cave. From the latter he learns to trace what would today be called a *genealogy* of heresy. Cave's *Historia Literaria* divides (all too neatly) into fourteen 'saecula' of heresy, which follow the first age, the 'Apostolicum'. The heresies begin with the 'Saeculum Gnosticum', then 'Novatianum', 'Arianum', 'Nestorianum', 'Eutychianum', 'Monotheleticum', and so on up to 'Scholasticum'. Newman's own account of ecclesiastical epochs shares another thing with Cave's, and that is the choice of heroes and villains. Most of the heroes are Greek Fathers—Origen, Athanasius, Basil, and Cyril—who fought against the 'Syrian' and 'Latin' heresies of Cave's list.[94] High Anglicans were less willing to defend the Latin Fathers than to defend their Greek counterparts. Consider, for instance, Novatian: Cave describes the heretical 'saeculum Novatianum', and Bull readily admits that this Latin Father is 'no great authority in the Church' (*Defensio* ii. 476). This view of the Latin Fathers probably had to do with their association with the Catholic Church of later times. Moreover, of the pre-Nicene Latins who were venerated by Anglicans in the early modern era, Cyprian was a favourite precisely because he opposed the Latin extremism of Novatian and the papalism of Stephen. Newman in *Arians of the Fourth Century* continues within this trajectory of feeling no great veneration for the Latin Fathers, although upholding those Fathers was traditionally understood as important. As he planned the book, he wrote to Hugh Rose that his focus would be the 'Councils . . . on the Trinity and Incarnation, i.e. those of the *Greek* Church (to speak

[94] A High Church origin for Newman's historiography is more convincing than the claim that Newman demonstrates 'the great Augustinian perspective', following history 'across the centuries of the city of God'. See O. Berranger, 'Pour une lecture théologique de l'histoire chez Newman', in C. Lepelley and P. Veyriras (eds.), *Newman et l'histoire* (Lyons: Presses Universitaires Lyon, 1992), 13–38.

generally of them)', and Rose agreed that the Latin Councils would be a distraction (*LD* ii. 352; cf. ii. 358–9). In the book, he implies a continuity between the Catholic schools of later times and the schools of both heretical sophists and the Antiochene Church.[95]

On Platonism and ousia

While Petavius said that the pre-Nicene Fathers were more Platonic than orthodox in their Trinitarian doctrine, Newman is intent on defending them, particularly those of the Alexandrian school, from Petavius's charges. Cudworth was also opposed to Petavius, albeit his motive for defending the pre-Nicenes was very different from Newman's. Cudworth's focus is primarily Platonism not patristics. He finds ways to 'plead their excuse, who had no Scripture Revelation at all, to guide them'—meaning the Early and Middle Platonists. His main plea here is that, if 'the generality of Christian doctors, for the first three hundred years after the apostles' times' could do no better than turn to Plato, why should others be blamed for following the master philosopher (*TIS* 595)?

Newman does not agree with any of his seventeenth-century sources about the early Church's use of *homoousios*. Sometimes he follows Bishop Bull, in arguing for continuity between the pre- and the post-Nicenes. For instance, he argues that the idea of the consubstantiality of Father and Son was an early one: 'The term *homoüsion* is first employed for this purpose by the author of the *Paemander*, a Christian of the beginning of the second century. Next it occurs in several writers at the end of the second and the beginning of the third.' But, as he continues, crucially, in 'the middle of the third century, a change took place in the use of it and other similar words', as a result of the Council of Antioch called to condemn Paul's heresy (*Ari* 188–9). The question is whether, in saying the change took place in 'words', Newman thinks change took place in ideas also? Bull did not believe the idea signified by the word

---

[95] The Sophists' 'science of argumentation provided the means, their practice of disputing for the sake of exercise or amusement supplied the temptation, of assailing received opinions. This practice, which had long prevailed in the Schools, was early introduced into the Eastern Church' (*Ari* 31). Cf. Introduction n. 19, above.

homoousios changed *at all* in this period. He wrote that there was no more than an

apparent contradiction between the councils of Antioch and Nice[a] ... The fathers of the council of Antioch with good reason abhorred [Paul's] inter- pretation of the word; and therefore, not caring much for words in a question of such moment, they were content to suppress the term itself in silence, in order to cut off all occasion for the cavils of the heretics, provided only that the thing was agreed on, i.e. the true divinity of the Son. (*Defensio* i. 78)

It has been seen how important language and its proper theological use is for Newman, never depicting the pre-Nicenes as 'not caring much for words'. In contrast to Bull, Newman conceived the con- tinuity between pre- and post-Nicene Alexandrians as employing an 'ecology' of doctrinal language. However, Newman did not fully recognize that terminology might depend on changing ideas. As different from Cudworth and Bull as he tried to be, he regarded 'orthodoxy' with post-Nicene eyes even as he affirmed the dynamism of pre-Nicene doctrine.

On Alexandria and orthodoxy

Bull accuses Petavius of too quickly maligning Origen. Petavius seems to think himself 'bound' by 'his religion' to uphold the ana- themas of the Second Council of Constantinople, says Bull, rather than defending Origen as many 'illustrious men of the Church of Rome' have done—such as Erasmus and Pico della Mirandola (*Defensio* i. 221). This seems to be a standard way of defending Origen among seventeenth-century Anglicans, for Cave cites the good things Erasmus and Haymo of Halberstad had to say about him (*Apostolici* 234, 238). Newman, by contrast, does not cite any Catholic authorities in Origen's defence.

Both Newman and Cave set up an Alexandrian lineage that fixes their heroes in a particular school, with a particular way of reading and arguing about the scriptures. That method is spelled out in Origen's *Letter to Gregory*, which Cave paraphrases thus:

[Origen] lets [Gregory of Neocaesarea] know, that he instructed him mainly in those sciences and parts of philosophy, which might be *introductory* to the

Christian religion; acquainting him with those things in geometry and astronomy, which might be useful for the understanding and explaining the Holy Scriptures, these things being as *previously* advantageous to the knowledge of the Christian doctrine...[and] advising him before all things to read the Scripture, and that with the most profound and diligent attention, and not rashly to entertain notions of divine things, or to speak of them without solemn premeditation. (*Apostolici* 271, my italics)

From this letter, Newman recounts how Origen drew Gregory into the Church:

While professedly teaching him Pagan philosophy, his skilful master insensibly enlightened him in the knowledge of the Christian faith. Then, leading him to Scripture, he explained to him its difficulties as they arose; till Gregory, overcome by the force of truth, announced to his instructor his intention of exchanging the pursuits of the world for the service of God. (*Ari* 67)

Newman extrapolates from the letter's method, by which Origen taught a few scholars whom he gathered around himself in Caesarea, Gregory among them, into a whole curriculum for everything taught at the school in Alexandria. Newman overlooks the discontinuities in the Alexandrian school in the third century—many of which were the result of Origen's feuds with his bishop. Rather, he describes the Alexandrian school as 'a pattern to other Churches in its diligent and systematic preparation of candidates for baptism', as well as 'carefully examining into the doctrines revealed in Scripture, and of cultivating the habit of argument and disputation' (ibid. 41).

Orthodox language works, for Newman, by suppressing heresy and in the pre-Nicene era one heresy was suppressed at a time. Origen's pupils, Gregory of Neocaesarea and Dionysius of Alexandria, were taught by their master to defend against two forms of Sabellianism, 'the Patripassian and the Emanative'. Yet, in so doing, they have unfairly 'incurred odium in a later age, as if they had been forerunners of Arius' (ibid. 125). Newman also argues that until any particular Christian doctrine was refined in the fire of controversy the pre-Nicenes were free to explore those areas of doctrine whose bounds the Church had not yet set. This has been shown to be a traditional notion among Anglican writers, who consistently defended Origen for his speculations in uncharted theological territory.

On Antioch and heresy

Petavius and Cudworth see the '*ad extra*' subordinationism within
Platonism to be the source of Arius's depiction of the Trinity. But,
whereas Petavius blames the Neoplatonists, Cudworth seeks to understand them, albeit without letting their mistakes be 'dissembled,
palliated or excused' (*TIS* 592). It has become clear that Newman
was closer to Cave's account of Arian heresy, however, than to either of
these commentators. Although Rowan Williams gives a brief recapitulation of the different accounts of Arianism's genealogy given by
Cave and Newman, he neglects four similarities between them. These
similarities show Cave and Newman to be closer than Cave and
Cudworth, even though Williams invokes the latter when discussing
Cave.

Firstly, Williams fails to mention the connections between Cave
and Newman in the anti-Jewish and anti-female perspective on
heresy they share with their sources. Secondly, Cave and Newman
stress the role played in Arianism by Lucian of Antioch (whom, by
the way, Bull defends). Williams argues that, compared to Newman,
whose genealogy of Arianism tended to play down Neoplatonists in
favour of Antiochenes, Cave mentions Paul and Lucian only fleet-
ingly.[96] But Paul and Lucian are nevertheless mentioned by Cave, and
not simply passed over. Regarding the role of Lucian, Williams
writes: 'Ever since Newman', Arius's letter to 'fellow Lucianist' Eusebius of Nicomedia 'has produced some very questionable reconstruc-
tions of Arius's intellectual background'.[97] Yet it was Cave who used
Lucian as evidence of proto-Arianism in Antioch, even when that
evidence was in fact empty of content. Thirdly, both lay most of the
blame for Arius's success on Eusebius of Nicomedia. Admittedly,
Cave does follow Cudworth's argument in perceiving Eusebius of
Nicomedia as the wrong type of Platonist, whose doctrine of the
Trinity was too subordinationist, whereas Newman portrayed the
pupils of Lucian as part of an Antiochene school of theology. Here
the difference between Newman and Cave masks a fourth and final

[96] Williams thinks it significant that 'Only at the end of a longish disquisition on
[philosophy] does Cave add that Arius had been predisposed to such views by his
apprenticeship to Lucian' (*Arius*, 3).
[97] Ibid. 30.

similarity. Newman and Cave are furthest apart in an area in which, above all, they agree: both think that the schools of the ancient Church explain the rise of the Arian heresy. For Cave, the philosophy of Alexandria found common cause with the school at Antioch under Lucian, while for Newman philosophy and theology came together in Antioch under Paul.

Newman recognizes with Cave that Alexandrian Platonism at the time of Origen (but never under Origen) delved too far into the mystery of the Trinity; but this, for Newman, was not the source of Arianism. Instead, the family tree of heresy begins in Antioch, even when its branches spread into Alexandria, as in the case of Aetius and Eunomius: 'Aetius came from the School of an Aristotelian of Alexandria. Eunomius, his pupil, who re-constructed the Arian doctrine on its original basis, at the end of the reign of Constantius, is represented by Ruffinus [*sic*] as "pre-eminent in dialectic power"' (*Ari* 30). In a very unspecific footnote here—though one which acknowledges the debt Newman owes—he cites 'Cave, *Hist. Literar.* vol. i.'

The role of Athanasius

The final sentence of *Arians of the Fourth Century*, of course, made explicit his view that the English Church shared in the ancient concerns of Athanasius. This has led subsequent interpreters to read a love for Athanasius into the start of the book as well.[98] But this chapter has sought to read the book forwards, not backwards, beginning where Newman does with the pre-Nicene Fathers. Newman argued in his first chapter that the Antiochene school was the key to understanding Arius, and in the doctrinally rich second chapter that the best of orthodoxy was to be found in the pre-Nicene Church. At the time, Newman saw these two chapters as his great contribution to scholarship, while the rest of the book he suggested was derivative.[99] These two chapters spoke to the situation in

---

[98] e.g., Marriette Canévet has argued that Newman recognized his affinity with Athanasius when he wrote *Arians of the Fourth Century*. See 'Newman et l'utilisation de l'histoire dans *Les Ariens du quatrième siècle*: un example, Athanase', in Lepelley and Veyriras, *Newman et l'histoire*, 124.

[99] He noted at the start of ch. 3: 'The rest of this volume is drawn up from the following authorities: Eusebius, Vit. Const., Socrates, Sozomen, and Theodoret, Hist. Eccles., the various historical tracts of Athanasius, Epiphanius Haer. lxix. lxxiii., and

contemporary England, by comparing the schools of Paul of Samosata and Origen, just as much as the last page. *Arians of the Fourth
Century* was finished in 1832, when the leaders of his own day, firstly
the rabble-rousing political or religious reformers, and secondly the
Anglican statesmen and bishops in parliament, had in Newman's
mind renounced truth. A rabble-rouser like Arius was probably a
'tool of deeper men' at court, like Eusebius of Nicomedia in the
Emperor Constantius's court or Prime Minister Grey in the court
of St James (*Ari* 39). Paul of Samosata and Arius are seen creating a
'public debate' among those least able to judge right from wrong,
which Newman thought would be the fruit of extending the suffrage
(ibid. 139).[100] Moreover, inferior as it was to the pre-Nicene faith that
preceded it, if the bishops had rallied to the Nicene faith all the strife
of the fourth-century controversies could have been averted. So too
could the bishops have opposed the Reform Act.

The Antiochene schools of philosophy and theology bred a
method of disputation (sophistry) and biblical interpretation (literalism) which Newman blames for the Arian heresy. By contrast,
Alexandria had a catechetical school that had taught sound doctrine
and exegesis for many years. England's school of orthodoxy was, of
course, Oxford. What was needed in Oxford was a return to the
teaching offered by Origen, in order that future bishops who were
schooled there might be superior to the current crop. For only then
'our Athanasius and Basil will be given us in their destined season,
to break the bonds of the Oppressor, and let the captives go free'
(ibid. 394).

the Acta Conciliorum. Of moderns, especially Tillemont and Petavius; then, Maim-
bourg's History of Arianism, the Benedictine Life of Athanasius, Cave's Life of
Athanasius and Literary History, Gibbon's Roman History and Mr. Bridges' Reign
of Constantine' (*Ari* 236 n. 1).

[100] Cave, writing at the end of the seventeenth-century upheavals in regime, was
also keen to show that Arius was 'mingling himself with every company' (*Ecclesiastici*
156).

3

Preaching and Researching an Alexandrian Christology (1834–40)

Changes in Newman's view of the person and work of Christ were the result of three summer vacations spent researching different patristic writings on Christ in 1834, 1835, and 1839. Coming between the publication of *The Arians of the Fourth Century*, which relished the teaching of the pre-Nicene Alexandrians, and Newman's first insights into doctrinal development, which recognized that it was necessary to interpret the pre-Nicenes 'by the times which came after', these three summers help to explain not only his Christology but also the major shift in his thought about doctrine after 1839 (*Dev* 13). Indeed, research undertaken that summer made him aware that the doctrine of Christ only became fully present to the mind of the Church in the sixth, seventh, and eighth centuries, with the trio of Leontius of Byzantium, Maximus the Confessor, and John of Damascus. This awareness of the trio may have caused Newman's move from conceiving doctrine as static to it developing, although he did not begin to write about his new idea until correspondences with his brother late in 1840. Not one of three was an Alexandrian. Nevertheless, Newman saw the need to situate them within an orthodox tradition that 'developed' from Origen and Dionysius of Alexandria to Athanasius and Cyril.

Throughout his book *Newman and Heresy*, Stephen Thomas uses archive material to demonstrate how Newman shaped his rhetoric in Oxford controversies around comparisons between his contemporaries and ancient heretics. This chapter will supplement Thomas's valuable work by re-examining the papers in the Birmingham Oratory, showing that Thomas neglected Newman's quest to date the purported Confession against Paul of Samosata. This chapter will also use a source that Thomas often overlooks: Newman's Christological sermons.[1] The influence of what he discovered each summer can be discerned in his preaching during the academic year that followed (1834–5, 1835–6, and 1839–40). Examining the sermons on Christ, and doing so chronologically,[2] has two advantages. Firstly, unlike the heresies upon which Thomas focuses—explaining what is *not* orthodox—the sermons reveal Newman's positive doctrine of Christ's person and work. Secondly, an examination of the sermons reminds us that his writings were driven not only by the controversies of contemporary Oxford, but also by the Church year. The preaching calendar meant that Newman pondered Christ's incarnation every Christmas and Christ's suffering and death at the end of every Lent. For example, notes in the Oratory archive on the Manichees, a page of which is dated 24 December 1835, cite Athanasius's *On the Incarnation*—an ideal text to ponder for Christmas.[3] His Christological musings also interacted with his thoughts on the nature of doctrine throughout the 1830s. What he expressed in the pulpit and on paper had a broadly 'Alexandrian' shape.

THE HIGH CHURCH CONTEXT:
(3) INTERPRETING THE ALEXANDRIANS

The previous chapter showed how Newman's *Arians of the Fourth Century* shaped an Anglican historiography that divided Alexandrian and Antiochene theology, and he did this based in part on the ancient

---

[1] Thomas does show 'The Humiliation of the Eternal Son' to be a repost to the rationalism of Newman's teacher Whately and friend Blanco White (*Newman and Heresy: The Anglican Years* (Cambridge: Cambridge University Press, 1991), 84–6).

[2] Roderick Strange jumps around chronologically in his examination of the sermons. See 'Newman and the Mystery of Christ', in Ian Ker and Alan G. Hill (eds.), *Newman after One Hundred Years* (Oxford: Clarendon Press, 1990).

[3] OM B.3.5, the dated page is called 'For the Ante Nicene Incarnation Controversy'.

schools' different methods of scriptural interpretation. Newman seems to have been the first to argue for a pre-Nicene school of theology in Antioch contemporaneous with that which earlier commentators had discerned in Alexandria. By the time he wrote *Development of Christian Doctrine* in 1845, Newman had widened the sweep of his thesis to cover a period from the third to the fifth centuries, arguing of the Antiochene 'Exegetical School... on the one hand that it devoted itself to the literal and critical interpretation of Scripture, and on the other that it gave rise to the Arian and then the Nestorian heresy' (*Dev* 282).[4] Countering the heresies of Antioch across these years were the heroes of Alexandria, especially Origen, Dionysius, Athanasius, and Cyril, and their followers.

Since the nineteenth century, the subtleties of the Alexandrian–Antiochene division have been closely examined,[5] showing, in the words of Rowan Williams, that 'Newman's own perspectives and proposals are often flawed by a colossally over-schematic treatment and a carelessness in detail'.[6] This was true even by the standards of High Churchmen of his own day, who criticized him for misunderstanding Clement and Origen. His unprecedented view of the Antiochenes was not deemed worthy of criticism by High Churchmen, according to Newman in 1871, recalling that Edward Burton, Regius Professor of Divinity at Oxford, said no more than: 'Of course you have a right to your opinion' (*Ari* 403). In spite of these flaws, Newman introduced many to Alexandrian doctrines through his writings and sermons; for instance, deification ($\theta\epsilon o\pi o i\eta\sigma\iota\varsigma$) or the teaching that the Son's incarnation is the Father's way to raise humanity up, in the power of the Spirit, into the very life of God. Andrew Louth writes, quoting from Newman in 1838 (*Jfc* 150):

[4] *Dev* 281–93 was appended to the 1871 edition of *Arians of the Fourth Century* as Note I, The Syrian School of Theology. Here Newman offers no account of why 'St. Chrysostom pointedly contradicts the doctrine of Theodore, though his fellow-pupil and friend; as does St. Ephrem though a Syrian also' (*Dev* 286/*Ari* 410).

[5] Recently, Frances M. Young showed in *Biblical Exegesis and the Formation of Christian Culture* (Cambridge: Cambridge University Press, 1997) that the division was not one of allegory versus literalism. And J. D. Dawson showed that Origen's interpretations depended as much on the 'literal' sense as on the allegorical in *Christian Figural Reading and the Fashioning of Identity* (Berkeley, Calif.: University of California Press, 2002).

[6] Williams, introduction, *Ari* (p. xxxvi).

'*This* is really and truly our justification, not faith, not holiness, not (much less) a mere imputation; but through God's mercy, the very Presence of Christ': here, in a sentence which sums up the central theme of his *Lectures on Justification*, Newman gives expression to this central conviction of the Oxford Movement, the conviction that as we respond to God in Christ, God Himself is present to us, in our hearts, drawing us to Himself: a conviction which expresses... the heart of the patristic doctrine of deification.[7]

Alexandrian Christology was propounded through the *Lectures on Justification*, all about God's transformation of the Church and her people, and 'it appears that Newman never felt that his *Lectures* had been seriously challenged'.[8] By the late 1830s, indeed, he was much less deferential about his interpretation of the Alexandrians than he had been earlier in the decade.

Sensitive to the criticisms that his first book received, Newman's first impulse was to justify what he wrote in *Arians of the Fourth Century* against criticism from the High Church Bishop of Lincoln, John Kaye, in January 1834. Newman also sought to correct *Arians of the Fourth Century*, and his 'Letters on the Church Fathers' published in the *British Magazine* from October 1833 and the Records of the Church that he edited from November 1833 afforded him the opportunity to examine the Fathers more closely. The Records focused on the pre-Nicene Church, while the 'Letters' focused on the fourth century. The latter period provided Newman with information about the former period. For instance, *Arians of the Fourth Century* stated: 'later writers, and even Basil himself, do not scruple to complain of

---

[7] Andrew Louth, 'Manhood into God: The Oxford Movement, the Fathers and the Deification of Man', in Rowan D. Williams and Kenneth Leech (eds.), *Essays Catholic and Radical* (London: Bowerdean Press, 1983), 74–5. C. S. Dessain has made a similar point: 'The East has always emphasized that the grace of justification is a personal union with God, the result of our deification. In the West grace has tended to be thought of as more a remedy for sin and as a quality of the soul. Newman's emphasis, in his sermons and in his treatises, is on our deification and on the indwelling of the Holy Trinity that follows from it' ('Cardinal Newman and the Eastern Tradition', *Downside Review*, 94 (1976), 95).

[8] This is the view of Peter Toon, *Evangelical Theology, 1833–1856: A Response to Tractarianism* (London: Marshall, Morgan and Scott, 1979), 168; here he surmises: 'If the Evangelicals had responded by examining the roots of Newman's views (that is the teaching of the Greek Fathers) and challenged these roots by the teaching of the Apostle Paul and James, then the whole controversy (and perhaps the development of Evangelical theology) would have taken on a different character.'

Dionysius as having sown the first seeds of Arianism; Basil confessing the while that his error was accidental, occasioned by his vehement opposition to the Sabellian heresy' (*Ari* 127). But no footnote in *Arians of the Fourth Century* explained where Basil said this (*Epistle* 9) about Dionysius of Alexandria (d. *c*.264); Newman had probably gathered this insight second hand. Writing the 'Letters' in late 1833 and early 1834 gave Newman an opportunity to read Basil's epistles at first hand; he even commented to the *Magazine*'s editor, Hugh James Rose: 'My *translations* of Basil etc are not over exactly literal... [but] the meaning is his, as near as I could give it' (*LD* iv. 162). Then, in March 1834, Newman began editing the fragments of Dionysius's *Refutation and Defence* for the University Press at Oxford, and he found the perfect means of investigating the pre-Nicenes by the way of the later Fathers (*LD* iv. 202).

Edward Burton's offer that Newman edit Dionysius gave him the chance to prove his credentials to those who doubted his scholarship in *Arians of the Fourth Century* by requiring him to write a Latin commentary (*LD* iv. 274). By late July, he realized that he would also have to 'write out the whole of the Greek' (ibid. 311); so, by early August, he had decided to put *Arians of the Fourth Century* behind him for the foreseeable future, writing to John Bowden, 'pray give yourself no great trouble about [procuring] the German Athanasius—when I shall have an opportunity of correcting my Arians is of course very uncertain and of distant date' (ibid. 320).[9] But he could still address some of its supposed errors about the pre-Nicenes by examining Dionysius in depth, and over the next few years Newman continued to defend the existence of a pre-Nicene 'secret tradition', described in Chapter 1 above. For instance, he wrote to Hugh Rose in December 1835 that

you need not fear I should fidget about the Disciplina Arcani—though I have had no reason to change my mind about it—and find the Bishop of Lincoln grants that Clement holds it. Faber too has deduced the same from

[9] The 'German Athanasius' is J. A. Möhler's *Athanasius der Grosse und die Kirche seiner Zeit* (1827), of which Rowan Williams writes: 'Newman was as ignorant of German as most of his Oxford contemporaries, but was provided by J. W. Bowden with a list of the contents of Möhler's book [*LD* iv. 302–3]; his appetite was sufficiently whetted for him to consider making a serious beginning with German, but no more about Möhler appears' ('Newman's *Arians* and the Question of Method in Doctrinal History', in Ker and Hill, *Newman after One Hundred Years*, 274–5).

Origen's writings. At the same time I never meant it was a *Church* rule, but a discretionary selfimposed rule for individuals. (*LD* v. 178)

Rose needed the assurance that Newman would not be taking the notion of *disciplina arcani* any further, for, like most High Churchmen, Rose was suspicious of it. In fact, Newman was wilfully misinterpreting the Bishop of Lincoln's writings on the subject. In 1826, Bishop Kaye had stressed how wary Tertullian was of any *disciplina arcani*.[10] By 1835, Kaye's opposition to the notion could not have been clearer, writing of the one Church Father' whom he acknowledged, in 1826, to have praised secret tradition: 'Clement's Esoteric system agrees only in one respect with the Romish Disciplina Arcani; it is equally destitute of solid foundation.' Kaye writes that rather than 'rely on unwritten tradition, Clement says, "that they who are labouring after excellence, will not stop in their search of truth, until they have obtained proof of that which they believe from the Scriptures themselves"'.[11] Therefore Newman was not quite honest when, in the letter to Rose, he claimed of the unwritten tradition that 'the Bishop of Lincoln grants that Clement holds it' (*LD* v. 178). Newman also cited to Rose the moderate Evangelical, G. S. Faber, in defence of Origen's catechetical method (the 'economy' of teaching the faith gradually rather than all in one go).[12] Kaye weighed in on pedagogy in early Alexandria, too: 'The authority of Clement has been quoted in support of a mode of interpretation κατ᾽ οἰκονομίαν [i.e. according to the economy], but in my opinion, erroneously.'[13] These words could well have been directed at Newman's account in *Arians of the*

[10] 'Having already delivered our opinion respecting the mischievous consequences which have arisen to the Church, from the countenance lent by the writings of Clemens Alexandrinus to the notion of a Disciplina Arcani—we shall now only express our regret that Protestant divines, in their eagerness to establish a favourite point, should sometimes have been induced to resort to it' (John Kaye, *The Ecclesiastical History of the Second and Third Centuries, Illustrated from the Writings of Tertullian* (Cambridge: J. Deighton and Son, 1826), 251).

[11] Ibid., *Some Account of the Writings and Opinions of Clement of Alexandria* (London: Rivingtons, 1835), 368.

[12] Faber wrote: 'according to their progress in theological knowledge, the collective body of believers was divided into two classes: the class of *Those who were as yet instructed only in the shadow of the Word*, as Origen speaks; and the class of *Those who had been made acquainted with the true Word in the opened heaven*' (G. S. Faber, *The Apostolicity of Trinitarianism*, 2 vols. (London: Rivingtons, 1832), ii. 43).

[13] Kaye, *Clement of Alexandria*, 397.

Fourth Century, which praised the Alexandrians for their 'economical' methods of teaching and exegesis of scripture, as could Kaye's warning about allegory: 'To follow Clement through all his allegorical interpretations [of scripture] would be a wearisome and unprofitable labour.'[14]

Newman had drafted a memorandum in January 1834, responding to specific criticisms of *Arians of the Fourth Century* that Kaye had made to Rose. There is evidence neither that the memorandum was sent nor that it would not have satisfied Kaye, for Newman apologized only 'if I have any where implied that the Disciplina was a strict rule' (*LD* iv. 169 n. 1). He would not stop propounding a secret tradition, but contrary to the fears of Bishop Kaye, Newman's aim was not 'Romish',[15] but to reclaim pre-Nicene antiquity for Anglicans. While Roman Catholics began with doctrine as it *is* found in the present and tried to trace it back to its origins, using the secret tradition to explain the differences between what scripture says and what tradition does, for Newman that was to start at the wrong end.[16] Newman was saying something radical not Romish, as Rowan Williams notices of a letter from Archdeacon Lyall: 'Lyall wrote to Rose that "a secret tradition is not tradition at all", and this sums up the anxieties of orthodox High Church theologians. Newman is apparently granting that pre-Nicene formulations actually *are* compatible with something other than Nicene orthodoxy.'[17]

In spite of what Newman wrote to Rose in December 1835, he did not stop espousing the *disciplina arcani*, nor continuing to alarm

---

[14] Ibid. 376.

[15] The 'Romish' use of secret tradition, wrote Kaye, attempts 'to account for the total silence of the first ages of Christianity respecting certain doctrines which it now requires its followers to believe, as necessary to salvation' (ibid. 367).

[16] Owen Chadwick shows that Newman had in mind the seventeenth-century Catholic, Emanuel Schelstrate, and his followers (*From Bossuet to Newman* (2nd edn.; Cambridge: Cambridge University Press, 1987), 68–9).

[17] Williams, introduction, *Ari* (p. xxxi). In fact, Lyall wrote: 'Mr Newman's notions about tradition appear to me directly adverse to that which Protestant writers of our own Church have contended for—according to them a "secret tradition" is no tradition at all, [Vincent of Lérins's] quod semper, quod ubique, quod ab omnibus, is the very definition of authentic tradition. Mr. Newman's views seem to me more favourable to the Romanist writers' (*LD* iii. 105). Lyall's letter to Rose dated 19 Oct. 1832 was forwarded to Newman.

some High Churchmen. In Tract 71, published in May 1836, Newman bemoaned that, in the Church of England, 'we have argued for the sole Canonicity of the Bible to the exclusion of tradition, not on the ground that the Fathers held it (which would be an irrefragable argument) but on some supposed internal witness of Scripture to the fact, or some abstract and antecedent reasons against the Canonicity of unwritten teaching'. To reject the unwritten tradition on 'supposed' or 'abstract' arguments was a mistake, cried Newman. No wonder the High Churchmen continued to fidget.[18] The same month as Tract 71, Newman reviewed *The Life of Archbishop Laud* (1836), concluding of its author, Charles Le Bas (b. 1799), 'that for honest and manly pursuit of truth, no living writer has a greater claim on our reverence' (*Critic* 19: 379–80). But, in *The Life of Archbishop Cranmer* (1833), this same High Church historian criticized unwritten tradition as opposing the Reformer's teaching that scripture alone contained all that was necessary for salvation.[19]

Newman upheld the pedagogy of the early Alexandrians before the High Churchmen because he saw himself and them on the same side in 'the battle of the University' against an alternative pedagogy that was threatening Oxford in 1834–6 (*LD* iv. 360). That was the modern pedagogy of the so-called Oriel Noetics, against which the Oriel friends, Newman, Froude, and Keble propounded the notions of reserve and of a secret tradition to promote the right ethos. 'When Whately departed from Oxford in 1831', writes one commentator, 'the Noetic torch passed into the hands of R. D. Hampden'.[20] Hampden would be resisted twice during this period—successfully keeping

[18] In 1838, High Churchman Edward Hawkins, Newman's Provost at Oriel, wrote *The Duty of Private Judgment* in response to Tract 85's appeal to Hawkins's earlier sermon *The Use and Importance of Unauthoritative Tradition* (1819).

[19] 'It is concluded [by Cranmer] that if traditions are to be received at all, it should be simply in the spirit of modest acquiescence, not of implicit faith; and that no one thing could be named which more urgently demanded the jealous vigilance of Kings and Princes, than the attempt to invest such *Unwritten Verities* with the same dignity as the *written* word of God' (Charles Le Bas, *The Life of Archbishop Cranmer*, 2 vols. (London: Rivingtons, 1833), ii. 4).

[20] Tod E. Jones, *The Broad Church: A Biography of a Movement* (Lanham, Md.: Lexington Books, 2003), 83.

subscription to the Thirty-nine Articles as a requirement for admission to Oxford in 1835 and unsuccessfully opposing Hampden's appointment as Regius Professor of Divinity in 1836—with Newman's arguments from Christian antiquity. Subscription at Oxford may have been related in Newman's mind to early Christian initiation rites. Perhaps he saw subscription to the Thirty-nine Articles to be a necessary test of admittance, as the Creed was for those to be baptized, after which the secrets of a rich secondary tradition awaited initiates; this tradition was 'the privilege of the Christian when admitted', he wrote to Froude in August 1835, adding in parenthesis that the 'Disciplina Arcani comes in here' (*LD* v. 102). Controversy arose when Newman learned of Hampden's pamphlet in August 1834 entitled *Observations on Religious Dissent*, which Newman told Rose 'calls all articles impositions on human authority, and advocates their removal as a test on matriculations' (*LD* iv. 323). Such prizing of 'human authority' over ecclesiastical authority was, for Newman, comparable with Antiochenes who prized the literal (human) over the allegorical (spiritual) interpretation of scripture and thus rejected established tradition and ethos.

THE QUEST OF THREE SUMMERS: DIONYSIUS AND THE CONFESSION AGAINST PAUL

Newman's extensive research for the edition of Dionysius, which mainly took place over three summer vacations, remains unpublished in the Birmingham Oratory archive.[21] In 1834, Newman worked on the fragments of Dionysius that were extant; in 1835, he examined fourth-century writers for information about Dionysius; in 1839, he looked at debates from the fifth and following centuries, although by now Dionysius was at the back of his mind. Each summer took him further into the early Church's Christological controversies with Paul of Samosata, Apollinarius of Laodicea (*c.*310–*c.*390), Nestorius (d. *c.*451), and Eutyches (*c.*378–454), and each summer made him think of other books to write instead of

---

[21] OM B.2.4. For a description of contents, see Thomas, *Newman and Heresy*, 70.

Dionysius. In August 1835, he was considering 'a volume on the Incarnation to accompany the Arians', which he considered to have been about Trinitarian doctrine (*LD* v. 118). In April 1839, planning ahead for the summer, he intended 'to put notes to our [i.e. A Library of the Fathers'] Translation of Theodoret's Heresies etc, to translate S. Cyril against Nestorius, and to finish (if possible) my edition of S. Dionysius' (ibid. vii. 65).[22] These threads of research appear disparate, but one particular quest connected them all: from the time he began working on Dionyius, Newman wanted to date the so-called Confession against Paul of Samosata.

Pondering the Dionysius volume in March 1834, Newman needed to discern two things in particular. He knew from Eusebius's *History of the Church* that Dionysius, although invited to attend the first session of the Council of Antioch, was prevented by old age and ill health and instead wrote a letter (*Ecc Hist* 7. 27). Firstly, Newman needed to discern whether the letter to which Eusebius referred was genuinely the one known to Burton;[23] or was it, together with the *Ten Questions* that Paul asked in response to the letter, and Diony- sius's answers, a forgery? Secondly, the *Ecthesis* or Confession sup- posedly against Paul of Samosata required an accurate date. Newman wrote to Burton on 1 March 1834 to oppose the 'arguments con- tained in the Roman Preface to Dionysius and sent by you to Mr Faber on the subject of the abandonment of the ὁμοούσιον at Anti- och' (*LD* iv. 194).[24] The preface to Simon de Magistris's Greek and Latin edition of Dionysius's works, printed in Rome in 1796 by the Congregation for the Propagation of the Faith, claimed that this Confession, which included '*homoousios*', proved the word was used at Antioch; Newman was correct to say that the word was abandoned

[22] He failed in all of these projects. R. Scott's translation of Theodoret's *Compen- dium of Heresies and Dialogues* and Newman's of *St Cyril Against Nestorius* were advertised in the prospectus of A Library of the Fathers until, respectively, 1850 and 1845 (*LD* vii. 66 n. 1).

[23] Burton quoted this letter in *Testimonies of the Ante-Nicene Fathers to the Divinity of Christ* (2nd edn.; Oxford: Clarendon Press, 1829), 399; the source for the letter (ibid. p. xix) was Simon Maria de Magistris, *S. Dionysii Alexandrini episcopi cognomento Magni* (Rome, 1796).

[24] Newman disagreed with Burton's analysis in Faber, *Apostolicity of Trinitarian- ism*, ii. 302–7, and perhaps saw this letter as the start of his research into Dionysius and Paul, preserving it with his notes in OM B.3.5.

and the Confession came later. He had already expressed the opinion, in *Arians of the Fourth Century*, that Paul was condemned at the Council of Antioch for his particular use of 'consubstantial' to describe the relation of the Father and the Son, leading the Fathers to abandon that word.[25] By contrast, Burton argued (wrongly) that *homoousios* was not abandoned at the Council and claimed that the dubious Confession was indeed from Antioch even though it was found in the *Acts* of the Council of Ephesus (431).

The President of Magdalen College thought the Confession was a later forgery. Martin Routh, who recorded the Confession in his *Reliquiae Sacrae*,[26] said that it actually arose from debates with Nestorius, which is why it is found in the *Acts* of Ephesus in which Nestorius was condemned. Another piece of evidence in support of Routh's dating was a fragment of a Creed, purportedly from the Council of Antioch, that appeared in 428 on a placard against Nestorius, put around Constantinople by the Eusebius who was later the bishop of Dorylaeum.[27] It seemed to Routh too much of a coincidence that all of these accounts of Paul appeared at the time of the Council of

[25] Newman continues to use an argument from *Arians of the Fourth Century*: 'we have … an exact parallel to this perversion and abandonment of the ὁμοούσιον in the instance of the προβολή; which is used (προβοληθὲν γέννημα) by Justin, usurped by the Gnostics, vindicated from them for the Church by Tertullian, given up (abandoned) to them by Origen. And it would be natural in Gregory Neocaes[area] and Athenodorus, as being Origenists, to do so (if necessary) in the case of ὁμοούσιος … [when] Paul perplexed the Fathers of Antioch with a quibble on the word' (*LD* iv. 196). Cf. *Ari* 190.

[26] Martin Routh, *Reliquiae Sacrae*, 5 vols. (New York: Olms, 1974.), iii. 366–7. Confusingly, although supposed to date from the Council of Antioch and found in the *Acts* of Ephesus, the Confession itself claims to belong to a gathering of bishops 'in Nicaea'. Tillemont suggested the Confession 'does not combat Consubstantiality with regard to those who would say that Jesus Christ, in as much as he is man, is Consubstantial with the Father, and it establishes very strongly the Catholic sense of the Council of Nicaea' (*Mémoires pour servir à l'histoire ecclésiastique des six premiers siècles*, 16 vols. (2nd edn.; Paris: Charles Robustel, 1701–12), iv. 301); therefore, 'it appears rather to have been made by some later Council against Nestorius and Eutyches' (ibid. vi. 814 n. 11).

[27] For the details of this public posting and the content of some of Eusebius's claims—e.g., 'Paul said, "Mary did not bear the Word." Agreeing with this, Nestorius said, "My good man, Mary did not bear the divinity"'—see Timothy E. Gregory, *Vox Populi: Popular Opinion and Violence in the Religious Controversies of the Fifth Century* (Columbus, Ohio: Ohio State University Press, 1979), 90.

Ephesus for them to be genuinely from the Council of Antioch. The charge on the placard was preserved by Leontius of Byzantium (*c*.490–*c*.545), alongside fragments of the Antiochene *Acts*, in order to tar Leontius's opponents with the brush of Nestorius and Paul of Samosata.[28] In being asked to edit the writings of Dionysius, then, Newman found himself in the middle of a conundrum of the date of the Confession against Paul, upon which question the two senior historians at Oxford, Routh and Burton, held different opinions, and to solve which would require immersion in later Christological debates. Newman's quest to date the Confession against Paul had begun; and it would end with a different answer from them both.

Newman worked hard on gathering the various fragments of Dionysius together in the summer of 1834. In July, he asked one of the younger Tractarians, Benjamin Harrison, who was studying in Paris, to examine some supposed writings of Dionysius on Luke and Job (*LD* iv. 294–5, 310). In return, Harrison, needing reinforcements in a public correspondence with Jean-Nicholas Jager that August, 'got [Newman] into controversy with [the] Parisian Abbé' (ibid. iv. 360). Newman returned to Dionsysius the following summer, telling Froude on 21 July 1835 of his frustrations at the slow pace of research, interrupted as it was by the correspondence with Jager (ibid. v. 104). He wrote to Froude again, on 9 August, that he was still 'hard at Dionysius—i.e. at the Apollinarian Controversy. Afterwards will follow the Nestorian' (ibid. 118).

Stephen Thomas puzzles over the letters of early August 1835, in which Newman, deep in his research on Dionysius, announces his expectation of writing about the Apollinarian controversy. 'But why does he "expect" this?' Thomas asks.[29] Thomas's solution to the puzzle is that Newman was developing a theory of heresy, in which he saw his friend Blanco White's conversion to Unitarianism as a similar 'defection' to that of Apollinarius of Laodicea, a friend of Athanasius whose pursuit of speculative truth led to secession from the Church and then condemnation at the Council of Constantinople

---

[28] The fragments of the *Acts* from Leontius's *Adversus Nestorianos et Eutychianos* are also in Routh, *Reliquiae Sacrae*, iii. 309–12.

[29] *Newman and Heresy*, 88.

(381).[30] A simpler explanation than Thomas's would be to connect Dionysius with Apollinarius by way of the Confession against Paul, the authorship of which Newman had been investigating since the letter to Burton in March 1834. Rather than focusing on Newman's remarks to Froude about 'poor Blanco' in the letter of 9 August, as Thomas does, this explanation focuses on the previous sentences about Newman's research:

in a certain Creed given to the Council of Antioch A.D. 264 occurs the word πρόσωπον [person] as applied to the σύνθετον or union of the δύο φύσιες [two natures] in our Lord. Now I think to be able to prove it was not so used till A.D. (say) 390. You see what investigations this must lead to. (*LD* v. 118)

Newman had concluded that this 'certain Creed' (the Confession against Paul) dated from *before* the word πρόσωπον came to be replaced by hypostasis in the fifth century.[31] This Confession would have been useful to the Apollinarians in claiming the authority for their arguments from the terminology with which the heresiarch Paul was condemned.

An examination of Newman's unpublished notes at the time reveals Newman's hunch about the Confession. A page entitled 'Paulus Samosatenus', written the day after the letter to Froude, names Apollinarius.[32] It suggests the wide field of investigation into which Newman had already entered on Paul, citing Athanasius, Theodoret, Epiphanius, and Leontius of Byzantium. With it, although undated, is a page listing available sources for 'Paul's opinions', showing that Newman did not think Dionysius of Alexandria's

---

[30] 'Six days *before* Newman saw the transition from Sabellianism to Apollinarianism, he had begun to perceive the importance of Blanco's thesis that "Sabellianism is but Unitarianism in disguise"... Three days later [writing to Rose on 6 Aug. 1835 (*LD* v. 115)], referring again to Blanco's book, he was beginning to see its value "as a witness to the tendency of certain views". Then, to Froude on 9 August, came the first of his declarations that study of Dionysius leads inevitably to Apollinarian controversy' (ibid. 89). On 15 August, Newman began with 'a rough draft written on the "defection of Apollinaris"' (ibid. 90).

[31] What he writes to Froude is almost word for word the same as in a set of undated notes with a series of questions in OM B.3.5, the first being: 'Qn. on Cyril's μία φύσις σεσαρκωμένη.' In these notes, Newman compares 'Evidence pro the use of Persona' with 'Evidence against the use of it' as the basis for his statement at Apoll 2 n. 1: 'Cyril calls it... ὑπόστασις, though not πρόσωπον.'

[32] OM B.3.5, dated 10 Aug. 1835.

purported communications with Paul were genuine.[33] Moreover, a note at the top of this page tells him to see 'the comparison of Paul and Nestorius in the Contestation' (meaning the charges on Eusebius of Dorylaeum's placard)—a hint at Newman's future course of study in Nestorianism, mentioned in the letter to Froude. Such study was necessary to check that Routh was wrong to date the Confession against Paul from the same time as Eusbius's placard, but would wait until the summer of 1839.

Newman's research into the Apollinarian controversy in 1835 exists in two major papers, 'Apollinaris' history' of 19 August[34] and 'Apollinarianism' of 22 August.[35] The first paper, a narrative, would be published the following July, with some alteration, under the title 'Life and Ideas of the Heresiarch, Apollinaris' as part of Newman's series of 'Letters' for the *British Magazine* and later in *The Church of the Fathers* (1840) and in volume i of *Historical Sketches* (1872). The second paper (herein called Apoll) is an engagement with Apollinarian Christology that was not published until 1874 in *Tracts Theological and Ecclesiastical*, by which stage it had undergone major modifications (shown in the comparisons to *TT* which follow). The second paper was printed and bound together with an abstract of 'Monophysite Heresy' from 23 August 1839 for private circulation.[36] Perhaps the parallels between the two summers of research appealed to Newman; in any case, the bibliographies in this bound volume helpfully show his reading matter in the summers of 1835 and 1839.

The question of dating the Confession against Paul led to Newman's engagement in the summer of 1835 with *On the Sects*. This work, attributed to Leontius, included a comparison of the followers of Paul with those of, on the one hand, Nestorius and, on

---

[33] OM B.3.5, dated 10 Aug. 1835.untitled page, listing: '1. The Bishops, as by their Synodal letter... 2. The Bishops in their letter to Paulus... 3. Pseudo-Dionysius.' In thinking the third source (Dionysius's letter and his response to Paul's *Ten Questions*) a forgery, Newman agreed with Mosheim (*de reb* ii. 232) and Cave (*Hist Lit* 98) against Tillemont (*Mémoires*, iv. 660–2 n. 8, discussing the French scholarship) and Burton (*Inquiry into the Heresies of the Apostolic Age*, 580), who believed them to be genuine.

[34] OM B.2.5.

[35] OM B.3.5 no. 1.

[36] The editors of *LD* suggest this printing may relate to Newman's proposed preface 'on Apollinarianism' to Charles Daman's edition of Athanasius's *Tracts on the Incarnation and the Holy Spirit* for A Library of the Fathers (*LD* vii. 371 and n. 2).

the other, Sabellius.[37] Here was one option for authorship of the Confession: perhaps those who rejected the Nestorian 'two sons' formula wrote it to connect Nestorius with the heresiarch Paul of Samosata? Yet Leontius said that the Christologies of Nestorius and Paul were different, the latter not accepting that the pre-existent Word dwelt in Christ. Perhaps, instead, the Apollinarians forged the Confession, in order to claim that their opponents were 'Paulianists'? Such a surmise underlies Newman's comment, on 22 August 1835, that the Apollinarians 'accused Catholics of holding two sons, the Son of God and the son of Mary, instead of the One Person of Emmanuel; an imputation in which they often indulged, comparing them to the Paulianists' (Apoll 4).[38] Various pieces of patristic evidence were pointing at Apollinarian authorship of the Confession that summer. Another work by Leontius gathered together Apollinarian forgeries, among them one which spoke of 'the ἄκρα ἔνωσις [perfect union], the *summa unio* of the Word of God with his human nature' (ibid. 4).[39] Theodoret preserved an Apollinarian fragment showing that this phrase meant something similar to the Confession's 'one compound person (σύνθετον πρόσωπον)', which Newman

---

[37] *de Sectis* 2 (PG 86: 1213 D8–1216 B7). Apoll 1 shows that Newman used the Latin translation of sixteenth-century humanist Johannes Leunclavio (in the ten-volume edition of Marguerin de La Bigne's 'Bibl[iotheca Veterum] P[atrum], Paris 1624', which Pusey had bought for him in Germany in 1827). Here the work is attributed to Leontius of Byzantium, as it was by Migne, who used Leunclavio's translation in PG 86, but Marcel Richard has shown it to be by a different Leontius ('Le Traite "De Sectis" et Léonce de Byzance', *Révue d'histoire ecclésiastique*, 35 (1939), 695–723).

[38] *TT* 311 omitted 'an imputation in which they often indulged'.

[39] For ἄκρα ἔνωσις, see *Adversus Fraudes Apollinaristarum* (PG 86: 1965 D1–6). Newman used Latin because he only had available the sixteenth-century translation of Leontius by the Spanish scholar Francisco Torres (which he read in the Bodleian in Marguerin de La Bigne's *Bibliotheca Patrum*, published in fourteen volumes by the University of Cologne (cited by Newman as 'Bibl. P. Col. 1618', Apoll 1), to which a one-volume supplement was added in 1622. La Bigne's first edition was published to oppose French Protestants in 1575, and was added to in later editions. A twenty-seven-volume 'Maxima' edition was published (Lyons, 1677) and then rearranged by the Maurist Nicholas Le Nourry (Paris, 1715) and by André Galland (Venice, 1765–81). Leontius's Greek texts were finally published by Angelo Mai (Rome, 1833 and 1844), which Migne used alongside Torres's Latin in PG. My thanks to Brian Daley for his help with Leontius.

had cited to Froude on 9 August.[40] Newman quoted from Ephrem the Syrian (*c*.306–73) on August 22 that the Apollinarians held to a union of human and divine in Christ that resulted in one 'compound nature, different from both' natures of which it was comprised (ibid. 10).[41] Three days earlier he was convinced that Athanasius's *Letter to Epictetus* revealed the folly of this position.[42] Desperate to legitimize themselves, had the Apollinarians forged the Confession against Paul? Newman may still have been pondering the Confession when he made notes 'For the Ante Nicene Incarnation Controversy' on 24 December 1835, but he would make no further progress on the question until 1839.[43]

The final breakthrough came during his third summer working on Dionysius, recorded in a letter of 12 July 1839. Newman wrote to Frederic Rogers that he had finally '*proved*, as I think, what I have long believed, that the word *Persona*, or Πρόσωπον, was not a technical word in the controversy of the Incarnation till after 350–360. This last hit enables me at once to finish Dionysius' (*LD* vii. 105). Newman's notes from July 1839, which provided the background to his paper on 'Monophysite Heresy',[44] show him to have examined the Greek words for

---

[40] 'The testimony of Apollinaris from his "Summary"... "If the complex [σύνθετον] is also one, as man, then he who on account of the union with the flesh says the Word was made flesh, means the one in complexity [σύνθεσιν ἕν]" ' (*Eranistes* 1 (trans.: NPNF)).

[41] *TT* 317 has: 'a compound nature, a σύνθετος οὐσία, which was neither the one nor the other.' The Greek phrase is in Apoll 11 n. 6, quoting the record of Photius, *Bibliotheca* cod. 229 (PG 103: 992 A2) of Ephrem's description of the Apollinarian view of the union. Newman does not question the authenticity of this phrase, even though it is a ninth-century Greek record of a fourth-century writer of Syriac.

[42] The paper on 19 Aug. said of the *Letter*: 'Apollinaris is still unnoticed by name; but tenets kindred to his are described in it', proceeding to translate Athanasius before adding: 'I leave the arrangement and interpretation of these positions, which are shocking to relate, for a proper place' ('Apollinaris' history', 8–9; cf. *HS* i. 395 where this and the translation from *ad Epictetum* 2 are omitted). That proper place was Apoll, dated three days later.

[43] OM B.3.5, e.g., 'Extracts from Beausobre on Manicheeism', referring to Isaac de Beausobre's *Histoire critique de Manichée et du Manichéisme* (1734). Newman had originally used Beausobre's argument to show that 'The history of the word *probole* or *offspring* is parallel to that of the *consubstantial*' (*Ari* 190 n. 7); both words, having been orthodox, were abandoned, the latter at the 'celebrated Council held at Antioch against Paulus of Samosata' (ibid. 192). Was Newman revisiting Beausobre with that Council in mind?

[44] OM B.2.5 (henceforth Mon).

'person' (πρόσωπον and hypostasis) to discern their different meanings at different times.[45] In the pre-Nicene era, from which this Confession was purported to come, Newman found that πρόσωπον did not have any technical meaning with respect to Christ's person, for Clement of Alexandria used it to describe the Son as 'the person of the Father'.[46] But 'person' took on a specific Christological meaning, Newman thought, in the debates raging around the Apollinarian controversy. Thus, of the two words from the Confession's formula, πρόσωπον σύνθετον, Newman's research now showed that the first word carried an Apollinarian meaning, just as his research four summers before showed that the second word did.

The quest was complete and the following summer Newman began his translation and annotation of Athanasius for A Library of the Fathers, drawing on all that he had learned of Dionysius and Paul of Samosata. He wrote to Pusey on 28 July 1840:

I expect the four Orations [against the Arians] will not take much more than 200 pages, to judge by the one I have done ... It seems then expedient to add the De Decretis. *Then* two are left of a doctrinal character, the de Incarnatione Verbi Dei and the de sententia Dionysii. Of these the latter may be dispensed with, as being in part long quotations from Dionysius ... and I would add [instead] a third treatise the De Synodis. (*LD* vii. 371)

Having decided that he would indeed add *On the Councils* (*de Synodis*) to his edition, Newman followed it with an extended note 'On the alleged Confession of Antioch against Paul of Samosata'. In it, he doubted that Malchion's description of Christ as a 'composition' (σύνθεσις) in the fragments of the *Acts* of the Council of Antioch was genuine, even though Leontius recorded it (*Ox Frs* viii. 170).[47] So, although by the early 1840s Newman had lost all

[45] OM B.3.5 e.g. a page dated 13 July 1839 entitled 'Persona', and a piece dated 5 July 1839 entitled 'Eutychianism'.

[46] Newman quoted Clement in *Ox Frs* viii. 172, while annotating Athanasius 1840–2. These annotations will be discussed in Ch. 4, below. There it will be seen that in 1832 Newman took pre-Nicenes like Clement to have understood that the Son represented the Father's 'person'.

[47] OM B.3.5 contains pages dating from the early 1840s on forgeries. John Behr thinks Malchion did speak of the 'synthesis' of divine and human in Christ (*The Way to Nicaea* (New York: SVS Press, 2001), 231). See also ibid. 226 n. 72 for the division among twentieth-century scholars over the authenticity of the *Acts*, G. Bardy agreeing with Newman that they are Apollinarian forgeries.

enthusiasm for quoting Dionysius, he had succeeded in his quest to date the Confession against Paul.

DIONYSIUS OF ALEXANDRIA OR PAUL OF SAMOSATA? (SUMMER 1834–EASTER 1835)

Given that Newman was working on Dionysius and Paul of Samosata in 1834–5, it is not surprising that Newman's preaching about Christ in this period showed a preference for Dionysius's Christology over that of Paul. A Lenten sermon from 8 March 1835 called 'The Humiliation of the Eternal Son' ends with a warning that *all* heresy reduces to a rejection of Christ's divinity. The example that he gives—the reduction of Sabellianism, via Nestorianism, to Ebionitism—mentions the heresies that various Fathers likened to Paul's teaching: Hilary suggesting Paul was Sabellian in his interpretation of *homoousios*,[48] Eusebius of Dorylaeum comparing him to Nestorius, and Eusebius of Caesarea calling him Ebionite.[49] In the sermon, he preaches against those who distinguish, through their 'reason, and dispute',

> between the Christ who lived on earth and the Son of God Most High, speaking of His human nature and His Divine nature so separately as not to feel or understand that God is man and man is God ... I fear I must say (to use the language of ancient theology), that they begin by being Sabellians, that they go on to be Nestorians, and that they tend to be Ebionites and to deny Christ's Divinity altogether. (*PS* iii. 12: 592)

Such rationalists sound like would-be followers of Paul of Samosata, whose sophistry led him to espouse a human Jesus adopted by a 'Sabellian' God, which is to say a God who subsists as different modes or emanations rather than in three hypostases. (Only when reading *de Sectis* in the summer of 1835, did Newman learn the difference,

---

[48] See Hilary's *de Synodis* 81. Ch. 4, below, has more on this.

[49] Burton recorded that in *On the Theology of the Church*, written against Athanasius, 'Eusebius speaks of the doctrine, "which the Ebionites long ago, and Paul of Samosata lately, and those who after him are called Pauliani, had maintained"' (*Inquiry into the Heresies of the Apostolic Age*, 585).

unknown to him in *Arians of the Fourth Century*, between the
Sabellian and the Paulinian Christ.) These rationalists also sound
like those against whom Newman was arguing about subscription to
the Thirty-nine Articles from November 1834 until May 1835.

In Dionysius's writings, by contrast, Newman found Christ
depicted as a fully divine hypostasis. Newman learned from Athanasius that Dionysius

> taxes and corrects those who accuse him of having said that God was the
> creator (of Christ), in that they failed to notice that he had previously
> spoken of God as Father, in which expression the Son also is implied. But
> in saying thus, he shews that the Son is not one of the creatures, and that
> God is not the maker but the Father of His own Word.[50]

Like Origen his teacher, Dionysius argued that the existence of the
'Son', who was revealed in the flesh, is constitutive of what it means
for God to be 'Father'. In other words, there is no God without the
Son of God. When the divine Son became human, he did not cease to
be divine, the divine nature taking to itself a human nature.[51] The
same truth was expressed in opposition to Paul in the Letter of
the Six Bishops during the Council of Antioch: in Christ, they said,
'the body from the Virgin, containing "the whole fullness of divinity
bodily", was united immutably to the divinity and was deified.'[52]
Christ is Son of God become human, the human body only becoming divine by virtue of the Son uniting with it. Neither Origen (who
was dead) nor Dionysius (who died soon after it began) attended the
Council, but other pupils of Origen influenced the Council, among
them Gregory of Neocaesarea and his brother Athenagoras, and
Firmilian of Caesarea (*Ecc Hist* 7. 28). Although the latter would

[50] *de Sententia Dionysii* 21 (trans.: NPNF).

[51] Origen wrote, 'First we must know this, that in Christ there is one nature, his
deity, because he is the only-begotten Son of the Father, and another human nature,
which in very recent times he took upon himself to fulfil the divine purpose. Our first
task therefore is to see what the only-begotten Son of God is, seeing he is called by
many different names according to the circumstances and beliefs of the different
writers' (*de Principiis* 1.2.1).

[52] (Trans. Behr, *Way to Nicaea*, 223.) Given that six of the signatories of the
Synodal Letter also wrote the so-called 'Letter of the Six Bishops', and that Dionysius
and Firmilian had been invited to attend the Council, John Behr writes: 'it is to be
expected that the critics of Paul based themselves on Origen, and thus not surprising
that characteristic elements of Origen's theology are reflected in this letter' (ibid. 221).

die before the conclusion of the Council, the final Synodal Letter
aligns itself with Firmilian's and Dionysius's teachings—and therefore with Origen's—concerning Christ (*Ecc Hist* 7. 28.3). At the
Council, then, Newman thought that Origen's Christology overthrew
Paul's. In what follows, one theme of Origen's Christology in
particular, found in Newman's sermons from Christmas 1834 and
Eastertide 1835, will be discussed.

Following the 'pattern' of Christ's life

An example of Newman preaching the Christology of Origen and
Dionysius in this period came in his Christmas sermon of 1834 called
'The Incarnation'. He preached: 'Ten thousand times more dazzling
bright than the highest Archangel, is our Lord and Christ. By birth
the Only-begotten and express Image of God; and in taking our flesh,
not sullied thereby, but raising human nature with Him...Man shall
judge man at the last day' (*PS* ii. 3: 252). Here is a divine hypostasis
taking on human flesh. And in taking it on, Christ raises human
nature and opens the possibility for the human flesh to be divinized.
This fundamental Alexandrian insight sets divinization ($\theta\epsilon o\pi o\iota\eta\sigma\iota\varsigma$)
as the goal of human life, expressed by Origen as 'knowing God'. As
Andrew Louth paraphrases Origen's *Commentary on John*: 'Knowing
God is being known by God, and that means that God is united to
those who know him, and gives them a share in his divinity.'[53] This
mystical coming-to-know is suggested in Newman's sermon by the
more Augustinian term 'Beatific Vision', although this is not a vision
awaiting death. Newman still expresses the idea propounded in
Arians of the Fourth Century that heretics forced the Church to
formularize her faith into creeds, rather than continue with this
deeper sort of knowing:

For instance, the Athanasian Creed confesses that Christ is 'God of the
substance of the Father'...Such are the terms in which we are constrained
to speak of our Lord and Saviour...We intreat His leave, and we humbly
pray that what was first our defence against pride and indolence, may

[53] Louth, *The Origins of the Christian Mystical Tradition: From Plato to Denys*
(Oxford: Clarendon Press, 1981), 73.

become an outlet of devotion, a service of worship... He will illuminate our earthly words from His own Divine Holiness, till they become saving truths to the souls which trust in Him... And we, while we make use of it, will never so forget its imperfection, as not to look out constantly for the True Beatific Vision. (*PS* ii. 3: 251)

According to Newman's sermon, faith is the fruit not of human formulae but of divine illumination of the words of scripture and creeds. This is similar to Origen's view of the scriptures as able to open up to give a 'spiritual' meaning. To discern this spiritual meaning requires the exegete to learn from Christ the 'spiritual' meaning of the 'carnal' words of scripture. As Origen said in the *Commentary on John* (1. 10), for instance, the spiritual meaning of Isaiah 52: 7 is to praise 'the feet of those who walk in the intellectual way of Christ Jesus, and through that door go into God [i.e. θεοποίησις]. They announce good tidings, those whose feet are beautiful, namely, Jesus'.[54]

The illumination of the intellect, which Origen and Newman desire, is made possible only by the resurrected Jesus. As Origen put it in *Against Celsus* (2.1) with reference to the Jewish law, after the resurrection the Apostle Peter 'learned from Jesus to ascend from the law that is regulated according to the letter, to that which is interpreted according to the spirit'. Such learning is Christological, for Origen, because those like the Ebionites who misunderstand Christ misunderstand scripture too and cannot therefore go through the door to God.[55] It has already been seen that Newman's research into the relation of Ebion to Paul of Samosata led him to mention Ebionite Christology in a Lenten sermon of 1835 directed against the rationalists of his own days. It is also possible that he saw a likeness between the pagan philosopher Celsus, who mocked the fables of the Bible, and the rationalists.

---

[54] (ANF trans.) Although Newman had not read much Origen for *Arians of the Fourth Century* he was able to use the past tense in Oct. 1836 to praise 'what I read of his "against Celsus"' (*LD* v. 368). I have no proof that he read the *Commentary on John*, but he knew enough about the gospel commentaries to describe Origen's exegetical method.

[55] Origen notes here that, in Hebrew, the name 'Ebion signifies "poor" among the Jews, and those Jews who have received Jesus as Christ [*i.e. but have remained under the Jewish law*] are called by the name of Ebionites' (ANF trans.)

Against the rationalists who, in using their intellect, misunderstood Christ, Newman followed Origen in making the resurrected Christ his intellectual pattern of life. Roderick Strange has shown how important the idea of Christ as a 'pattern' was to Newman in connecting Christ's life with our growth in holiness in imitation of him, but does not speculate whence the idea came.[56] Origen's use of 'pattern' seems to lie behind Newman's engagement with questions of how the Son of God can suffer, and how in our sufferings are we like the Son. For example, Origen wrote in *Against Celsus* 2.42:

not understanding that the Logos had become the man Jesus, [Celsus] would have Him to be subject to no human weakness, nor to become an illustrious *pattern* to men of the manner in which they ought to bear the calamities of life … seeing that he regards labour to be the greatest of evils, and pleasure the perfect good. (ANF trans., my italics).

There are similarities here with Newman's equally rhetorical sermon on the Third Sunday after Easter 1835, entitled 'Bodily Suffering', in which he calls upon his hearers to follow the 'pattern' of Christ and renounce the pleasure of worldly goods:

Pain, which by nature leads us only to ourselves, carries on the Christian mind from the thought of self to the contemplation of Christ, His passion, His merits, and His *pattern*; and, thence, further to that united company of sufferers who follow Him and 'are what He is in this world.' He is the great Object of our faith; and, while we gaze upon Him, we learn to forget ourselves. (*PS* iii. 11: 577, my italics)

The ascetical disciplines adopted by Newman, which he considered as integral to the ethos of the Oxford Movement, reflect Origen's teachings on union with Christ.[57] Newman's concern with ethos was patterned not only on Christ, therefore, but on Christ's person and words as interpreted by Origen.

[56] Roderick Strange, *Newman and the Gospel of Christ* (Oxford: Clarendon Press, 1981), 52.
[57] Christ 'ever chose the good, even before he knew the evil at all … so, too, should each one of us, after a fall or a transgression, cleanse himself from the stains by the example set before him, and taking a leader for the journey proceed along the steep path of virtue, that so perchance by this means we may as far as is possible become, through our imitation of him, partakers of the divine nature' (*de Principiis* 4.4.4).

CYRIL OF ALEXANDRIA OR APOLLINARIUS?
(SUMMER 1835–EASTER 1836)

In a letter to his Aunt Elizabeth on 9 August 1835, Newman explained why he could not focus all of his attention on the edition of Dionysius. 'I have far graver objects in view,' he wrote, 'I mean, one must expect a flood of scepticism on the most important subjects to pour over the land, and we are so unprepared, it is quite frightful to think of it. The most religiously-minded men are ready to give up important doctrinal truths because they do not *understand their value*' (*LD* v. 120). Yet this sent him not away from patristic research, but deeper into it. The devaluation of Christian doctrine, as he saw it, by the 'religiously-minded'—indeed by Oxford dons like Hampden and Blanco White—made clear to Newman the need for a return to orthodoxy in the face of contemporary 'scepticism'. And this was because he saw in the life of Apollinarius what would happen if 'the speculations of a self-willed and presumptuous intellect' were not kept in check by 'the range which Scripture had prescribed, and the Church Catholic witnessed'.[58]

What most troubled Newman about Apollinarius was his use of logic at the expense of scripture and tradition. In *Arians of the Fourth Century*, he made this charge against Paul of Samosata and Arius, who ignored the Rule of Faith when interpreting scripture. Writing in 'Apollinarianism', Newman now laments that Apollinarius thought he was opposing Arianism with 'a strong and (what may be called) intelligible doctrine, asserting with more or less clearness...not merely that Christ was more than man, but that he was simply the Eternal Son, either without the addition of a human nature, or with only its nominal addition' (Apoll 2). The Apollinarians forgot the richness of scriptural truth and tradition, taking instead 'a plain and broad view of the subject which, while rescuing them from

[58] 'Apollinaris' history', 11. This became in 1840: 'While indulging in the speculations of a private judgment, he might still endeavour to persuade himself that he was not outstepping the range which Scripture had prescribed, and the Church Catholic witnessed' (see alterations at *CF* 635) and in 1872: 'he was not outstepping the teaching of the Catholic Church' (*HS* i. 396).

Humanitarianism, saved them also from the irritation of mind occasioned by that subtle orthodox phraseology which had been rendered
necessary by Arianism itself' (ibid. 2). In this one complex sentence,
Newman is dealing with three of his favourite themes: his rejection
of interpreting scripture only at a surface level; his opposition to
R. D. Hampden and Blanco White, whose 'humanitarianism' left
them irritated by orthodoxy; and his nostalgia for pre-Nicene
doxology before Arianism had forced the 'subtle phraseology' of a
formulized faith. These three become a unified argument: while
rightly opposing the Arians' sophistry, Apollinarius nevertheless
replaced their arguments with sophistry of his own, ignoring the
Rule of Faith as much as any nineteenth-century rationalist.

Certainly there was an aspect of Apollinarius's thought that
appealed to Newman, as Thomas has pointed out.[59] Both thinkers
began with the 'Church's "great article": that the Personality of God is
his Divine Essence, so that his manhood is "but an addition to his real
nature" '.[60] However, in the work of Cyril, Newman found a far more
fruitful way than that of Apollinarius to pursue a Christology built on
this Alexandrian foundation. After all, Apollinarius had gone on from
this great article of faith to 'a denial of the intellectual principle, or
νοῦς, in our Lord's human nature', so that he might guard 'against the
doctrine of a double personality, or what was afterwards called Nestorianism' (Apoll 6–7; cf. *TT* 310). From summer 1835 to spring 1836,
Newman came to realize *why* Apollinarius's opposition to a (Nestorian) idea of two Sons in Christ was illegitimate and *why* Cyril's idea of
the 'hypostatic union' was right. Cyril had used this terminology in
his second letter to Nestorius, arguing that, in the incarnation, the
divine hypostasis of the Son united full humanity to himself, which is
to say a humanity comprised of body *and* soul. But the locus of
Christ's 'personhood' was not the body and soul but the hypostasis.
In preaching this, Newman espoused the broadly Alexandrian Christology that he could trace back to Origen.[61]

[59] Thomas describes Newman, in his affinity for Apollinarius, as 'very close to the
heretic' (*Newman and Heresy*, 143).

[60] Ibid. 99, quoting Apoll 2.

[61] Origen had written: 'we must believe that there did exist in Christ a human and
rational soul, and yet not suppose that it had any susceptibility to or possibility of sin'
(*de Principiis* 2.6.5).

The change that this focus on the hypostatic union wrought in
Newman's Christology between 1835 and 1836 will be considered
here by comparing four Lenten sermons—two from either side of his
research into Apollinarius and Cyril. 'The Humiliation of the Eternal
Son' and 'Tears of Christ at the Grave of Lazarus' were preached in
Lent 1835, while 'The Incarnate Son, a Sufferer and Sacrifice' and
'Christ, the Son of God Made Man' date from Lent 1836. All four
sermons are based on a series of presuppositions that he considered
Alexandrian. But it is also the case that Newman's Christology had
changed in a year, as will be shown in three areas: his shifting opinion
of the term 'instrument' (ὄργανον), his language regarding Christ's
human mind (νοῦς), and his use of the 'communication of idioms' in
depicting Christ's person.

The human in Christ as an instrument

Apollinarius, as a follower and friend of Athanasius, shared many of his
opinions. Indeed, Newman judged, in 'Apollinaris' history' on 19
August 1835, that the pain which Athanasius felt at Apollinarius's
defection led him to avoid mentioning the latter's name in three letters
on Apollinarian themes and 'in a work written by Athanasius on the
same subject in the very end of his life with the vigor and richness of
thought of his which distinguish his earlier writings', meaning *On the
Incarnation against Apollinarius*.[62] As Newman noted three days later,
here Athanasius challenged his friend's description of Christ's outward
'form as but an organ, an instrument of manifesting Him [σχῆμα
ὀργανικόν]...and having no value or use except as effecting this'
(Apoll 5).[63] Yet the problem was that Athanasius had earlier in

---

[62] 'Apollinaris' history', 9; cf. *HS* i. 395. In Mar. 1879, in a letter to William Bright
concerning the provenance of various works attributed to Athanasius, Newman
wrote: 'I have never felt...the contra Apollinarem [was not by Athanasius]' (*LD*
xxix. 75). Although Bright and, after him, Robertson (NFPF [series 2] 4: lxiv) agree
with Newman, J. F. Bethune-Baker in 1903 thought it 'probably not the work of
Athanasius', on the basis of late nineteenth-century German scholarship (see *An
Introduction to the Early History of Christian Doctrine to the Time of the Council of
Chalcedon* (5th edn.; London: Methuen, 1933), 240 n. 1).

[63] *TT* 313 rearranges word order and, in the note, instead of Apoll n. 3's correct
citation of *Contra Apollinarem* 1.2, 15, mistakenly cites *Contra Apollinarem* 1.2, 14.

his writings used the idea of Christ's body as an 'instrument' and as a garment 'surrounding him' ($\pi\epsilon\rho\grave{\iota}$ $\alpha\grave{\upsilon}\tau\acute{o}\nu$)—and so, in a sermon earlier that year, had Newman.

In his anti-Arian writings, Athanasius interpreted 'He created me' from Proverbs 8: 22 with words that Apollinarius could draw upon. The patriarch wrote: 'we must not conceive that the whole Word is in nature a creature, but that He put on the created body and that God created Him for our sakes, preparing for Him the created body.'[64] Newman's sermon of March 1835, 'The Humiliation of the Eternal Son', conceives the human nature of the divine Son in Athanasian terms as an instrument which the Son uses to save us. He preaches: 'The flesh which [Christ] had assumed was but the instrument through which He acted for and towards us . . . having clothed Himself with a created essence, He made it the instrument of His humiliation; He acted in it, He obeyed and suffered through it' (*PS* iii. 12: 588–9). The *work* of salvation is a key Athanasian insight, and Newman only uses the idea of an instrument when referring to the Son's work in the flesh.[65] In this enterprise, the flesh is an instrument of God, which is precisely *not* to hold the Arian position that the Son is an instrument of the Father. Newman says that, even in the incarnation, 'In [the Son's] eternal union with God there was no distinction of will and *work* between Him and His Father; as the Father's life was the Son's life, and the Father's glory the Son's also, so the Son was the very Word and Wisdom of the Father, His Power and Co-Equal Minister in all things' (ibid. 587, my italics).

However, after his research, Newman recognized that Athanasius's image could be misunderstood—as it was by Apollinarius—to mean that Christ 'was the Logos, clad in a human body' rather than hypostatically united to full humanity (Apoll 7; omitted from *TT*). As a result, in his 1836 Lenten sermons, Newman tried to protect against Apollinarius's misunderstanding. The sermon 'Christ, the Son of God Made Man' says that, in Christ taking humanity upon him,

---

[64] Discourse II. 47.

[65] Newman continued to preach this in 1836: 'He took upon Him our nature, as an instrument of His purposes, *not as an agent in the work*' (*PS* vi. 5: 1225, my italics). The agent in this work is divine.

it must not be supposed, because it was an instrument, or because in the text [Heb. 9: 11] it is called a tabernacle, that therefore it was not intimately one with [the Son], or that it was merely like what is commonly meant by a tabernacle, which a man dwells in, and may come in and out of; or like an instrument, which a man takes up and lays down. Far from it; though His Divine Nature was sovereign and supreme when he became incarnate, yet the manhood which He assumed was not kept at a distance from Him (if I may so speak) as a mere instrument, or put on as a mere garment, or entered as a mere tabernacle, but was really taken into the closest and most ineffable union with Him. (*PS* vi. 5: 1227)

Firstly, notice that the focus has shifted from the Son's 'union with God' in 1835 to the Son's own 'ineffable union' with humanity in 1836, suggesting that the hypostatic union is uppermost in Newman's Christology at the later date. Secondly, the sermon stresses the *difference* inherent in analogies between human life and God's life. For while Athanasius writes that the Logos 'put on a created body', he did not do so in the same way a human puts on, say, a boiler suit, or a spacesuit, to do a special job.[66] The difference in the two terms in any analogy, especially an analogy predicated of a divine nature, prevents Athanasius being taken to mean that the Logos is the same as a space traveller and his flesh merely a suit. Newman, here, shows his continuing interest in the rules of speech. Having (he hopes) properly safeguarded the image of the garment, Newman goes on: 'He surrounded Himself with it' ($\pi\epsilon\rho\grave{\iota}$ $\alpha\grave{\upsilon}\tau\acute{o}\nu$), as well as, 'He lodged it within Him; and thenceforth the Eternal Word, the Son of God, the Second Person in the Blessed Trinity, had two natures' (*PS* vi. 5: 1228). The second statement subverts the garment image by suggesting it is just as correct to say that the flesh had the Logos surrounding it (which would again be $\pi\epsilon\rho\grave{\iota}$ $\alpha\grave{\upsilon}\tau\acute{o}\nu$).

In 1836, Newman wants the human, whom the Logos assumes, to be *fully human*, agreeing with Cyril that this means it must be substantive, but not so as to replace the divine person (hypostasis) with a human one. This is a difficult position to hold, and seems to be forced on Newman just as much as on Cyril by the fear of

---

[66] The spacesuit image is the old chestnut of R. P. C. Hanson (*The Search for the Christian Doctrine of God* (Edinburgh: T. & T. Clark, 1988), 448).

accusations of Apollinarianism. One way to avoid such accusations was to accept that the human Jesus had a mind of his own and to be truly human that mind must be born ignorant. The sermons that followed his work on Apollinarianism reveal that Newman became aware of the shortcomings of Athanasian language and trying to find a way to make him safe. In the face of Apollinarius's arguments, Newman recognizes two directions he might take in clarifying his Christology: Cyril or Nestorius? Either, like Cyril, he could stress that the two minds of Christ, human and divine, were coextensive in a single person. Or, he could take a Nestorian line that there were two Sons in Jesus Christ, one divine and one human, and that the twain need never meet.

The ignorance of Christ in his human mind

In further reaction to the Apollinarian heresy, then, Newman accepted in his 1836 sermons that Christ could be ignorant in his human intellect ($\nu o\hat{\upsilon}s$) without that threatening the omniscience of his hypostasis. He would later discover, to his surprise, that preaching a Christ capable of ignorance was also heresy. Looking back in a letter of March 1846 to his old friend Henry Wilberforce, he recalls his 'own mistake' at this time 'was saying that our Lord was "allknowing as God, ignorant as man." Almost all the Fathers of the Fourth Century, I believe, say the same—but the Church has since determined such doctrine to be heresy' (*LD* xi. 135). In 1835–6, Newman was unaware that such doctrine was heretical, and preferred Athanasius's arguments against the Arians, which allowed Christ to grow in wisdom, to those of Apollinarians, who in denying Christ a human intellect denied any capacity for growth. Various Arians made much of the scripture reference to Christ's growing in wisdom (Luke 2: 52). How could the Son 'grow' in knowledge if he were unchangeably God? Obviously, Arius said, the Son was not God, arguing along the lines rehearsed by Williams both that the Son is free to grow but 'that God, in endowing the Son with [the] dignity of heavenly intimacy from the very beginning of his existence . . . know[s] that his firstborn among creatures is and always will always be worthy of the highest degree of grace, a perfect channel for creative and redemptive action'.[67] Williams suggests that to Athanasian ears such logic 'may sound rather tortuous'. Athanasius tried to portray Arius as holding that grace *came to* the Logos in his incarnate ministry, advancing him from a human to a quasi-divine status. Athanasius thus accused the Arians of thinking like the 'Samosatene'.[68]

While Arian Christology interpreted Luke 2: 52 to show that the Logos was a creature, it was of the utmost importance for Athanasius to demonstrate that the text showed something else. But Athanasius recognizes the interpretive problem with which he is faced, arguing that the text cannot mean what it seems to mean because, 'If He advanced when He became man, it is plain that, before He became man, He was imperfect'.[69] Neither Athanasius nor, admittedly, Arius wanted to accept imperfection in the Logos. So the text must be interpreted alternatively. For Athanasius, because the wisdom of the Logos was continuously being revealed in the human, it appeared to those around him *as if* Jesus Christ were increasing in wisdom. Really, of course, he only advanced in his human nature, for 'how did Wisdom advance in wisdom?' and 'how did He who to others gives grace . . . advance in grace?'[70]

But still Athanasius is open to the charge that 'natural' growth of the human soul is irrelevant to Christ, and therefore Christ's humanity is not like others' humanity. In spite of Athanasius's claim that all humanity advanced when 'He promoted the things which needed promotion',[71] is the human Jesus really growing in wisdom as any human would, and in any way that we (even with grace) could follow? Rather, he is advancing by virtue of the Logos. Even if Jesus's soul does grow in wisdom in a way that other humans can follow, when it comes to those moments which require divine insight—for instance, at Lazarus's tomb, or on the cross—then the Logos takes over and trumps human ignorance and suffering with divine knowledge. This seems to be Newman's own position in the 1835 sermon, 'Tears of Christ at the Grave of Lazarus', that Christ *in his humanity* was filled with the knowledge that he had as Logos. For in this Lenten sermon he said:

[67] Williams, *Arius* (2nd edn.; London: Student Christian Movement, 2001), 114–15.

[68] Discourse I. 38.   [69] Discourse III. 51.

[70] Ibid.   [71] Discourse I. 38.

Here was the Creator of the world at a scene of death, seeing the issue of His gracious handiwork. Would not He revert in thought to the hour of creation, when He went forth from the bosom of the Father to bring all things into existence? There had been a day when He had looked upon the work of His love, and seen that it was 'very good.' Whence had the good been turned to evil, the fine gold become dim? (*PS* iii. 10: 568–9)

If these were Christ's thoughts upon seeing the grave of his friend Lazarus, this would imply that the human mind had access, as it were, to divine omniscience. But then did the human mind of Jesus fulfil any function? How is the divine mind not imposing itself upon the human? From here it was a small step to Apollinarianism, a danger Newman seems to have realized later that year. In his work in August 1835, he wrote of the heretics: 'they alleged, that a human soul was unnecessary to the Son of God, who was already provided with an infinite intelligence, which supplied every need' (Apoll 5).[72]

In two unpublished sermons from 1836, Newman faced up to the theological difficulty of conceiving divine omniscience in a fully human Christ. Such sermons are like thought experiments, as Roderick Strange observes (although the latter misses the reaction to Apollinarianism which they contain).[73] The first of these unpublished sermons argues:

That our Blessed Lord and Saviour took upon Him a human soul as well as a body is proved, if it be necessary to prove it, by His fearing, sorrowing, being in an agony, praying the cup might pass from Him, and feeling Himself forsaken by the Father. The Son of God in His original nature never could have these feelings—they are human—they are feelings of a human soul— they are not bodily feelings. They are neither of the body, nor again of the Son of God—they evidence the presence of a human soul, which He took to Himself as His own as well as the body, even a perfect manhood—and acts

---

[72] *TT* 312 has: 'they said that a human intellect was unnecessary to the Incarnate Word, whose infinite intelligence would supply every need which a human mind could answer.' The later Newman often changed his earlier use of 'Son of God' to 'Word' and vice versa (see Ch. 5, below).

[73] Strange writes of sermons 407 and 408 that 'Newman posed the difficulty and in each he offered not a solution—"I will not presume to decide how really is the case"—but an account which illustrated how the statements affirming the two minds in Christ could be reconciled' (*Newman and the Gospel of Christ*, 72, quoting sermon no. 407: 14).

according to it, being inseparably united to it, when and as far as He pleased.[74]

The inseparability of this union is Cyrilline, for the person who is the subject of this union is 'the Son of God in His original nature'. The divine person is the locus of all the actions and feelings and memories of the human Jesus:

As a man of self-control can turn away from his own thoughts, suspend his memory, make unknown to himself what he knows, not have what he has, then take it again, as he knows how to *let out* his feelings, how to *repress* them, and how to be serious, and how to be mirthful, so in some unknown way did our Saviour rule that manhood, which He had made part of Himself, though ever distinct and entire in itself in His one indivisible person.[75]

The human Jesus experiences these feelings and memories, for instance his growth in wisdom; nevertheless, in this analogy it is the Logos who chooses when to 'suspend his memory... to let out his feelings [and] to repress them'.

On the face of it, here Newman appears close to the Apollinarian position he described the previous summer, for Christ was not 'a man' in the strict sense that he was more properly the Word 'clad in a human body' (Apoll 7). In fact, he was preaching the ideas of Cyril. In 'Christ, the Son of God Made Man', from Lent 1836, he preached that Christ 'was not, strictly speaking, in the English sense of the word, *a* man... As He had no earthly father, so has He no human personality' (*PS* vi. 5: 1225). In other words, because Jesus Christ is a person only by virtue of the divine Word—he is the second hypostasis of the Trinity rather than '*a* man'—and this hypostasis is Son of God, not son of Joseph. But, although Christ has no human personality, the Son took on humanity '(if we may dare so to speak) almost as a new attribute of His Person' (*PS* vi. 5: 1227). The cautionary parenthesis is perhaps for the sake of his audience, for Newman himself endorsed the idea of a communication of properties (ἀντίδοσις ἰδιομάτων) that he found in Cyril. The sermon states shortly after: 'He acted through both of [the natures], sometimes

---

[74] Sermon no. 407: 1 (quoted ibid. 71).
[75] Sermon no. 407: 15 (quoted ibid. 73).

through both at once, sometimes through One and not through the other, as Almighty God acts sometimes by the attribute of justice, sometimes by that of love, sometimes through both together' (*PS* vi. 5: 1228). With the incarnation, according to Cyril and his followers like John of Caesarea, humanity became another of the divine person's attributes (ἰδιομάτα). The origins of this teaching will now be explored.

The communication of idioms

Scripture predicates both divine and human attributes of Jesus. Origen pondered the metaphysics behind this:

the Son of God is said to have died, in virtue of that nature which could certainly admit of death... And for this reason, throughout the whole of scripture, while the divine nature is spoken of in human terms[,] the human nature is in its turn adorned with marks that belong to the divine prerogative.[76]

The way in which Christ is 'spoken of' here expresses something of the mystery of his person: 'if [a human mind] thinks of God, it sees a man; if it thinks of man, it beholds one returning from the dead with spoils after vanquishing the kingdom of death.'[77] It is not that the natures swap their properties—so that divinity can die and humanity can vanquish death—but, rather, that both divine and human properties can be predicated of (and only of) Christ's *person*. Newman placed himself in this tradition in Lent 1836, commenting on various texts from John's gospel:

take the following passages of scripture: 'I do nothing of Myself;' 'He that sent Me is with Me;' 'the Father hath not left Me alone;' 'My Father worketh hitherto, and I work;' 'Whatsoever I speak, even as the Father said unto Me, so I speak;' 'I am in the Father, and the Father in Me.' Now, it is true, these

---

[76] *de Principiis* 2.6.3. On Origen as the first to use this manner of speaking, see Brian E. Daley's entry 'Idioms, Communication of', in Lacoste, *Encyclopedia of Christian Theology*, ii. 747–8. As far as I can find, Newman did not use the phrase 'communication of idioms' until his translation of Athanasius at *Ox Frs* xix. 348 n. i; 443 n. h.

[77] *de Principiis* 2.6.2.

passages may be understood of our Lord's human nature; but, surely, if we confine them to this interpretation, we run the risk of viewing Christ as two separate beings, not as one Person; or, again, of gradually forgetting or explaining away the doctrine of His Divinity altogether. (*PS* vi. 5: 1223–4)

Newman thinks that Christ's human properties are better predicated of his person than 'of our Lord's human nature'.[78]

By the time of Cyril, Basil of Caesarea had also developed this tradition, distinguishing between the *ousia* of God on the one hand and the properties or idioms predicated of God on the other. Those idioms included Christ's designation as 'way, truth, and life' as well as the Trinitarian names 'Father' and 'Son'.[79] Basil employed the terminology of metaphysics to argue that such idioms were predicated of God in an analogous way to the particulars predicated of individual humans, while the *ousia* of God was predicated analogously to a universal nature: idioms 'do not reveal the nature of Paul *qua* human, but do characterize him as a particular individual'.[80] Thus Basil set the scene for Cyril to show how one of the Trinitarian hypostases, differentiated by his properties or idioms as Son, had preserved the divine *ousia* of his hypostasis while uniting with a human nature—what Cyril called the 'hypostatic union'. As John McGuckin puts it: 'up to the time of Cyril it would be fair to say that the [tradition] had been able to clarify its doctrine of the "Eternal Logos" (the Trinitarian relationships) far more satisfactorily than it had its conception of how the Logos entered into full communion with a particular historical and relativised life in the incarnation'.[81] Cyril changed all that by, among other strategies, portraying the hypostatic union as

---

[78] Not viewing Christ as two separate beings nor forgetting his divinity were themes 'in his first unpublished sermon of the set in 1836, [when] he noted the way some heretics had denied the true humanity of Christ, others his true divinity, and others again had denied "that God *became* man, considering the Son of God and the Son of man to be two distinct beings, the one condescending to dwell in the other." He commented: "None of the three took in the true notion of the *Christ*, the one Christ, at once God and man"' (*Newman and the Gospel of Christ*, 62).

[79] See Lewis Ayres, *Nicaea and its Legacy: An Approach to Fourth-Century Trinitarian Theology* (Oxford: Clarendon Press, 2004), 191–207.

[80] Ibid. 201, paraphrasing *Contra Eunomium* 2.4.

[81] John McGuckin, *Saint Cyril of Alexandria and the Christological Controversy* (Crestwood, NY: SVS Press, 2004), 178.

analogous to the union of body and soul in a human, a useful analogy given that the soul, because incorporeal, was held to be impassible yet still subject to bodily passions.[82] Newman agreed with Cyril.[83]

Preached on Palm Sunday 1836, 'The Incarnate Son, a Sufferer and Sacrifice' represents Newman at his most Cyrilline. He says that the Son 'added a new nature to Himself, yet so intimately, that it was *as if* He had actually left His former self, which He did not' (*PS* vi.6: 1231–2). Here, the divine person has become so intimate with the flesh he took on it was 'as if' humanity were his *only* nature. The consequences are clear:

> As the soul acts through the body as its instrument,—in a more perfect way, but as intimately, did the Eternal Word of God act through the manhood which He had taken. When He spoke, it was literally God speaking; when He suffered, it was God suffering. Not that the Divine Nature itself could suffer, any more than our soul can see or hear; but, as the soul sees and hears through the organs of the body, so God the Son suffered *in* that human nature which He had taken to Himself and made His own. (*PS* vi. 6: 1232)

Newman makes it plain here that to say God's Son was among us is 'not a figurative way of speaking, or a rhetorical form of words'; rather 'it is a literal and simple truth'. Based on a communication of idioms, divine speech is predicated of the person of Christ so that as the human vocal chords move, God 'literally' speaks.[84] The actor in the flesh was none other than God's eternal Son.

Notice that the unity of human and divine in Christ's person is analogous to the 'soul act[ing] through the body'. Newman needs to speak analogically because inherent within such modes of speech, of

---

[82] See Frances M. Young, *From Nicaea to Chalcedon: A Guide to the Literature and its Background* (London: Student Christian Movement, 1983), 261. Young provides a good introduction to the relationship of the Christologies of 'Cyril, Athanasius and Apollinarius' (pp. 258–63).

[83] He had already used this analogy (preserved in the Athanasian Creed) in Lent 1835: 'Just as we speak of seeing our friends, though we do not see their souls but merely their bodies, so the Apostles, Disciples, Priests, and Pharisees, and the multitude, all who saw Christ in the flesh, saw, as the whole earth will see at the last day, the Very and Eternal Son' (*PS* iii. 12: 588).

[84] See Thomas Weinandy, *Does God Suffer?* (Edinburgh: T. & T. Clark, 2000), esp. 199–206.

course, is the *difference* that prevents one saying that the human flesh
assumed by the Logos is the mere instrument or garment posited by
Apollinarianism. A recapitulation of Newman's criticism of Apollinarianism shows the difference between a heretical use of the communication of idioms and Cyril's use. Newman recognized that
Apollinarian heretics did not use the analogy for the hypostatic
union of the human body and soul, but instead saw in that union a
new compound of divinity and humanity: 'Let it be observed, they
did not merely say that the Incarnation was *analogous* to the union of
soul and body, as the Athanasian Creed says, and the Eutychians after
their time, but that it *was* such a union (Apoll 9).[85] The result,
Newman thought, was to introduce *change* into Christ's human
and divine natures, which 'go together to make up a new third', 'a
compound nature' (ibid. 10; cf. *TT* 317). Cyril recognized that there
must be difference between the natures in order for them to be in
'union' at all, or else they would collapse into sameness.[86] Cyril is
implied with this mention of Cyril's follower Eutyches. At this stage
of his thought, Newman saw Eutychian heresy as superior to the
Apollinarian heresy: Eutyches followed Cyril in using the body–soul
analogy properly of the union of human and divine in Christ. Some
have suggested that is because Newman was Eutychian himself,[87]
which might explain why in 1839 he engaged so fully with the
Eutychians' faults.

[85] *TT* 317 sounds more confident about the right and wrong sides on this
question: 'he did not merely say that the Incarnation was analogous to the union
of soul and body, as the Athanasian Creed rightly teaches, and as the Eutychians
afterwards perversely maintained, but that it was an actual instance of that union.'
This reflects what he wrote in 1844: 'The Athan[asian] Creed compares the Hypostatic Union to that of soul and body in one man, which, as taken literally by the
Monophysites became their heresy' (*Ox Frs* xix. 359 n. f).

[86] It is by no means certain that Apollinarius did not mean something very similar
to Cyril when using the analogy. See John Behr, *The Nicene Faith*, 2 vols. (New York:
SVS Press, 2004.), ii. 391.

[87] Strange says David Newsome, Hilda Graef, and Gabriel Daly hold that Newman
was a near Monophysite ('Newman and the Mystery of Christ', 323). For the same
reason, Yngve Brilioth claims that Newman 'finds it difficult to account for the tears
at Lazarus' grave' (*The Anglican Revival: Studies in the Oxford Movement* (London:
Longmans, 1925), 223).

LEO OR EUTYCHES—OR LEONTIUS OF
BYZANTIUM? (SUMMER 1839–EASTER 1840)

Newman later recalled of the summer of 1839: 'About the middle of
June I began to study and master the history of the Monophysites.
I was absorbed in the doctrinal question ... It was during this course
of reading that for the first time a doubt came upon me of the
tenableness of Anglicanism' (*Apo* 108). In spite of the doctrinal
focus of the second sentence, the point has been made that Newman's
doubts about 'the tenableness of Anglicanism' related to the mode of
decision-making employed by the Council of Chalcedon rather than
to 'the doctrinal question' of Christ's person in the Council's Definition.[88] Were not those who opposed the Council's decisions, who
argued that they were the *real* upholders of the truths of Cyril and
Athanasius, just like those who opposed Roman innovation with the
argument that Anglicanism held unchangingly to the truths of the
Fathers? Which left Newman's own Tractarian party 'in the position
of the Oriental communion, Rome was, where she now is; and the
Protestants were the Eutychians' (ibid.). This *ex post facto* account of
Newman's first doubts about the Church of his birth sounds like it
was influenced by Wiseman's comparison of Anglicanism with
Donatism in the *Dublin Review*, which, when Newman read it in
September 1839, gave him a 'stomach-ache ... at the end of' his
Monophysite research (*LD* vii. 154).[89] Yet the connection that New-
man claims to have seen thereafter (*Apo* 110), between the Donatist–
Anglican analogy and Monophysitism, hardly appears in Newman's
work at the time.[90]

---

[88] See, e.g., M. Svaglic's n. 108 at *Apo* 540 and Thomas, *Newman and Heresy*,
204–5.

[89] At the time, judging by a letter to Cardinal Wiseman from Oct. 1841 that he
never sent, Newman's patristic work was not drawing him from the Church of
England but rather was 'in the interests of Catholic unity among us. Though we
cannot conciliate our people to you, we can dispose their minds towards conciliation
by recalling them to primitive truth' (*LD* viii. 297).

[90] The only connection that Thomas can find in late 1839 is the 'might seem' of the
first sentence of this quotation from the 1840 article 'The Catholicity of the English
Church' (*Critic* 27): 'The Monophysites got possession of whole districts, and might
seem, if any men, identified with the local Churches in those districts'—the point

This section will oppose the view that Newman saw in Pope Leo the ecclesiastical decision maker *par excellence* and that the history of Chalcedon was an impetus to Newman's movement towards Rome. Moreover, without speculating on the role comparisons between Monophysitism and Anglicanism played in Newman's conversion, it is wrong to claim that such comparisons were not 'a doctrinal question' for him. The 1839 research showed that when the 'doctrinal question' of the composition of Christ's person was posed at Chalcedon, the Definition of 'two natures in one person' represented a *development* away from Cyril's formula 'one incarnate nature', which the Monophysites upheld. Before Newman, Anglicans had not bothered much with either the Monophysites or their 'Chalcedonian' rivals, because the Church of England was committed only to the formularies of the first four ecumenical Councils, ending with the Chalcedon Definition as the classic expression of Christology. It was probably Martin Routh who directed him towards the later Chalcedonians, Leontius of Byzantium, Maximus the Confessor (580–662), and John of Damascus (*c.*660–*c.*750),[91] but there was no existing Anglican map of these theologians for Newman to follow. Newman was venturing into unknown historiographical waters; and in charting them he crystallized his own unique historiography of doctrinal development. He discovered that Chalcedon was not the end of developments concerning Christ's person, but a new beginning that required the interpretation of later commentators, especially Leontius (who opposed Severus of Antioch (*c.*465–538) by comparing him to Eutyches). Newman discovered, in the words of *Development of Christian Doctrine*, that it was necessary to interpret earlier Fathers, including Leo, 'by the times which came after' (*Dev* 13).

The first indication of the interpretive method at the centre of Newman's new historiography came in a review of a book on the Apostolic Fathers for the *British Critic* in January 1839. He compared the interpretive powers of the Fathers with those of contemporary

being that Anglicanism 'might seem' to be identified with a district too—'Yet they are named from Eutyches, from Severus, from Jacob, from Gaianus and from Theodosius' (quoted at *Newman and Heresy,* 221).

[91] Newman used Michel Lequien's edition of the Damascene and the edition of Maximus by François Combefis, according to the bibliography of the abstract of 'Monophysite Heresy' dated 23 Aug. 1839 (Apoll 17).

sceptics: 'while to a modern Protestant [Ignatius of Antioch] is so unmeaning, a disciple of Irenaeus, Athanasius or Cyril of Alexandria, will be in no perplexity as to what his words mean' (*Critic* 25: 66).[92] That summer, Newman became aware that the earlier Fathers who needed interpreting were not simply Ignatius or even a pre-Nicene like Dionysius, but also Cyril himself and Leo.[93] As a result, Newman's research that summer was broad in focus. He wrote to John Bowden on 11 July 1839: 'I am busy with the theology of the 5th century at present, preparatory (I trust) to finishing my edition of Dionysius of Alexandria—and editing (for the Library of the Fathers) Theodoret, Leo and Cyril. Also we hope to begin publishing a translation of Fleury', specifically Fleury's volumes relating to the period 381–456 (*LD* vii. 102). These were diverse projects, which found convergence in the Christological disputes leading to the Council of Chalcedon (451). But it would be wrong to think that Newman stopped his reading with the fifth century. It was not that Newman came across Pope Leo's *Tome to Flavian*, espousing the 'two natures in one person' formula, and found that it solved all Christological questions. Leo's formula did not even satisfy Newman, as the next section will show by examining his preaching the following year. His research into the history of Chalcedon did not represent the beginning of the end of Newman's searching, no matter what he said in later years. Rather, Leo's formula was just a beginning: it started a new round of Christological dispute that required the clarification of later Chalcedonian Fathers.

The largest piece of research from this period extant in the Oratory archive is an unpublished paper on 'Monophysite Heresy' dated 23 August 1839.[94] Here Newman tells largely the same story for the Monophysites as he had for the Apollinarians: both grew out of a

---

[92] In the 1870s (the neo-Thomist-tending) Newman synthesized all Catholic fathers with one another, strengthening this to 'no perplexity at all' (*EH* i. 247). See Ch. 5, below.

[93] He expressed a hunch that he was moving away from the pre-Nicenes when he wrote to Frederic Rogers on 12 July: 'now that I am in the Monophysite controversy, I think I shall read through it, and then back to the Nestorian, before I go to [Dionysius]. I should not wonder if this opened other questions, which on fresh grounds threw Dionysius off again just as before' (*LD* vii. 105).

[94] OM B.2.5, as well as Mon, also contains eight pages beginning 'No controversy of ancient times lasted through so long a period as the Monophysite', and three pages beginning 'Having considered in outline the doctrine of the Monophysites'.

corruption of Alexandrian teaching; both set out to confute a heresy (Arianism and Nestorianism) which ended up taking them to an opposite extreme; both flourished in Antioch and therefore ultimately had more to do with the theology of the 'East' than with Egypt; and, together with the contemporary rationalist, both put more emphasis on logic than traditional teaching. Newman had maintained since *Arians of the Fourth Century* that the trouble with heretics is that they prefer sophistry to traditional teaching.[95] In August 1835, he wrote that 'Apollinaris...like Arius, preferred abstract reasoning to Scripture' (Apoll 3). In August 1839, he says that the Monophysites shared with other heretics 'an allowance of abstract reasoning, in other words, that is, maintenance of intellectually conceived first principles in a matter which was purely of faith' (Mon 4). Newman does not explain why a matter 'purely of faith' is not open to being discussed 'intellectually', whereas a heresy can have its 'first principles' analysed by his own rigorous logic.[96] In this paper, all Monophysites, whether Apollinarius who started the heresy (ibid. 1), or the Eutychians (ibid. 7–22), or the Theopaschites, whose position that God suffered was the consequence of Christ's one divine nature (ibid. 23–46), or the 'more subtle and more argumentative form' of Semi-Eutychians (ibid. 49), are forced by Newman's logic

---

[95] Aloys Grillmeier writes: 'Eutyches...only accepted the formula "from two natures" under pressure and gave it a twist which prevented his opponents from using the expression and set it up as a Monophysite catchword: "I acknowledge that the Lord was *from two natures* before the union, but after the union I acknowledge only *one nature.*" According to Grillmeier, therefore, the 'two natures' of Flavian's proposed formula were not what divided him from Eutyches, but the 'temporal and genetic connotation' in the phrase '*from* two natures' (*Christ in Christian Tradition: From the Apostolic Age to Chalcedon (451)*, trans. J. S. Bowden (New York: Sheed and Ward, 1965), 458).

[96] Newman uses the logic that he learned from Whately to connect the errors of all heretics: 'Opinions apparently very opposite, or rather those which are apparently most so, agree in the major premiss or principle of which they rest, and differ in the minor. Hence they are much more connected than at first might be supposed' (Mon 9 n. ++). I would add to Thomas's point in *Newman and Heresy* (p. 209) that Newman's method is suggestive of what G. C. Stead describes as 'reductio rhetorta', which 'saddles the opponent with the very proposition which [the opponent] regards as evidently false' ('Rhetorical Method in Athanasius', *Vigiliae Christianae*, 30 (1976), 134). Whately (who had accused Newman of 'Arianizing' in 1827 (*Apo* 25)) was himself reduced, by Newman's rhetoric, to a position of denying the divinity of Christ.

into the doctrinal position of denying both Christ's full divinity and his full humanity. He concludes:

as this tenet of the μία φύσις [one nature] derogated from our Lord's Godhead, it could not but impair the doctrine of His manhood... In order that God might certainly be received as man, and man held to be God, it seemed to teach that Christ came short of being God in that He was man, and of man in that He was God. (Mon 77)

Admittedly, Newman distinguishes the more from the less dangerous versions of the heresy. He had done this in his work on Apollinarianism in 1835, too, making a distinction between Apollinarius and those in Antioch who took up his heresy. Likewise, the Antiochenes who followed Severus were the most dangerous Monophysites.[97] But distinctions among heretics do not negate the logical similarity that connects them all.

In 1841, Newman deployed this very logic to oppose a joint Lutheran–Anglican bishop in Jerusalem, who would be nominated alternately by the monarchs of Prussia and Britain. Newman thought that distinctions among heretics—'Jews (whether converted or not) Lutherans etc. whether conformed or not, Druses who are half Mahometans, and the Monophysites of Mesopotamia'—did not negate their similarity, and that therefore 'our Church' should remain aloof (*LD* viii. 299). He wrote to Miss Giberne in October 1841, 'What a miserable concern this Jerusalem Bishoprick is!' before continuing, 'I am engaged with Athanasius, and shall be giving some years to him, Leo, Cyril, Theodoret etc. for the Library of the Fathers; they will be very difficult reading for English people' (ibid.). Newman thought that these Fathers shone a light on the contemporary English Church's error in consorting with heretics; but he was not going to leave the Church yet.

It has already been shown that Newman found it necessary to correct Athanasius's Christology where Apollinarius had taken it to heretical extremes. Between 1836 and 1840, Newman came to realize

---

[97] These he calls 'Semi-Eutychian' because they 'held that the Divine Nature of the Word had the addition of what viewed by itself was a human nature, but viewed in the Word thereby ceased to be a separate nature, but formed one nature with the divine' (Mon 53).

that Cyril also needed some correction. Although he follows Cyril's Christology closely, Newman also criticized him in 1836. In the 'Lectures on the Prophetical Office', first delivered that spring in St Mary's, Cyril is accused of hot-headedness in the speed with which he conducted affairs at the Council of Ephesus. But the squabbling and mutual recriminations between Cyril and John of Antioch do not invalidate the truth that Cyril established at the Council, just as the way in which the English Reformation was carried out does not invalidate the truth of its cause:

Cyril and Nestorius, with their respective partisans, arrived at Ephesus at the time appointed, before John, Bishop of Antioch, and the Orientals. After waiting for a fortnight, Cyril opened the Council, as President, without them; in spite of the earnest representations of the Imperial Officer, who intreated him to allow a further delay. Its proceedings thus unsatisfactorily commenced, were concluded within the space of a single day... [A]t the end of several years John and Cyril, making mutual admissions and explanations in points of doctrine, were reconciled to each other, and jointly assented to the condemnation of Nestorius. From that time Nestorius has been accounted a heretic by the Church... But, anyhow, the scandals of the Council of Ephesus are an effectual hindrance to any over-delicate and fastidious criticisms by Roman writers of our Reformation. (*VM* i. 346–7)[98]

Notice the criticism in 1836 is not about Cyril's doctrine but about his ethos. Newman recognizes for the first time that good doctrine could coexist with bad behaviour, three years before Stephen Thomas says that Newman discovered that the opposite was true in the case of Eutyches. Thomas finds, in the research from the summer of 1839, 'a certain sympathy with the Monophysite *ethos*',[99] especially when Newman compares it with earlier heresies: 'As the Monophysite heresy is contrary to Arianism in doctrine, so, as might be expected, is it in its ethical character. It was far more subtle, specious and attractive to pious minds' (Mon 2). Thomas contends that Newman 'pulls back ultimately from the paradox—good *ethos* : false

[98] In his *Letter to the Duke of Norfolk* (1874) Newman reshaped this same argument in response to Gladstone's criticism of the lack of unanimity at the Vatican Council: 'Anglicans, who are so fierce against the Vatican, and so respectful towards the Ephesine, should consider what good reason they have for swallowing the third Council, while they strain out the nineteenth' (*Diff* ii. 306).

[99] *Newman and Heresy*, 206.

doctrine'[100]—by saying that Eutyches went against the Church's authority. But, in the spring of 1836, Newman had already met the opposite paradox in Cyril—bad ethos : true doctrine—and not pulled back from that.[101]

Doctrinally, moreover, could not Cyril be accused of opening up the possibility of heresy for his follower Eutyches, as Athanasius had for Apollinarius? Cyril was as responsible for Eutychianism, Newman says in the 'Lectures', as Gregory of Nyssa was for giving Catholics a justification for the doctrine of transubstantiation. But this is to say Cyril was not really blameworthy at all for what is, Newman thinks, a pernicious outcome. He writes, as he did in *Arians of the Fourth Century*, that these openings for later heretical teachings occur when the Fathers speculate as individuals rather than when their doctrine is guided by collective tradition:

St. Cyril might afford a handle to Eutyches... Origen might deny the eternity of future punishment; yet all such instances, whatever be their weight from other circumstances, still, as not professing to be more than expressions of private opinion, have no weight at all, one way or other, in the argument from Catholic Tradition. (*VM* i. 52–3)

Newman was as sympathetic to Cyril as he was to Origen, drawing back from a direct criticism of the opportunities Cyril afforded Eutyches, just as in *Arians of the Fourth Century* he had forgiven Origen for his private speculations.

Aware of the Monophysites when researching Apollinarianism in August 1835,[102] it is probable that Newman was already attempting to avoid Eutychianism in the sermon 'Christ, the Son of God made Man' in Lent 1836. He wrote of Christ: 'This is what His unity consists in,—not unity of nature, but in this, that He who came on earth, was the very Same who had been from everlasting' (*PS* vi. 5: 1228). Not a single unified nature, but a union of the hypostasis of

---

[100] *Newman and Heresy*, 212.

[101] In 1860, Newman again wrote of Cyril's 'un-saintly doings' in 'The Trials of Theodoret' (*HS* ii. 341).

[102] He first encountered both Entyches and Severus briefly during his research into Apollinarius in 1835. 'Apollinaris' history' argued that 'the later Apollinarians and their successors the Eutychians sheltered themselves behind the names of orthodox writers' (p. 19). More cryptically, Newman mentioned 'Severus?' at Apoll 3 n. 2.

the Son with a full humanity of soul and body. The hypostatic union was Newman's focus after the summer of 1835, but he was not sure of what this meant for the human nature of Christ until after the summer of 1839, as will now be seen in the discussion of a final theme, the suffering of the Son.

Predicating suffering of the Son

It is important in this section to compare Newman's Christology with that of Leo, whose legates judged Eutyches a heretic at Chalcedon. It is an important comparison because Newman's own Christology after August 1835 did not follow either Leo on one side or Eutyches on the other; rather it followed Leontius's Christology from nearly eighty years after Chalcedon. Newman discovered in 1839 that he did not favour the Christology of Leo. The Pope's *Tome to Flavian* argued for symmetry in the natures of Christ and this symmetry came to define the terms of Chalcedon: two natures coming together to form one person (πρόσωπον) and one hypostasis. The Chalcedonian Definition did not say whether this hypostasis was the same as the second hypostasis of the Trinity, an omission which offended many followers of Cyril.[103] Thus, Chalcedon did not put an end to the Christogical controversies; instead, the violent rejection of the Definition marked a new beginning to them. Leontius of Byzantium defended Chalcedon in the 530s and 540s. His *Against the Nestorians and Eutychians*, written in controversy with Severus, came to understand the Definition differently from the way Leo had; and it is this later Chalcedonianism that Newman read in 1839 and which his Christology in 1840 most resembled.

---

[103] For what the Definition did not say, see Sarah Coakley, 'What Does Chalcedon Solve and What Does it Not? Some Reflections on the Status and Meaning of the Chalcedonian Definition', in Stephen T. Davies, Daniel Kendall, and Gerald O'Collins (eds.), *The Incarnation* (Oxford: Clarendon Press, 2002), which challenges modern interpreters of the Definition: on the one hand Richard Norris and George Lindbeck for interpreting the Chalcedonian Definition 'figuratively', thus dodging its ontological implications, and on the other hand Thomas Morris and David Brown for taking the Definition too 'literally'. Coakley interprets it in a third way: 'it sets a "boundary" on what can, and cannot, be said' about Christ (p. 161).

In the summer of 1839, Leontius and fellow Chalcedonian thinker John of Damascus impressed Newman. It has already been suggested that Routh had directed Newman to Leontius in 1835; and whereas John was popular among High Churchmen as a source for earlier patristic teaching, Newman was one of the first Anglicans to engage with the Damascene's Christology found variously in the writings on heresy and orthodoxy. Newman accepted John's view that 'Arians, Sabellians, Nestorians and Eutychians all agreed in assuming as a first principle that nature and person were the same [in Christ]—or that no nature but what was a person' (Mon 4). John, and now Newman, corrected this mistaken first principle by drawing on Leontius. Newman goes on to describe the 'Catholic' position, which is opaquely described thus:

> the Catholics distinguished between *hypostasis* and *enhypostaton*, individual & individualized or in individuality. They allowed that no *physis* or *ousia* could exist except [as] at least individualized, but they denied that it need be an individual, since it might belong to an individual. (Mon 70)

Here Newman describes Leontius's distinction,[104] as expressed in the words of Brian Daley, between:

> a *hypostasis* and that which is simply hypostatic (*to enhypostaton*): the latter term is precisely *not* predicated of concrete individuals as such, but of the universals (essence, nature) encountered in them, to indicate that they are concretely realized. So one must say that divinity and humanity, as complete and functional natures, are both 'hypostatic' (*enhypostata*) in the person of Christ, but not in themselves.[105]

Leontius's formulation avoided the Nestorians' two individuals in Christ, the human one and the divine one, by specifying that Christ's

---

[104] PG 86: 1277 C14–D6. According to the bibliography at Apoll 17, Newman read the Latin translation of Francisco Torres, which differentiated 'hypostasis, & enypostaton [*sic*]', in J. Basnage, *Thesaurus Monumentorum Ecclesiasticorum et Historicorum*, i (Antwerp: Wetstenii, 1725), 538. This rearrangement of Henricus Canisius's *Antiquae Lectiones* (1603), with additional observations by Basnage, was available in the Bodleian. There Newman may also have read Leontius's work in Greek in MS Laud 92B, but no record of this exists.

[105] Brian E. Daley, 'Anhypostasy' in Lacoste, *Encyclopedia of Christian Theology*, i. 40–2. For further discussion of the relationship of Leontius's thought with John of Damascus's, see Richard Cross, 'Individual Natures in the Christology of Leontius of Byzantium', *Journal of Early Christian Studies*, 10 (2002), 245–65.

only person/hypostasis is the second hypostasis of the Trinity. The formulation also avoided the Eutychians' reduction (after Cyril) of the divine and human to 'one nature incarnate'; for, given that natures exist hypostatically in the person, 'it is precisely "union, not nature", that serves as the foundation of the subject's inner identity'.[106] Leontius was correcting Cyril's 'one nature' formula by emphasizing Cyril's other great insight: the importance of the hypostatic union. To have a union at all, as Cyril had shown, there must be different substances to join together (there would be no need for union if there were sameness). But, because of their difference, it is not 'natural'—not according to their nature—for these two substances to come into union, according to Leontius.[107] This union, which is the central mystery of who Christ is, therefore occurs at the level of Christ's person not nature.

For Newman, following Leontius, Christ is fully human, but his human nature is 'individualized' in the divine hypostasis. This was permitted within the bounds of the Chalcedonian Definition. Leontius, however, was so helpful to Newman in clarifying the Definition because he went as far as to say that, even after the union, the only hypostasis was that of the second person of the Trinity. The difference between the divine and human, in this account, is that Christ *always was* a divine individual, who only recently has 'taken to Him a manhood, but so that it became attached to his individuality as a part of Him' (Mon 70). As Newman put it elsewhere in his 1839 notes: Christ 'was God; He became man. He ever had the divine nature; He added on to it the human'.[108] As a result of the hypostatic union, then, the Son is a hypostasis with divine nature (conceived as a bundle of properties or idioms, such as impassibility) of whom a human nature (conceived as a different bundle of properties, such as passibility) can now be predicated.

---

[106] Daley, 'Nature and the "Mode of Union": Late Patristic Models for the Personal Unity of Christ', Davies, Kendall, and O'Collins, *The Incarnation*, 170, quoting the twenty-sixth of Leontius's *Hypothetical Propositions* against Severus. At 166 n. 2, Daley points out a similar phrase in *Contra Nest et Eut* 5, which Newman certainly read: 'That which is said to be one by union is not the same as that which is one by nature'.

[107] Ibid. 169.

[108] OM B.2.5. Untitled MS beginning 'No controversy...', 2.

It can be no coincidence that, for the first time in Newman's sermons, Christ's humanity seems fully individualized in 'Christ's Privations a Meditation for Christians' of Lent 1840. In this sermon Christ is portrayed as a divine individual who experiences pain in his humanity, opening up the difficulty of how to predicate suffering of the second hypostasis of the Trinity. In the summer of 1839, Newman became aware that the Eutychians' 'real objection [to Christ's human nature] lay, not against the word nature, but against the humiliation which the assumption of that nature applied; and whether consciously or not, they objected to the word, in order to mask the force of the shock which the humiliation gave to their feelings' (Mon 28). In other words, the Eutychians were unwilling fully to countenance the 'humiliation' that, in becoming incarnate, the divine hypostasis had to undergo. Thus, Newman's preaching in 1840 gives an account of the humiliation of Christ, depicting a fully suffering Son. But how can a divine hypostasis be described as suffering?

Newman first noticed the dilemma here in the 1835 sermon 'The Humiliation of the Eternal Son'. This sermon criticizes modern forgetfulness of the ancient doctrines of Christ:

we have well-nigh forgotten the sacred truth, graciously disclosed for our support, that Christ is the Son of God in His Divine nature, as well as His human; we have well-nigh ceased to regard Him, after the pattern of the Nicene Creed, as 'God from God, and Light from Light', ever one with Him, yet ever distinct from Him. We speak of Him in a vague way as God, which is true, but not the whole truth; and, in consequence when we proceed to consider His humiliation, we are unable to carry on the notion of His personality from heaven to earth. (*PS* iii. 12: 591)

Newman's desire 'to carry on the notion of His personality from heaven to earth' led him to a Cyrilline solution in 1836, preaching in 'Christ, the Son of God made Man': 'When He poured out His precious blood upon the Cross, it was not a man's blood, though it belonged to His manhood, but blood full of power and virtue, instinct with life and grace, as issuing most mysteriously from Him who was the Creator of the world' (*PS* vi. 5: 1226). Notice that 'it was not a man's blood', because Christ was not strictly speaking '*a* man' (ibid. 1225); but it was human blood, for 'it belonged to his manhood', and not the blood of a composite being like that proposed by Apollinarius.

Yet Newman may have seen in 1839 that, rather like Eutyches's description, the Christ he described in 1836 does not experience real humiliation. Human properties like passibility and mortality are predicated here of the Creator of the world. It is God who bleeds in emulation of Cyril's teaching, opening Newman to the criticisms described by John McGuckin: 'God wept. God died. God . . . suckled. To [Cyril's] opponents, especially Nestorius, this language broke the very foundations of their Christological scheme, and they attacked it as akin to mythology.'[109] Is Newman engaging in mythology too? How can Christ suffer in the flesh, when the person doing the suffering is the second hypostasis of the Trinity rather than a human person?

To many at the time, Cyril's language seemed dangerous. Given the impassibility of God, a point on which both Cyril and his opponents agreed, it was incoherent to predicate human properties like the weeping of the divine Son. But Cyril wanted to stress the unity of natures in the divine hypostasis. Thus, when Antiochene opponents accused Cyril and his followers of overvaluing Christ's suffering by projecting it into God—asking, for instance, how can God weep?— Cyril answered that God suffers impassibly ($\dot{a}\pi a\theta\hat{\omega}s$ $\ddot{\epsilon}\pi a\theta\epsilon v$). To sort out the incoherence of Cyril's language, followers like Eutyches went further and spoke as if Christ's human nature had gained divine attributes and the human suffering was really only illusory. James Antony Froude (Hurrell's brother) recalled seeing Newman as one such heretic after the 1836 sermon 'The Incarnate Son of God, a Sufferer and a Sacrifice'.[110] To some of those who heard him that Palm Sunday, Newman tended towards Monophysitism.

Just as the possible dangers of Cyril's Christology were overcome by Leontius's Chalcedonianism, so were the possible errors of New- man's 1836 sermons overcome by his reading of Leontius in 1839.

---

[109] McGuckin, introduction to Cyril of Alexandria, *On the Unity of Christ* (Crest- wood, NY: SVS Press, 1995), 45.

[110] Strange draws attention to this in 'Newman and Mystery of Christ' (p. 328), before explaining that 'Froude's memory may suggest Monophysitism, but Newman's teaching is Chalcedonian' (p. 329). Given the previous week's 'Christ, the Son of God Made Man', I do not agree that Froude was wrong to detect a Monophysite tone in Newman's sermons at the time, even if Froude was mistaken in recollecting the exact words. Moreover, Strange does not recognize the difference Newman's reading of Leontius made to what he understood by 'Chalcedonian'.

After Leontius, it was no longer incoherent to predicate sufferings of a human nature that was individualized in a divine hypostasis. In Lent 1840, instead of Christ's suffering lacking human characteristics, Newman preached about 'the overwhelming fear He had of His sufferings before they came. This shows how great they were; but it would seem besides this, as if He had decreed to go through all trials for us, and, among them, the trial of fear' (*PS* vi. 4: 1217). Notice this is still a divine hypostasis who knows beforehand what sufferings he faces; for this reason, Christ voluntarily accepted all 'He had decreed to go through' in a way that no other human being could; more on this shortly. Nevertheless his 'terror' drives him to have second thoughts during the Agony in Gethsemane and then on the cross comes the Cry of Desolation:

both in soul and in body was this Holy and Blessed Saviour, the Son of God, and Lord of life, given over to the malice of the great enemy of God and man. Job was given over to Satan in the Old Testament, but within prescribed limits; first, the Evil One was not allowed to touch his person, and afterwards, though his person, yet not his life. But Satan had power to triumph, or what he thought was triumphing, over the life of Christ, who confesses to His persecutors, 'This is your hour, and the power of darkness.' (Lk 22:53) His head was crowned and torn with thorns, and bruised with staves; His face was defiled with spitting; His shoulders were weighed down with the heavy cross; His back was rent and gashed with scourges; His hands and feet gored through with nails; His side, by way of contumely, wounded with the spear; His mouth parched with intolerable thirst; and His soul so bedarkened, that He cried out, 'My God, My God, why hast Thou forsaken Me?' (Mt 27:46). (*PS* vi. 4: 1217–18).

The mention of Christ's soul, of course, underscores the point made already in this chapter: that Newman was avoiding any Apollinarian implications that Christ had no human soul. But new in 1840 is the real threat that this soul might give in to the 'dark' forces. Moreover, Christ's back is rent with scourges and his feet are gored with nails— language suggestive not of God's blood pouring forth, but of pain and passible human blood. Newman's preaching of the passion became more passionate after 1839, in the face of the Eutychians' opposition to Christ's humiliation.

Christ's free acceptance of humiliation led to another thorny question, however, concerning Christ's will. What role did Christ voluntarily going through suffering and death have to play in the redemptive action of the cross? Again, Newman alluded to this question in the 1835 sermon 'The Humiliation of the Eternal Son'. His text is Hebrews 5: 7–8: 'This, then, is the force of the words, "Though He was a Son, yet had He experience of obedience." He took on Him a lower nature, and wrought in it towards a Will higher and more perfect than it. Further, "He learned *obedience* amid *suffering*", and, therefore, amid temptation' (*PS* iii. 12: 587). In 1839, however, Newman discovered a new way to make sense of what it means for Christ's will to be subjected to 'a Will higher than it'. Pope Leo taught, in the words of Grillmeier, that 'the human will of Christ is the means by which he is proved before God', in a way that made sense of the Chalcedonian Definition of Christ's two natures, each with its own will.[111] This stood against the way in which the Alexandrians had understood the role of Christ's will in the passion: Athanasius, again in the words of Grillmeier, 'ascribes victory in Gethsemane to the divine will in Christ, while the weakness of the flesh asks to be freed from suffering'.[112] Newman discerned in 1839 that developments at Chalcedon veered away from Alexandrian teaching. Yet in the theology of Maximus and John of Damascus, who picked up on Maximus, Christ was understood to have two wills (one human, one divine) but never to the detriment of his unified person, who is the divine Son.[113] While Jesus could, humanly, have chosen in Gethsemane not to suffer on the cross, the mystery of the incarnation is that Christ humanly willed to do what he (and the Father and the Spirit) divinely willed that he should

---

[111] 'Leo sees in the struggle of Christ the *manifesta distinctio* of the nature that takes and the nature that is taken and shapes a clear dyotheletic formula... "*Superiori igitur voluntati voluntas cessit inferior*" (*Serm*. 56, 2),' (*Christ in Christian Tradition*, 471).

[112] Ibid.

[113] Andrew Louth writes: 'Maximus is heir to... the Alexandrian Christological tradition of Athanasius and Cyril. He is heir to this principally because it was the dominant tradition in Byzantine theology from the sixth century onwards... Maximus' defence of two wills in the Incarnate Christ is not intended to suggest that there are two subjects in Christ, but to safeguard the full humanity in which the Second Person of the Godhead lives out a human life' (*Maximus the Confessor* (London: Routledge, 1996), 27–8).

do. So Christ's human will, while remaining real and created, freely chooses what God wills.

Such divinely willed suffering, which he humanly chooses to accept, appears in 'Christ's Privations a Meditation for Christians' from Lent 1840. Newman preached: 'how little is our pain, our hardships, our persecutions, compared with those which Christ *voluntarily* undertook for us!... How base and miserable are we, for understanding them so little, for being so little impressed by them!' (*PS* vi. 4: 1218, my italics) On the cross, Christ absorbs suffering into a divine hypostasis, which being impassible can soak it all up. The divine hypostasis remained the focus of Newman's preaching, perhaps more so when he became a Catholic,[114] in spite of Leo's two-nature Christology. Yet, since his reading of Leontius, Maximus, and John of Damascus, he could be more 'impressed by' sufferings that were experienced by a fully human Christ.

CONCLUSION: WHAT NEWMAN'S SERMONS SHOW ABOUT HIS CHRISTOLOGY

Finally, some of the threads from this chapter can be tied together. Newman's sermons in this period, to a lesser or greater extent, show a method of scriptural exegesis that *Arians of the Fourth Century* had claimed was Alexandrian. Nevertheless, it has become clear that the way he interpreted Christ's actions in certain texts changed. As Newman shifted from the view of Christ's flesh as merely an instrument for the Logos, to an emphasis on the Logos as the actor doing the divine work, to allowing the human Jesus fully to experience suffering that it might be absorbed into the divine hypostasis, so Newman continually revised his interpretation of various portions of scripture. For instance, in the 1835 sermon 'Tears of Christ at the Grave of

---

[114] Newman preached this more clearly in 'Mental Sufferings of Our Lord in His Passion' in 1849: Christ's 'passion was an action ... God was the sufferer; God suffered in His human nature; the sufferings belonged to God, and were drunk up, were drained to the bottom of the chalice, because God drank them' (*Mix* 331).

Lazarus', Christ's grief is a sign for us, more than the result of affection for Lazarus. Because 'it is the very sight of sympathy in another that affects and comforts the sufferer', in weeping for Lazarus Jesus showed us the sympathy God has for us (*PS* iii. 10: 567). There is a communication of idioms at work here, enabling a property not usually applied to God (sympathy) to be seen in the person of Jesus. But is the divine really being sympathetic? Rather, is the 'instrument' of Jesus's flesh being manipulated? And, if so, are human observers being deceived by Jesus's tears?

By comparison, in his 1840 sermon 'Christ's Privations a Meditation for Christians', a different interpretation is given of Jesus weeping for a dead friend. Now

Lazarus was His friend, and He lost him. He knew, indeed, that He could restore him, and He did. Yet still He bitterly lamented him, for whatever reason, so that the Jews said, 'Behold how He loved him.' But a greater and truer bereavement, as far as we dare speak of it, was His original act of humiliation itself, in leaving His heavenly glory and coming down on earth. This, of course, is a great mystery to us from beginning to end; still, He certainly vouchsafes to speak, through His Apostle, of His 'emptying Himself' of His glory. (*PS* vi. 4: 1216–17)

For Newman in 1840 the weeping over Lazarus is part of the self-emptying (*kenōsis* from the verb in Philippians 2: 7) by which the Son humbled himself to become incarnate. This self-emptying is the basis upon which the weeping and dying of Christ ultimately depend. Such an argument is itself a Cyrilline one, for, even as he corrected Cyril with the writings of later Chalcedonians, he was beginning to think in terms of their 'developing' the Alexandrian patriarch.[115] Moreover, a Christology with a more passionate passion in 1840 was rhetorically useful. His preaching of Christ's suffering in the 1840s is more moving than his earlier Christological sermons and a

---

[115] Cyril wrote in his *Third Letter to Nestorius*: 'The Only begotten Word... came down for the sake of our salvation and abased Himself into emptying [*kenōsis*] and was incarnate... not indeed casting off what He was, but even though He became Man by the assumption of flesh and blood He still remained God in nature [*physis*] and in truth' (trans. T. H. Bindley and F. W. Green (eds.), *The Oecumenical Documents of the Faith* (London: Methuen, 1950), 213–14, quoted at Coakley, *Powers and Submissions*, 13). Coakley argues that this represents no real emptying at all, seeing as the Logos loses nothing but rather *adds* a human nature.

reminder of the relationship between Newman's research and preaching in this period.

It was not until he was translating Athanasius from 1840 that Newman, much to his shock, discovered the Agnoetae, 'a sect of those very Eutychians, who denied or tended to deny our Lord's manhood with a view of preserving His divinity, being characterized by holding that He was *ignorant*' (*Ox Frs* xix. 295–6 n. o).[116] Beforehand, he had no difficulty conceiving that Christ had incomplete knowledge in his human soul, and that he could therefore grow in wisdom as Luke's Gospel taught (Luke 2: 52). However, he admitted in the letter to Dodsworth in 1852: 'When I read more, I found the view condemned (or the substance of it) in the case of the heresy of the Agnoitae [*sic*], *after* St Athanasius's day' (*LD* xv. 56).[117]

His reading of the Agnoetae had made him alter his Christology, as can be seen in his annotations to the *Select Treatises of S. Athanasius* (1842–4), where he rejected the idea of an ignorant human mind in the Son. Glossing Discourse III. 43, Newman wrote of Christ's soul, 'which left to itself had been partially ignorant, as other human souls, yet as ever enjoying the beatific vision from its oneness with the Word, it never was ignorant really, but knew all things which human soul can know' (*Ox Frs* xix. 461 n. b). Enlightened by the Beatific Vision though it was, Christ's soul chose to fear what any human would (a choice only a divine person could make). Therefore Newman sees Christ's not knowing more than any human as part of the 'economy' of God. As was the case in 1835 and 1839, the patristic research from 1840 to 1844 brought shifts in his sermons; however, it is not until 'Mental Sufferings of Our Lord in His Passion' in 1849 that the Christological change can be seen, Newman preaching that 'it was the soul and not the body which was the seat of the suffering of the Eternal Word' (*Mix* 325). He explains that this was no ordinary human soul: 'He Himself created the soul which He took on Himself,

---

[116] Here Newman's recognition that the Agnoetae taught ignorance in Christ's *human* nature showed him a more perceptive reader than Suicer, who wrote: 'These taught that the *divine* nature of Christ was ignorant of certain things, like the hour of the last judgement' (my italics). See entry on ’Αγνοηταί in Johann Kaspar Suicer, *Thesaurus Ecclesiasticus*, 2 vols. (Amsterdam: Westenium, 1728), i. 65.

[117] Newman refers here to what he now realizes was a mistake in an 1835 sermon, corrected in the 1868 edition of *PS*. Cf. *PS* (1st edn.) iii. 12: 139.

while He took His body from the flesh of the Blessed Virgin, His Mother' (ibid. 324). Thus Christ could do what others could not because his soul was different from other human souls, and he could choose to suffer pain.[118]

This chapter ends near to where it began, with a quotation from the 1838 *Lectures on Justification*. Written between his summers researching the Apollinarians and the Monophysites, these Lectures are in many ways the summation of his Anglican thought on the ramifications for humans of the doctrines relating to the incarnation. They show the sorts of rhetorical flourishes that have been seen in the Christological sermons, including the communication of idioms, which he uses in these Lectures to prevent the kind of 'spiritualizing' of the Atonement found in Evangelical preaching. Newman accepted that the Atonement required the sacrifice of Christ's material body and blood, but also insisted that our justification required a participation in the body and blood of Christ made present by the Spirit in the Eucharist. The Atonement is made real in humans only through the Spirit and in the Eucharist: the doctrines of Trinity, Christology, and deification complement each other, and do so in a way that even a modern critic of the idea that Origen, Athanasius, or Cyril were distinctively 'Alexandrian' in their biblical exegesis, might describe as doctrinally 'Alexandrian'.[119] Newman argues:

as Christ really 'came in the flesh', which none but deceivers and antichrists can deny, and suffered in the real body and blood of man;—so on the contrary the communication of this great and adorable Sacrifice to the individual Christian, is not the communication of that Body and Blood

[118] Another example from Cyril, quoted by Newman in 1844, is Christ's grief: 'When grief began to be stirred in Him, and His sacred flesh was on the verge of tears, He suffers it *not to be affected freely*, as is our custom, but "He was vehement in the Spirit", that is, He in some way chides His own Flesh in the power of the Holy Ghost' (*Ox Frs* xix. 477 n. a, quoting fragment). Newman preached in this same sermon in 1849: 'withdrawing the support of the God-head from His soul, distress, terror, and dejection at once rush in upon it' (*Mix* 334).

[119] Frances Young writes: 'Cyril spoke for the many faithful who received the eucharist as the flesh of the incarnate Logos and trusted that in this way they were assured resurrection by participating in the new humanity sanctified by the presence of the Logos himself... He was wedded to the Alexandrian tradition of θεοποίησις, of deification realized by the saving initiative of God himself' (*From Nicaea to Chalcedon*, 262).

such as it was when offered upon the Cross, but, in a higher, glorified, and spiritual state. The Son of God suffered as the man Christ Jesus, 'with strong crying and tears',—'in weakness' and a body of 'flesh;' the crucified Man, the Divine Son, comes again to us in His Spirit. (*Jfc* 205)

For Newman, it is vital 'for our individual justification' that the crucified is the Divine Son, that the crying and tears of Jesus are the manifestation of God's Logos. It is vital for us that this is so. For, in Alexandrian fashion, the body of Christ is not only the crucified, risen, and ascended flesh of the Son, but also the Eucharistic body on which the Church feeds.

4

Newman on the Trinity before and after Nicaea (1840–58)

Beginning to translate Athanasius in the summer of 1840, New-man found in him the standard of orthodoxy by which all other Fathers, before or after, could be judged. Having Athanasius as a standard of orthodoxy explains some of Newman's peculiar judge-ments about the Fathers in the 1840s and 1850s. On the one hand, reworking the essay 'Life and Ideas of the Heresiarch, Apollinaris' for a third edition of *The Church of the Fathers* (1857), Newman puts his former hero Origen alongside Nestorius as worse heretics than Apollinarius (*HS* i. 392). This is because Origen and Nestorius conform less to Athanasius's version of orthodoxy than Apollinarius. On the other hand, in the essay 'On St Cyril's Formula, μία φύσις σεσαρκωμένη' (1858)—about the one-nature formula for Christ's incarnate person which errs by the standards of Chalcedon—Cyril is praised because his use of 'nature' (*physis*) is held by Newman to replicate Athanasius's use of hypostasis, as will be seen below. Newman's description of orthodoxy, which in *Arians of the Fourth Century* had considered the move to fixed terminology at Nicaea as a loss, from 1840 became fixated on Athanasius. As a result, previously drawn dis-tinctions between theological positions are collapsed into a rather flat account of orthodoxy. The Athanasius that Newman depicted therefore had to be a strange composite of Greek and Latin post-Nicene orthodoxy.

THE LITTLEMORE CONTEXT:
IN EXILE WITH ATHANASIUS

Already in May 1840, Newman was preparing himself for an experiment in monastic living at Littlemore. Unsurprisingly he saw this experiment in Greek terms, telling Thomas Mozley, 'We have bought nine acres, and want to build a μονή or refuge (*LD* vii. 328).[1] This was nine months before the publication of Tract 90 precipitated a national debate over Newman's place in the Church of England. After Tract 90, Newman could focus fully on the translations of Athanasius, a project 'to which I had long wished to devote myself' (*LD* viii. 504).[2] His absorption with the project is best explained in his words to Keble, that Athanasius was 'a great refuge after other things' (*LD* viii. 259). Newman was mentally and physically exhausted by the reaction to Tract 90. The refuge of his work and the refuge of a monastic life coincided in April 1842, when, to escape public attention, he formally established residence at Littlemore, being joined over time by a group of young disciples.[3] From 1840 to 1844, Newman translated Athanasius's *On the Decrees of Nicaea* (*de Decretis*), *On the Councils of Ariminum and Seleucia* (*de Synodis*), and the four Discourses against the Arians. Newman's edition of the first two works, together with Discourse I, was published in 1842 as volume viii of A Library of the Fathers, of which he, Keble, Pusey, and

[1] He continues, 'I want a cell to contain three rooms: 1, a sitting-room 12 by 9 (say); 2, a bed-room 6 by 6?; and 3, a cold-bath room 6 by 3?'.

[2] Written to the Bishop of Oxford in Apr. 1842: 'A year since I submitted myself entirely to your Lordship's authority... I not only stopped the series of the tracts on which I was engaged, but withdrew myself from all public discussions of Church matters of the day... I turned myself at once to the preparation for the press of the translations of St Athanasius... As to my intentions, I propose to live [in Littlemore] myself a good deal... I do not understand what "cells of dormitories" means. Of course I can repeat your Lordship's words, that "I am not attempting a revival of the Monastic Orders in anything approaching the Romanist sense of the term".' (LD viii. 504–7). Newman's reassurance of the bishop contradicts his letter to Mozley in n. 1.

[3] Sheridan Gilley writes: 'The first, in spring 1842, was John Dobrée Dalgairns, an unstable enthusiast... The next, in July, was William Lockhart... [who] promised to stay with Newman three years; others, like Mark Pattison and Hurrell Froude's younger brother James Anthony, were occasional visitors who took part in the religious observance of the place' (*Newman and his Age* (London: Darton, Longman and Todd, 1990), 211).

Marriott were the editors. Discourses II–IV were published in 1844 as volume xix.[4] In between the publication of these two volumes of *Select Treatises of S. Athanasius in Controversy with the Arians*, a volume called *S. Athanasius Historical Tracts* was published in 1843. This latter was translated by M. Atkinson, with a historical preface and notes by Newman.

The Tractarians' A Library of the Fathers was conceived a full year after Newman was in discussion with the High Churchmen Rose and Palmer about a series of books on early Church history in August 1835. Rose suggested that this should be based upon a translation of the *Histoire Ecclésiastique* of the Catholic Abbé, Claude Fleury (1640–1723), as an alternative to the Protestant narrative of Johann Lorenz von Mosheim (1694–1755). Newman wrote to Bowden that Palmer and Rose 'are clear that any other plan of a history than what they propose will never be executed—I do not deny this—but at the same time think their plan will never sell' (*LD* v. 124). In fact, the translation of Fleury would not be accomplished until 1842, under Newman's direction at Littlemore, and the comments he would make about Fleury in the introduction are contained in embryo in this letter's remarks about 'a dull work'.

A Library of the Fathers was closer to Newman's heart. In August 1836, Newman wrote that 'Pusey and I think of giving our names as joint Editors to a "Library of the Catholic Fathers", which will consist of Translations from St. Austin, St. Crysostom etc., etc.' (*LD* v. 345). Although Newman translated and annotated Athanasius's anti-Arian works for the series, one wonders how different would things have been if Pusey had not prevented Newman from including Origen in A Library of the Fathers in October 1836? In a fascinating reply to Pusey's doubts about including Origen in the series—a surprised Pusey asked of *Contra Celsum*, 'you mean to say you knew and liked it?'—Newman wrote: 'what I read of his "against Celsus", seemed to me full of matter for reflection and very valuable... Is

---

[4] Henceforth these two works will be referred to as *Ox Frs* viii and *Ox Frs* xix to distinguish them from Newman's later (freer) translation of these works in *Ath* i. Many of the notes in *Ath* ii repeat the text of the footnotes to the volumes of *Ox Frs*. Newman called these the 'third edition' (1881) to distinguish them from a second edition (1853) for A Library of the Fathers.

his Commentary on St Matthew impossible [for inclusion]? though fanciful it is full of beautiful thoughts. Williams of Trinity has read it, and might give an opinion' (*LD* v. 368).[5]

In the mid-1830s, the vicar of St Mary's and his curate, Isaac Williams, revered Origen; yet by the early 1840s that changed for Newman. It was the period of seclusion at Littlemore (from where, in September 1843, he resigned from St Mary's and preached his last Anglican sermon (*SD* 395–409)) that enabled Newman to immerse himself not simply in Athanasius's writings but in the writings of his Alexandrian predecessors, leading to new doubts about Origen. Newman also researched the details of Athanasius's life, which feature in the preface to the *Historical Tracts*, including the chronology of Athanasius's exiles in the face of Arian antipathy (e.g. *Ox Frs* xiii, p. xvi). It is tempting to picture Newman in these years seeing his self-inflicted exile at Littlemore, in the face of Anglican antipathy, as the equivalent of Athanasius's exile hiding in the desert with Antony of Egypt.[6]

This focus on Athanasius in the early 1840s enabled Newman to revisit themes from the previous decade in order to correct some of his earlier arguments. In *An Essay on the Development of Christian Doctrine* (1845), Newman reassessed the position of Origen and began to place his former hero outside of orthodoxy. The orthodoxy by which Origen is judged is what Newman previously saw as the formulized faith of Nicaea; specifically, Origen is judged by one word, *homoousios*. Origen thought that, as a signifier for God, the word was too materialistic and thus rejected it. Athanasius thought it provided the only alternative to an Arian depiction of God by signifying that the Son was equal to the Father.[7] But even Athanasius had his doubts about the viability of this word in the wake of Nicaea, doubts which Newman took into account when he wrote *Arians of the Fourth Century*.

---

[5] Reading 'through' as 'though'; *LD* v. 368 n. 1 has Pusey's concerns.

[6] Benedicta Ward has shown the influence of Desert Fathers like Antony of Egypt on the Tractarian leaders. 'A Tractarian Inheritance: The Religious Life in a Patristic Perspective', in Geoffrey Rowell (ed.), *Tradition Renewed* (London: Darton, Longman and Todd, 1986), 214–25.

[7] Newman saw two alternatives: 'The Arians maintained that the very word "Son" implied a *beginning*, or that our Lord was not very God; the Catholics said that it implied *connaturality*, or that He was Very God as one with God' (*Ox Frs* viii. 272).

In *Arians of the Fourth Century*, Newman conceived an 'Alexandrian' style of theology, which Origen and Clement began, and which after Nicaea became the language of orthodoxy. It was not just Athanasius who used this language: Newman's first book showed that the Cappadocian Fathers and Cyril of Alexandria confuted Arian heresy with it as much as Athanasius did (e.g. *Ari* 208). Alexandrian theology was rich and diverse, Newman argued, precisely because it made room for shifting terminology and allegorical interpretation of scripture. This was not quite the argument of Newman's Anglican predecessors who read the Alexandrians, although it was similar to aspects of Bull, Cudworth, and Cave. While Petavius saw Origen as a step not towards the Council but to Arianism, Newman followed Bull's view of pre- and post-Nicene continuity. While Petavius and Cudworth both argued that Origen said different things from Nicaea, only Cudworth thought that Origen could still be considered orthodox and Newman agreed. But, in the 1840s, Newman distanced himself from Cudworth and Bull.

Although this might sound like Newman's thesis of pre- and post-Nicene continuity shifted to a thesis of change, akin to Petavius's, in fact Newman was striking out on a third course. In the 1840s, he was espousing an idea of doctrinal development that upheld both continuity and change. As the section below, 'The Eclipse of Origen', will show, *Development of Christian Doctrine* (1845) was dressed up in the clothes of Bull's argument, but his new doctrine widened differences from Bull that were already present in *Arians of the Fourth Century*. And different from Petavius, the idea of development acknowledged that Origen sowed the seeds of Athanasius's teaching, even though the pre-Nicene theologian fell short of post-Nicene orthodoxy.[8] Pious teachers can spawn developments of orthodoxy, but also corruptions that become heresy. The second section, 'The Rise of Athanasius', will demonstrate the ironic result of Newman's new thesis to be that development was actually less open to historical dynamism than was his first book. Newman's 'development' is shorthand for the triumph of Athanasian orthodoxy—an orthodoxy

---

[8] Moreover, in the words of Chadwick, 'it is a mistake to suppose that Petau possessed either a sense of historical change or any idea of development' (*From Bossuet to Newman* (2nd edn.; Cambridge: Cambridge University Press, 1987), 59).

which, in the way he presents it, allows little room for complexity or dynamism. Cyril among Greeks and Augustine among Latins are portrayed not as enriching a tradition but as merely reiterating the teaching of Athanasius.

THE ECLIPSE OF ORIGEN

Origen is not the only pre-Nicene Father whom Newman invokes in his discussions, in the 1840s and 1850s, of *ousia*-language used of God. Yet Origen is of particular interest because it has been shown how important Origen's rich reading of scripture was in the forma-tion of Newman's teaching and preaching. Beginning with his trans-lation of the writings of Athanasius, Newman started to change his mind about Origen. Indeed, the shift in sympathies away from Origen, which will be traced in this section, was based on Newman's view of the word *homoousios*. This will introduce the question of how important Bishop Bull was to Newman's thought in this period, especially in relation to the Council of Antioch at which Origen's pupils abandoned the word *homoousios*. Finally, Origen will be examined as he appears in *Development of Christian Doctrine*, playing a far more ambiguous role than in previous depictions.

Origen and *homoousios*

In pursuing his research for the Athanasius translation, Newman realized he was wrong in thinking that Origen had the same notion of God as the Council of Nicaea. Origen might have used the word *homoousios* but, if he did, he gave it a different meaning from the Nicene Creed.[9] Athanasius quoted Origen approvingly to show Father and Son were coeternal in *de Decretis* 27; but coeternal is not the same as coequal (a point already made by Cudworth). Equality as well as

---

[9] Eusebius and Pamphilus use *homoousios* in their *Defence of Origen* (*Ox Frs* viii. 35 n. t). Of this work, however, only the first book remains, and that in the translation of the unreliable Rufinus.

eternity are the proper implications, for Newman in 1842, of the term *homoousios*. By Athanasian standards, the consubstantiality of Son and Spirit with the Father without coequality was an insufficient doctrine of God and vice versa.[10] Maybe here Newman had a pre-monition that Origen could be judged a precursor to the Arian heretics.

The annotations to his translation of Athanasius continue to uphold Origen as orthodox, yet there are signs that Newman's view was changing based upon Origen's interpretation of *ousia*-language. In a note on the term, *ousia*, Newman makes a division between on the one hand an 'Aristotelic sense' in which the word *ousia* 'seems to have stood for an individual substance, numerically one, which is predicable of nothing but itself' and therefore not a 'universal' to be shared, and on the other hand the Christian signification, which takes 'a sense of its own, such as we have no example of in things created, viz. of a Being numerically one, subsisting in three persons; so that the word is a predicable or in one sense universal, without ceasing to be individual' (*Ox Frs* viii. 152 n. a). As a rehearsal of what will be argued below, it is clear that Newman's annotation to *de Synodis* 51 does not accord with Athanasius's thought. Newman wants Christian theology to hold together a numerical oneness with something 'generic', like that found in other universals. But Athanasius is far more like Origen before him than Newman's (Aristotelian) terms allow: both patristic theologians held to a Platonic view in which Son and Spirit participate in the Father.[11]

---

[10] Newman argues of *de Synodis* 49: 'By "the Son being *equal* to the Father", is but meant that He is His "unvarying image"; it does not imply any distinction of substance' (*Ox Frs* viii. 149 n. x).

[11] Athanasius says in Discourse III. 15: 'when the Father says, *This is My Beloved Son* [Matt. 3: 17], and when the Son says that God is His own Father, *it follows that what is partaken is not external*, but from the substance of the Father. And as to this again, if it be other than the substance of the Son, an equal extravagance will meet us; there being in that case something between this that is from the Father and the substance of the Son, whatever that be' (*Ox Frs* viii. 203, my italics). As Anatolios helpfully points out about the language of participation here: 'Thus there is nothing in the Father in which the Son does not participate, and there is nothing in the Son other than what he has by participation of the Father. In this way, Athanasius transposes the mystery of the consubstantial generation of the Son from the Father into the terminology and framework of participation' (*Athanasius: The Coherence of his Thought* (London: Routledge, 1998), 107).

Of those who reject the true Christian sense, though, some do so because *ousia* 'either implied the parts of a *material* subject, or it involved no *real* distinction of persons, i.e. Sabellianism' (*Ox Frs* viii: 152 n. a). Shortly, in his section 'On the Alleged Confession of Antioch against Paul of Samosata', Newman will show this to be exactly the unfortunate choice which Paul presented to the Council of Antioch: either to understand the word *homoousios* to mean that Father and Son were divisions of some divine material, or to conceive of God as Sabellians did and argue there was but one 'being' in three self-identical modes (Paul's preferred option). As in 1833, Newman argues that the Fathers at the Antiochene Council (268), many of whom were Origen's disciples, rejected both of Paul's options. But, whereas in 1833, the rejection of *homoousios* was thus laid at the door of the disciples and not the master, now Newman suggests that Origen taught them to be 'very jealous of the corporeal ideas concerning the Divine Nature which Paul (according to Athanasius and Basil) imputed to the word ὁμοούσιον' (ibid. 166). To escape the material sense of the word, Newman implies that Origen held a Platonic theory. The Son and Spirit, in other words, participate in the *ousia* of the Father, an *ousia* which 'Platonists, in order to mark their idea of the perfection and simplicity of the Divine Nature ... consider ... "above substance"' (ibid.). In the paragraph that follows, Newman places Origen alongside Plotinus, whereas in *Arians of the Fourth Century* Plotinus was considered Origen's opponent. In 1842, Newman writes: 'The views of physical necessity too, which the material system involved, led [Plotinus] to speak of His energy and will being His substance. 6 Enn. viii. 13. And hence Origen; "Nor doth God partake of substance, rather He is partaken, than partakes" contr. Cels. vi. 64' (Ibid.).

Placing Origen alongside Plotinus need not mean that Newman considered Origen a Neoplatonist. Indeed, in 1845, he was still maintaining the position that he held in *Arians of the Fourth Century*, against Mosheim. In *Development of Christian Doctrine* Mosheim is again criticized for arguing that 'since there is a resemblance between the philosophical and the Catholic, there is certainly a very strong presumption that the Catholic were actually derived from the philosophical' views of Neoplatonists:

It is plain that, in the whole of this elaborate Essay [*de reb*], there are but two of [Mosheim's] statements which are at all of the nature of an argument in behalf of the matter of fact which he proposes to prove: the one, that Origen is said to have introduced Platonic doctrine into his writings; the other, that Synesius is charged with not renouncing his Platonism on becoming a Bishop. Of these, the instance of Synesius is an isolated one; while Origen was never countenanced by the Church even in his day, and has no distinct connexion with the Neo-platonists. (*Dev* 201–2)

Although there is 'no distinct connexion' with Plotinus, yet three years before writing this Newman opens the possibility that, in order to escape any notion of materiality in God, Origen described God the Father as *hyperousios*. The results for Trinitarian doctrine were clear. Around 1842, Newman saw what in *Arians of the Fourth Century* he had denied, that Origen, like Plotinus, might have conceived the Logos not as *homoousios* with, but subordinate *ad extra* to, the Father. Newman was opening himself to the realization that, in a Plotinian vein, Origen could have meant that, while God's 'energy and will' might be hypostases in the 'material' sense, the Father was beyond 'substance' (*Ox Frs* viii. 166). Even if Origen's likeness to Plotinus were not enough, there was also the frightening similarity to Arius's teaching of three separated hypostases.

Development in opposition to Bishop Bull

Newman's interpretation of the Council of Antioch is that the Fathers there not only objected to the material sense of *homoousios*, as Origen had taught them, but also to the Sabellian sense. In this respect, at least, in both *Arians of the Fourth Century* and his notes on *de Synodis*, Newman differs significantly from Bishop Bull. The details of this difference deserve attention for two reasons: firstly, what Newman wrote in *Arians of the Fourth Century*, in opposition to Bull, would undergo changes in 1842 and 1845; secondly, Stephen Thomas does not think Newman differed from Bull until *Development of Christian Doctrine.*[12] Already, in 1833, Newman was presenting

---

[12] Thomas notices *Dev*'s 'fantastic description of Bull's methodology. The attempt to transmute Bull's ponderous form into something fleeter shows how desperate [Newman] is to avoid giving the impression of a total reversal of his earlier "Via

a different thesis from Bull. Ostensibly Newman agreed with Bull's analysis of the word as 'formally recalled (as from exile), and inserted in [the Nicene] Creed, this most fitting expression, which, as they were aware, had been received and approved by holy fathers prior to the council of Antioch' (*Defensio* i. 79). Unlike Bull, however, he was more prepared to see the dynamism of pre-Nicene theology.

Even Newman's apparent agreements with Bull can be deceptive, as when he cites an account of the Council of Antioch that Bull plainly drew from Athanasius (*Ari* 28 n. 5). According to Bull, in the section of *Defensio* that Newman cites, Athanasius (and Basil who followed him) gave the real reason why the Council of Antioch opposed *homoousios*. That reason, said Athanasius, was Paul's sophistry, which deliberately laid stress on the material sense of the word in order for it to be rejected.[13] Bull thinks the account of Hilary, which puts the blame for its rejection on Paul's use of the word in the Sabellian sense, cannot be correct. Newman sees the tension between the accounts of Hilary and Athanasius but synthesizes them, and thus differs subtly from Bull.[14] Yes, he agrees with Bull and Athanasius that Paul was cunning, 'striving by every means to overthrow the received doctrine of the divinity of the Son', and, moreover, that such sophistry was copied by the Arians (*Defensio* i. 78). But Paul could also have been a Sabellian. Indeed, in *Arians of the Fourth Century* Newman thought Paul's heresy both denied Christ's full divinity and implied a form of Sabellianism. As well as discussing Paul's Artemonian and Ebionite credentials, Newman considered that his 'heresy was derived from the emanative school' of Sabellianism, which

Media" approach, in which the *Defence of the Nicene Faith* had been a mainstay of the Tractarian position' (*Newman and Heresy: The Anglican Years* (Cambridge: Cambridge University Press, 1991), 246). However, this section will show that while using Bull's book Newman never fully agreed with its argument.

[13] Bull wrote: 'It therefore follows, that the assertion of Athanasius is quite true, that Paul framed an argument for impugning the divinity of Christ out of the word ὁμοούσιος, which he was aware was in use among Catholics (and possibly so explained by some of them, as to give occasion [at the Council of Antioch] to its being spoken ill of) and that the fathers, accordingly, determined on the suppression of it altogether' (*Defensio* i. 75).

[14] Newman notes in his translation of *de Synodis* 45: 'while S. Basil agrees with Athan[asius] in his account of the reason of the Council's rejection of the word, St Hilary on the contrary reports that Paul himself accepted it, i.e. in a Sabellian sense, and therefore the Council rejected it' (*Ox Frs* viii. 144 n. p).

conceived of Christ as an emanation of God (*Ari* 128). As Newman presented the two kinds of Sabellianism—one Patripassian, the other Gnostic or 'emanationist'—it became clear that he thought the latter kind very similar to adoptionism. Newman's exemplary 'emanationist'

would speak of the presence rather than the existence of God in His chosen servant; and this presence, if allowed to declaim, he would represent as a certain power or emanation from the Centre of light and truth; if forced by his opponent into a definite statement, he would own to be but an inspiration, the same in kind, though superior in degree, with that which enlightened and guided the prophets. (*Ari* 123)

This exemplary emanationist also bears resemblance to Paul as countered by the Letter of the Six Bishops, as Newman explains (wrongly calling it the 'Synodal Letter' (*Ari* 129)).

According to Bull, heretics insist on the 'sophism' of misinterpreting the *homoousios* in a material way, whether 'Sabellians, followers of the Samosatene, or, lastly, Arians', which is why Nicaea 'subjoined immediately, God of God, light of light' (*Defensio* i. 78). But if before Nicaea the Sabellians had accepted the material meaning of the word in order to criticize *homoousios*, he argues, 'it is no way credible' that the Nicene Fathers would have accepted it too, for Nicaea anathematized Sabellianism (*Defensio* i. 67). But Newman thinks the opposite: that the threat of Sabellianism was indeed present at Antioch.[15] In this he followed Hilary's claim about Paul's use of *homoousios*, that 'by attributing this title to God he had taught that He was single and undifferentiated, and at once Father to Himself'.[16]

When Newman comes to clarify his thoughts, in 1842, he employs his argumentative skills to the utmost to weave two accounts together to portray one supremely cunning Samosatene:

Paul then might very naturally have urged this dilemma upon the Council, and said, 'Your doctrine implies the ὁμοούσιον, which is Manichaean, unless it be taken, as I am willing to take it, in a Sabellian sense.' And thus it might be at once trite as Athanasius says, that Paul objected, 'Unless Christ has of

---

[15] '[I]n the course of the third century, the word *Homoüsion* became more or less connected with the Gnostic, Manichaean, and Sabellian theologies' (*Ari* 129).

[16] Hilary, *de Synodis* 81 (trans.: NPNF).

man become God, it follows that He is One in substance with the Father; and if so, of necessity there are three substances' [in a material sense, *de Synodis* 45]. (*Ox Frs* viii. 167)

Here, Newman employs not just adoptionist-sounding words in Paul's mouth (Athanasius's suggestion), but also makes him admit Sabellianism (Hilary's suggestion). Thus, Newman makes the case for the rejection of *homoousios* differently from Bull—though no less fancifully.[17] As Newman acknowledges in 1842, some 'learned writers' denied altogether 'the rejection of the word ὁμοούσιον in the Antiochene Council' (*Ox Frs* viii. 165). Among them was Edward Burton, with whom Newman disagreed in a letter discussed above (*LD* iv. 194–7; see Ch. 3). Some scholars were suspicious of Athanasius's accuracy in *de Synodis* 45 and 51 when he depicts Paul—already by the fourth century considered the archetypal heretic—as questioning the use of *homoousios* with the very argument the Arians were supposed to have used.[18] Although, in 1842, Newman does not express any doubt about Athanasius, he does recognize the similarity of the heretics' arguments, noting in his translation that Paul's opposition to the materialist meaning of *homoousios* was 'the objection which Arius argues against the One in substance . . . when he calls it the doctrine of Manichaeus' (*Ox Frs* viii. 143 n. p). Newman is too much in awe of Athanasius to doubt the patriarch's account, and thus mixes Paul's heresy with both an Arian denial of Christ's divinity and also, following Hilary, with Sabellianism.[19]

[17] John Behr argues: 'Given Paul's insistence on the human character of Christ's existence, it is unthinkable that he could have taught a unitary God existing as both Father and Son' (*The Way to Nicaea* (New York: SVS Press, 2001), 219).

[18] 'The credibility of Athanasius' account, however, is severely undermined by the fact that he attributes exactly the same argument as he puts on Paul's lips to his own opponents' (ibid.). Here Behr follows De Riedmatten in arguing that any condemnation of *homoousios* at the Council of Antioch must have been highly qualified since the Synodal Letter was sent for confirmation to Dionysius of Rome, a supporter of the word (ibid. 220).

[19] Given all of Newman's research, he gives surprisingly little detail when annotating Athanasius's *de Decretis* 24 thus: 'Paul of Samosata, Sabellius, and Arius, agreed in considering that the Son was a creature, and that He was called, made after, or inhabited by the impersonal attribute called the Word or Wisdom' (*Ox Frs* viii. 41–2 n. e).

What has become clear is that, on the subject of *homoousios*, Newman was still less 'Athanasian' than Bull even in 1842. Were the reports of Hilary and Athanasius to be separated along a scale and the commentators who followed them placed on that scale according to whether they favoured Hilary or Athanasius, then Newman would fall in the middle, whereas Petavius would be on the side of Hilary and Bull on the side of Athanasius.[20]

In *Arians of the Fourth Century*, unlike Bull, Newman followed Hilary's account of the Nicene Council to the extent that he presented Paul of Samosata as a Sabellian. But, unlike Petavius, Newman followed Athanasius's report just as much as Hilary's. In 1842, Newman put yet more distance between himself and Bull, this time with respect to Origen. In 1833, Newman had thought that, due to the growth at the end of the third century of two kinds of Sabellianism, it was Origen's disciples who had opposed predicating *ousia* language of the Father and Son, not their master. Among these disciples was Dionysius of Alexandria, and Newman shares Basil's criticism of—as well as his explanation for—Dionysius's opposition to *homoousios* (*Ari* 127). In 1842, he notes that, in the *Commentary on John* (20.16), Origen would 'object to the phrase' that the Son was from the Father's *ousia* (*Ox Frs* viii. 167). At this stage, perhaps because of Origen's antipathy to Paul's cunning use of *homoousios*, Origen is not criticized for rejecting it. But Newman is far from mounting the sort of defence of Origen that he shared with Bull in 1833.

Before seeing how Origen is treated in *Development of Christian Doctrine*, it is important to see how Bull is treated there. Nicholas Lash's close analysis shows that Newman was aware of the limitations of writing any history, including his own, which required the historian 'imposing a view' before seeing whether events lined up with this narrative. Newman reveals the limitations of all historiography when he writes of Bull:

[20] Although claiming not to oppose 'the venerable Hilary', surely Bull does just that when he opposes Petavius (and Sandius). Bull argues that even were it granted 'the Samosatene heretic held precisely the same opinion touching the Son of God as Sabellius (a position, however, which might with good grounds be questioned) yet surely Sabellius himself would never have willingly affirmed that the Son is consubstantial ($\delta\mu oo\acute{u}\sigma\iota o\varsigma$) with the Father, but rather identically-substantial ($\tau a\upsilon\tau oo\acute{u}\sigma\iota o\varsigma$)' (*Defensio* i. 67).

the title of his work, which is a 'Defence of the Creed of Nicaea', shows that he is not seeking a conclusion, but imposing a view. And he proceeds both to defend the Creed by means of the Fathers against [the Unitarian] Sandius, and to defend the Fathers by means of the Creed against Petavius. He defends Creed and Fathers by reconciling one with the other…In other words, he begins with a presumption, and shows how naturally facts close round it and fall in with it, if we will but let them. He does this triumphantly, yet he has an arduous work; out of about thirty writers whom he reviews, he has, for one cause or other, to explain nearly twenty. (*Dev* 158–9)

Although Newman suggests *Defensio* is carried out 'triumphantly' yet there is the barbed suggestion that the Fathers are being 'explain[ed]' rather than speaking for themselves. Lash notes that Newman 'heightened the critical tone' for the 1878 edition, changing his description of Bull's method.[21] Here, Bull's title 'shows that he is not investigating what is true and what false, but explaining and justifying a foregone conclusion' (*Dev* [1878] 134). As has been seen, less-direct criticism of Bull began with the first edition of *Arians of the Fourth Century* and deepened when he annotated Athanasius in the early 1840s.

Origen in *An Essay on the Development of Christian Doctrine*

Origen is presented as a more ambiguous figure in *Development of Christian Doctrine* than in Newman's earlier writings. In 1845, Newman thinks that Origen led to later heresy. In some ways the story is the same as in *Arians of the Fourth Century*, with Origen shown to be a great bible scholar, 'the first writer who distinctly mentions' the letter of James (*Dev* 159). 'Origen and others' were responsible for the 'allegorical' method of scriptural interpretation dominant in Alexandria; this was used to discern the 'Catholic doctrine of the Holy Trinity' in texts 'which do not obviously refer to that doctrine…On the other hand, the School of Antioch, which adopted the literal interpretation, was the very metropolis of heresy'

[21] Lash, *Newman on Development: The Search for an Explanation in History* (London: Sheed and Ward, 1975), 23. For an account of other changes made for the 1878 edn. see 'Newman's Revisions', Ottis Screiber's Appendix to *An Essay on the Development of Christian Doctrine*, ed. C. F. Harrold (London: Longmans, 1949).

(ibid. 324). The division between Alexandrian orthodoxy and Antiochene heresy is installed once more. But there is a difference, for each city now plays a role in the idea of development, with Origen's teachings bridging the two cities. Doctrines grow, according to *Development of Christian Doctrine*, but they can overripen. Whereas in Alexandria, Cappadocia, and the West, Origen's teachings 'developed' into orthodoxy, in Antioch and the East they 'corrupted' into heresy.

Origen's teachings 'developed' in the minds of some of the finest Eastern and Western Fathers. Newman writes, 'St. Gregory Nazianzen and St. Basil digested into form the theological principles of Origen; St. Hilary and St. Ambrose are both indebted to the same great writer in their interpretations of Scripture' (*Dev* 352–3). Origen is included with Clement in the list of Fathers who recognized the faith was 'Catholic'—which is to say, in line with Newman's 'first test' of development—as is Tertullian, who influenced Pope Leo the Great (ibid. 249). However, in his 'application of the second and third tests' Newman indicates that Origen and Tertullian are 'inferior' authorities to those who learned from them; their ideas needed sifting by greater authorities: 'Doctrine too is percolated, as it were, through different minds, beginning with writers of inferior authority in the Church, and issuing at length in the enunciation of her Doctors' (ibid. 352). They are not, it seems, inferior simply because they represent the 'beginning' of a doctrine set to develop, but because their minds are too innovative. The 'Doctors' of the Church, by contrast, repeat and refine their theological views, rather than inventing new ones:

St. Athanasius, St. Augustine, St. Leo are conspicuous for the repetition *in terminis* of their own theological statements... Here we see the difference between originality of mind and the gift and calling of a Doctor in the Church; the holy Fathers just mentioned were intently fixing their minds on what they taught, grasping it more and more closely. (*Dev* 353)

The pattern for true development seems to be conservative rumination rather than speculative innovation.

In the School of Antioch, by contrast, Origen's teachings 'corrupted' into what Newman calls a 'Syrian' brand of theology, which connects Arianism and Nestorianism. This theme of

Development of Christian Doctrine is completely different from *Arians of the Fourth Century*, in which Origen had no influence in Antioch. In 1833, Newman mounted a sixfold defence against those who blamed Origen for the Arian heresy, his first line of defence being Origen's habitual opposition to heresy (*Ari* 98–9). This first defence is not mentioned in 1845, for now Newman thinks teachings 'percolate' in ways that their authors cannot control; thus, even if Origen did not teach heresy there himself, 'Palestine abounded in Origenists' (*Dev* 244). Newman defended Origen in a second way by saying that his 'speculations... related to points not yet determined by the Church'. It should be added that Newman conceived a difference in *Arians of the Fourth Century* between private and public speculation. Thus, he argued, thirdly, that '[Origen's] opinions... were imprudently made public by his friends' and, fourthly, the texts he did write have become corrupt. Private speculation was acceptable, but putting that speculation into writing and making it public was unacceptable; and, in 1833, Newman thought Origen only speculated in private. In 1845, by contrast, Newman implies that Origen made public thoughts he should have kept private, which is why Demetrius, bishop of Alexandria, 'could banish Origen for speculations which developed and ripened... in Syria' (*Dev* 282). Fifthly, Newman had said 'the doctrine of the Trinity is clearly avowed [by Origen], and in particular, our Lord's divinity energetically and variously enforced' (*Ari* 58). It has already been seen that Newman began to have doubts about Origen's 'doctrine of the Trinity' in 1842. As for Christology, Newman thinks that Origen shares much in common with later 'Syrian' views:

As it tended to the separation of the Divine Person of Christ from His manhood, so did it tend to explain away His Divine Presence in the Sacramental elements... Some countenance too is given to the same view of the Eucharist, at least in some parts of his works, by Origen, whose language concerning the Incarnation also *leans* to what was afterwards Nestorianism. (*Dev* 287, my italics)

Newman's sixth point was that, if Fathers like Athanasius defended Origen, how can later generations criticize? But while Newman took Origen at his best in *Arians of the Fourth Century*, it is clear from the last two quotations from 1845 that he now believes Origen could 'lean', or be 'ripened in Syria', towards heretical ends. In his ambiguous views of Origen in 1845, while holding him in esteem because Athanasius did, Newman is newly critical of his 'leanings' to heresy.

THE RISE OF ATHANASIUS

The 1831–2 correspondence with Hugh James Rose, one of the editors of the series of which *Arians of the Fourth Century* was intended to be part, provides a yardstick to measure how far Newman had moved towards Athanasius a decade later. In these letters, Newman can be seen hazarding ideas that, after Rose's input, would either end up in his first book or be rejected. One idea that was rejected was Newman's original plan, in August 1831, to discuss any Church Council 'which will at all illustrate the phraseology or doctrines of our Articles' (*LD* ii. 353). On Rose's advice, Newman was 'let off the consideration of the Council of Trent—(which I shall count a great gain)—for in no sense can it be said to confirm our Articles' (ibid. 359). The shift could not be clearer—from Newman's rejection of the Latin Church and its Councils in 1831 to his position in Tract 90 ten years later, that the Thirty-nine Articles could accord with Trent.

Newman's 'Latinization' can also be seen in his doctrine of God by comparing the Rose correspondence with the translation of Athanasius made at Littlemore. He wrote to Rose in August 1832 that it was

difficult to conceive God one Person as Three, the difficulty being deeper than people suppose... And, in my own mind, I think it is clear that the whole is an Economy—everyone grants that much of the Scripture account is such—e.g. His being angry, repenting—or resting—etc. etc.—for these, and such like, *make up* the idea of a Personal God, as distinct from a mere system or Anima Mundi. (*LD* iii. 78)[22]

---

[22] In Tract 73 in May 1836, Newman described what he means by Anima Mundi as 'universal essence, who has no known existence except in His works, as an all-pervading power or principle, not external to the created world, but in it, and developed through it' (*EH* i. 81).

Two points of special interest come from this sentence. The first is *who* Newman conceived God to be in 1832. He uses an expression, 'God one Person as Three', which might seem odd when judged by the standards of post-Nicene orthodoxy. God is 'one Person', rather than the more typical designation: 'God is three persons in one substance.' Such an expression runs counter to later orthodoxy but does not, it should be noted, contradict the teachings of Athanasius, in spite of what Newman came to believe from 1841. When putting the finishing touches to *Arians of the Fourth Century*, Newman's letter to Rose emphasizes the *personal* dimension of God: the Father is the 'one person' who, by the Word and Spirit, is revealed as 'angry' and then 'repenting' of anger in the Old Testament, and 'resting' after creation. God's person is revealed to us by sending forth the Word and Spirit. *Monarchia*, as Newman went on to explain in *Arians of the Fourth Century*, was the pre-Nicene teaching that the Word and Spirit derive their unity from their one Source. He wrote there that the pre-Nicenes discerned in scripture that the Son was a messenger of the one God, whose 'personality' derived from the Father's person, professing a doctrine that Newman had shown, in the letter to Rose, to be his own.[23]

At this early stage, Newman also believed that Athanasius upheld the doctrine of the *monarchia*. In *Arians of the Fourth Century*, he portrays the Father as 'the God' (ὁ Θεός) of the Creeds, also stating that God could be no Father without a consubstantial Son.[24] At Littlemore in the 1840s, however, Newman's opinions shifted.

---

[23] 'The very name of Son, and the very idea of derivation, imply a certain subordination of the Son to the Father, *so far forth as we view Him* as distinct from the Father, or *in His personality*: and frequent testimony is borne to the correctness of this inference in Scripture, as in the descriptions of the Divine Angel in the Old Testament, revived in the closing revelations of the New' (*Ari* 163, my italics).

[24] 'Hence it is, that the Father is called "the only God", at a time when our Lord's name is also mentioned, John xvii.3, 1 Tim. i.16, 17, as if the Son was but the reiteration of His Person ... The Creed, called the Apostles', follows this mode of stating the doctrine; the title of God standing in the opening against the Father's name, while the Son and Spirit are introduced as distinct forms or modes (so to say) of and in the One Eternal Being. The Nicene Creed, commonly so called, directed as it is against the impugners both of the Son's and of the Spirit's divinity, nevertheless observes the same rule even in a stricter form, beginning with a confession of the *"One* God"' (*Ari* 176).

Here, Newman de-emphasized *monarchia* in favour of a more Latin depiction of the Trinity, increasingly worried about the doctrine's tendency to subordinate the Son to the Father.[25] Moving away from the 'God one Person as Three', in which the Son and Spirit derive from 'the One God' of ancient Israel, Newman took Athanasius with him.

In the annotations, the Athanasius translation is glossed with texts from Augustine, the Cappadocians, and Cyril of Alexandria, turning Newman's hero into a composite of these post-Nicene Fathers. For Newman at Littlemore, Nicaea was not orthodox enough. Thus, below, Basil supports the view that God could be simultaneously One and Three, by stressing that each person was the One God, whereas Athanasius held that the Father is the One God. Augustine's appearance in the annotations is of particular interest given the Latin direction in which Newman was heading. In Rome in 1847, Newman expressed suspicion of Nicaea's teaching on God's unity in the paper he wrote privately for the Catholic theologian, Giovanni Perrone. He writes that the Nicene Council, grounded in the derivation of Son and Spirit from one Source, was eclipsed once the Latin Church had come to grips with the threat of Sabellianism:

Sabellius attempted to uphold more clearly the numerical unity of the Godhead, and fell into heresy. After some time which enabled the Church to find the exact formula for this great mystery, Augustine, doctor of the Church, finally enunciated the dogma most fully, the Creed *Quicunque* confirmed it, and the Fourth Lateran Council defined it'. (Perrone 102)

As will be seen, Augustine, the *Quicunque*, which Newman knew to be wrongly called the Athanasian Creed,[26] and the Fourth Lateran were already shaping the composite picture of Athanasius in the

[25] By 1845, Newman 'questioned whether any Ante-nicene father distinctly affirms either the numerical Unity or the Coequality of the Three Persons; except perhaps the heterodox Tertullian, and that chiefly in a work [*Adversus Praxean*] written after he had become a Montanist' (*Dev* 14).

[26] *Arians of the Fourth Century* cited Daniel Waterland's *Works* (Oxford, 1823). The first chapter of Waterland's *A Critical History of the Athanasian Creed*, ed. J. R. King (Oxford and London: James Parker and Company, 1870) examines seventeenth- and eighteenth-century scholarship, most of which assigned this Creed to the Western Church not earlier than the fifth century.

1842–4 annotations. Bishop Kaye criticized Newman's annotations not for Latinizing but for 'Lateranizing' Athanasius.[27]

A second point in the letter to Rose is Newman's view that even though Christians have some grasp of *who* God is there can be no revelation of *what* God is—the divine *ousia*. This is what Newman considers to be the scriptural doctrine of 'economy'. In *Arians of the Fourth Century*, Newman made clear that Clement and Origen saw this as the way scripture reveals the truth about the God who remains a mystery. Clement and Origen were Newman's guides in the 1830s, rather than Athanasius. Newman is touching on the doctrine of divine simplicity in the letter: the teaching that, unlike creatures, God is not made of anything but is simple, and thus all attributes are predicated of God in a way that befits uncreated *ousia*. As creatures, we cannot know or speak of what God is like—*ousia* thus expresses a negative theology, something humans cannot know. For Athanasius, Newman writes in 1842, it is God as Father whom humans cannot know 'as such' and therefore, predicated of the Father's simplicity, the words 'Person' and 'Substance' do not convey separate notions:

it must be ever borne in mind that we are contemplating divine things according to *our notions*, not in *fact*: i.e. speaking of the Almighty Father, *as such*; there being no real separation between His Person and His Substance. It may be added, that, though theologians differ in their decisions, it would appear that our Lord is not the Image of the Father's person, but of the Father's substance; in other words, not of the Father considered as Father, but considered as God. (*Ox Frs* viii. 211 n. 1 [in fact, f])

This quotation reveals the heart of Newman's new position on the Trinity. While admitting that 'theologians differ in their decisions', Newman does not put Athanasius with those who say the Son is indeed 'the Image of the Father's person', which is where it will be argued the patriarch belongs. For this would be unity based on

[27] Kaye noted, specifically against Newman, that 'Cudworth states the doctrine of the ancient orthodox Fathers to be, that the essence of the Godhead, in which three persons or hypostases agree, as each of them is God, is not one singular and individual, but one common essence ... [*TIS*] 601. He states the notion of the Lateran Council to be, that there is a Trinity of persons, numerically the same, or having one and the same singular essence'. As will be seen, Newman held the Lateran notion (*Some Account of the Council of Nicaea* (London: Rivingtons, 1853), 246–7 n. 1).

derivation, which Origen and Athanasius held in common. In a derivation view, it was Sonship that differentiated the Son *of God* (a title of derivation) from God the Source, or as Newman put it in a Lenten sermon in 1836: 'He is God, not *though*, but *because* He is the Son of God', suggesting Christ's divinity is derived from his Father (*PS* vi. 5: 1222). Instead of a derivation view, in 1842 Newman introduces a 'generical' view of substance in which 'God's' substance is where Father, Son, and Spirit find their unity.[28] On the face of it, Newman's position in the early 1840s looks in line with what he wrote to Rose, for, predicated on God's unknowability, it seems just as correct to say 'one Person as Three' as to speak of 'a triple Personality'.[29] But, in fact, the latter signifies an account of God which is not found in the writings of Athanasius that Newman was annotating.

In what follows, these two themes recur: the *oneness* of God as it derives from the one Source (the Father) and the *economy* by which this truth is expressed, but as the means by which loyalty shifts from Origen to Athanasius in the 1840s. Firstly, Newman's conflation of generical and numerical unity will reveal that, increasingly in the 1840s, Newman privileged the latter (Lateran) notion. A crucial passage on God's Trinity will then be examined from 1842, when Newman was crystallizing his own thoughts around those of Athanasius. Finally, the new trajectory, which saw the post-Nicenes as one with Athanasius in considering *ousia*-language as 'economic' with the truth (because the true being of God is unknowable), will be

[28] Richard Cross explains the difference in 'On Generic and Derivation Views of God's Trinitarian Substance', *Scottish Journal of Theology*, 56 (2003), 464–80. Cross argues that, contrary to Athanasius, the Father's monarchy is better sustained if *ousia* is conceived as 'the "place" at which the persons overlap'; in other words, if *ousia* somehow precedes the persons as in the 'generic' view of substance (ibid. 470). Athanasius's derivation view 'is simply incoherent, accepting both that the Father possesses, and that he does not possess, the property of being the generator of the Son' (ibid. 469). The important point of Cross's observation for my purposes is that, incoherent as it might be, Athanasius holds a derivation view of God's unity— something that Newman forgets in the 1840s—in which 'consubstantiality is an asymmetrical relation, and Athanasius persistently claims that the Son is *homoousios* with the Father, but not vice versa: the Father is not *homoousios* with the Son' (ibid. 467).

[29] A phrase from University Sermon XV in 1843; God's 'triple Personality, in the sense in which the Infinite can be understood to have Personality at all' (*US* 350).

traced from the Athanasius translation to the 1858 essay 'On St Cyril's Formula'.

How God is one

Newman's writings published in 1833 and in 1842 favoured two different couplets when talking about the oneness of God. Each of the two terms in these couplets complements the other (though they might appear to be opposites) in Newman's account to give as full a description of God's one *ousia* as possible. The couplet used in *Arians of the Fourth Century* describes the divine unity as both 'of God' and 'in God' (*Ari* 172). The first half of this couplet led (Newman does not say when) to the doctrine known as the *monarchia*, in which God's oneness derives from a single source; hence, for the Son and Spirit to be 'of God' means to be 'of the Father'. However, Newman was keen to balance this with the other half of the couplet, the unity 'in God', which led (again, Newman does not say when)[30] to the doctrine of the coinherence or *perichoresis* of the Son and Spirit 'in the Father'. This twofold way of referring to God's unity was favoured in *Arians of the Fourth Century* at the time when Newman conceived of the Father as the 'One God'. By 1842, although this couplet continued to appear, it was mainly in the texts that Newman quoted and only rarely in his annotations.[31] For example, the doxology with which Athanasius ends *de Decretis* shows the doctrines of *perichoresis* and *monarchia*, for the Son and Spirit are one in the God who is Father: 'to *God and the Father* is due the glory, honour, and worship with His co-existent Son and Word, together with the

---

[30] Verna Harrison finds no evidence for the Trinitarian use of the word *perichoresis* until the concept was disseminated in John Damascene's *de Fide Orthodoxa*. 'Through John, the concept achieved currency in both East and West' ('Perichoresis in the Greek Fathers', *St Vladimir's Theological Quarterly*, 35 (1991), 53). Moreover, she cites the work of August Deneffe, arguing that it was medieval Latin doctrine that translated the Greek περιχώρησις as, alternatively, the dynamic *circumincessio* ('interpenetration') or the static *circuminsessio* ('coinherence') (ibid. 54).

[31] e.g., Athanasius follows Dionysius of Rome in arguing that God's unity derives from the one Source or Father in *de Decretis* 26. Newman notes that 'the Monarchy . . . is one of the especial senses in which God is said to be one' (*Ox Frs* viii. 45 n. h).

All-holy and Life-giving Spirit, now and unto endless ages of ages'
(*Ox Frs* viii. 58, my italics).

The way of expressing God's unity that Newman favoured had
shifted to another couplet, 'numerical' and 'generical' oneness, which
he had encountered in Ralph Cudworth. When researching *Arians of
the Fourth Century*, he had learned from Cudworth

> that when the ancient orthodox fathers of the Christian church maintained,
> against Arius, the Son to be *homoousion*, coessential or consubstantial with
> the Father, though that word be thus interpreted, Of the same essence or
> substance, yet they universally understood thereby, not a sameness of sin-
> gular and numerical, but of common or universal, essence only; that is, the
> generical or specifical essence of the Godhead. (*TIS* 608)

In other words, for Cudworth, the substance of God is one and the
same, but the persons are three. The unity of the divine persons came
from their substance—the substance of the one God or Father—and
not from their number. Alternatively, argued Cudworth, since 1215,
Catholics have taught numerical unity in which each of the divine
persons is the one God, 'a doctrine, which seemeth not to have been
owned by any public authority of the Christian church, save that of
the Lateran council only' (*TIS* 601). Newman in the 1840s disagrees
with Cudworth, but expresses his disagreement by citing Edward
Gibbon not Cudworth. Gibbon claimed that numerical oneness
was stressed by the Latin Fathers (a 'Trinitas' suggesting *one* triad)
whereas Greeks stressed what was generic to the three Persons (τριάς
suggesting a substance shared among *three*).[32] Newman shares Gibbon's (and Cudworth's) view that the doctrine of generical unity is
'Greek', while differing from Gibbon in thinking that the Greeks also
'taught the doctrine of "a one" or a numerical unity' (*Ox Frs* viii. 46
n. k). In the 1840s, Newman wants to see the Latin doctrine of
numerical unity in the Greek Fathers, whereas he had previously
not thought this doctrine important. In *Arians of the Fourth Century*,

[32] Gibbon, *Rise and Fall of the Roman Empire*, ed. J. B. Bury (2nd edn.; London:
Methuen, 1909), ii. 374 n. 74. Gibbon wrote humorously of the two doctrines
Newman formerly preferred: 'The περιχώρησις or *circumincessio* is perhaps the
deepest and darkest corner of the whole theological abyss' (ibid. 369 n. 59) and,
regarding Bishop Bull's discussion of the 'pre-eminence of the Father', or *monarchia*,
'some of his antagonists have called [it] nonsense and others heresy' (ibid. n. 60).

the doctrine of economy prevented speculation on God's *ousia*, and thus excluded any human understanding of 'number and comparison' in the Godhead (*Ari* 155). What brought the change to a more Latin perspective?

The reason Newman shifted his expressions of divine unity had something to do with his change of mind on who the Church means by 'the one God'. He seems, in 1842, to be uncomfortable with the idea that this refers primarily to the Father and only derivatively to the Son and Spirit, hence he rarely emphasizes the *monarchia*. He criticizes the Second Confession of Sirmium (AD 357) for 'declaring that the One God is the God of Christ, [which] implies that our Lord is not God' (*Ox Frs* viii. 123 n. u). This 'Arian' Creed, which Athanasius recorded, suggests to Newman that Arianism arose from a view of the Father alone as 'the one God'. Newman thinks instead that each person is 'the one God', and, as a consequence, tries to discern the new couplet of numerical and generical oneness in scripture. Thus he argues: 'when S. Paul says "God was in Christ"; he does not mean absolutely the Divine Nature, which is the proper sense of the word [i.e. 'God'], but the Divine Nature as existing in the Person of the Son' (*Ox Frs* viii. 155 n. f). In other words, 'God' does not mean the one God or Source for Newman here, which Paul's original ὁ Θεός did.[33] Rather, 'God' for Newman means the 'Divine Nature', which is at this stage the same as saying God's substance, the 'generical' *ousia* which Father and Son share. While researching Athanasius at Littlemore, Newman became concerned to depict a robustly coequal Father, Son, and Spirit, a coequality he believed to be the key signification of *homoousios*. To this end, he played down what Athanasius took for granted—the *monarchia* of the Father—and played up what he did not—a generical and numerical unity within the Godhead.

In order to portray a numerical unity in the Athanasius translations, Newman had to gloss what the patriarch said with annotations citing Augustine. For instance, Athanasius writes in Discourse III. 9: 'For as the Father is First, so also is [the Son] both First, as Image of the First, and because the First is in Him, and also Offspring from the Father, in whom the whole creation is created and adopted into

---

[33] Paul only once refers to Christ by this name, in Rom. 9: 5, and the interpretation of this passage is greatly disputed, as is shown by Behr (*Way to Nicaea*, 58–9).

sonship' (*Ox Frs* xix. 412–13). Augustine had a wholly different notion of how coequality might be described, a fact which Newman fails to mention in annotating this text. While the Greek is speaking of the Son as 'Image of the First' (the doctrine of *monarchia*) and coinhering with the First (*perichoresis*), the gloss Newman gives from Augustine is as follows: 'The question has almost been admitted by S. Austin, whether it is not possible to say that God is *One* Person, (Trin. vii. 8.) for He is wholly and entirely Father, and at the same time wholly and entirely Son, and wholly and entirely Holy Ghost' (*Ox Frs* xix. 412 n. d).[34] Here the Son is equally the 'One person' who is God, rather than derivatively sharing in the Source's divinity as Son *of* God. In his annotations, Newman emphasizes the similarities between Athanasius and Augustine, while playing down the differences.

A comparison of Newman's thought with Athanasius's theology reveals the manipulation the patriarch's writings were undergoing in the early 1840s. In *On the Decrees of Nicaea*, written probably thirty years after the Council of Nicaea, Athanasius named God both 'Father' of the Son and 'Fountain of Wisdom' (*de Decretis* 15). As such, 'God's Wisdom' or Son derives from the Father who is Source ($\pi\eta\gamma\dot{\eta}$), which is why it is the Father who is 'God' with the Greek article ($\dot{o}$ $\Theta\epsilon\acute{o}s$) whereas the Son is 'Son *of* God' ($\tau\grave{o}\nu$ $Y\grave{\iota}\grave{o}\nu$ $\tau o\hat{v}$ $\Theta\epsilon o\hat{v}$, PG 25: 441 A6–B3). For Athanasius, the Son is derived from a Source, according to the doctrine of the *monarchia*; nevertheless, for God to be 'Father', there must always have been a Son to make God so. During the battles over doctrinal language that resulted from the Council of Nicaea, Athanasius became convinced that only the extra-biblical word *homoousios*, which is to say the Son is 'consubstantial' with the Father, was sufficient to describe this relationship. But, warns Athanasius, this is not 'substance' (*ousia*) in a material sense of the word, for God is not a compound; nor is God ($\tau\acute{o}\nu$ $\Theta\epsilon\acute{o}\nu$) knowable when we use names like 'God' ($\Theta\epsilon\acute{o}\nu$) and 'Father' (*de Decretis* 22, PG 25: 456 A11–14). '[I]f God be simple,' Newman

---

[34] Newman's 'almost' here is telling, because it was actually the Fourth Lateran Council which stated that the persons are numerically the same. Augustine finally refuses to describe God as 'One person' because the term is not relational. See Cross, 'Quid tres? On What Precisely Augustine Professes Not to Understand in *De Trinitate* 5 and 7', *Harvard Theological Review*, 100 (2007), 215–32.

translates, 'as He is, it follows that in saying "God" and naming "Father", we name nothing as if about Him, but signify His substance itself' (*Ox Frs* viii. 38). It is only in the incarnation that the Son makes known the unknowable God, a theme of Discourses I–III, which date from Athanasius's second exile between 339 and 346. Newman translated Discourse II. 14 thus: '*God* being good and *Father* of the Lord, in pity, and desiring to be known by all, makes His own Son put on Him a human body and become man, and be called Jesus, that in this body offering Himself for all, He might deliver all from false worship and corruption' (*Ox Frs* xix. 300, my italics). Notice that the Father is God (ὁ Θεός) whereas the Son is the one who is sent by the Father so that the unknowable God might be known in the flesh.

But Newman's theology is in some ways blind to Athanasius's own terminology. Worried about the connotations of calling the Father alone the one God, Newman forces Athanasius into a later version of Latin orthodoxy. 'The one God' now signifies the 'unity of substance', meaning both generical and numerical unity, and ignores the unity based on derivation from the Source. While in the translation of the Discourses Athanasius compares the sun and its radiance to God and the Logos (the sun's 'substance is whole and its radiance perfect and whole, yet without impairing the substance of light, but as a true offspring from it'), Newman's gloss, using Basil, moves away from the unity of derivation that underlies this analogy (*Ox Frs* xix. 326–7). He writes: 'there are two Persons, in Each Other ineffably, Each being wholly one and the same Divine Substance, yet not being merely separate aspects of the Same, Each being God as absolutely as if there were no other Divine Person but Himself... Basil. contr. Eun. i. 10' (*ibid.* n. g).[35] Newman's focus is on 'one substance' rather than on Sonship, a combination of numerical (each is the 'one' divine person) *with* generical ('substance') unity that Cudworth's talk of substance precluded. But Cudworth's was just one of many Anglican teachings that Newman had rejected by the early 1840s.

---

[35] Another Cappadocian, Gregory of Nazianzus, preserved the *monarchia* in *Oration* 31.14. See Christopher A. Beeley, 'Divine Causality and the Monarchy of God the Father in Gregory of Nazianzus', *Harvard Theological Review*, 100 (2007), 199–214.

How God is three

In relation to the doctrine of God's threeness, or Trinity, Newman's views were expressed most clearly in the extended note in *Select Treatises* on the meaning of 'hypostasis' in the Nicene Anathema. Here Newman heads towards a position that considers Origen a step on the way to Arianism in the East. In the same note, he says Athanasius was saved from this error in part by his association with the West. Even if this argument is not yet fully formulated, it was—to use an image of development used by Newman—a Latin direction in which his writings were looking.[36] But, to explain how he got there, it is important to see how he conceived Origen and Arius as specifically 'Eastern' in their Trinitarian views, and Athanasius as somehow 'Western'. Newman first expresses the difference between Eastern and Western views of the 'Trinity' in a definition in one of his annotations to *de Decretis*, where he writes:

> The word τριάς translated Trinity, is first used by Theophilus, ad Autol [ochum] ii. 15 . . . It is certain that the Latin view of the sacred truth, when perverted, becomes Sabellianism; and that the Greek, when perverted, becomes Arianism; and we find Arius arising in the East, Sabellius in the West . . . It is important, however, to understand, that 'Trinity' does not mean the *state* or *condition* of being three, as humanity is the condition of being man, but is synonymous with 'three persons'. Humanity does not exist and cannot be addressed, but the Holy Trinity is a three, or a unity which exists in three. (Ox Frs viii. 46 n. k)

Three things in particular stand out from Newman's definition quoted here, culminating in his reflections on why East and West suffered different heresies.

First is the questionable way Newman presents the word 'Trinity' as the true development in English of the word τριάς ('three') in the pre-Nicene Church. Not only is Newman suggesting the word was a relatively early signifier for God, but in trying to substantiate this claim, here by quoting a late second-century Bishop of Antioch, Newman proves less discriminating of the word 'Trinity' than he

---

[36] The image is Newman's in his final letter to William Froude in 1879: 'which way does [the letter] B look? to the left or to the right?' (*LD* xxix. 116).

had been in his first book. As I have shown in Chapter 2, *Arians of the Fourth Century* interpreted the second and third centuries as a period of shifts and clarifications in doctrinal language of the Trinity. Reflecting the fact that doctrinal terms had not been formulated, Newman rarely uses the word 'Trinity' in relation to early doctrine in *Arians of the Fourth Century*, except as a gloss to express the divine Object the pre-Nicenes found themselves encountering in scripture and prayer.[37] This implies Newman was aware how little his Alexandrian heroes themselves used even 'three' when talking of God. Among pre-Nicenes, Newman quotes the word only from Gregory of Neocaesarea in the East, and from Tertullian in the West; he also quotes Dionysius of Rome's mention of 'Trinity' from Bull but here in defence of 'Divine Monarchy' (*Ari* 173–4). His annotations in 1842 seem less sensitive to the rarity of τριάς than *Arians of the Fourth Century*. Although Theophilus used it Newman does not warn his reader that this bishop's 'three' were God, Word, and Wisdom. He is similarly quick to conclude that Athanasius's use of 'Father, Son, and Spirit' represented a fully worked-out 'Trinitarian' doctrine when, in fact, the word 'Trinity' appears much more frequently in Newman's notes than in Athanasius's own writings.[38] Although Newman finds Cyril speaking of the 'ineffable unity of the Trinity', Cyril more usually follows Athanasius in talking of Father, Son, and Spirit (*Ox Frs* viii. 251 n. f). Newman seems to have grown overconfident, since *Arians of the Fourth Century*, of the role the word played and its continuity of meaning in pre-Nicene and post-Nicene doctrine.

---

[37] 'Thus the systematic doctrine of the Trinity may be considered as the shadow, projected for the contemplation of the intellect, of the Object of scripturally-informed piety: a representation, economical; necessarily imperfect, as being exhibited in a foreign medium, and therefore involving apparent inconsistencies or mysteries; given to the Church by tradition contemporaneously with those apostolic writings, which are addressed more directly to the heart; kept in the background in the infancy of Christianity, when faith and obedience were vigorous, and brought forward at a time when, reason being disproportionately developed, and aiming at sovereignty in the province of religion, its presence became necessary to expel an usurping idol from the house of God' (*Ari* 145).

[38] Only a few times can Newman catch Athanasius writing of the 'Trinity'. In the notes, he quotes from Athanasius's letter *ad Serapion* 1.14 and 4.6 (*Ox Frs* viii. 33 n. r, 184 n. k). In Newman's translations, Athanasius also uses the word in Discourses I. 17–18, I. 58, III. 15 (*Ox Frs* viii. 205–6, 264; *Ox Frs* xix. 421–2).

Secondly, what stands out from the quotation above is Newman's view that the English word 'Trinity' signifies no earthly three, but only the divine 'unity which exists in three'. How this unity-in-three comes about has solely to do, in 1842, with his conception of the word *homoousios*. Once again, in *Arians of the Fourth Century* he avoided the word as much as possible, aware how dangerous it was for many of the pre-Nicenes (although he believed they conceived the relationship of Son to Father in such a way as came to be called *homoousios*). Indeed, around the time of Nicaea, when proper talk about God's *ousia* became a theme of the Council, Athanasius was himself wary of such language. Even though the Council had declared the credal way for it to be used, Newman recognized that 'for whatever reason[,] Athan[asius] avoids the word ὁμοούσιον, in these Discourses' (*Ox Frs* viii. 210 n. d).[39] Yet, in annotating 'these Discourses', Newman did not refrain from using the word in a way that signified the generic unity of the τριάς.

Michel René Barnes has suggested that in the aftermath of Nicaea Marcellus of Ancyra was able to use the Creed as grounds for a renewal of Sabellianism. For Marcellus, there could not be two any-things in God—not two lights or hypostases or *ousiai*—if there was but one God, and this the credal language of 'light from light' and 'of the *ousia* of the Father' affirmed.[40] Newman might be alluding to this very problem with *homoousios* after Nicaea when he mentions, in the quotation, the influence of 'Sabellius in the West'. Another of Barnes's

[39] He changed this opinion slightly in 1858: '[Athanasius] introduces the word, I think, only once into his three celebrated Orations, and then rather in a formal statement of doctrine than in the flow of his discussion, viz. *Orat.* i. 4' (*TT* 337). Newman does not follow through to suggest that the Creed was probably not of first importance to those attending the Council.

[40] Barnes explains why Marcellus liked *homoousios*: ' "of the *ousia*" may sound now to express a relationship ("*from* the essence") but it was at the time universally taken by supporters and critics alike to express divine unity. An identical understanding attaches to the famous phrase "*homoousios* with the Father" and may fairly be judged to have been the intention behind the phrase: the unity theology intimated in the use of the same language—God, Light, true God—of both Father and Son is expressed and explained in the creed's *ousia* language' ('The Fourth Century as Trinitarian Canon', in L. Ayres and G. Jones (eds.), *Christian Origins: Theology, Rhetoric and Community* (London: Routledge, 1998), 51). Barnes also argues that in Rome Athanasius may have taken from Marcellus the idea of calling 'Arians' all those who opposed *homoousios* (ibid. 55).

suggestions is that for polemical purposes Athanasius depicted those like Eusebius of Caesarea, who opposed Marcellus, as the continuation of Arius.[41] Like many orthodox writers, Newman accepted Athanasius's polemic and referred to the 'Semi-Arians' as Arius's successors. Newman copied Athanasius's depiction of the triumph of *homoousios* as the only word capable of confuting on the one hand Arius and on the other hand Semi-Arians like Eusebius of Nicomedia and Eusebius of Caesarea. In the 1840s, the formula *homoousios* was the orthodox standard, but the generical signification that he gave the word was not found in Athanasius.[42]

This brings up the third and final point: Newman's interpretation of why the East and West were plagued by different heresies—'Arius arising in the East, Sabellius in the West'. Newman gives this question greatest consideration in the extended note on the meaning of 'hypostasis' in the Nicene Anathema. This note integrates Newman's changing views on Origen with his shifting views on Athanasius. Put starkly, and without Newman's detailed qualifications, the note shows that Origen used *ousia* language in order to stress God's threeness—a tendency which led to division among the three, as in Arianism. He writes: 'Three Hypostases are spoken of by Origen, his pupil Dionysius, as afterwards by Eusebius of Caesarea . . . and Athanasius' (*Ox Frs* viii. 71); but Athanasius, under the 'influence of the West', also used hypostasis to speak of God's one *ousia* (ibid. 72). Latins, like Jerome, took Greeks, like Origen, to be speaking of three 'hypostases' as if the word meant the same as *ousia*, thus implying

---

[41] Barnes writes: 'until recently, authority has settled on Athanasius' understanding that the immediate post-Nicene trinitarian crisis was occasioned by Arius' theology instead of Eusebius' understanding that the immediate post-Nicene trinitarian crisis was occasioned by Marcellus of Ancyra's theology. Among Athanasius' greatest polemical triumphs was his development of and promulgation of the rhetorical strategy of identifying his opponents as "Arians"' (ibid. 54).

[42] If Behr is correct about *de Decretis* 22, then Newman is un-Athanasian to speak of generical unity: 'Titles such as "God", "Father", "Lord", and "I am" are held, by Athanasius, to indicate not something "about God", but "his essence itself", which, though signified, remains "incomprehensible". That the title "Father" is here listed with other titles indicative of the "essence" of God is significant. It demonstrates that the term "essence" is not used by Athanasius in a generic sense, as referring to the kind of being God is, but to indicate the very being of God, God himself. Yet that God is essentially Father . . . entails there being a Son' (*The Nicene Faith*, 2 vols. (New York: SVS Press, 2004.), i. 232).

that God was divided into three essences—the doctrine that, it is claimed, is common to all 'Arians'. By attaching 'no fixed sense to the word', on the other hand, Athanasius could use it in a way suitable to the West, writing elsewhere that 'hypostasis is substance' or *ousia* (ibid. 70, quoting *ad Afros* 4). Therefore, the patriarch could be judged correct by the standards of Jerome, who 'uses strong language' against those who speak only of 'Three Hypostases'.[43] This is not to say that Newman now considered Jerome in the West as the judge of all things orthodox, just that he had lost his former respect for Origen. Newman's trajectory is taking him away from his former Alexandrian heroes, Origen and Dionysius, and towards a Latin-friendly depiction of Athanasius.[44] In this depiction, the patriarch becomes the point of contact between East and West, thus holding together the tendency towards oneness without Sabellianism in the Latin Church *and* threeness without Arianism in the Greek.

The extended note demonstrates another theme discussed already—the way Newman distanced himself from Bull. The whole note is a critique of Bull. *Defensio* argued that the mention of both '*ousia*' and 'hypostasis' in the Nicene Anathema shows that there was already a distinction between the two words which approached later orthodox usage, another area of dispute with Petavius. (On this issue, by the way, Routh and Burton also opposed Bull (*Ox Frs* viii. 66)). Bull followed Basil's analysis of the Anathema 'in his 78th epistle', placing his 'trust...in the great Basil rather than in the modern Jesuit, Petavius' (*Defensio* i. 240). Newman, by contrast, employs the full range of historical-critical methods to argue that the use of

---

[43] Jerome writes: 'If you desire it, then be a *new* faith framed *after* the Nicene, and let the orthodox confess in terms like the Arian' (*Ox Frs* viii. 70, quoting *Epistle* 15. 4). Also, in 1845, Newman supported Jerome's opposition to Origen in *contra Rufinus* (*Dev* 279).

[44] In 1858, Newman added historical detail to this depiction of Athanasius, noting that the shift in his use of 'hypostasis' occurred when, as secretary to Alexander of Alexandria, he is presumed to have written in 'AD 320–324, two formal letters against Arius, one addressed to [Alexander's] namesake of Constantinople, the other encyclical', the second of which changes from an Alexandrian to a Latin use of hypostasis. 'I am not supposing [Athanasius] did this without Alexander's sanction. Indeed, the character of the Arian polemic would naturally lead Alexander, as well as Athanasius, to be jealous of the formula of the τρεῖς ὑποστάσεις, which Arianism was using against them; and the latter would be confirmed in this feeling by his subsequent familiarity with Latin theology' (*TT* 342–3).

hypostasis to mean 'person' 'was little more than Alexandrian till the middle of the fourth century' (*Ox Frs* viii. 72). Newman can thus present the Alexandrians as presaging later orthodoxy, while also giving centre-stage to the greatest of their number, Athanasius, who presented the true doctrine of God where Origen veered towards Arianism.

The language of *ousia*

From the perspective both of God's unity and Trinity, then, in the early 1840s, Newman changed his interpretation of Athanasius from one in which 'the one God' signified the Father to one in which each of the three persons is equally the one God. Nevertheless, he consistently followed the patriarch's reticence when speaking of *what* God is. Even when Athanasius refers to God as 'three', the words are predicated in a unique way, which recognizes that the divine *ousia* can never be known.

In 1842, Newman writes of this unique sort of predication in his annotations. Athanasius uses 'nature' (*physis*) at the end of *de Synodis* 52, writing of the '*nature* of Son', where he might be expected to use 'hypostasis of Son'. Newman explains Athanasius's expression with reference to Cyril. (As in the 1858 essay 'On St Cyril's Formula', it was a device of Newman's scholarship to refer one Alexandrian patriarch to the other in instances of untypical terminology.) Cyril, arguing against Nestorius, says:

'three Natures' is the One Eternal Divine Nature viewed in that respect in which He is Three... These phrases mean that the Son *who is* the Divine Substance, is from the Father *who is* the [same] divine substance. As (to speak of what is *analogous* not parallel) we might say that 'man is father of man', not meaning by man the same individual in both cases, but the same nature, so here we speak not of the same Person in the two cases, but the same Individuum. (*Ox Frs* viii. 155 n. f; square brackets unidentified)

Therefore, Newman argues, for both Alexandrian patriarchs the substance which Father and Son share brings numerical unity. A Latin term is even used for this numerical unity, 'Individuum'. But, in spite of the ways in which such a conception has been shown

to be unlike Athanasius, Newman is making a very Athanasian assertion to say that God remains unknown in speaking of the generical
ousia or numerical Individuum because these words are '*analogous*,
not parallel' to human usage. God's unity and Trinity remain a mystery, for, though humans can come up with analogies which attempt to
make sense of them, they are predicated of a simple (divine) substance
rather than a creaturely substance. Newman is clear: this difference
means that humans can in no way be considered 'parallel' to God.

This lack of divine–human parallels is the ground upon which
Newman will base the argument of his 1858 essay 'On St Cyril's
Formula' which draws together what he sees to be Athanasius's two
senses of hypostasis and Cyril's two senses of *physis*. The essay strives
to bring together these two Alexandrians' use of *ousia*-language, and
might therefore be accused of over-simplification. It is also a confusing piece, continuously moving between the subject matter of Trinitarian doctrine (the three hypostases/natures in one hypostasis/
nature) and of Christology (the unity of human and divine in
Christ's hypostasis/nature). But this confusing argument is explained
by Newman's peculiar purpose in the essay: to draw on Athanasius's
writing on the Trinity in order to suggest reasons why Cyril could
write of one nature (*physis*) in Christ, even though at face value this
contradicted Chalcedon's definition that Christ was one person in
two natures. Roderick Strange summarizes the argument thus:
'according to Newman, a correct understanding of the technical,
Alexandrian use of *physis* prohibited its predication of the humanity
of Christ in the same parallel sense in which it is predicated of his
divinity.'[45] This was similar to the argument Newman had already
formulated in 1842 on Athanasius's use of *physis* and hypostasis.
There Newman showed that the *ousia* of God and humanity are in
no way 'parallel'. This, of course, has the consequence in Christology
of making it difficult to speak of Christ having two separate natures,
human and divine, as if these were comparable in their respective
substances, and is the reason why Newman continued a 'Monophysite' in Cyril's sense throughout the 1840s and 50s.

[45] Roderick Strange, *Newman and the Gospel of Christ* (Oxford: Clarendon Press,
1981), 59.

CONCLUSION: DEVELOPMENT WITHOUT
DYNAMISM

With the idea of development, maybe noticed in 1839 but formulated while in his cell at Littlemore, Newman found a means to prevent theological language after Nicaea and Chalcedon ever becoming static. Shifting terminology is integral to doctrinal development.[46] It was seen in Chapter 2 that in *Arians of the Fourth Century* Newman held that formulae impoverished doctrine. His *Development of Christian Doctrine* continued to hold this to be true; nevertheless, here the golden age of dynamism in terminology came after Nicaea, not before. This readjustment of the *Arians of the Fourth Century*'s argument was the result of two shifts in Newman's own thought: firstly, in his view of *homoousios* and secondly, in his view of Origen and Athanasius.

By the 1840s, Newman thinks that at the Council of Nicaea a test of orthodoxy was necessary and that the Creed provided it. In 1833, Newman had been less of an advocate of *homoousios* than he became later, but back then he was also sure of Origen's orthodoxy in respect of the unity of Father and Son, even when the pre-Nicenes did not use the credal word. Secondly, then, it is Newman's change in his view of this word that causes his change of focus from the hero of the pre-Nicene era, Origen (and those whom he taught, like Dionysius) to the hero of the post-Nicene era, Athanasius (and those who are conflated with him: Augustine, the Cappadocians, and Cyril). Yet, what is so extraordinary about this change of focus is the way Newman makes so similar an argument about Athanasius as he had previously made about Origen—each was able to uphold the richness of tradition precisely by avoiding fixed terminology. For, beyond *homoousios*, which Athanasius understood rightly as an 'obscure' word, post-Nicene doctrine was far from formulaic. Following on

---

[46] As Ian Ker has rightly pointed out 'although [an idea] has to undergo change, this is not for the sake of change itself—if this were the case, then it would be the kind of change which Newman calls a corruption—but in order for the idea *to remain the same*' ('Newman, Councils and Vatican II', in Terrence Merrigan and Ker (eds.), *Newman and the Word* (Louvain: Peeters Press, 2000), 134).

from his arguments in *Development of Christian Doctrine*, by 1858, Newman thought 'no better illustration can be given of that intrinsic *independence of a fixed terminology* which belongs to the Catholic Creed, than the writings of Athanasius himself, the special Doctor from whom the subsequent treatises of Basil, the two Gregories, and Cyril are derived' (*TT* 339, my italics). Newman has taken what he previously saw as the special grace of Origen—a richness in doctrinal language—and applied this to Athanasius, while at the same time opposing it to what in 1845 he saw as Origen's weakness—his innovation and speculation.

Why has this change come while Newman was at Littlemore? Perhaps Athanasius holds together two aspects of doctrine which Newman found in tension within himself in those years of being an 'outsider' within the Church of England: how to reflect the riches of a tradition without making it static (which he thought was Bull's crime) and how to uphold 'orthodoxy' even when faced with charges of being false. Above all, Newman found refuge in a certain fixity of Trinitarian doctrine that he ascribed to Athanasius.

This chapter has traced the development of Newman's doubts about Origen, specifically in the way that, once he realized Origen had no notion of 'unity of substance', the three hypostases seemed to divide. Does Newman think Origen is to blame for later Arian interpretations of him? Based on the evidence of *Development of Christian Doctrine* this is a difficult question to answer because of Newman's ambiguous stance on Origen. The scope of his argument leaves room for Origen to be rescued. In defence of the lack of continuity between pre-Nicene and post-Nicene doctrine, Newman writes of the former:

Stray heterodox expressions, Sabellian or Unitarian, or what was afterwards Arian, Platonisms, *argumenta ad hominem*, assertions in controversy, omissions in practice, silence in public teaching, and the like, such as alone can be adduced, can be made up into no system. They are 'a rope of sand', to use the familiar phrase, not a *catena*; each stands by itself, with an independence, or an irrelevancy, which precludes the chance of assimilation or coalition. (*Dev* 389)

Origen's occasional inconsistencies with later orthodoxy would surely include his writing within this description. But, in the 1840s, Newman showed himself far less flexible about what is and is not 'orthodoxy' than previously.

Owen Chadwick argues that in *Development of Christian Doctrine*

Newman wished to apply later evidence to an earlier epoch, not as an old-fashioned argument *de praescriptione* ('The Church has always believed the same and she believed *x* in the fifth century, therefore she believed *x* in the third'), but as a genuine use according to the strict canons of historical scholarship.[47]

Newman's friend James Mozley would not have agreed with Chadwick. Mozley, in his review of *Development of Christian Doctrine* for the Tractarian journal, *Christian Remembrancer*, of which he was editor, argued that Newman was rejecting historical scholarship. Whereas Newman previously (following seventeenth-century Anglicans Cudworth and Bull) accepted that some sort of subordination of Son and Spirit to their Source was part of patristic doctrine, he now opposed any subordination of Son to Father; but Mozley showed this was an anachronistically 'modern' mode of understanding the Trinity:

[Newman] has one mode of holding the doctrine of the Trinity which puts aside the doctrine of the subordination of the Second Person; the Fathers had another mode of holding it, which put forward that doctrine. Their theology on the subject was different from his. But it is a further question, if this doctrine is true, as it undoubtedly is, and the Fathers held the doctrine of the Trinity with, and the modern interpreter without the appeal to it, whether their theology is, therefore, less sound and less perfect than his.[48]

In *Development of Christian Doctrine* on the one hand Newman showed how the earlier epoch could lead to the later; on the other

---

[47] Chadwick, *From Bossuet to Newman* (2nd edn.; Cambridge: Cambridge University Press, 1987), 147. Chadwick thinks Newman followed Cannop Thirlwall (1797–1875) and Barthold Georg Niebuhr (1776–1831) in 'suggest[ing] a theoretical pattern into which the facts might rationally fit: and this theoretical pattern could not be constructed out of the facts alone ... but must also be affected by probabilities arising from the later and better-known developments of the Greek states or the Roman republic' (ibid. 145). However, Newman compared his own history writing with those around him, inventing the verb 'to Niebuhrize' to describe the false neutrality which Niebuhr claimed (Günther Biemer, '«Neibuhriser?»' L'historiographie selon Newman', in C. Lepelley and P. Veyriras (eds.), *Newman et l'histoire* (Lyons: Presses Universitaires Lyon, 1992), 152).

[48] Anon. [James Mozley], 'An Essay on the Development of Christian Doctrine', *Christian Remembrancer*, 13 (1847), 241.

hand he criticized the earlier by those later standards. The first part of this process saw Origen's influence on the orthodox and heretical alike, but the second part judged him an inferior authority who fell short of later orthodoxy. What was and was not adequate before Nicaea, however, is wholly different from what was adequate or not when judged after the Council. Moreover, Newman's judgement of the pre-Nicenes is not even based on the language of the Council so much as on his interpretation of what Athanasius signified by *homo-ousios*. For, indeed, in the aftermath of the Council, Athanasius himself avoided the word, and when he did use it, as has been argued, it was to the exclusion of the numerical way of understanding unity in the Trinity, which had nevertheless become Newman's own.

5

The Athanasius 'With Whom I End'
(1864–81)

Newman went to Rome to be made a cardinal in 1879, taking him away from the work he had begun of revising the translation of Athanasius that he made at Littlemore in the early 1840s. Although he became a cardinal, it should not be forgotten that his view of Church history was unacceptable to those who taught at the Roman Schools when Newman first went there in 1846–7. The reception awaiting him in Rome each time, one as convert and one as cardinal, was very different; also different each time was his doctrine. Both differences were the result of Newman's increasing engagement with scholastic theology, especially after the Church's rejection of his 1859 *Rambler* article 'On Consulting the Faithful' made him painfully aware of the gap between his own patristic views and views acceptable in Rome. Newman turned to the Schools, specifically to theologians from the Roman College, to help bridge that gap. He found a 'synthesis' between the Fathers and Thomas Aquinas that came to be reflected in Newman's patristic writings, even in the retranslation of Athanasius published in 1881.

THE ROMAN CONTEXT: ENGAGEMENT
WITH THE SCHOOLS

An Essay on the Development of Christian Doctrine (1845) held that the 'Doctors' of the Church repeat and refine their theological views, rather than invent new ones. 'St. Athanasius, St. Augustine, St. Leo are conspicuous for the repetition *in terminis* of their own theological statements... the holy Fathers just mentioned were intently fixing their minds on what they taught, grasping it more and more closely' (*Dev* 353). The pattern for true doctrinal development was, for Newman at the time of his conversion, conservative rumination rather than speculative innovation. Athanasius was prized, alongside the Latin Doctors, for 'fixing' his mind rather than thinking expansively, which is perhaps surprising considering Newman was arguing for doctrinal growth. In spite of its conservatism, however, many in the Catholic Church that he entered did not accept *Development of Christian Doctrine*.

In Rome to study for Catholic ordination at Propaganda Fide in 1846–7, Newman quickly discovered that his historiography alienated him from prominent theologians in his adopted Church, especially the Jesuit trio at the Roman College: Giovanni Perrone, Carlo Passaglia, and Johannes Baptist Franzelin. Passaglia (1812–87), the Rector of the Roman College, whom Newman considered 'almost the only divine of Rome', invited him to attend disputations there; at one disputation, Newman realized that he was the one 'spoken against' by Passaglia (*LD* xii. 36).[1] Newman may also have attended the lectures of Perrone (1794–1876) at the same time that Franzelin did.[2] Perrone held the Chair of Dogmatic Theology at the Roman College and at Newman's request annotated a short paper that attempted to bring the theory of development into line with Catholic writers, including Perrone himself. Newman had written that 'Until the Church has given dogmatic form to this or that part of her deposit, she may not be fully conscious of what she thinks on the subject. In this sense... the Church possesses greater theological knowledge now than in former times' (again, the stress is on rumination), to which Perrone responded, 'I would not dare to speak thus'

---

[1] Passaglia left the Jesuits in 1859, becoming increasingly involved with Cavour in the movement for Italian unification. He was only reconciled to the Church a few months before his death.

[2] For an account of Franzelin's time at the College, including Perrone's lecture style, see Nicholas Walsh, *John Baptist Franzelin, SJ, Cardinal Priest of the Title SS. Boniface and Alexius: A Sketch and a Study* (Dublin: M. H. Gill and Son, 1895), 84–108.

(Perrone 76–7).[3] Franzelin (1816–86), a Jesuit from the Tyrol, succeeded Perrone in the Chair of Dogmatic Theology in 1857 and became a cardinal in 1876. Although admitting that he enjoyed Newman's writings,[4] when replying to the suggestion of the Institut Catholique's Monsignor d'Hulst of some parallels between the two cardinals' views of doctrine, Franzelin still maintained that Newman's teachings on development were not to be 'in nostras scholas transferendae'.[5]

Newman could not make his theory of development acceptable in Rome in the 1840s and 50s, no matter how many baroque scholastics he quoted.[6] To compare Newman's remarks on heresy with Perrone's reveals considerable difference in their history of the Fathers. Newman wrote: 'When some heresiarch introduces his proposition into the public arena, the minds of the bishops are stunned—at first, they do not know how to respond.' Perrone disagreed:

The process is not like this at all, but just the opposite. At the appearance of some controversy or heresy, theologians in the place where it arose discuss it first. Then the bishops examine it, and defer it to the Roman Pontiff, who brings forth a definitive judgment. This is from history. (Perrone 77)

---

[3] I am grateful to Carleton Jones OP for permission to quote his unpublished translation of the 'Newman–Perrone Paper on Development'. Jones himself tries to minimize the differences between Newman and Perrone: 'Although it is doubtful that Perrone accepted the analogy that Newman goes on to make between the mind of an individual believer and the "mind" of the Church, it is certain that Perrone agreed with Newman's (and Möhler's) emphasis upon revelation as a living idea in the minds of the faithful' (introduction, Perrone (p. 37)).

[4] According to Walsh, 'we have by [Franzelin's] own word that he sufficiently understood [English] to read the works of Cardinal Newman and to enjoy them' (*John Baptist Franzelin*, 190).

[5] This exchange is recorded in Edgar Hocedez, *Histoire de la théologie au XIXe siècle*, 3 vols. (Brussels: L'Edition Universelle, 1947–52), iii. 162–3.

[6] There is much to support Owen Chadwick's judgement in *From Bossuet to Newman*, that, encountering Roman theology for the first time, Newman made digestible excerpts of the scholastics rather than a 'strenuous attempt to penetrate the[ir] mind' (p. 174). Excerpts made in 1847 appear in *Thèses de Fide* in support of his own University Sermons (from the baroque Jesuits Francisco Suarez, Juan de Lugo, Gregory of Valencia, Domenico Viva, and the Dominican Charles-René Billuart) and in the novel *Loss and Gain* (from Lugo's *de Virtute Fidei Divinae* and Zaccaria's *Anti-Febbronio*, an eighteenth-century discussion of infallibility (*LG* 217 n.; 224 n.)). Excerpts from Lugo's *Disputationes de Mysterio Incarnationis* appear as footnotes to an 1849 sermon (*Mix* 306–7).

Perrone's thoughts on what was clear 'from history' did not change
Newman's mind on how doctrine was formed, however, as can be
seen in the infamous article the latter wrote for the *Rambler* in 1859.
Calling it, 'On Consulting the Faithful in Mattters of Doctrine',
Newman continued to play down the historical role of bishops in
doctrinal disputes: 'the Nicene dogma was maintained during the
greater part of the 4th century, 1. not by the unswerving firmness of
the Holy See, Councils or Bishops, but 2. by the "consensus fidelium"' (*Cons* 77). In other words, the priests and laity sometimes
upheld orthodoxy when bishops erred. It was at Perrone's suggestion,
in 1867, that Newman took the opportunity to explain his meaning
when republishing the article in response to the news that Franzelin
had lectured against Newman.[7] He did this in Note V to a new
edition of *Arians of the Fourth Century* (1871), and soon after
depicted Catholic bishops, especially the Pope, as successors of the
exemplary fourth-century bishops Ambrose and Basil.[8]

Although Newman's historiography of doctrine found little ap-
proval in the Catholic Church, things began to change right at the
end of the 1860s. Newman grew in confidence when he discovered
that Pope Pius IX thought favourably of his writing. In a note dated
1872, Newman recalled '[t]he Pope having sent to Dr. Cullen [Car-
dinal Archbishop of Dublin, in 1867] to ask about the character and
drift of my writings, and Dr. Cullen having reported to him most
favourably... and then two years later having invited me as a theologian to the Ecumenical Council'—an invitation, it should be emphasized, that Newman rejected because he did not consider himself
a theologian.[9] His theological reading deepened to include Josef

[7] Ward, *The Life of John Henry Cardinal Newman*, 2 vols. (London: Longmans,
1912), ii. 174.

[8] He wrote in the *Letter to the Duke of Norfolk* (1874): 'I say the Pope is the heir of
the Ecumenical Hierarchy of the fourth century, as being, what I may call, heir by
default. No one else claims or exercises its rights or its duties. Is it possible to consider
the Patriarch of Moscow or of Constantinople, heir to the historical pretensions of
St Ambrose or St Martin? Does any Anglican Bishop for the last 300 years recall to
our minds the image of St Basil?' (*Diff* ii. 207).

[9] Ward, *Life of John Henry Cardinal Newman*, ii. 192. In a letter to Miss Giberne of
Feb. 1869, Newman explained: 'Recollect, I could not be *in* the Council, unless I were
a Bishop—and really and truly I am *not* a theologian. A theologian is one who has
mastered theology—who can say how many opinions there are on every point, what

Kleutgen's *La Philosophie Scholastique* (1868), a lightly marked-up copy of the first volume of which is found in Newman's library and where he may have discovered the so-called 'medieval synthesis'.[10] As teacher of the future Leo XIII, Kleutgen (1811–83) was one of the founders of the revival of the study of Thomas Aquinas, and Pope Leo made him prefect of studies at the Roman College. One of the hallmarks of this neo-Thomism[11] was to read all Church Fathers—patristic and medieval—as if they represented a single metaphysical system in opposition to modern philosophy. Newman did the same in 'Causes of Arianism' (1872) in *Tracts Theological and Ecclesiastical*.[12]

Newman's status as a theologian received a further boost with the coronation of Leo XIII in February 1878. Newman's revisions to the Athanasius translation that year coincided with the discovery that the new Pope appreciated his work. In December 1878, he heard from Margaret Dunn, whose confessor was Newman, that

authors have taken which, and which is the best—who can discriminate exactly between proposition and proposition, argument and argument, who can pronounce which are safe, which allowable, which dangerous—who can trace the history of doctrines in successive centuries, and apply the principles of former times to the conditions of the present. This it is to be a theologian—this and a hundred things besides—which I am not, and never shall be' (*LD* xxiv. 212–13). Notice that here the theorist of development is not even claiming to be able to trace the history of doctrines, so unconfident was he of his grasp on theology.

[10] An example of Kleutgen's synthesis comes in a discussion of Cappadocian teachings as reported by John of Damascus: 'Dans cet enseignement de saint Jean Damasène, nous trouvons donc absolument les mêmes principes que saint Thomas et avec lui la plupart des scholastiques défendent, non seulement sur la distinction des divers attributs de Dieu, mais encore sur l'unité que nous affirmons des créatures de même espèce' (*La Philosophie scholastique exposée et défendue*, i (Paris: Gaume frères et J. Duprey, 1868), 374).

[11] According to Roger Aubert, neo-Thomists differ from their neoscholastic predecessors: 'La néo-scolastique n'est toutefois pas le néo-thomisme, car la plupart des néo-scolastiques du XIXe s., surtout avant 1870, sont des éclectiques' ('Aspects divers du Néo-Thomisme sous le pontificat de Léon XIII', in Giuseppe Rossini (ed.), *Aspetti della Cultura Cattolica nell'Età di Leone XIII* (Rome: Edizioni Cinque Lune, 1961), 134). This older 'eclecticism' was in evidence in Rome in 1846, when Newman learned in a conversation with 'one of the Jesuit fathers' that ' "St Thomas was a great saint—people don't dare to speak against him, but put him aside." I asked what philosophy they did adopt. He said *none*. "Odds and ends—whatever seems to them best—like St Clement's Stromata" ' (*LD* xi. 279).

[12] Newman plays down Augustine's own reference to the Son's derivation from the monarchical Father in *Contra Maximum* 2. 3, interpreting the Bishop of Hippo in line with medieval doctrine: 'the tendency of [Augustine's] theology—certainly that

the 'Holy Father took [her] two hands in his and pressed them affectionately for your sake' (*LD* xxviii. 435 n. 1). Also in December, Newman stated that while he was 'no theologian' yet he did 'not anticipate' his understanding of Aquinas upsetting the new Pope (ibid. 431). By this stage, in fact, Newman had become what he did not feel qualified to be—a Catholic theologian, of the sort of which Leo approved.[13] In October 1878, Newman had told Pusey that 'the direct aim' of this new translation (unlike his Library of the Fathers original) would be 'the sacred doctrine itself to which [Athanasius] devoted his life, which implies and indeed requires, if one would be honest, fidelity to his theological teaching, but not necessarily to his controversial text' (ibid. 406). From the perspective of Athanasius's theology, Newman's focus on doctrine was precisely the problem. This was not the doctrine of Athanasius but of those reviving the study of Thomas Aquinas. As will be shown, Newman read Athanasius through the neo-Thomistic synthesis, so he was unable to stay faithful to Athanasius's 'theological teaching'.

Even in his Oriel days, Newman possessed all of Thomas Aquinas's works.[14] *That* he read Aquinas is not in question; *how* he read Aquinas is. Here it will be argued that by the 1870s Newman read Aquinas through neo-Thomist lenses. In a telling letter to the Pope in December 1879, half a year after Newman was made a cardinal, he writes of the Catholic Church:

---

of the times that followed—was to throw that doctrine [*monarchia*] into the background. The abuse of it by the Arians is a full explanation of this neglect of it. Moreover it was out of keeping with the doctrinal system of the medieval Church' (*TT* (1st edn.) 132–3). Newman, endlessly tinkering, removed this last sentence for the 1883 edition (*TT* 178).

[13] Leo XIII, although considering Aquinas the pre-eminent theologian, was not interested in Thomas alone. The Pope shared Newman's interest in making the Fathers one with Thomas. Of his encyclicals, *Aeterni Patris* (1879) holds Origen to have 'graced the chair of the school of Alexandria' and praises Athanasius, Chrysostom, and the Cappadocians before saying 'Augustine would seem to have wrested the palm from all'; while *Providentissimus* (1893) describes Origen as, among exegetes in 'the Eastern Church, the greatest name of all' and in the West selects Augustine as 'so marvellously acute in penetrating the sense of God's word'. See <http://www.vatican.va/holy_father/leo_xiii/encyclicals/> for Leo's encyclicals.

[14] Newman had all twenty-eight volumes of the 1781 *Editio Altera Venetia* (*PN* i. 235 n.).

that the mental creations of her theologians, of her controversialists and pastors, should be grafted on the Catholic tradition of philosophy, and should not start from a novel and simply original tradition, but should be substantially one with the teaching of St Athanasius, St Augustine, St Anselm and St Thomas, *as those great doctors are in turn with each other.* (*LD* xxix. 212, my italics)

Newman propounds a synthesis of the 'great doctors' as if they represented a single metaphysical system. Newman's 1881 translation exhibits this synthesis, sometimes interpreting Athanasius's theology in Latin-patristic and at other times in Thomistic categories (although this 'Thomism' did not accurately reflect Aquinas either). The problem with the neo-Thomism of Kleutgen is that the historical differences between fourth-century Alexandrians and Latins, let alone between patristic and medieval writers, are collapsed. That is what is found in Newman's translation too. The Athanasius 'in whose name and history years ago I began to write, and', Newman claimed in 1881, 'with whom I end', looked a lot more like a neo-Thomist than had the Athanasius whom he translated in the early 1840s (*Ath* i, p. ix).

ARIANISM REVISITED AND ORIGEN REHABILITATED

The famous Anglican essayist, Dean Inge of Westminster Abbey, chose to view Newman's patristic writing as autobiographical. In 1912, Inge claimed 'Newman's writings, and his life, are a "human document" in a very peculiar degree ... Even his historical portraits are constructed from his inner consciousness; hence their historical falsity—all ages are mixed in his histories—and their philosophical truth'.[15] While this book has shown that Newman was a more serious historical scholar than Inge allowed, nevertheless the closeness in his mind of historical characters to his personal events has also become clear. Changes in his view of Arianism in the 1870s, as well as his revised translation of Athanasius, likewise seem connected to events in his life. The connections begin when Newman responded to Charles Kingsley's (1819–75)

---

[15] W. R. Inge, *Outspoken Essays*, First Series (2nd edn.; London: Longmans, 1921), 182.

'What, Then, Does Dr. Newman Mean?' in March 1864, with a series of pamphlets giving the 'History of My Religious Opinions', styled an 'Apologia'. He wrote in the preface for the heavily edited volume based on these pamphlets in 1865 that 'its original title of "Apologia" is too exactly borne out by its matter and structure' for him not 'to prefix to my Narrative some account of the provocation out of which it arose' (*Apo* 1). Newman did not mention in the preface the provocation of Kingsley's novel *Hypatia* (1853), which criticized the fifth-century Alexandrian Church, particularly her patriarch Cyril; he reserved until the appendix dealing with the provocation Kingsley's attack on Greek patristic teaching on *economia* (ibid. 439–43). Newman's choice of title was itself an invocation of the Church Fathers—Athanasius among others writing *Apologias* for events in their lives (*contra Arianos, ad Constantium, de Fuga*). In defence of his conversion to Catholicism and against Kingsley's libels, Newman wrote of an analogy that was confirmed in his mind in the summer of 1841, he said, when working on his translation of Athanasius, that 'the pure Arians were the Prot-estants, the Semi-Arians were the Anglicans, and that Rome now was what it was then. The truth lay, not with the *Via Media*, but in what was called "the extreme party" ' (*Apo* 130). Athanasius and Newman were both members of the 'extreme party', he claimed of his earlier self, looking to Rome for affirmation; Anglicans like Kingsley were, by contrast, Semi-Arians.

Connections Newman saw between himself and Athanasius, and between Anglicans and Semi-Arians, might explain some of the content of 'Causes of Arianism' in 1872 as well as certain revisions he made to the Athanasius translation in the late 1870s. In 'Causes of Arianism', Newman is careful to differentiate Arians from Semi-Arians. The latter (whom he considered analogous to Anglicans) appeared as a compromise to the Arian heresy (Protestantism), but from the perspective of Athanasius (Catholicism) the Semi-Arians were all the more dangerous for that.[16] The teachings on God among these various positions will receive a quick recapitulation.

[16] According to Ian Ker, with respect to the Anglican Church, Newman in this period had no 'hint of the later understanding of the Second Vatican Council that other churches are not devoid of ecclesiastical significance . . . But on the other hand, Newman had none of the harsh intolerance of so many of his co-religionists' (*John Henry Newman: A Biography* (Oxford: Clarendon Press, 1988), 696).

The problem of Arianism, thought Newman in an extended note in the 1842 Athanasius translation, was its heretical view of Christ's Sonship. The word 'Son' was taken by Arius to imply that Father and the Son had different 'natures' or 'substances', because a child is not the same being as its parent (*Ox Frs* viii. 272). Newman's argument had evolved by 1872 to show the ways in which the Arians were assisted in this misinterpretation of scripture by the writings of the pre-Nicene Fathers. Up until then, he had argued that most pre-Nicenes at least accepted the 'connaturality' of Son and Father ('consubstantiality', as it were, *avant la lettre*), but in 'Causes of Arianism' he noticed that such a doctrine did not protect the Son's coeternity with the Father. Rather, by interpreting the prologue of John's gospel to mean that the Word existed in the bosom of the Father before 'going forth' as the Son, the pre-Nicenes could be seen as holding to a temporal 'birth' of the Son. The only ancient school to oppose this view was that of Alexandria. Notably, Origen taught the need to protect the Son's coeternity with the Father, as did the Council at Antioch, because 'the most eminent members of the Council were closely connected with Origen as a teacher' (*TT* 263). The Fathers' abandonment at Antioch of the word *homoousios* is not as much of a problem for Newman in the 1870s as was in the 1840s. This is because of his new focus on the doctrine of coeternity as a better protection against heresy than either connaturality or consubstantiality (upheld so vigorously in the 1840s to the point of criticizing Origen for his ambiguity). Without the doctrine of coeternity, the language of Sonship could again be misunderstood, the Semi-Arians teaching a 'temporal gennesis': a begetting that occurred after, not at the same time as, the Son's conception as though '[f]rom eternity He was conceived, as if "in utero"', but only 'before time and creation He was born' (*TT* 254). This had been the pre-Nicene position of Justin and it gave cover, Newman thought, to the Semi-Arians' heresy. The pre-Nicenes outside of Alexandria are shown to be the precursors of Semi-Arianism, with the exception, of course, of Dionysius of Rome. He is the one pre-Nicene who held to both coeternity and the word *homousios*: 'a still more authoritative Voice issued about the same time' as the Antiochene Council, whose teaching Newman thinks demonstrates the 'Infallible' Papacy (*TT* 296).

With this focus on coeternity in God came a shift in how Newman apportioned blame for the troubles that beset the Church in the fourth century. It is noticeable, compared with works from the 1830s and 40s, how little mention is made in 'Causes of Arianism' of the heretical archetype, Paul of Samosata, probably because the debate over *homoousios* had ceased to be Newman's prime concern (*TT* 262). Newman also refused the connection between Arius's theology and those 'fellow-Lucianists', Eusebius of Caesarea and Eusebius of Nicomedia (*Ari* 238): Arius's true successors took thirty years to emerge, he wrote in 1872, gathering 'under the name of Anomoeans, Aëtius and Eunomius being its leaders' (*TT* 147).[17] The two Semi-Arian Eusebii, by contrast, had a confession of their own, expressed in the creeds of the various Councils that Athanasius reported in *de Synodis*. Newman discerned—from the fact that 'out of the Eusebian Councils which followed the Nicene, two only, or rather one, actually absolved Arius'—that the Eusebians were not in agreement with Arius's theology (ibid.). They taught that the Son's being was 'like' the Father's, *homoiousios*.

The Semi-Arian position was an advance on Arius's rejection of *homoousios*, appearing as a compromise to keep everyone happy. But the Semi-Arians were so dangerous precisely because they veered so little from the language of orthodoxy, in the same way Newman in 1839 had considered the Semi-Eutychians worse than Eutyches (see Chapter 3). Having likened Semi-Arians and Monophysites to Anglicans in the *Apologia Pro Vita Sua* of 1864, was Anglicanism in his mind when he thought about Semi-Arianism in 1872? Newman's depiction of Hilary suggests that it might have been. Hilary 'did not hear of the Nicene Council or Creed till thirty-one years after the Council was held' (*TT* 288). When Hilary heard of it, he initially interpreted the Nicene Anathema just like the Anglican George Bull did: that the Council legitimized the doctrine of the begetting (γέννεσις) of the Son for the purpose of creation.[18] In Bull's opinion,

---

[17] The Anomoeans maintained that the Son's *ousia* was 'unlike' the Father's, in accord with Arius.

[18] The early Hilary 'tells us that He who was the Word from eternity, became the Son in order to creation. "The Word," he says, "was in the beginning God, and with God from the beginning. He was born from Him who was, and He that was born had this prerogative, viz. that He it is who *erat antequam nasceretur*; that is, there is the same eternity of Him who begat, and of Him who is begotten." Matt. xxxi. 3' (*TT* 289).

the Nicene Council anathematized those who taught the Son was not before his generation, but not those who held that 'the Son, indeed, a little before the creation of the world, proceeded forth in a certain inexplicable manner from the Father... and that in respect of this going forth also, he is called in Scripture *the Son of God*, and, *the First-born*' (*Defensio* ii. 485). However, in Newman's 'contrary view', expressed in 1842, the Catholics at Nicaea held no belief that the Son was 'born' of the Father (*Ox Frs* viii. 274). Hilary only realized the danger of this birth language 'after his visit to Asia Minor... and at Alexandria [where] he became the personal friend of Athanasius, who inherited the Alexandrian antagonistic and true teaching' (*TT* 289–90). Two things should be noticed here as unusual for someone who would soon become a Catholic cardinal. Firstly, a Latin like Hilary is not the guarantor of orthodoxy, but rather Athanasius is. Secondly, by analogy, Latins like Hilary who learned from Athanasius could escape the danger of Semi-Arianism; Anglicans like Bull who did not learn from the Alexandrian remained heretics.[19] The Alexandrians were still Newman's favourites in the 1870s.

With the Semi-Arians portrayed as the real criminals for refusing the coeternity of Father and Son, Origen is rehabilitated in Newman's eyes. The Alexandrians were the ancestors of Latin truth. The life of Hilary shows how close the West came to being Semi-Arian, while Tertullian's cosmology also led to Semi-Arianism. Newman acknowledged that, at the time of Tertullian and Origen, the regnant philosophy precluded the universe from having been created 'after' the Son came to be:

From this common ground, two schools took their start, but in opposite directions; the one holding that each of the Divine acts, the other that neither of them, was from eternity... Origen affirmed that the creation was from eternity, as well as the *gennesis*, and Tertullian affirmed that the *gennesis* had a beginning as well as the creation. (*TT* 232)

---

[19] 'For myself, returning to Bull, I would rather avoid his word "subordination" in its application to our Lord... [I]n keeping with St. Hilary's felicitous paradox, that "The Father is the greater without the Son being the lesser," *vid.* Hil. *de Trin.* ix. 56'. Therefore 'instead of the "subordinatio Filii", let us speak of the "Principatus Patris"' (*TT* 174). For 'Principatus Patris', see below.

Instead of following Origen, the Semi-Arians conceived the universe in similar terms to Tertullian: because neither the Son nor creation was eternal, the Son must have a temporal *gennesis* and so is not coeternal with the Father.[20]

It was Origen's teaching on the coeternity of Father and Son that provided the right answer, even if it brought with it the corollary that the universe was eternal too. But Newman used his knowledge of scholasticism to help Origen out here, for 'as to Origen's notion of the eternity of the Universe, it must be recollected that, though in matter of fact creation is not from eternity, yet it might have been, had God so willed. At least so says Suarez... [and] St. Thomas' (*TT* 234). Newman glosses Origen's theology to avoid classing him as a father of heresy. Thanks to his acquaintance with Perrone's scholastic theology, Newman was aware that 'if a Council has condemned the work of Origen or Theodoret, it did not in so condemning go beyond the work itself; it did not touch the persons of either' (*Diff* ii. 326).[21] Thus, in the 1870s, Origen escapes condemnation through scholastic loopholes. More positively, Origen's influence on Athanasius and the Cappadocians is made explicit.[22]

If Athanasius and, through his teaching of coeternity, Origen are the ancestors of Catholic doctrine, and Semi-Arianism is the ancestor of Anglicanism, then Newman can imagine himself as the Athanasius of his own time combating Anglican heresy. For instance, in the retranslation of *Select Treatises of Athanasius Against the Arians*, Newman put words into Athanasius's text: 'The quarrel then between us and them' perhaps identifying himself with Athanasius ('us') against his opponents ('them', *Ath* i. 245). Newman often uses the first person where it is not found in Athanasius's original Greek,

---

[20] G. H. Williams shows that Eusebius was probably an Origenist in his 'philosophical background': 'A cascade of decreasingly divine potencies from the Supreme, impassible, transcendent One, through the Logos–Son and the Holy Spirit, the chief of spirits, to angels and men... Eusebius [of Caesarea] understood the self-disclosure of the Logos incarnate to be little more than the reminder that man is immortal if he will but confirm to the eternal law of the Logos' ('Christology and Church–State relations in the Fourth Century', *Church History*, 20/3 (1951), 16).

[21] This section from the *Letter to the Duke of Norfolk* (1874) contains quotations from the works of his old friend Perrone.

[22] Newman writes: 'Basil and Gregory of Nazianzen of the school of Origen... took up the work which Athanasius had so long carried on before them' (*TT* 245).

such as, 'As I have said' (ibid. 313). While on the one hand this might appear a simplification aimed at helping the reader, on the other Newman thought he spoke for Athanasius. Who were their joint opponents? Pursuing the parallel of Anglicans like Kingsley with Semi-Arians like Asterius the Sophist suggests an explanation for some of Newman's revisions to Athanasius's words. As opposed to Catholic universality, Anglicans (Semi-Arians) share with Protestants (Arians) a private judgement, standing them 'in their private heresy' (ibid. 209)—a different description from that given in 1842, which had merely 'their own heresy' (*Ox Frs* viii. 228). Just after this, Newman translates that Asterius and others 'imply that the Word is a work to their own private satisfaction' (*Ath* i. 209), not 'a work after their own measure' (*Ox Frs* viii. 228). Thus, unlike Catholics, 'such men' should be named Arians because they 'derive the faith which they profess from private persons' (*Ath* i. 157) changed from 'which they profess from others' (*Ox Frs* viii. 180). The later translation sounds similar to the argument in the *Apologia Pro Vita Sua* that—as Augustine, Athanasius, and Leo attest—'the deliberate judgment in which the whole Church at length rests and acquiesces, is an infallible prescription and a final sentence against such portions of it as protest and secede' (*Apo* 117).

More speculatively, Kingsley's attack that led to the *Apologia Pro Vita Sua* may provide an explanation for Newman's revisions to Athanasius's language about women in Discourse I. Kingsley's accusations of Newman's effeminacy and duplicity led to a new reluctance in the Athanasius translation to connect femininity and sophistry. Chapter 2 showed that, in *Arians of the Fourth Century*, Newman was happy to imply a connection between the demagogic Arius and the women who surrounded him. In so doing, Newman was following a trope within patristic writing found in his original translation of Athanasius, where Arius is accused of having 'an effeminate soul' (*Ox Frs* viii. 183). This phrase is omitted from his later translation (*Ath* i. 159). Likewise, twice in the original translation Athanasius draws an analogy between the serpent deceiving Eve and Arius's deception, alluding once more to Arius's connection with femininity (*Ox Frs* viii. 187, 189); twice the analogy is left out of the later translation. Allusions to the effeminacy of heresy were too close to the Anglican Kingsley's polemic against the Catholic Newman.

Like 'Causes of Arianism', the Athanasius translation suggests New-man's ongoing difficulties with Anglicanism.

GENERAL CHANGES TO THE ATHANASIUS TRANSLATION

In February 1840, two years before his first volume of Athanasius translations was published, in his 'Advertisement' to *The Church of the Fathers*,[23] Newman gave an insight into the difficulty of being a translator:

if a translator be conscious to himself, as he may well be, of viewing either his original or his version differently, according to the season or the feeling in which he takes it up, and finds that he never shall have done with correcting and altering except by an act of self-control, the more easy will it be for him to resign himself to such differences of judgment about his work as he experiences in others. (*CF* 593)

Over the seasons of his life, Newman indeed took up his Athanasius translation, not so much because of the criticism of others but of self-criticism. Its themes appear to be a constant agitation. By November 1878, having just decided upon a 'free translation' of *Select Treatises*, Newman wrote about the business of being a translator to fellow Athanasius scholar, William Bright, in words that match his musings from 1840:

the [Library of the Fathers] *translation* is so unsatisfactory. I have felt sure that, if I compared it with the Greek I should in fact so alter it as to be publishing a fresh translation. I should be unable to keep my hands off it— and it is coming to pass! and after all, as in the case of mis-prints, I shall not be making it better. (*LD* xxviii. 420)

Newman was correct to be wary of what he was beginning. What seems to have obstructed Newman's view were the theological lenses through which he translated Athanasius. The changes he made by the

[23] The 'Advertisement' to the first and second editions is described in later editions of *CF* as 'with a few literary corrections'; it was not printed in *HS* i or ii. Here it is quoted from the Birmingham Oratory Millennium Edition, where it appears in an appendix.

time of publication, in 1881, reflected a Thomistic theology of the
sort Leo XIII might relish.

This is not to claim that Newman's original translation of *Select
Treatises* was made without lenses. As a leader of the Oxford Movement, he was seeing Athanasius as the supreme upholder of a conciliar
orthodoxy that was, in fact, far less unified at the time of Nicaea than
Newman wanted it to be. The assumption of a unified orthodox version
of truth found expression in his original version near the start of
Discourse I, when Athanasius writes of Arius's condemnation by the
Ecumenical Council. In Newman's original translation, Athanasius asks
questions of those who think that Arius's doctrines are 'little different
from the Truth' (*Ox Frs* viii. 188). It is noticeable, however, that the
second translation has people (Anglicans among them?) falsely holding
Arius's teachings to be 'an indifferent matter in relation to the Truth'
(*Ath* i. 162). There is a subtle strengthening of dogmatic tone in the
later version, as seen near the end of Discourse I in the words, 'This is
what they [the Arians] urge against the orthodox doctrine' (ibid. 238).
This sentence is not even found in the Greek, but with it Newman
depicts a unitary body of 'orthodox doctrine', as in Discourse II. 12
when ὀρθήν is translated as 'orthodox teaching' instead of what previously read 'orthodoxy' (*Ath* i. 265/*Ox Frs* xix. 298).

In his second translation, then, Newman inserted his own phrases
in the text and subtly changed his tone and wording from the first
translation. Thirty-four years after finishing his first translation, Newman wrote to Bright that 'literalness was a first duty in the "Library of
the Fathers" from the circumstances of the time', probably because of
Anglican suspicions of Newman and the Tractarians (*LD* xxviii. 420).
In the second translation, by contrast, he felt comfortable 'allowing
myself in abbreviation where he [Athanasius] was diffuse, and in
paraphrase where he was obscure' (*Ath* i, p. vii). Newman transposed
Discourse III. 58–67 to Discourse I—'what seems its more natural
place', he wrote—as if that is where Athanasius always intended it
(ibid. 154). He reorganized Athanasius's text in Discourse I. 55–62
entirely.[24] Further changes made Athanasius's text accord with the
orthodoxy that followed him.

---

[24] The sections, which follow Newman's numeration in *Ox Frs* viii. 259–69,
are reordered thus: §§ 5, 3 (omitting the first half), 6, 7, 8, 10, 4, 11, 9, 12 to make
§§ 89–98 in *Ath* i. 238–47.

Newman's struggle to make Athanasius consistent with later dogma began five years before *Development of Christian Doctrine*. In spite of arguing for doctrine's propensity to change, as the bastion of orthodoxy Athanasius was somehow to be immune from ever looking doctrinally out-of-date. The Anglican patristic scholar and Bishop of Lincoln, John Kaye, criticized the first translation's notes for finessing the way Athanasius held that Christ was ignorant in his human nature, a later heresy.[25] In one annotation to the first translation, Newman said that Athanasius's teaching, that the Son advanced in wisdom, was only '*primâ facie*' inconsistent with the subsequent teaching of the Church. Kaye complained: 'What is here meant by *primâ facie* I do not understand; the language of Athanasius is as express as language can be'.[26] Kaye knew as well as Newman that it was not until the sixth century that Pope Gregory I, after the controversy with the Agnoetae, declared it heretical to claim Christ was ignorant in his human soul.[27] But, asked Kaye, what had that to do with Athanasius, who was writing two centuries before? Had Kaye lived to see the 1881 translation, he would have thought that worse followed, for now Newman's finessing occurred not in the footnotes but in the translation.[28] Athanasius's Christology must be made safe from subsequent heresy, to which end Newman amends the patriarch's argument, so that now it is not Christ whose knowledge is perfected over time, but ours who are 'looking at Him'. To this end, Newman moved a sentence of III. 53 and relocated it to III. 52, and in so doing reshaped

[25] Although III. 43 holds that 'as man He is ignorant', Newman states that the advance of Christ's human mind did not happen gradually over his lifetime, because 'it was from the first taken out of its original and natural condition and "deified" by its union with the Word' (*Ox Frs* xix. 461 n. b).

[26] John Kaye, *Some Account of the Council of Nicaea* (London: Rivingtons, 1853), 251 n. 1.

[27] See Ch. 3, above.

[28] In 1847, Newman translated most of *Ox Frs* xix. 464 n. f into Latin (Perrone 98–100) to use as evidence for the ninth thesis he put to Perrone—that 'since the truth is one, and was given to the Church from the beginning, even the less catholic expressions of the truth which Catholics give will have such an uncertain and ambiguous tone that, where the matter is important, it will not be difficult to give them a devout interpretation' (ibid. 79–80). Newman would give Athanasius such an interpretation in the 1881 translation.

Athanasius's Christology. The two versions are worth quoting in full to understand their contexts. In the first translation, the sentence appears in parenthesis in III. 53:

> For *Jesus advanced in Wisdom and grace*; and, if we may speak what is explanatory as well as true, He advanced in Himself; for *Wisdom hath builded Herself an house*, and in Herself She gave the house advancement. (What moreover is this advance that is spoken of, but, as I said before, the deifying and grace imparted from Wisdom to men, sin being obliterated in them and their inward corruption, according to their likeness and relationship to the flesh of the Word?) For thus, the body increasing in stature, there progressed in and with it the manifestation of the Godhead also, and to all was it displayed that the body was God's Temple, and that God was in the body. (*Ox Frs* xix. 474)

In the 1881 version, the sentence has been moved out of a discussion of how the human 'Jesus advanced in Wisdom' (Luke 2: 52) and placed into the previous section, to become the last sentence of what is quoted below:

> for all things advance by looking at Him; and He, being One and Only, is in the Only Father, out of whom never does He reach, but in Him abideth ever. To men then belongs advance; but the Son of God, since He could not advance, being perfect in the Father, humbled Himself for us, that in His humiliation we rather might have capacity to increase. This is the real advance, the deifying and grace imparted from Wisdom to men, sin being obliterated in them and their inward corruption, according to their likeness and relationship to the flesh of the Word. (*Ath* i. 420)

In its original place, any advance humans made towards God was dependent upon Christ's advance in human wisdom. Christ's ignorance was reversed that ours might be also.[29] Already in 1844, Newman had been dubious about the Son's advancement in human

---

[29] Anatolios gives a good account of how, in fact, human salvation depends upon divine wisdom 'reversing' human ignorance in Christ; for without this reversal, humans could not reorient themselves to God: 'especially with regard to "negative" experiences of fear, ignorance, death, etc., Christ's appropriation of these simultaneously constitutes their very reversal' (*Athanasius: The Coherence of his Thought* (London: Routledge, 1998) 154).

knowledge. In 1881, Christ saves us from ignorance without ever being ignorant himself.

Another theme of Athansius's Discourses is to make sure that, in saying the Son is derived from God and sent from God in one eternal procession, it does not mean the Son is 'a creature' of God. In II. 12, Athanasius argues that when Peter says Jesus was 'made' Lord, in Acts 2: 36, it is in the sense that Jesus demonstrated himself to be Lord already, through his works in the flesh (ἀπεδείκνυε διά τῶν ἔργων, PG 26: 172 C8). But here it is worth noticing what Newman does with his second translation. Rather than coming on mission from the Father, in the 1881 translation Jesus manifests Godhead seemingly on his own initiative—making *himself* God—'For the Lord did not then fashion Himself to be God, nor indeed is a made God conceivable, but He made Himself God by manifesting Himself in the works' (*Ath* i. 265). The first translation had run, 'For the Lord did not then fashion Himself to be God [θεόν]...but He manifested it by the works' (*Ox Frs* xix. 298). Here Athanasius seems to be at one with the New Testament tradition described by Karl Rahner, in which using 'θεός...without the article...suggests a kind of conceptual generality'.[30] In 1844, Newman had inserted the ambiguous 'it' to imply that this conceptual generality of divinity was manifested by the Son, and not that the Son was himself ὁ θεός, a title which Chapter 4 showed that Athanasius reserved for the Father. Yet Newman changed his original translation in order to proclaim that each of the divine Persons was equally ὁ θεός.

The *Quicunque* was a Latin Creed from after Athanasius's time, yet the more Newman thought about the development of doctrine, the more he became convinced that this Creed better expressed the truth about the coequality of persons than that upheld by Athanasius after Nicaea. Newman admitted this in his paper for Perrone in 1847:

must we not say that the structure of the Nicene Creed shows that the most ancient Church, the most holy witness to the truth, was less intellectually accomplished in its divinity than the Church which produced the Creed *Quicunque*...? It is not that the dogma of the Most Holy Trinity as it is

---

[30] Karl Rahner, 'Theos in the New Testament', *Theological Investigations*, i (Baltimore, Md.: Hellicon, 1965), 136.

found in the Creed *Quicunque*, did not live in the mind of the Church, but that it dwelt there as a kind of secondary aspect of the truth, of which the first was, 'One God, the Father Omnipotent, His consubstantial Son, and the Spirit-Paraclete, proceeding from the Father'. Nor was it otherwise when, in the Apostolic age, 'One God, one Mediator, Christ' was preached. (Perrone 96–7)

For Newman, what was 'secondary' in the pre-Nicene and Nicene Fathers' teaching on God became primary only when developed into the Latin Creed. This later Creed expressed the fullness of God because it did not describe the Father alone as the 'One God'. Thus, in the revised translation, Newman read this Creed into Athanasius, even though the patriarch held to the earlier depiction of the Father as the one God with a consubstantial Son and Spirit.

Athanasius did not quite share the terminology of later orthodoxy. Athanasius wrote of the Son as divine, not human, in person (hypostasis) and in nature (*physis*). In 'On St Cyril's Formula' (1858), Newman was right that words like hypostasis and *physis* were largely interchangeable for Cyril of Alexandria and Athanasius, as signifiers, like *ousia*, of the unknowable divine substance.[31] Therefore Cyril could write of the Son as possessing only one nature, that of God, even though shortly after Cyril's death the Council of Chalcedon taught the incarnate Son is one person (hypostasis) with two natures (*physeis*), divine and human. In order to bring the Alexandrians into alignment with Chalcedon, Newman omits the first sentence of Discourse II. 65, in which Athanasius uses *physis* in his and Cyril's sense: 'the truth declares the Word is not by nature a creature' (*Ox Frs* xix. 373, PG 26: 285 A1–3; cf. *Ath* i. 334). For Athanasius, the statement is true because the Word is by nature God, but, for Newman, to say so would undermine later teaching that Christ had two *physeis*. Also in the earlier translation, in III. 63, the Word was 'by nature the proper Offspring of God's Substance' (*Ox Frs* xix. 491). In the revised translation, however, Newman describes the Word as 'by God's nature the proper Offspring of God's Substance', because, by his mother's substance, Christ is properly human too (*Ath* i. 198, a

---

[31] 'The words οὐσία, ὑπόστασις, φύσις, and εἶδος, among the Alexandrians of the fourth and fifth centuries [were used] as denoting fully and absolutely all that the natural theologian attaches to the notion of the Divine Being—as denoting the God of natural theology' (*TT* 353).

section moved to Discourse I).[32] For Athanasius, through the Son taking on human nature, we have been adopted by the Father and our natures divinized by the Spirit. In 1881, Newman wants to be clearer about this process even than Athanasius, adding the words 'nature' and 'gift' to III. 24, to stress the difference between our natures and God's: 'our being in the Father is not ours by nature, but is the Spirit's gift', replacing the earlier, 'our being in the Father is not ours, but is the Spirit's which is in us' (*Ath* i. 387/*Ox Frs* xix. 433, cf. PG 26: 373 C3–4). While Athanasius's writings may not have been contrary to later Church teaching, they were undoubtedly framed in different theological terms from those Newman uses.

THEOLOGICAL CHANGES TO THE ATHANASIUS TRANSLATION

Newman's argument in 'Causes of Arianism' emphasizes Christ's eternal Sonship as the best safeguard against the Arian notion of a beginning to the Son. He makes this argument based on a new genealogy of Arianism, or more specifically Semi-Arianism: 'the *Syncatabasis* of the Son...as well as the *Principatus* of the Father, accidentally suggest and favour that form of Arianism, which had such a sudden and wide extension in Christendom on the conversion of the Empire' (*TT* 198). According to Newman, these two pre-Nicene doctrines, the *Principatus Patris*, which he previously called 'the *Monarchia*' of the Father, and the *syncatabasis*, which he previously called the 'condescension'[33] of the Son from the Father, left the door open to Arian heresy. To keep that door closed, the *monarchia* needed to be combined with the doctrine of 'coinherence' (*perichoresis*), a lesson he claims the Church learned from Latin pre-Nicenes, among whom only Pope Dionysius held both of these doctrines together and in so doing properly understood the monarchy of the Father. As for *syncatabasis*, he thinks the only pre-Nicenes who

---

[32] The genitive 'God's' does not appear in PG 26: 456 C13–14.

[33] Newman uses '*monarchia*' repeatedly in 1833 (described at *Ari* 175) but only uses 'condescension' once in his discussion of the Son's '*gennesis*' (*Ari* 198).

escaped heresy were those taught by Origen that the Son's condescension was eternally from the Father and had no temporal beginning.[34] But here Newman is reading Origen through Athanasius's terminology, '*syncatabasis*' being a transliteration of a word that only appears in Discourse II. 62.[35] Athanasian theology is regnant even when describing Origen. The details of Newman's argument regarding each doctrine will now be examined in relation to his 1881 translation.

The monarchy of the Father

This doctrine is introduced near the beginning of 'Causes of Arianism' as the third point in the following:

[Selected pre-Nicene] passages coalesce and form one whole, and a whole in agreement with the subsequent teaching on the subject of the fourth and fifth centuries; and their doctrine, thus taken as a whole, will be found to contain these four main points:—(1) Each of the Three Divine Persons is distinct from each; (2) Each is God; (3) One proceeds from Another in succession; (4) Each is in the Other Two. In other words, the primitive ecclesiastical tradition concerning the Divine Being includes the doctrines of [1] the Trinity, of [2] the Unity, of [3] the *Monarchia* or *Principatus*, and of [4] the *Circumincessio* or Co-inherence. (*TT* 160)

With respect to (2), each person of the Trinity being ὁ θεός, Newman alludes to the tension here with (3), the *monarchia* of the Father.[36]

---

[34] For Origen, seeing as God is outside time, God cannot 'begin' to be the Creator of the world in any sense we can understand because 'begin' is a temporal term. From the beginning, God already is the Creator together with the Word, for 'as will proceeds out of the mind, and neither tears the mind nor is itself separated or divided from it, in some such manner must we conceive that the Father has begotten the Son, who is His Image' (*de Principiis* 1.2.6 (Newman's translation from *Ari* 170)).

[35] According to G. W. H. Lampe, Origen uses συγκαταβαίνω to describe: Christ's descent into Hades (*Commentary on John* 6. 35), Christ's incarnation (*Contra Celsum* 4. 6), teachers imparting knowledge to their students by way of economy (ibid. 12, 41), and these last two ideas combined (ibid. 14); Athanasius follows Origen in combining the ideas at Discourse II. 78 (*A Greek–Patristic Lexicon* (Oxford: Clarendon Press, 1961), 1267).

[36] He describes the *monarchia* thus: 'of the Three, the Father is emphatically... spoken of as God. Thus St Justin and St Clement speak of Him as the God of the Universe; thus Athenagoras speaks of "God, His Son and Word, and His Spirit"; Irenaeus of "God and His Hands"' (*TT* 161).

However, (4), the *circumincessio* eases the tension because each person inheres in the others as the one God. This is in some ways a return to *Arians of the Fourth Century*, when *monarchia* and coinherence, respectively, combined to uphold both Son and Spirit as 'of God' and 'in God'. In *Arians of the Fourth Century*, although the 'Ante-Nicene school of Rome [was] still more explicit' in its doctrine of coinherence than the Greeks, still Athenagoras, Clement, and Gregory of Neocaesarea were shown to be upholders of this doctrine too, because in 1833 Newman was more favourable to Greeks than Latins (*Ari* 173). By 1872, Newman no longer liked the doctrine of *monarchia*, arguing that it was largely Greek patristic writers who held it, whereas Latins held the doctrine of coinherence. Unless complemented by the Latins' *circumincessio*, in fact, the doctrine of *monarchia* 'might be perverted into a Semi-Arian denial of the proper divinity of Son and Spirit, if ever They were thought, by reason of Their derivation, to be emanations, and therefore external to the Essence of the Father' (*TT* 169). In 'Causes of Arianism', Newman looks to Tertullian, Dionysius of Rome, and Augustine. Having contrasted their accounts of coinherence as ways to protect Christ's eternal Sonship, he finds Augustine the best.

The key is what each Latin Father does with Christ's words in John's gospel, 'I and the Father are *one*', which was commonly translated by the neuter 'unum'. Tertullian gave this gloss: 'They are all one (unum), by unity of substance'; but the problem was 'that it seemed to imply a fourth reality in the Divine Being over and above the Three Persons, of which the Three Persons partook' (*TT* 169–70). Such a problem, writes Newman, had led the Council of Antioch to oppose 'unity of substance' (*homoousios*) for its materialistic implications, and also led Eusebius of Caesarea to oppose the word's reappearance at Nicaea. Dionysius of Rome translated Jesus's words with the masculine 'unus' instead, 'saying definitely that the Father is the "Unus Deus", with the explanation or understanding that the Son and Spirit are in Him' (*TT* 171). But this caused the opposite problem, suggesting 'a sort of subordination to the Son and the Spirit, which, scriptural though it was, became a handle to Semi-Arianism' (*TT* 172). The third alternative was Augustine, who understood the translation "unus" [as] expressing any one or other of the Three Persons, since Each of Them (no matter which of Them is taken) is the One God' (*TT* 170). Given 'the experience of [Semi-Arian] heresy', Newman thinks only Augustine's alternative was safe from the charges of materialism or subordination in the Godhead (*TT* 172). Newman brought this interpretation to the Athanasius translation.

Even though the *monarchia*, as 'St. Irenaeus, St. Athanasius, and St. Basil taught, never can be put aside', Newman in the revised translation did just that (*TT* 178). Rejecting the importance of the doctrine, in 1881, Newman translates as 'Son' the one Athanasius deliberately called 'Son *of* God'. Thus, in II. 31, he translates 'the Son is the Word' instead of 'the Word is the Son of God' (*Ath* i. 289/*Ox Frs* xix. 323). Athanasius wrote 'the Son of God' because he conceived the Son as derived from ὁ θεός and 'proper' (ἴδιος) to that God's nature and substance (PG 26: 212 B10–11).

Newman's preference for Latin over Greek doctrine is perhaps no surprise given the Thomistic revival that was beginning in the 1870s. In 1872, Newman had glossed Augustine in scholastic terms: ' "unus" stands indeterminately for Either of the Three, somewhat in the sense of an *individuum vagum*' (*TT* 172).[37] What did Newman do then with Athanasius's own Trinitarian doctrine? In the words of the first translation of Discourse I. 18, 'it belongs to Greeks to introduce a generated Trinity... but the faith of Christians acknowledges the blessed Trinity as unalterable and perfect and ever what It was' (*Ox Frs* viii. 206–7). By 'Greeks' Athanasius meant Neoplatonist philosophers. In 1881, Newman decided to translate what these philosophers affirmed as 'a Triad' from the Greek τριάδα: 'it belongs to Greeks to introduce a Triad which is generate... but the faith of Christians acknowledges the blessed Trinity as unalterable and perfect and ever what It was' (*Ath* i. 177, PG 26: 49 B5–12). Even if it was not wholly accurate to translate τριάδα as 'Trinity' in 1842, it was at least consistent to compare a Greek 'generated Trinity' with a Christian 'blessed Trinity'. Less consistent is to compare a Greek 'Triad' with a Christian 'Trinity', in 1881, when Athanasius uses the same

---

[37] 'Individuum vagum', comes from medieval commentaries on the famous passage distinguishing primary from secondary substance in Aristotle's *Categories* 2a. 11–19. For a discussion of what Aristotle might have meant in this passage, see G. C. Stead, *Divine Substance* (Oxford: Clarendon Press, 1977), 57–9.

word for both. But Newman seems to have been following his Catholic contemporaries by implying in the revised translation that the doctrine of God divided into *de Deo uno* (on God's unity) and *de Deo trino* (on God's Trinity).[38] 'Greek' Neoplatonic philosophers discerned by their intellect that God was one, *de Deo uno*, a God beyond being who made a Logos and Spirit that were less than God, resulting in 'a Triad which is generate'. The 'blessed Trinity' was only known through revelation which Arian philosophy misunderstood.

In 'On St Cyril's Formula' (1858), Newman claimed that Athanasius and Cyril used *ousia* words, in some instances, 'as denoting the God of natural theology' (or of the philosophers) and, in other instances, these words were 'applied to the second Person of the Blessed Trinity, meaning simply that same Divine Being, Deus singularis et unicus, in persona Filii' (*TT* 353–4).[39] In Christian theology, *ousia* words had both a universal sense in keeping with the natural theology of *de Deo uno*, and an individual sense when applied to the Trinitarian persons of *de Deo trino*, so that—as Newman put it in 1872—'the Three Persons are Each *really* identical with the One Divine Essence... yet Each *really* distinct' (*TT* 172). But, for Athanasius, the hypostases differed because God's very essence (*ousia*) was the Father's alone, from whom the Son and Spirit were eternally derived in the doctrine of the *monarchia*. Athanasius uses this doctrine, as Newman first translated I. 17, to argue that 'God [ὁ θεός] is not Maker, if He had not His proper Framing Word which is from Him' (*Ox Frs* viii. 205, PG 26: 48 A6–7). In 1881, Newman retranslated this passage: 'if God be Maker of all things by means of His Son, to deprive the Son of this necessary prerogative is, in fact, to deprive the Eternal Father of His creative power' (*Ath* i. 176). For the later Newman, it seems, Athanasius's language did not sufficiently stress the coequality of God and 'His proper Framing Word'. Instead of Athanasius's derivation language of a Word who is 'from' God, the new translation stresses the dependancy on one another of 'Father' and 'Son', though neither title is found in the Greek, to demonstrate their coequality.

---

[38] A useful introduction to this division occurs in Karl Rahner, 'Remarks on the Dogmatic Treatise "De Trinitate"', *Theological Investigations*, iv (Baltimore, Md.: Hellicon, 1966), 77–102.

[39] In 'St Chrysostom' (1859) Newman admitted that 'a treatise *de Deo*' appealed to him less, at this stage, than the lives of Christ and the saints (*HS* ii. 218).

The condescension of the Son

In 'Causes of Arianism', Newman is concerned to make safe the doctrine of the Son's 'going forth' (*syncatabasis*) from the Father. In pre-Nicene theology, the doctrine appeared in three forms that could suggest the Son had a beginning: 'first, the Logos in the bosom of the Father, or... Endiathetic, which I shall denote by the letter A; next, the Logos born to be a Son, or Prophoric, B; and, lastly, the Logos Prototocos [First-born], C' (*TT* 245). By contrast to any such 'temporal *gennesis*', argues Newman, Athanasius followed the teachings of Origen's 'eternal *gennesis*', which held the going forth to occur in a series of stages, from the speaking of the Word, to the creation which that speaking brought about, to the Word's entering into creation as a human (*TT* 201–7). This was one process, in the sense of the Son *proceeding* from the Father, but one that is from all eternity, with no temporal beginning even though time was brought to birth by it. The 'necessary safeguards' against the heretical ABC were, therefore, in place: (A) the Son's *gennesis* from God is eternal and unchanging, (B) so he was not Word before he became Son, and (C) his condescension is as 'first-born of all creation', a different notion from the heretical-sounding, 'first-born of God'. These safeguards led, in turn, to revisions in his translation.

(A) In 1881, Newman is more reluctant than before to call Christ Logos or 'Word'. In Discourse I. 17, which Newman introduces in the revised translation with an invented phrase, 'coming back then to the eternity of the Son' (*Ath* i. 175; cf. *Ox Frs* viii. 204), Newman replaces Athanasius's Logos with 'Son'. Thus, the following sentence:

if the Word is not with the Father from everlasting, the Trinity [τριάς] is not everlasting; but a One was first, and afterwards by addition it became a Three [τριάς]; and so as time went on, it seems what we know concerning God grew and took shape. (*Ox Frs* viii. 205, PG 26: 48 A12–B2)

becomes:

if the Son was not, then the Triad is not from eternity, but was a Monad first, and afterwards a Triad, and so the true knowledge which we have of God grew, it seems, and took shape. (*Ath* i. 176)

This is the opposite move from what a reader of *Arians of the Fourth Century* might expect, where 'Son' was held to be a more dangerous title than 'Word' because 'Son' implied a begetting (γέννεσις) in the manner of humans, which is to say materially and temporally. As to 'Word', he wrote in 1833: '[n]o appellation, surely, could have been more appositely bestowed to counteract notions of materiality and of distinct individuality, which the title of Son was likely to introduce into Catholic doctrine' (*Ari* 169). By the time of 'Causes of Arianism', Newman has come to hold that 'Word' is the more dangerous title. Describing the 'Word' as from all eternity might imply the Logos ἐνδιάθετος, a 'Wisdom' or 'Reason' not sufficiently differentiated from God, and so the translation had to be changed.

(B) In 'On St Cyril's Formula' (1858), Newman had quoted Discourse II. 35 to show the care which was needed when predicating terms like 'pronounced Word' and 'fiat' of the Son: ' "God's Word is not merely προφορικός, nor by His Son is meant His command", e.g. Fiat lux' (*TT* 365). The later Newman is allergic to the view he attributes to Justin in 'Causes of Arianism': 'From eternity He was conceived, as if "in utero", and before time and creation He was born. He was not born from eternity' (*TT* 254). Looking once more at the revised translation of I. 17, the reader is prevented from seeing any sort of birth of the Son, for the Son goes forth from the Father eternally. This coeternity is emphasized by reducing Athanasius's argument to a single point, that God cannot first be One and then Three, for such a change would imply some notion of time in which the change took place. The first translation had:

And further, if the Son is not proper Offspring [γέννημα] of the Father's substance, but of nothing has come to be [γέγονεν], then of nothing the Trinity consists, and once there was not a Three, but a One; and a Three once with deficiency, and then complete; deficient, before the Son was generated [γένηται], complete when He had come to be [γέγονε]. (*Ox Frs* viii. 205–6, PG 26: 48 B2–7).

In the revised translation, this becomes: 'Then again, if the Son has come out of nothing, I suppose the whole Triad came out of nothing too' (*Ath* i. 176). Perhaps Newman avoids calling the Son 'Offspring', in 1881, in case it is taken to be a synonym for the 'generated' Son proclaimed by Athanasius's opponents. Both English words imply 'birth', an idea that Newman is trying to avoid. Indeed, shortly before this point, in the 1881 version, Athanasius asks of his opponents, 'Was He, or was He not? ever [i.e. eternally], or not before His generation', instead of, 'Was He... always, or not before His birth'? (*Ath* i. 165/*Ox Frs* viii. 192) The Son's going forth must be seen as a process that begins eternally and becomes temporal only when the Son assumes flesh; but even then Newman wants to guard against the idea that the incarnation was a 'temporal *gennesis*'. On the knotty problem of the Christological interpretation of Proverbs 8: 22 ('The Lord created me'), Newman originally translated II. 67 as: 'Not of His substance then is *He created* indicative... but of His bodily gener-ation [γενέσεως]' (*Ox Frs* xix. 376, PG 26: 289 A15–B1).[40] The later Newman changed the last words to 'His bodily coming into being', an equally good translation but one that precluded the idea of a gener-ation (*Ath* i. 336).[41] To be utterly sure that Athanasius is seen to hold that the Son proceeds eternally, Newman even invents for III. 28: 'He is more than eternal; He is co-eternal' (*Ath* i. 393, cf. *Ox Frs* xix. 439).

(C) The way that Newman uses language in his revised translation makes a clear distinction between what has come into existence, which is to say, creation, and what exists from all eternity, the Son who condescends to become creation's first born. Tracing his shifting translation of Discourse II. 64 in three iterations—1844, 1872, 1881—shows Newman progressively widening the gap (*diastema*) between on the one hand God's creative Word and on the other creation itself; between the eternal *gennesis* of the Son and the temporal beginning of creation. Athanasius's conception of the

---

[40] For why this scripture presents a knotty problem, see Frances M. Young, 'Proverbs 8 in Interpretation (2): Wisdom Personified; Fourth-century Christian Readings: Assumptions and Debates', in D. F. Ford and G. Stanton (eds.), *Reading Texts, Seeking Wisdom: Scripture and Theology* (London: Student Christian Move-ment, 2003), 102–15.

[41] This new sensitivity in giving different translations for becoming-words (with one Greek 'ν') and begetting-words (with 'νν') is strange given Newman's statement in the notes that 'at this time, γένετον and γέννετον seem to be one word, whatever distinction was made at a later date' (*Ath* ii. 398). The 1842 basis for this note ran: 'Athanasius does not distinguish between γένετον and γέννετον, in spite of such distinction in the reading, as Montfaucon adopts... [Athanasius] allows that γέννημα *may* be taken as synonymous with κτίσμα, and only argues that there is a *special* sense of it in which it applies to the Word, not *as one of a number*, as the Arians said, but solely, incommunicably, as being the μονογενής' (*Ox Frs* viii. 261 n. e).

diastema plays an important role in his theology, as was shown in Chapter 2, but it is a role that Newman increasingly emphasized. The 'Word' in each of these translations remains, as it were, in the same place while creation moves further away in each iteration. In 1844, Newman had: 'the Word...condescended to things generate [γέννητοῖς], that it might be possible for them to come to be [γενέσθαι]' (*Ox Frs* xix. 372, PG 26: 284 A12–13). In 1872, the same text is quoted in 'Causes of Arianism' thus: 'The Word, when in the beginning He framed the creatures, condescended (συγκαταβέβηκε) to them, that it might be possible for them to come into being' (*TT* 202). By 1881, it has become: 'the Word... condescended to things which were to have a beginning' (*Ath* i. 333). Each translation carries more theological freight, culminating with the Word being so clearly coeternal with the Father that only at some point in the future is creation 'to have a beginning'. Newman sets the poles of God and creation so far apart that they can only be bridged, firstly, by the coeternal Son's condescension in the act of creation itself—what 'Causes of Arianism' calls 'the first act of His *Syncatabasis*' (*TT* 202)—and, secondly, the incarnation, for 'by this condescension of the Word, the creation too is made a son through Him, that He might be in all respects First-born of it' (*Ath* i. 333/*Ox Frs* xix. 372). This latter idea is crucial to Newman's writings in the 1870s, emphasizing creation's need for Christ to become 'First-born of it', rather than regarding him heretically as First-born of God.[42] In making the gap between God and creation larger in the revised translation than it was at first, moreover, Newman shows the condescension to be a twofold process in the way Aquinas did. 'Causes of Arianism' notes that Aquinas separated the eternal and temporal procession.[43] As Newman makes clear, the second phase of the

[42] The 1871 edition of *Arians of the Fourth Century*, Note II explains: 'Nor are such expositions of the title "First-born of creation", as Athanasius has so beautifully given us, to the purpose of Bull. Bull takes it to show that γέννεσις may be considered to be a mission or forthcoming; whereas Athanasius does not mean by the "First-born" any γέννεσις of our Lord from the Father at all, but he simply means His coming to the creature, that is, His exalting the creature into a Divine sonship by a union with His own Sonship' (*Ari* 419).

[43] 'The phrase "*temporalis procession*" is used by St Thomas, Qu. 43. art. 2, of the Son's Incarnation' (*TT* 196 n. 1). Aquinas wrote that as well as eternally, 'He may proceed temporally, to become man as well, according to his visible mission; or He

condescension, must not be mistaken for a temporal *gennesis*, but rather is the outworking of the eternal *gennesis*.

Newman's exemplars of Catholic truth in 'Causes of Arianism' are no surprise. When explaining *syncatabasis*, he writes:

This doctrine, expounded by St. Athanasius, confirmed by St. Augustine and St. Thomas, is in tone and drift very unlike Arianism, which had no sympathy with the mysticism and poetry of Plato; but it had a direct resemblance to the Semi-Arian edition of the heresy, and, if put forward without its necessary safeguards and corrections, as we find them in those great doctors, was likely to open the way to it. (*TT* 207)

Thanks to these doctors, spoken of as if they all say the same thing, Newman thought the danger in Platonic language was overcome. It is, however, likely that Athanasius had more in common with the Platonizing pre-Nicene Alexandrians who taught him than with later Latins who read (and misread) him.

CONCLUSION: A LATIN ATHANASIUS FOR A CATHOLIC CARDINAL

In his criticisms of the first translation, John Kaye uncovered Newman's Latinized (or Lateranized) depiction of the Trinity. However, during 1842–4, it was only in the annotations that Newman attempted to tidy up the differences between the Alexandrian East and Latin West. Only within the annotations could a composite Athanasius be seen. In 1881, within the translation itself, made with scholastic doctrines of God in mind, a confused Athanasius is seen.

A comparison of the later translation with the earlier gives an insight into the mind of a convert still after many years trying to explain himself to his adopted Church, as he did in the *Apologia Pro Vita Sua*, but now with more confidence in Roman theology. In November 1876, when Newman was considering in what form to

may proceed temporally by dwelling in man according to His invisible mission' (*ST* Ia.43.2).

republish his Athanasius volumes, Pusey wrote to him: 'If you could have revised your translation and notes (not that I know that there is any thing to revise) it would have been pleasant to have printed them in common; but your authorities might not have liked it' (*LD* xxviii. 138 n. 3). Here the Anglican Pusey misunderstands the Catholic Newman because he assumes 'your authorities' would prevent Newman publishing jointly with Pusey.[44] The authorities were at work on Newman's translation in ways Pusey did not understand, however, for his friend was aligning Athanasius with the Thomistic revival. This is the real irony: Newman, as a Catholic, maintained he was a historian not a theologian, and yet, by the 1870s, he was less interested in the historical Athanasius than in Catholic theology. His revised translation exhibits what Gerard McCool has described, referring to Leo XIII's encyclical *Aeterni Patris* (1879), as 'the serene conviction of the nineteenth-century neo-Thomists that scholastic philosophy was a single metaphysical system, common to all the scholastic doctors, and that scholastic philosophy could gather up, preserve, and represent the essence of patristic thought which it has superseded'.[45] By the time of publication in 1881, while it is not Athanasius 'in whose name I write' (*Ath* i, p. ix), it does not seem to be Aquinas's name either. Rather, Newman's translation properly reflects neither doctor but is a theological synthesis of a neo-Thomistic kind.

[44] Newman replied to Pusey: 'it never entered into my head to fancy that my own people, high or low, would be surprised at my having a joint edition' (*LD* xxviii. 138).

[45] Gerard McCool, *Catholic Theology in the Nineteenth Century: The Quest for a Unitary Method* (New York: Seabury Press, 1977), 233.

6

Conclusion

This conclusion will examine the Anglophone scholars who came after Newman in order to show the ways in which he changed the paradigms for their understanding of the Alexandrian Fathers. Limiting the scope to seven scholars from Oxford in the 200 years since Newman's birth will be sufficient to show how he shaped doctrinal history for these Oxonians and for those who read them into the late twentieth century.

William Bright and Charles Bigg were successive Regius Professors of Ecclesiastical History at Oxford, Bright from 1868 until his death in 1901 and then Bigg until his death in 1908. Their writings are a good place to begin to trace Newman's influence on depictions of the Alexandrians. Bright's Greek edition of *The Orations of St Athanasius Against the Arians* will be examined here,[1] not least because it led to a correspondence with Newman, together with Bigg's 1886 Bampton lectures, *The Christian Platonists of Alexandria*.[2] Next on the list is Archibald Robertson who, though never a Professor in Oxford, was principal of Hatfield Hall, Durham and principal of King's College, London before becoming bishop of Exeter. In the 1870s, he was educated at Newman's undergraduate college, Trinity, where he became a fellow, just when theology became a subject for examination in Oxford.[3] The importance at Oxford of Alexandrian theology can

---

[1] William Bright, *The Orations of St Athanasius Against the Arians* (Oxford: Clarendon Press, 1873).

[2] Charles Bigg, *The Christian Platonists of Alexandria: Eight Lectures* (Oxford: Clarendon Press, 1886).

[3] Pusey worked for the establishment of the Honour School of Theology in 1869 even though he opposed such an innovation in 1854, because he came to see that in

be seen from the fact that Athanasius's *On the Incarnation* was a prescribed text for the first examination in the Oxford Honour School of Theology in 1870 and from 1878 onwards,[4] while Cyril's *Letters to Nestorius*, the third of which included the Twelve Anathemas, were prescribed in 1872. Robertson himself went on to lecture in Oxford on Athanasius from 1879 to 1881, publishing a Greek edition of the *On the Incarnation* (1882) for use in the School. He then published an English translation of this text (1885), before including it with Newman's Oxford translations (1842–4) among *Select Writings and Letters of Athanasius, Bishop of Alexandria* (1891), which will be examined here for Robertson's comments in the introduction.[5]

Moving to the twentieth century, B. J. Kidd, who had been taught by Bright and became Warden of Keble College, gives insight into the continued use of a variety of Newman's patristic writings in his three-volume *A History of the Church to AD 461*.[6] Next, Frank Cross, who is best known as the first editor of the *Oxford Dictionary of the Christian Church*, spoke highly of Newman in his inaugural lecture as Lady Margaret Professor of Divinity on the state of Athanasian scholarship a century after the publication of the second volume of Newman's Library of the Fathers translation. Finally, to bring us to the present day, Maurice Wiles (Regius Professor of Divinity, 1970–91) and Rowan Williams (Lady Margaret Professor, 1986–91), though both

Schools examinations 'unsound views would be rejected—not because they were unsound, but because they were erroneous'. These words of Maurice Wiles are supported by the evidence that he gives from early papers: 'In 1876 [the candidate] is asked to "Maintain the position of the English Church as to the sufficiency of the Holy Scriptures for Salvation" and in 1878 to "Shew, with instances, that the Ante-Nicene Christian writers held Nicene doctrines"' ('Jerusalem, Athens and Oxford: An Inaugural Lecture as Regius Professor of Divinity in the University of Oxford' in Wiles, *Working Papers in Doctrine* (London: Student Christian Movement, 1976), 167–8). Newman's discussions with Pusey were formative of the Oxford view that patristic study was the ground of Anglican doctrine.

[4] F. L. Cross, *The Study of St Athanasius: An Inaugural Lecture* (Oxford: Clarendon Press, 1945), 10.

[5] See NPNF ser. 2 iv. 34 for Robertson's explanation and dates of his translation of *de Incarnatione*.

[6] Kidd, *A History of the Church to AD 461*, 3 vols. (Oxford: Clarendon Press, 1922). E.g. for the *Syncatabasis* of the Son and the *Principatus* of the Father discussed in Ch. 5 above, see ibid. i. 360 n. 3 and ii. 39 n. 6, both citing *TT* 174.

educated at Cambridge, continued the Oxonian tradition of drawing from Newman even as they criticized him. Newman's influence will be traced in three doctrinal areas that have been explored in this book: firstly, the legacy of *Arians of the Fourth Century*; secondly, the status of Origen's teachings; and thirdly, the use of Athanasius as a composite for post-Nicene views on the Trinity.

THE LEGACY OF *THE ARIANS*
OF THE FOURTH CENTURY

Newman had set out in 1831 to write an introduction to the doctrine of the Thirty-nine Articles to be included in Rose and Lyall's Theological Library; he ended up with a narrative of why Nicaea was in some ways a gain and in other ways a loss in the history of doctrine. Chapter 2 showed that *Arians of the Fourth Century* depended upon traditional High Church scholarship on the pre-Nicene Fathers to make this argument, but managed to offend contemporary High Churchmen Archdeacon Lyall and Bishop Kaye by suggesting that something had been lost at Nicaea. Moreover *Arians of the Fourth Century* helped insure that into the twentieth century British scholars would consider Antiochenes and Alexandrians as polar opposites, Alexandria making saints while Antioch spawned heretics like Paul of Samosata and Arius.

In spite of criticisms of its accuracy from the very beginning, Newman's first book continued to receive praise from Oxonians. The occasion for such praise from Bright was a response to criticism of *Arians of the Fourth Century* by the Cambridge Professor of Ecclesiastical History, H. M. Gwatkin, in *Studies of Arianism* (1882).[7] Bright wrote that Gwatkin's *Studies* 'falls below the high level of the *Arians* in theological depth, keenness, and richness, such as appear so wonderfully in Newman's sections on the "Scriptural"

---

[7] The preface to the first edition had: 'Of Newman's *Arians* let it suffice to say that his theories have always been scrupulously examined; so that if they have not been accepted, it is only because there is usually good reason for rejecting them' (Gwatkin, *Studies of Arianism* (2nd edn.; Cambridge: Deighton Bell & Co., 1900), p. xv).

and the "ecclesiastical" doctrine of the Trinity, and on "variations of ante-Nicene theological statements" '.[8] Robertson called it 'an English classic, unrivalled as a dogmatic and religious study of Arianism, although unsatisfactory on its purely historical side. (Obsolete chronology retained in all editions.)'[9] It was probably the 'unsatisfactory' history—the oversimplified story, the heroes, and villains— that allowed *Arians of the Fourth Century* to become a doctrinal 'classic'. Thus, Newman in *Arians of the Fourth Century* achieved what he set out to do, described in the Introduction above as making doctrinal history available in the present not as antiquarian scholarship but as living wisdom.

Indeed, the polemical purposes for which *Arians of the Fourth Century* was written in the first place should not be overlooked. Hindsight shows how much the work depended upon its time, and looking from this perspective reveals rich ironies that were missed by those who treated Newman's book as a straightforward history and forgot its original context. Written at the start of the 1830s, *Arians of the Fourth Century* was arguing for the role of 'secrecy' or 'reserve' in the Church in a growing public square.[10] Newman was taking advantage of the national role of the Church *precisely when* he argued for distancing the Church from national politics.[11] In a book that

---

[8] Anon. [William Bright], 'Gwatkin's Studies of Arianism', *Church Quarterly Review*, 16 (1883), 381. Soon after, Newman wrote to thank Bright (*LD* xxx. 239–40), who replied: 'Mr Gwatkin's presumed to be a student of the theological history of a great period; and his curt sentence, therefore, required something like a gentle castigation' (OM Newman–Bright Correspondence, quoted at Roderick Strange, *Newman and the Gospel of Christ* (Oxford: Clarendon Press, 1981), 13 n. 29).

[9] NPNF ser. 2 iv, p. xiii.

[10] Rowan Williams, introduction, *Ari* (p. xlvi). Jürgen Habermas has shown that the public square was of growing importance in the nineteenth century. See Frank Turner, *John Henry Newman: The Challenge to Evangelical Religion* (New Haven, Conn.: Yale University Press, 2002), 53–5.

[11] He wrote in 1835: 'One chief part of political power confessedly consists in the display of power.... If anyone says that a modest and retiring influence is the peculiar ornament of the Church, I answer that it is her privilege in peaceful, not her duty in stirring times' (Suff 47–8). This parallels the language of *Arians of the Fourth Century*: 'Enough has now been said, by way of describing the condition of the Catholic Church, defenceless from the very sacredness and refinement of its discipline, when the attack of Arianism was made upon it; insulting its silence, provoking it to argue... and in consequence requiring its authoritative judgment on the point in dispute' (*Ari* 141).

came out simultaneous to early Tracts proclaiming the authority of the successors of the apostles, Newman implied that English bishops 'timorously or indolently, kept in the background' in the face of reform (*Ari* 294). Above all, the collapse of the *ancien régime* in 1829–32—a collapse that Newman felt diminished the role of the English Church in the life of the nation—opened the possibility for him to express these radical views about the Church. Scholars who read *Arians of the Fourth Century* fifty or a hundred and fifty years later lived in a completely different context.

Given that Newman aimed for his history book to foster principles that would come to be identified with the Oxford Movement, it is not surprising that scholars shaped by the Movement continued to praise the book. The antithesis at the heart of *Arians of the Fourth Century* between Alexandrian and Antiochene methods of scriptural interpretation, described in Chapter 2, was also about the principles of authority as embodied by a particular ethos. Respect for the authority of tradition meant a rejection of rationalist or sceptical argument; it also meant an asceticism and spiritualism opposed to worldly materialism. Newman's teaching on Antiochene rationalism and materialism became the dominant interpretation of Eastern Christianity among his Oxford Movement successors. A comparison between two Oxford scholars—Edward Burton at the time of *Arians of the Fourth Century* and B. J. Kidd nearly a century later—suggests how much difference Newman made to who was held responsible for the Arian heresy. Burton had thought it obvious that the blame for Arianism fell upon the home of its founder, Alexandria (*Ari* 403); Kidd would quote Newman on the rationalism and sophistry of Arianism that showed blame lay with Antioch.[12]

Cambridge scholars did not agree with Newman's depiction of Arianism as an Antiochene heresy; but, then, according to the caricatures of both universities, it was natural that they would not. Gwatkin thought it was the Arians (not their Alexandrian opponents) who were anti-rational, for they 'upheld the Lord's divinity by

[12] Kidd, *A History of the Church to AD 461*, ii. 37, 39 quoting *Ari* 221. On the objections at Nicaea to *homoousios* (ibid. 32 n. 8) Kidd cites *Ari* 184–5 and *Ath* ii. 438, 454. For events after Nicaea, regarding Valens (ibid. 166 n. 3), the Homoeans (ibid. 151 n. 8), and the Council of Seleucia (ibid. 168 n. 5), Kidd also cites *Arians of the Fourth Century*.

making the Son of God a creature, and then worshipped him to escape the reproach of heathenism', while Athanasius was a great intellect.[13] Turning on its head Newman's depiction of Alexandrian–Catholic tradition versus Antiochene–Arian rationality, Gwatkin suggested that it was the Arians who had the greater claim to be traditionalist. In so doing, Gwatkin presented the Oxonians, whom he knew to be jealous of that label,[14] with a view that proved to Bright that Cambridge was opposed to 'churchly spirit'.[15] Bright complained: 'Mr. Gwatkin, we think, was led away by the charm of an antithesis when he said that "the victors of Nicaea leaned on scripture, the Arians on tradition throughout the controversy".'[16] Newman's antithesis in *Arians of the Fourth Century* was more charming to Bright than, it seems, was Gwatkin's.

But, while the successors to the Oxford Movement supported what *Arians of the Fourth Century* had to say about tradition and ethos, they shared the suspicions of earlier High Churchmen concerning Newman's praise for the Alexandrians' use of allegory and the secret tradition. Newman's departure for Rome confirmed in their eyes what from the beginning Bishop Kaye had taken to be the 'Romish' doctrine of the *disciplina arcani*. Chapter 1 showed that Newman's fondness for the secret tradition, which *Arians of the Fourth Century* claimed had operated in the pre-Nicene Church, was an aspect of Newman's radicalism not 'Romanism'. Yet, just as High Churchmen reacted suspiciously when they read *Arians of the Fourth Century*, so Bigg lectured in 1886 that no such 'secret tradition' existed.[17] Nor

[13] Gwatkin, *Studies of Arianism*, 2–3.

[14] Gwatkin wrote that the 'general principles' of 'the Oxford school' are 'reverence for tradition' and 'utter condemnation of the Reformation as little better than pure and simple wickedness' (*The Knowledge of God and its Historical Development*, 2 vols. (2nd edn.; Edinburgh: T. & T. Clark, 1909), ii. 317.

[15] Bright wrote of 'The Cambridge school': 'if any bias is ever observable in its language, this would be rather in the direction of a suspicion of what our American brethren call the "churchly" spirit, as if it involved narrowness or bigotry' ('Gwatkin's Studies of Arianism', 379).

[16] Ibid. 386.

[17] Bigg writes in *Christian Platonists of Alexandria*: 'It is possible to defend the practice of Reserve, if it be taken to represent the method of a skilful teacher, who will not confuse the learner with principles beyond his comprehension. This however is by no means what the Alexandrines intended. With them it is the screen of an esoteric belief' (pp. 144–5), noting: 'It is so defended by J. H. Newman, *Arians*, i. 3 pp. 40 sqq. 3rd edn.; see also the *Apologia pro Vita Sua*; and by Origen himself, *Contra Celsum*, 3. 52 sqq.' (ibid. 145 n. 1).

was it a good idea for Newman to suggest that allegorical readings of scripture, when guided by the secret tradition, were the best way of 'conveying instruction to believers' (*Ari* 59). Bigg continued that Newman 'considers [allegorical interpretation] to have been the bulwark of orthodoxy against the sceptical literal method of the school of Antioch... As regard the Old Testament, it is a dangerous and in its actual use a delusive method, delusive because it proceeds upon the exaggeration of a truth'.[18] Similar doubts about Old Testament allegory were expressed in the early examination papers for Oxford's Honour School of Theology,[19] and in 1903 the standard British textbook of the period by Bethune-Baker would warn that the economical teaching of the early Alexandrians might 'easily lead to a perversion of the true paedagogic reticence', expressing a view that could have been addressed to Newman seventy years before.[20] Yet, there remained something enticing to inheritors of the Oxford Movement about the depiction in *Arians of the Fourth Century* of an early Church following practical rules that led to rich secondary teaching. Nicaea, and the Councils which followed, saw both a loss of richness—with practical rules of faith replaced by propositional ones—and a gain of clarification. Today, Rowan Williams seems to follow Newman in his description of doctrine as artificially (but necessarily) regulated at Nicaea and subsequently.[21]

Even as later historians criticized aspects of Newman's history, they also depended upon it. *Arians of the Fourth Century* is in some ways the first textbook of the history of doctrine from 'St. Mark,

[18] Bigg 148, with n. citing *Dev* 1878 7.4.5 (which is also *Arians of the Fourth Century* (1871) Note I).

[19] The fact that 'Early examination papers...invite criticism of Athanasius's exegesis of the Old Testament' suggests lingering High Church suspicion of allegorical interpretation in the Honour School of Theology (Wiles, 'Jerusalem, Athens, and Oxford', 168).

[20] J. F. Bethune-Baker, *An Introduction to the Early History of Christian Doctrine to the Time of the Council of Chalcedon* (5th edn.; London: Methuen, 1933), 40, citing Newman at 39 n. 1.

[21] Williams argues that 'Christological clarifications, Chalcedon above all, and the subsequent Christological clarifications of the Byzantine period, are indeed not *simply* regulative stipulations'—as Maurice Wiles claims—'but the result of applying regulative principles to the more chaotic language of pre-dogmatic *doctrina*' ('Doctrinal Criticism: Some Questions', in Sarah Coakley and David Pailin, *The Making and Remaking of Christian Doctrine* (Oxford: Clarendon Press, 1993), 250).

the founder of the Alexandrian Church' to the 'Creed of Constantinople... said to be the composition of Gregory Nyssen' (*Ari* 41, 392). It
depicts the road from the Evangelists to the Trinitarian creeds, recognizing the central role played by the Greek Fathers (the Alexandrians
and their allies from Cappadocia) in making sure that this road was
direct when heretics wanted to take wrong turns. Newman showed
both the integrity of this doctrine—the creeds were reiterations of the
truth about God not inventions—but also that doctrine had a lively
history before the 'imposition of the "*consubstantial*"' at Nicaea made
the faith 'consigned to arbitrary formulas' (*Ari* 234, 181). *Arians of the
Fourth Century* was the first roadmap of doctrinal history in the
British tradition, avoiding the sequential biographies of Cave or
the largely synchronic approach to specific doctrinal *loci* of Bull.
At the beginning of the twentieth century, histories of doctrine such
as Bethune-Baker's and Kidd's followed this model, extending the
roadmap to include the Councils of Ephesus and Chalcedon (this
Anglican focus on the first four councils was still in existence towards
the end of the century in the textbooks of J. N. D Kelly, Richard
Norris, and Frances Young).[22] These maps might account differently
for which territories fall either side of the road of orthodoxy, but they
still depict one road from the Apostles to Nicaea to Chalcedon, with a
few wrong turns taken along the way.

Maurice Wiles resisted such roadmaps of the period between the
Gospels and Chalcedon in his inaugural lecture as Regius Professor
of Divinity, wittily bemoaning in 1971 that 'it is still possible in
Oxford... to [study theology] as if the world went out of existence
in AD 461', ten years after Chalcedon.[23] Resisting a way of understanding doctrinal history in Oxford that went back to Newman,
Wiles said: 'our relation to past Christian tradition cannot be one of
identity nor even one of the preservation intact of some definable
inner core of that tradition.'[24] In other words, there is no continuous
road running through the history of doctrine; there is not even a clear

---

[22] J. N. D. Kelly, *Early Christian Doctrines* (London: A. and C. Black, 1958);
Richard A. Norris, introduction, *The Christological Controversy* (Philadelphia, Pa.:
Fortress, 1980); and Frances M. Young, *From Nicaea to Chalcedon: A Guide to the
Literature and its Background* (London: Student Christian Movement, 1983).

[23] Wiles, 'Jerusalem, Athens and Oxford', 179.

[24] Ibid. 177.

point of departure. As Wiles writes elsewhere, history teaches Christians to be unsure of their 'core' doctrine of the Trinity.[25] For this reason, Wiles regrets the high praise for Athanasius and Nicaea among nineteenth- and twentieth-century British scholars, and in this respect stresses the similarities of Newman and Gwatkin where Bright saw their differences.[26]

Judging by these remarks, what can Wiles possibly be said to take from Newman? Rowan Williams suggests that, like the radical author of *Arians of the Fourth Century*, Wiles recognizes 'that doctrine really does have a history', a recognition that has been 'painfully slow to dawn on theologians'.[27] Wiles's history is less integrated than that of Newman, but there are similarities between them. This book has suggested that Newman's *Development of Christian Doctrine* required the research of the summer of 1839, when he realized what most of his Oxford contemporaries neglected: that doctrinal history did not stop 'in AD 461'. Chalcedon was in many ways a new beginning on the question of who Christ was, not the end that Anglicans claimed. Unlike Wiles, however, Newman used this fact as evidence for a new roadmap in which a magisterium was needed to confirm true developments. The view of doctrine that took shape from 1840 to 1845 aimed to prove that 'a true development retains the *essential idea* of the subject from which it has proceeded' by charting Catholic teaching from the early Fathers until the end of the fifth century (*Dev* 204 and chs. 4–5). Although Newman did not tell the sixth-century story of Leontius and Maximus, whom he had read in 1839, he did allude to the strength of their opponents: 'While Monophysites or their favourers occupied the Churches of the Eastern Empire, Nestorianism was making progress far beyond it' (ibid. 316). This historiography did not have the same borders as earlier High Church doctrine. Moreover, the Anglicans who challenged Newman for asserting development 'under the continuous control

---

[25] Id, 'Some Reflections on the Origins of the Doctrine of the Trinity', *Working Papers in Doctrine*, ch. 1.

[26] Wiles criticizes the British scholarship of Athanasius in *Archetypal Heresy: Arianism through the Centuries* (Oxford: Clarendon Press, 1996), ch. 5.

[27] Williams, 'Doctrinal Criticism: Some Questions', 246; n. 10 refers to his 'Newman's *Arians* and the Question of Method in Doctrinal History', in Ian Ker and Alan G. Hill (eds.), *Newman after One Hundred Years* (Oxford: Clarendon Press, 1990).

of divine power, acting through a supernatural organization', reclaimed High Church historiography, explaining: 'It is not new doctrines to which Christians are bidden to look forward, but new and growing apprehension of doctrine.'[28] They had forgotten the lesson of *Arians of the Fourth Century* that doctrine has a history and reverted instead to the High Church view that the period from the Apostles to Chalcedon was seen as a period of static doctrinal verity, after which everything was an accretion. Although he had tried in the 1830s, Newman had never quite accepted the High Church view.

ORIGEN THE REDEEMABLE PRE-NICENE

The second area of Oxford scholarship in which Newman's influence can be traced is in his account of Origen's theology. Again, the account in his first book borrowed much from Cave and Bull, but went beyond them to give what Bright admiringly described as Newman's 'fervent vindication of Origen from the charge of antici- pated Arianism in *Arians*'.[29] Yet, when depicting orthodox teaching on the Trinitarian relation of Father and Son in the 1840s, Newman gave priority to the word *homoousios*, and not to Origen's doctrine of coeternity. Newman first made public his awareness that the Father was 'beyond substance' for Origen, and thus not *homoousios* with the Son, in an extended note for his translation in A Library of the Fathers (*Ox Frs* viii. 166). The result was that from *Development of Christian Doctrine* until 'Causes of Arianism' Origen's rejection of *homoousios* meant that the great theologian of the coeternity of Father and Son was judged heterodox. With 'Causes of Arianism' (1872) came Origen's rehabilitation. Newman's shifting view now held that coeternity was the mark of orthodoxy, whereas most pre-Nicenes taught the 'connaturality' of Father and Son and thus opened up the possibility of Arianism and Semi-Arianism,

---

[28] Bethune-Baker, *An Introduction to the Early History of Christian Doctrine*, 36; Kidd challenged *Dev* by using an argument of Newman's own from *VM* i. 228 not 'to ignore the distinction between explanatory and accretive developments' (*A History of the Church to AD 461*, ii. 35).

[29] [Bright], 'Gwatkin's Studies of Arianism', 381.

suggesting that the Son only came to be when 'going forth' from the Father. Origen was once more the best of pre-Nicene theologians.

Robertson relied on Newman's scholarship when he succinctly expressed Origen's view of the Son's relation to the Father as part of his introduction to Athanasius's writings. Robertson wrote of Origen's Christ: 'He is of one οὐσία with the Father as compared with the creatures; but as contrasted with the Father, Who may be regarded as ἐπέκεινα οὐσίας [beyond being], the Son is ὁ δεύτερος Θεός [the second God].'[30] Although the first edition of *Arians of the Fourth Century* had been wrong in some respects, Robertson appreciated its 'apology' for Origen, who was later held responsible for a heresy that took his name: 'What was the Origenism *of Origen*? To condense into the compass of our present purpose the many-sidedness of Origen is a hopeless task. The reader will turn to the fifth and sixth of Bigg's *Bampton Lectures* for the best presentation [and] to Newman's *Arians*' among Anglophones.[31] What different sides of Origen did Bigg and Newman offer Robertson's readers? The two are remarkably similar. Newman's fusion of Alexandrian Platonism, '*Via Media*' Anglicanism and English Romanticism, discussed above, was shared by Bigg, who sees in Origen 'a sweep of imagination reminding us of Hooker and Wordsworth [when] he regards the Natural Law [i.e. conscience], the "stern daughter of the voice of God", as swaying not men only but angels and stars'.[32] Like Newman, Bigg recognized Origen's rejection of rationalism: 'The Gospel is not the natural crown of Reason and the Law, but rather a remedy for their failure.'[33]

Until *Development of Christian Doctrine*, Newman had followed the seventeenth-century High Anglicans who taught that '*ad intra*' subordination of Son and Spirit to their Source was the acceptable consequence of the pre-Nicene doctrine of the Father's *monarchia*. Newman had even said in *Arians of the Fourth Century* that Origen was thus not a subordinationist but a believer that the Son was

---

[30] NPNF ser. 2 iv, p. xxvi. Regarding changes made to *Ari* 186 n. 2, which accorded with Robertson's statement here, the latter observed: 'the additions in brackets seriously modify [Newman's] statements in the text'.

[31] NPNF ser. 2 iv, p. xxv.

[32] Bigg, *The Christian Platonists of Alexandria*, 207, quoting Wordsworth's *Ode to Duty*.

[33] Ibid. 208.

homoousios with the Father. Perhaps Bigg was following the seventeenth-century Anglicans still when he argued that Origen's subordination of the Son to the Father was true to the Gospel, especially to Jesus's words of the Father: 'there is only one who is good' (Matt. 19: 17). More likely he was agreeing with Newman's position in 'Causes of Arianism' that, although pre-Nicene subordinationism was unquestionable, that does not diminish Origen's contribution to post-Nicene orthodoxy.[34] Such a view of Origen became the tradition of Oxford scholarship into the twentieth century. For instance, Kidd apologizes for Origen's errors by stating his larger contributions to doctrine, such as his teaching on *perichoresis*, for which Newman's scholarship is a reference: 'the Father is in the Son: and the Son in the Father. There is co-inherence. But Origen insists, with equal force, on the subordination of the Son to the Father. It was his way of getting rid of Modalism.'[35] The problem of modalist heresy had been a theme of 'Causes of Arianism', which argued that the teaching of an Endiathetic Logos or 'Inward Word betokened Sabellianism' (*TT* 209). Kidd is also suggestive of this 1872 essay when he writes of the Son: 'whereas according to [Justin Martyr] He was at first immanent in the mind of the Father and then put forth, according to Origen He was a Person co-eternal with God.'[36] For those who followed Newman, Origen continued to be a formative figure in orthodox doctrine. This may be why Rowan Williams's words are so reminiscent of *Arians of the Fourth Century* when explaining that it is unfair to judge Origen by later doctrinal standards.[37]

---

[34] Origen was 'struggling against his own principles and endeavouring to reduce the doctrine of Derivation and Subordination, which he had inherited from his predecessors, to the narrowest limits consistent with the direct teaching of Scripture. There is a sense even in which the Son may be called the Absolute Good, if not in respect of God yet in respect of man' (*The Christian Platonists of Alexandria*, 182 n.).

[35] Kidd, *A History of the Church to AD 461*, i. 421; n. 5 cites *Ath* ii. 72.

[36] Kidd, *A History of the Church to AD 461*, i. 422.

[37] Williams writes: 'In short, Origen's sense of what orthodoxy requires, because it is based upon a close connection between orthodoxy and the practice of systematic spiritual exegesis...is almost bound to appear heterodox in an age when the dominant discourse of theology is moulded by the pressure to agree formularies that can be communicated economically and authoritatively' ('Origen: Between Orthodoxy and Heresy', in W. A. Bienert and U. Kühneweg (eds.), *Origeniana Septima* (Louvain: Peeters Press, 1999), 13).

ATHANASIUS THE COMPOSITE POST-NICENE

This book has attempted to challenge the view that in his patristic writings Newman was primarily an Athanasius scholar. Praise for Athanasius was not rare in the nineteenth century in Britain or Germany. Bright wrote of Athanasius in 1873: 'in A.D. 359 he showed his characteristic "forebearance and tenderness towards the inconsistent"', a quotation from Newman, as was talk of the 'harmonious "combination of excellences", which enabled him to be "all things to all men", discerning, self-adapting and considerate'.[38] However, it was not only Newman whom Bright quoted: 'Möhler has reason to say that "the narrative of his life is a panegyric which words can only enfeeble".'[39] Gwatkin would become another great advocate of Athanasius in 1882, writing: 'my obligations to modern writers... are mostly due to the Germans', while 'English writers are fewer, and too many of them little better than copyists or partizans'.[40] Newman was, by implication, one such 'partizan', a criticism he had received earlier from another Cambridge man, Bishop Kaye.

Chapter 4 showed that the annotations to the anti-Arian writings (1842–4) presented a composite of Athanasius and later Fathers who did not agree with the patriarch on what was meant by 'the one God'. Newman's attempt to tidy up the differences between East and West actually re-inscribed those differences by shaping Athanasius's doctrine of the Trinity into a Latinized one: the annotations, as Kaye pointed out, presented an omniscient human nature in Christ that Athanasius would not have recognized. In 1881, not

---

[38] Bright, *Orations of St Athanasius*, pp. lxxvi and xcvii (Newman actually has 'in his judgment of the inconsistent... he evinces an admirable tenderness and forbearance', and 'this union of opposite excellences, firmness with discrimination and discretion' (*Ari* 356)).

[39] Bright, *Orations of St Athanasius*, p. xcvii. Duane W.-H. Arnold compares the praise for Athanasius in nineteenth-century Anglophone and German scholarship with the criticism he received later in *The Early Episcopal Career of Athanasius of Alexandria* (Notre Dame, Ind.: Notre Dame University Press, 1991), 11–23. Arnold makes the typical assumption that Newman held the same view of Athanasius throughout his life, beginning when he was 'a young and somewhat infatuated Oxford don' (ibid. 15).

[40] Gwatkin, preface to the first edition (2nd edn., p. ix).

just the annotations but also the retranslation itself confused matters further, as Chapter 5 revealed, through the neo-Thomistic synthesis that appears in *Select Treatises of Athanasius*. The Latin way in which Newman read the Eastern patriarch would influence generations of Anglophone readers through the widespread availability of the first translation in A Library of the Fathers and the Nicene and Post-Nicene Fathers series. Newman's second translation in volume 1 of *Select Treatises* and the amplified annotations gathered in volume 2, were less widely available. Yet, the notes in particular shaped the way Athanasius was interpreted; for instance, Kidd repeatedly cites them in his *History of the Church*.[41]

The influence of Newman's 'Latinized' view of Athanasius's doctrine of the Trinity can be seen where William Bright follows Newman's lead rather than John Kaye's *Council of Nicaea*. Bright's introduction to his Greek edition of *Orations of St Athanasius* says, 'The student should by all means make use of the very elaborate and important Notes (criticized, in some points, by Bp. Kaye) of Dr. Newman'.[42] When revising the translation in 1878, Newman saw this and wrote to Bright to ask what Kaye's criticisms were. Bright replied with the appropriate page numbers, to which Newman responded that Kaye's 'Platonic' Trinity is too divided ever to be One (*LD* xxix. 350).[43] Bright already agreed with Newman that the Son is 'the One God', and so is the Father. Unlike Athanasius's Greek, the English language has no way of differentiating 'God' for the Son and 'the God' for the Father, which explains this translation of Discourse I. 39 in Bright's introduction: 'It was not that the Son was Man, and then became God [Θεός], but that He was God [Θεός], and then became Man.'[44] Athanasius did differentiate the Father and Son, so that only the Father is God with the Greek article (ὁ Θεός), yet

---

[41] e.g., *A History of the Church to* AD *461*, ii. 20 n. 4, regarding Bishop Alexander's phrase 'peerless Image of the Father': 'On its inadequacy, see Newman [*Ath* ii. 370].' Also, *A History of the Church to* AD *461*, ii. 15 n. 3 calls Arius, 'the manner of the expert logician, afterwards so freely cultivated among his followers', citing, among other things, *Ath* ii. 22; *A History of the Church to* AD *461*, ii. 141 n. 8 cites *Ath* ii. 408 on human knowledge of God; and *A History of the Church to* AD *461*, ii. 151 n. 3 defends Athanasius for using *homoiousios* with *Ath* ii. 432–7.

[42] Bright, *Orations of St Athanasius*, p. lxxi n. 2.

[43] Referring to Kaye, *Council of Nicaea*, 246–7 n. 1.

[44] Bright, *Orations of St Athanasius*, p. lxix n. 4.

Bright and Newman in their commentary refused to acknowledge this (in the continuation of the passage, Athanasius wrote first of the Son and then of ὁ Θεός, distinguishing the two; see PG 26: 92 C1–2). On the rare occasions when Athanasius used the article for the Son's divinity he was quoting from only six verses in the New Testament that do so, Bright noting, for instance: 'Athanasius quotes Rom. ix.5 and 1 John v.20 as asserting Christ's Diety; i. 10, iii. 9, &c.'⁴⁵ Of the phrase in Paul's Letter to the Romans 9: 5 (ὁ ὢν πάντων Θεός), Bright mistakenly writes that it appeared in Discourse I. 10 (in fact I. 11), a section in which Athanasius calls the Son 'God *from* God' with no article (ἐκ Θεοῦ Θεός, PG 26: 32), as he did at the end of I. 39, laying stress on the derivation of the Son *of* God. Bright's version of the Greek text is still cited by scholars today, so all who follow his introduction risk conceiving Athanasius's doctrine of the Trinity in terms where each person is 'the one God'.

Bright, like Newman, wanted to play down the derivation of the Son from the Father in Athanasius. Both Oxonians held that a stress on the Son's derivation was found in Origen rather than in Athanasius, a view Archibald Robertson repeated in the 1890s.⁴⁶ But this book has argued that Athanasius was closer to Origen than Newman wanted to accept after 1840. By this stage, Newman began to see the Trinitarian doctrine of the pre-Nicenes as proto-Arian because of their rejection of *homoousios*. Newman's annotations to Athanasius (1842–4) presented the Nicene formula as all that could prevent the Arians from 'destroying the reality of that Fatherhood and Sonship', in the words of Bright.⁴⁷ Writing to Edward Burton in 1834, of course, Newman had seen no problem in the fact that *homoousios* was abandoned by Origen's disciples at the Council of Antioch; it was only in the 1840s, once the word had become Newman's standard of orthodoxy, that he had to explain why Athanasius's Discourses did

---

⁴⁵ Ibid. Karl Rahner points out: 'In St John's First Epistle ὁ Θεός so often certainly means the Father (1: 5–7; 4: 9.10; 4: 15; 5: 9–12; and υἱὸς τοῦ Θεοῦ [αὐτοῦ] in a good dozen instances) that it must be understood of the Father throughout the Epistle... [except] in a last emphatic utterance' ('Theos in the New Testament', *Theological Investigations*, i (Baltimore, Md.: Hellicon, 1965), 137 n.).

⁴⁶ Thus Roberson wrote that in Origen's theology, 'The Son is Θεός, the Father alone ὁ Θεός', NFPF (series 2) 4: xxvi.

⁴⁷ Bright, *Orations of St Athanasius*, p. x, with n. to 'See Newman, Arians, [201], ed. 1871'.

not use it more. Bright credited Newman with observing that 'the "Homoousion", although it occurs, is for the most part "avoided in these discourses" ';[48] although given the continuity in Alexandrian theology of the doctrine of the Father's *monarchia*, Athanasius's reluctance is perhaps not so surprising. Instead of seeing Athanasius as distinctively Alexandrian, however, Newman made him a composite of post-Nicene orthodoxy. Bright accepted the argument in 'On St Cyril's Formula' (which appeared first in the Catholic University's journal *Atlantis* in July 1858 and was excerpted in the 1871 edition of *Arians of the Fourth Century*) that Athanasius like Cyril and the Cappadocians used *ousia* words in 'two aspects'.[49] In other words, Bright agreed with Newman's view of Athanasius in the 1840s and 50s as the originator of the Greek doctrine that followed. Athanasius was also like later Latins for Bright, who thought the patriarch's doctrine 'Comp[arable to] the *Quicunque*', referring to the later Western Creed that he knew to be falsely attributed to Athanasius.[50] Thus, Bright's introduction to the *Orations* in 1873, drawing from Newman's published works to that date, depicted Athanasius's theology as a composite of Greek and Latin post-Nicene doctrine. By the 1870s, Newman's skills in Latin theology had changed the way he translated Athanasius so that the text that he published in 1881 looked more like the doctrine of the *Quicunque* than of an Alexandrian patriarch.

Speaking with wartime patriotism in 1944, in his inaugural lecture as Oxford's Lady Margaret Professor of Divinity, Frank Cross stated the influence of Englishmen—specifically Oxonians—on Athanasian studies. After Martin Routh (whose influence on Newman was seen in the

---

[48] Bright, *Orations of St Athanasius*, p. lxx, quoting *Ox Frs* viii. 210 n. d (Newman actually has, 'for whatever reason Athan[asius] ... avoids the word ὁμοούσιον, in these Discourses'). John Behr has argued that when in the later work, *de Synodis* 51, Athanasius writes that 'the fathers of Nicaea "said that the Son of God was from his essence, reasonably have they spoken of him as *homoousios*" [t]here is, therefore, an intrinsic asymmetry to their relationship: the Son is *from* the essence of the Father; he is the Son *of* God' (*Nicene Faith* i. 244).

[49] Bright writes, 'Generally [Athanasius] makes *hypostasis = ousia*. Dr. Newman, in the 3rd edn. of his "Arians" [432–44], considers that Athanasius did not use the word [hypostasis] in two substantially different senses, but in two aspects (so to speak) of one' (*Orations of St Athanasius*, p. xlvi n. 3).

[50] Bright, *Orations of St Athanasius*, p. xlvi n. 4.

Introduction and in Chapter 3), Cross listed 'John Henry Newman, Charles Marriott, and William Cureton'.[51] Marriott was the hardest working but least known of Newman's fellow editors of A Library of the Fathers, and Cureton discovered a long series of Athanasius's *Festal Epistles*.[52] Yet, among these four patristic scholars, Cross is clear who was pre-eminent on the patriarch: 'There was perhaps no one in any country who, in the first half of the nineteenth century, had a greater knowledge of Athanasius than Newman.'[53] However, this book has forced the question of whether Newman deserves the reputation as first among Athanasians for work done in four short years after 1840? It has been seen that beforehand Newman was probably more knowledgeable about the pre-Nicenes than about Athanasius. If knowledge acquired in a short period of time can lead to such a reputation, then based on his three summers of research in the 1830s Newman could be seen as expert on Dionysius of Alexandria or even Leontius of Byzantium. This book has shown that Cross and many others have swallowed the elderly cardinal's story that Athanasius was 'the great Saint in whose name and history I began to write, and with whom I end' (*Ath* i, p. ix). To take Newman at his word, however, falsely limits his contribution to the way that Greek and Latin Fathers have been understood in the Anglophone world.

[51] Cross, *Study of St Athanasius*, 10.

[52] John Marriott wrote of Charles: 'All who knew him well will remember how laboriously he worked at [the Library], and how, in one shape or another, it was always on hand' (Richard Church, *The Oxford Movement: Twelve Years 1833–1845* (London and New York: Macmillan, 1904), 86 n. 1). Newman challenged Cureton's contention, based on the Syriac text of three of St Ignatius's epistles that he discovered, that they were the only authentic ones, in 'On the Text of the Seven Epistles of Saint Ignatius' (*TT* 95–135). Newman's view has been vindicated.

[53] Cross, *Study of St Athanasius*, 10.

Bibliography

Acton, John, 'Doellinger's Historical Work', *English Historical Review*, 5 (1890), 700–44.

Allchin, A. M., 'The Theological Vision of the Oxford Movement', in John Coulson and A. M. Allchin (eds.), *The Rediscovery of Newman* (London: SPCK, 1967).

Allen, Louis (ed.), *John Henry Newman and the Abbé Jager: A Controversy on Scripture and Tradition 1834–1836* (Oxford: Oxford University Press, 1975).

Anatolios, Khaled, *Athanasius: The Coherence of his Thought* (London: Routledge, 1998).

Arnold, Duane W.-H., *The Early Episcopal Career of Athanasius of Alexandria* (Notre Dame, Ind.: Notre Dame University Press, 1991).

Aubert, Roger, 'Aspects divers du Néo-Thomisme sous le pontificat de Léon XIII', in Guiseppe Rossini (ed.), *Aspetti della Cultura Cattolica nell'Età di Leone XIII* (Rome: Edizioni Cinque Lune, 1961).

Ayres, Lewis, *Nicaea and its Legacy: An Approach to Fourth-Century Trinitarian Theology* (Oxford: Clarendon Press, 2004).

Bardy, G., 'Aux origines de l'école d'Alexandrie', *Recherches de science religieuse*, 27 (1937), 65–90.

Barnes, Michel René, 'De Régnon Reconsidered', *Augustinian Studies*, 26 (1995), 51–79.

—— 'The Fourth Century as Trinitarian Canon', in L. Ayres and G. Jones (eds.), *Christian Origins: Theology, Rhetoric and Community* (London: Routledge, 1998).

Barth, J. Robert., and John L. Mahoney (eds.), *Coleridge, Keats, and the Imagination* (Columbia, Mo.: University of Missouri Press, 1990).

Basnage, Jacques, *Thesaurus Monumentorum Ecclesiasticorum et Historicorum*, i (Antwerp: Wetstenii, 1725).

Beeley, Christopher A., 'Divine Causality and the Monarchy of God the Father in Gregory of Nazianzus', *Harvard Theological Review*, 100 (2007), 199–214.

Behr, John, *The Way to Nicaea* (New York: SVS Press, 2001).

—— *The Nicene Faith*, 2 vols. (New York: SVS Press, 2004).

Berranger, Olivier, 'Pour une lecture théologique de l'histoire chez Newman', in C. Lepelley and P. Veyriras (eds.), *Newman et l'histoire* (Lyons: Presses Universitaires Lyon, 1992).

Bethune-Baker, J. F., *An Introduction to the Early History of Christian Doctrine to the Time of the Council of Chalcedon* (5th edn.; London: Methuen, 1933).

Biemer, Günther, *Newman and Tradition*, trans. K. Smyth (New York: Herder and Herder, 1967).

—— '«Neibuhriser?» L'historiographie selon Newman', in C. Lepelley and P. Veyriras (eds.), *Newman et l'histoire* (Lyons: Presses Universitaires Lyon, 1992).

Bigg, Charles, *The Christian Platonists of Alexandria: Eight Lectures* (Oxford: Clarendon Press, 1886).

Bingham, Joseph, *The Antiquities of the Christian Church: Reprinted from the Original edn.*, 2 vols. (London: Henry G. Bohn, 1845).

Blehl, V. F., 'The Patristic Humanism of John Henry Newman', *Thought*, 50 (1975).

Bowden, John E., *The Life and Letters of Frederick William Faber, D. D.* (London: Thomas Richardson & Son, 1869).

Bright, William, *The Orations of St Athanasius Against the Arians* (Oxford: Clarendon Press, 1873).

—— [Anon.], 'Gwatkin's Studies of Arianism', *Church Quarterly Review*, 16 (1883), 375–402.

Brilioth, Yngve, *The Anglican Revival: Studies in the Oxford Movement* (London: Longmans, 1925).

Butler, Joseph, *The Analogy of Religion, Natural and Revealed, to the Constitution and Course of Nature* (2nd American edn.; Boston, Mass.: David West, 1809).

Burgon, John W., *Lives of Twelve Good Men*, 2 vols. (5th edn.; London: John Murray, 1889).

Burton, Edward, *An Inquiry into the Heresies of the Apostolic Age* (Oxford: Rivingtons, 1829).

—— *Testimonies of the Ante-Nicene Fathers to the Divinity of Christ* (2nd edn.; Oxford: Clarendon Press, 1829).

Canévet, Marriette, 'Newman et l'utilisation de l'histoire dans *Les Ariens du quatrième siècle*: un example, Athanase', in C. Lepelley and P. Veyriras (eds.), *Newman et l'histoire* (Lyons: Presses Universitaires Lyon, 1992).

Chadwick, Owen, *From Bossuet to Newman* (2nd edn.; Cambridge: Cambridge University Press, 1987).

—— *The Spirit of the Oxford Movement: Tractarian Essays* (Cambridge: Cambridge University Press, 1990).

Church, Richard, *The Oxford Movement: Twelve Years 1833–1845* (London and New York: Macmillan, 1904).

Coakley, Sarah, *Powers and Submissions: Spirituality, Philosophy and Gender* (Oxford: Blackwell, 2002).

—— 'What Does Chalcedon Solve and What Does it Not? Some Reflections on the Status and Meaning of the Chalcedonian Definition', in Stephen T. Davies, Daniel Kendall, and Gerald O'Collins (eds.), *The Incarnation* (Oxford: Clarendon Press, 2002).

—— 'Introduction: Disputed Questions in Patristic Trinitarianism', *Harvard Theological Review*, 100 (2007), 125–138.

Coleridge, Samuel T., *Biographia Literaria*, eds. James Engell and W. J. Bate, Bollingen Series LXXV (Princeton, NJ: Princeton University Press, 1984).

Coulson, John, *Newman and the Common Tradition: A Study in the Language of Church and Society* (Oxford: Clarendon Press, 1970).

Cross, F. L., *The Study of St Athanasius: An Inaugural Lecture* (Oxford: Clarendon Press, 1945).

Cross, Richard, 'Individual Natures in the Christology of Leontius of Byzantium', *Journal of Early Christian Studies*, 10 (2002), 245–65.

—— 'On Generic and Derivation Views of God's Trinitarian Substance', *Scottish Journal of Theology*, 56 (2003), 464–80.

—— 'Quid tres? On What Precisely Augustine Professes not to Understand in *De Trinitate* 5 and 7', *Harvard Theological Review*, 100 (2007), 215–32.

Daley, Brian E., 'Nature and the "Mode of Union": Late Patristic Models for the Personal Unity of Christ', in Stephen T. Davies, Daniel Kendall, and Gerald O'Collins (eds.), *The Incarnation* (Oxford: Clarendon Press, 2002).

—— 'Anhypostasy', in Jean-Yves Lacoste, *Encyclopedia of Christian Theology*, i (New York: Routledge, 2005).

—— 'Idioms, Communication of', in Jean-Yves Lacoste, *Encyclopedia of Christian Theology*, ii (New York: Routledge, 2005).

Davis, H. Francis, 'Newman and Thomism', *Newman Studien*, 3 (1957), 157–69.

Dawson, J. D., *Christian Figural Reading and the Fashioning of Identity* (Berkeley, Calif.: University of California Press, 2002).

Dessain, C. S., 'Cardinal Newman and the Eastern Tradition', *Downside Review*, 94 (1976), 83–98.

Dewey, Clive, *The Passing of Barchester* (London and Rio Grande, Ohio: Hambledon Press, 1991).

Dragas, George, 'Conscience and Tradition: Newman and Athanasios in the Orthodox Church', *Newman Studien*, 11 (1980), 73–84.

Edwards, Mark, 'Christ or Plato?', in L. Ayres and G. Jones (eds.), *Christian Origins: Theology, Rhetoric and Community* (London: Routledge, 1998).

Evans, G. R., 'Newman and Aquinas on Assent', *Journal of Theological Studies*, 30 (1979), 202–11.

Faber, G. S., *The Apostolicity of Trinitarianism*, 2 vols. (London: Rivingtons, 1832).

Franzelin, J. B., *Tractatus de Deo Trino secundum personas* (4th edn.; Rome: Typographia Polyglotta, 1895).

Fuller, Reginald, 'The Classical High Church Reaction to the Tractarians', in Geoffrey Rowell (ed.), *Tradition Renewed* (London: Darton, Longman and Todd, 1986).

Garrard, James, 'Archbishop Howley and the Oxford Movement', in Paul Vais (ed.), *From Oxford to the People: Reconsidering Newman and the Oxford Movement* (Leominster: Gracewing, 1996).

Gibbon, Edward, *Rise and Fall of the Roman Empire*, ed. J. B. Bury, ii (2nd edn.; London: Methuen, 1909).

Gilley, Sheridan, *Newman and his Age* (London: Darton, Longman and Todd, 1990).

Gilson, Etienne, Introduction, John Henry Newman, *An Essay Towards a Grammar of Assent* (New York: Image Books, 1955).

Gorce, Denys, *Newman et les Pères* (2nd edn.; Bruges: Editions Charles Beyaert, 1946).

Goslee, David, *Romanticism and the Age of Newman* (Athens, Ohio: Ohio University Press, 1996).

Gregg, R. C., and D. E. Groh, *Early Arianism: A View of Salvation* (Philadelphia, Pa.: Fortress, 1981).

Grillmeier, Aloys, *Christ in Christian Tradition: From the Apostolic Age to Chalcedon (451)*, trans. J. S. Bowden (New York: Sheed and Ward, 1965).

Gunton, Colin, *Theology through the Theologians: Selected Essays* (Edinburgh: T. & T. Clark, 1996).

Gwatkin, H. M., *Studies of Arianism* (2nd edn.; Cambridge: Deighton Bell & Co., 1900).

Gysi, Lydia, *Platonism and Cartesianism in the Philosophy of Ralph Cudworth* (Berne: Herbert Lang, 1962).

Hanson, R. P. C., *The Search for the Christian Doctrine of God* (Edinburgh: T. & T. Clark, 1988).

Harrison, Verna, 'Perichoresis in the Greek Fathers', *St Vladimir's Theological Quarterly*, 35 (1991), 53–65.

Harrold, C. F., 'John Henry Newman and the Alexandrian Platonists', *Modern Philology*, 37 (1940), 279–91.

Heine, Ronald, *Gregory of Nyssa's Treatise on the Inscriptions of the Psalms* (Oxford: Clarendon Press, 1995).

Hennessy, Kristin, 'An Answer to De Régnon's Accusers: Why We Should Not Speak of his Paradigm', *Harvard Theological Review*, 100 (2007), 179–97.

Hilton, Boyd, *The Age of Atonement: The Influence of Evangelicalism on Social and Economic Thought 1795–1865* (Oxford: Clarendon Press, 1988).

Hoegemann, Brigitte Maria, 'Newman and Rome', in Philippe Lefebvre and Colin Mason (eds.), *John Henry Newman in his Time* (Oxford: Family Publications, 2007).

Hooker, Richard, *Of the Laws of Ecclesiastical Polity; and other Works by and about Richard Hooker*, ed. John Keble, R. W. Church, and F. Paget, 3 vols. (Ellicott City, Md.: Via Media, 1994).

Imberg, Rune, *In Quest of Authority: The 'Tracts for the Times' and the Development of the Tractarian Leaders 1833–41* (Lund: Lund University Press, 1987).

Inge, W. R., *Outspoken Essays*, First Series (2nd edn.; London: Longmans, 1921).

Jones, Tod E., *The Broad Church: A Biography of a Movement* (Lanham, Md.: Lexington Books, 2003).

Kaye, John, *The Ecclesiastical History of the Second and Third Centuries, Illustrated from the Writings of Tertullian* (Cambridge: J. Deighton and Son, 1826).

—— *Some Account of the Writings and Opinions of Clement of Alexandria* (London: Rivingtons, 1835).

—— *Some Account of the Council of Nicaea* (London: Rivingtons, 1853).

Kelly, J. N. D., *Early Christian Doctrines* (London: A. and C. Black, 1958).

Ker, Ian, *John Henry Newman: A Biography* (Oxford: Clarendon Press, 1988).

—— *Newman on Being a Christian* (Leominster and Notre Dame, Ind.: Gracewing/University of Notre Dame Press, 1990).

—— 'Newman on the Consensus Fidelium as "The Voice of the Infallible Church"', in Terrence Merrigan and Ian Ker (eds.), *Newman and the Word* (Louvain: Peeters Press, 2000).

—— 'Newman, Councils and Vatican II', in Terrence Merrigan and Ian Ker (eds.), *Newman and Faith* (Louvain: Peeters Press, 2004).

Kerr, Fergus, *After Aquinas: Versions of Thomism* (Oxford: Blackwell, 2002).

Kidd, B. J., *A History of the Church to AD 461*, 3 vols. (Oxford: Clarendon Press, 1922).

King, Karen, *What is Gnosticism?* (Cambridge, Mass.: Harvard University Press, 2003).

Kleutgen, Josef, *La Philosophie scholastique exposée et défendue*, i (Paris: Gaume frères et J. Duprey, 1868).

Kolbet, P. R., 'Athanasius, the Psalms, and the Reformation of the Self', *Harvard Theological Review*, 99 (2006), 85–101.

Lacoste, Jean-Yves (ed.), *Encyclopedia of Christian Theology*, 3 vols. (New York: Routledge, 2005).

Lampe, G. W. H., *A Greek–Patristic Lexicon* (Oxford: Clarendon Press, 1961).

Lash, Nicholas, *Newman on Development: The Search for an Explanation in History* (London: Sheed and Ward, 1975).

—— Introduction, John Henry Newman, *An Essay Towards a Grammar of Assent* (Leominster and Notre Dame, Ind.: Gracewing/University of Notre Dame Press, 1979).

Louth, Andrew, *The Origins of the Christian Mystical Tradition: From Plato to Denys* (Oxford: Clarendon Press, 1981).

—— 'Manhood into God: The Oxford Movement, the Fathers and the Deification of Man', in Rowan D. Williams and Kenneth Leech (eds.), *Essays Catholic and Radical* (London: Bowerdean Press, 1983).

—— 'The Oxford Movement, the Fathers and the Bible', *Sobornost*, 6 (1984), 30–45.

—— *Maximus the Confessor* (London: Routledge, 1996).

Lubac, Henri de, *Scripture in the Tradition*, trans. Luke O'Neill (New York: Herder and Herder, 2000).

—— *History and Spirit: The Understanding of Scripture According to Origen*, trans. A. E. Nash and J. Merriell (San Francisco, Calif.: Ignatius, 2007).

McCool, Gerard, *Catholic Theology in the Nineteenth Century: The Quest for a Unitary Method* (New York: Seabury Press, 1977).

MacDougall, Hugh, *The Acton–Newman Relations: The Dilemma of Christian Liberalism* (New York: Fordham University Press, 1962).

McGrath, Francis, *John Henry Newman: Universal Revelation* (Tunbridge Wells: Burns and Oates, 1997).

—— Introduction, John Henry Newman, *The Church of the Fathers*, Birmingham Oratory Millennium Edition (Leominster and Notre Dame, Ind.: Gracewing/University of Notre Dame Press, 2003).

McGuckin, John A., Introduction, Cyril of Alexandria, *On the Unity of Christ* (Crestwood, NY: SVS Press, 1995).

—— *Saint Cyril of Alexandria and the Christological Controversy* (Crestwood, NY: SVS Press, 2004).

McPartlan, Paul, 'Person' in Jean–Yves Lacoste, *Encyclopedia of Christian Theology*, iii (New York: Routledge, 2005).

McRedmond, Louis, *Thrown among Strangers: John Henry Newman in Ireland* (Dublin: Veritas, 1990).

Magill, G., 'Newman's Personal Reasoning: The Inspiration of the Early Church', *Irish Theological Quarterly*, 52 (1992), 305–13.

Mead, Walter Russell, *God and Gold: Britain, America, and the Making of the Modern World* (New York: Alfred A. Knopf, 2007).

Merrigan, Terrence, 'Newman on Faith in the Trinity', in Terrence Merrigan and Ian Ker (eds.), *Newman and the Word* (Louvain: Peeters Press, 2000).

Meyer, Wendel M., 'The Phial of Blood Controversy and the Decline of the Liberal Catholic Movement', *Journal of Ecclesiastical History*, 46 (1995), 75–94.

Milman, H. H., *The History of Christianity: From the Birth of Christ to the Abolition of Paganism in the Roman Empire*, 3 vols. (London: John Murray, 1840).

Milner, Joseph, *The History of the Church of Christ*, ii (Boston, Mass.: Farrand, Mallory and Co., 1809).

Mozley, James [Anon.], 'An Essay on the Development of Christian Doctrine', *Christian Remembrancer*, 13 (1847), 117–265.

Neale, J. M., *A History of the Holy Eastern Church: The Patriarchate of Antioch (A Posthumous Fragment)* (Piscataway, NJ: Gorgias Press, 2003).

Newsome, David, *Two Classes of Men: Platonism and English Romantic Thought* (London: John Murray, 1974).

Nockles, Peter, *The Oxford Movement in Context: Anglican High Churchmanship 1760–1857* (Cambridge: Cambridge University Press, 1994).

——— ' "Church and King": Tractarian Politics Reappraised', in P. Vais (ed.), *From Oxford to the People: Reconsidering Newman and the Oxford Movement* (Leominster: Gracewing, 1996).

Norris, Richard A., *The Christological Controversy* (Philadelphia, Pa.: Fortress, 1980).

Oldcastle, John, *The Catholic Life and Letters of Cardinal Newman* (London: Burns and Oates, 1885).

Ottley, Robert L., *Lancelot Andrewes* (London: Methuen, 1894).

Palmer, William, *A Narrative of Events Connected with Publication of the Tracts* (rev. edn.; London: Rivingtons, 1883).

Parker, T. M., 'The Rediscovery of the Fathers in the Seventeenth-Century Anglican Tradition', in John Coulson and A. M. Allchin (eds.), *The Rediscovery of Newman: An Oxford Symposium* (London: SPCK, 1967).

Pattison, Robert, *The Great Dissent: John Henry Newman and the Liberal Heresy* (New York: Oxford University Press, 1991).

Perceval, A. P., *Collection of Papers Connected with the Theological Movement of 1833* (London: Rivingtons, 1842).

Pereiro, James, 'S. F. Wood and an Early Theory of Development in the Oxford Movement', *Recusant History*, 20 (1991), 524–53.

—— '*Ethos*' *and the Oxford Movement: At the Heart of Tractarianism* (Oxford: Clarendon Press, 2008).

Peterburs, Wulfstan, 'Scripture, Tradition and Development towards Rome: Some Aspects of the Thought of John Henry Newman', in Philip McCosker (ed.), *What is it that the Scripture Says? Essays in Biblical Interpretation, Translation, and Reception in Honour of Henry Wansbrough OSB* (Edinburgh: T. & T. Clark, 2006).

Prickett, Stephen, *Romanticism and Religion: The Tradition of Coleridge and Wordsworth in the Victorian Church* (Cambridge: Cambridge University Press, 1976).

Quantin, Jean-Louis, 'The Fathers in Seventeenth Century Roman Catholic Theology'; 'The Fathers in Seventeenth Century Anglican Theology', in Irena Backus (ed.), *The Reception of the Church Fathers in the West: From the Carolingians to the Maurists*, ii. (New York: E. J. Brill, 1997).

Rahner, Karl, 'Theos in the New Testament', *Theological Investigations*, i (Baltimore, Md.: Hellicon, 1965).

—— 'Remarks on the Dogmatic Treatise "De Trinitate"', *Theological Investigations*, iv (Baltimore, Md.: Hellicon, 1966).

Régnon, Theodore de, *Études de théologie positive sur la sainte trinité*, i (Paris: Retaux, 1892).

Reynolds, L. D., and N. G. Wilson, *Scribes and Scholars: A Guide to the Transmission of Greek and Latin Literature* (2nd edn.; Oxford: Clarendon Press, 1974).

Richard, Marcel, 'Le Traite "De Sectis" et Léonce de Byzance', *Révue d'histoire ecclésiastique*, 35 (1939), 695–723.

Routh, Martin, *Reliquiae Sacrae*, 5 vols. (New York: Olms, 1974).

Schreiber, Ottis, 'Newman's Revisions', Appendix to J. H. Newman, *An Essay on the Development of Christian Doctrine*, ed. C. F. Harrold (London: Longmans, 1949).

Selby, Robin C., *The Principle of Reserve in the Writings of John Henry Cardinal Newman* (Oxford: Clarendon Press, 1975).

Stead, G. C., 'Rhetorical Method in Athanasius', *Vigiliae Christianae*, 30 (1976), 121–37.

—— *Divine Substance* (Oxford: Clarendon Press, 1977).

Stern, J., *Bible et tradition chez Newman: aux origines de la théorie du développement* (Paris: Aubier, 1967).

Strange, Roderick, *Newman and the Gospel of Christ* (Oxford: Clarendon Press, 1981).

—— 'Newman and the Mystery of Christ', in Ian Ker and Alan G. Hill (eds.), *Newman after One Hundred Years* (Oxford: Clarendon Press, 1990).

Suicer, Johann Kaspar, *Thesaurus Ecclesiasticus*, 2 vols. (Amsterdam: Westenium, 1728).

Sykes, S. W., 'Newman, Anglicanism, and the Fundamentals', in Ian Ker and Alan G. Hill (eds.), *Newman after One Hundred Years* (Oxford: Clarendon Press, 1990).

Thomas, Stephen, *Newman and Heresy: The Anglican Years* (Cambridge: Cambridge University Press, 1991).

Tillemont, Louis-Sébastien le Nain de, *Mémoires pour servir à l'histoire ecclésiastique des six premiers siècles*, iii–vii. (2nd edn.; Paris: Charles Robustel, 1701–6).

Tokarsik, G., 'John Henry Newman and the Church Fathers', *Eastern Churches Journal*, 7 (2000), 101–16.

Tolhurst, James, Introduction, John Henry Newman, *Discussions and Arguments on Various Subjects*, Birmingham Oratory Millennium Edition (Leominster and Notre Dame, Ind.: Gracewing/University of Notre Dame Press, 2004).

Toon, Peter, *Evangelical Theology, 1833–1856: A Response to Tractarianism* (London: Marshall, Morgan and Scott, 1979).

Turner, Frank, *John Henry Newman: The Challenge to Evangelical Religion* (New Haven, Conn.: Yale University Press, 2002).

Vargish, Thomas, *Newman: The Contemplation of Mind* (Oxford: Clarendon Press, 1970).

Walsh, J. D., 'Joseph Milner's Evangelical Church History', *Journal of Ecclesiastical History*, 10 (1959), 174–87.

Walsh, Nicholas, *John Baptist Franzelin, SJ, Cardinal Priest of the Title SS. Boniface and Alexius: A Sketch and a Study* (Dublin: M. H. Gill and Son, 1895).

Ward, Benedicta, 'A Tractarian Inheritance: The Religious Life in a Patristic Perspective', in Geoffrey Rowell (ed.), *Tradition Renewed* (London: Darton, Longman and Todd, 1986).

Ward, Wilfrid, *The Life of John Henry Cardinal Newman*, 2 vols. (London: Longmans, 1912).

Waterland, Daniel, *A Critical History of the Athanasian Creed*, ed. J. R. King (Oxford and London: James Parker and Company, 1870).

Waterman, A. M. C., 'A Cambridge "Via Media" in Late Georgian Anglicanism', *Journal of Ecclesiastical History*, 42 (1991).

Weinandy, Thomas, *Does God Suffer?* (Edinburgh: T. & T. Clark, 2000).

Whately, Richard, *Elements of Logic, Comprising the Substance of the Article in the Encyclopaedia Metropolitana* (4th edn.; London: B. Fellowes, 1831).

Wheeler, Robin, *Palmer's Progress: The Life of William Palmer of Magdalen* (Berne: Peter Lang, 2006).

Wiles, Maurice, *Working Papers in Doctrine* (London: Student Christian Movement, 1976).

—— *Archetypal Heresy: Arianism through the Centuries* (Oxford: Clarendon Press, 1996).

Williams, George H., 'Christology and Church–State relations in the Fourth Century', *Church History*, 20/3 (1951), 3–33; 20/4 (1951), 3–26.

Williams, Rowan D., 'Person and Personality in Christology', *Downside Review*, 94 (1976), 253–60.

—— 'Newman's *Arians* and the Question of Method in Doctrinal History', in Ian Ker and Alan G. Hill (eds.), *Newman after One Hundred Years* (Oxford: Clarendon Press, 1990).

—— 'Doctrinal Criticism: Some Questions', in Sarah Coakley and David Pailin, *The Making and Remaking of Christian Doctrine* (Oxford: Clarendon Press, 1993).

—— 'Origen: Between Orthodoxy and Heresy', in W. A. Bienert and U. Kühneweg (eds.), *Origeniana Septima* (Louvain: Peeters Press, 1999).

—— *Arius* (2nd edn.; London: Student Christian Movement, 2001).

—— Introduction, John Henry Newman, *The Arians of the Fourth Century*, Birmingham Oratory Millennium Edition (Leominster and Notre Dame, Ind.: Gracewing/University of Notre Dame Press, 2001).

Young, Frances M., *From Nicaea to Chalcedon: A Guide to the Literature and its Background* (London: Student Christian Movement, 1983).

—— *Biblical Exegesis and the Formation of Christian Culture* (Cambridge: Cambridge University Press, 1997).

—— 'Proverbs 8 in Interpretation (2): Wisdom Personified; Fourth-century Christian Readings: Assumptions and Debates', in D. F. Ford and G. Stanton (eds.), *Reading Texts, Seeking Wisdom: Scripture and Theology* (London: Student Christian Movement, 2003).

Glossary

APOLLINARIANISM: a heresy named for Apollinarius (or Apollinaris, *c.*310–*c.*390), a friend of Athanasius who seems to have taught that the Word of God took the place of a soul/mind in the incarnate Christ. Apollinarius's opponents, however, asked how Jesus could be fully human if he had no human soul; they were concerned that a Christ who was not fully human as well as fully divine could not save humanity.

APOSTOLIC SUCCESSION: the early Church underscored the legitimacy of its ministry and teaching by saying that bishop handed on to bishop, in a line of uninterrupted succession, the commission that Jesus gave to the first apostles.

ARIANISM: a heresy named for Arius (*c.*250–*c.*336), an Alexandrian priest who, in asserting the unity and unknowability of God, taught that the Son of God was a creature. Moreover, because God created the Son, there "was [a time] when he was not". Although no group claimed Arius as their leader, Athanasius used the title "Arians" to describe various theologies opposed to the Nicene Creed's description of the Son as *homoousios* (q.v.) with the Father.

CHURCH COUNCILS: over the course of Christian history, certain gatherings of bishops and their representatives have been seen to be more authoritative than others in matters of Church law and teaching. Councils come together to judge certain questions; but then it remains for the Church to judge which councils are authoritative. The most important councils have been called "Ecumenical" (derived from the Greek for "the whole inhabited world"), beginning with the first Council of Nicaea (325).

COETERNAL: the teaching that Son and Spirit are fully one with the Father from all eternity.

COMMUNICATION OF IDIOMS: the teaching that, as a result of the union of human and divine natures in the person (hypostasis) of Christ, it is appropriate to "communicate" divine properties (idioms) to his person while speaking of his human nature, and likewise to "communicate" human properties while speaking of his divine nature. For example, "the Lord of glory was crucified" and "the Son of Man ascended into heaven".

CONSUBSTANTIAL: the teaching that Son and Spirit are "of the same substance" or being (*homoousios*, q.v.) as God the Father.

DONATISM: a heresy named for Donatus, the fourth-century bishop who was consecrated as a rival to the bishop of Carthage and thus brought division ("schism") to the African Church. Donatus's claim that the other bishop was improperly consecrated was based upon a rigorist position that the Church must not accept certain sorts of sinners back into its fold.

EBIONITISM: a very early heresy often grouped with that named for Cerinthus, both heresies teaching that Jesus was the human son of Mary and Joseph before the Holy Spirit came upon him at baptism. Some Fathers (and later commentators) thought Ebionitism was named for Ebion, but the name came from the Hebrew for "poor men" because this sect lived under strict ascetical discipline derived from the Jewish Law.

GENERICAL UNITY: a term used by seventeenth-century Anglican theologians who recognised that for Father, Son and Spirit to be "one" could mean different things. Generical unity describes the oneness of sharing the same substance (*ousia*). Conceiving the divine substance as resembling an Aristotelian "universal", this described God's unity as that of a genus held in common by three hypostases. Seventeenth-century Anglicans said that the Greek Fathers favoured generical unity to describe God, whereas the Latin Fathers favoured numerical unity (q.v.).

GEN(N)ESIS: a theological term for the coming-to-be of the Son from the Father. The two spellings of the term derive from two Greek verbs, *ginomai* "to become" and *gennaō* "to beget".

HOMOOUSIOS: a non-scriptural term meaning literally "of the same substance", *homoousios* gained theological resonance when it was used to express the unity of the Father and Son in discussions before and after Nicaea. There was initial disagreement about whether it was an appropriate term to describe the being of God, given that "*ousia*" could suggest material substance. Further disagreement arose over whether Father and Son were of the same substance or rather "of like substance" (*homoiousios*, q.v.).

HOMOIOUSIOS: a non-scriptural term meaning literally "of like substance," suggested after the Council of Nicaea as an alternative description for the relation of Father to Son. Although some of the upholders of Nicaea were not unfriendly to this term, it was rejected by those (the Homoeans) who claimed no more than that the Son was "like" the Father, and those (the Anomoeans) who saw the Father and the Son as "unlike" in substance.

HYPOSTATIC UNION: Cyril of Alexandria's expression for the unity of divine and human in Christ, in which the Son of God was the hypostasis ("person" but not in the human sense) who, in the incarnation, united full humanity with himself.

IMPASSIBILITY: the divine property of not being able to suffer or change.

MANICHAEISM: a heresy named for Mani, a third-century Persian teacher, who is thought to have blended ideas from Zoroastrianism, Buddhism and Christianity. Although we know little about Mani, Manichaeism is considered the archetypal "dualistic" heresy for dividing the world into spirit and matter, light and darkness. The Elect, through their ascetic rigour, aimed to release the particles of light trapped within their bodies.

MODALISM: a heresy teaching that Father, Son and Spirit were successive "modes" by which the one God was revealed. Versions of this heresy were attributed, among others, to those who taught Monarchianism (taking to an extreme the doctrine of *monarchia*, q.v.), and Sabellianism (q.v.).

MONOPHYSITISM: a heresy named for the teaching that Christ had "one nature" after his incarnation. The heresy took many forms after Eutyches, a friend of Cyril of Alexandria, was condemned at the Council of Chalcedon for his version of Monophysitism.

MONARCHIA: the teaching that emphasizes the primacy of God the Father as the One God from whom the Son and Spirit are derived. Such a teaching was integral to orthodoxy for—among others—Origen, Athanasius, and Gregory of Nazianzus, for whom the Father was the God (*ho theos*) and the Son was God (*theos*).

NEOPLATONISM: the successor of the philosophies that sprung from Plato (427–347 B.C.) and the "Middle Platonists" like Philo of Alexandria (*c.*20 B.C.–*c.* A.D. 50), various forms of Neoplatonism arose across the late-antique world from the third century onwards. Typically, Neoplatonism made God utterly transcendent, and thus beyond being, while conceiving of reality as a vast hierarchy of being that emanated from God. The most famous Neoplatonist, Plotinus (*c.* 205–70), studied in Origen's Alexandria before going to teach in Rome.

NESTORIANISM: a heresy named for Nestorius (d. *c.*451), a monk in Antioch and later bishop of Constantinople, who was condemned at the Council of Ephesus. He taught that Mary could not be described as "God-bearer" because she only gave birth to Christ's humanity not his divinity. He therefore taught two Sons in Christ—Son of God and Son of Mary.

NUMERICAL UNITY: a term used by seventeenth-century Anglican theologians who recognised that for Father, Son and Spirit to be "one" could mean different things. Numerical unity is the oneness that can be counted, rather than oneness that can be shared (generical unity, q.v.). This means that Father, Son and Spirit are the same individual, where "individual" means undivided internally and divided from everything else.

PERICHORESIS: a term describing the unity of God as a mutual indwelling of the three divine persons in one another. Newman thought it to be a very early teaching of the Church, complementing the *monarchia* (q.v.) by showing how the persons of the Son and Spirit might dwell in the God (*ho theos*) who is called Father. Scholars today, however, recognize that the term *perichoresis* itself, translated as "interpenetration," was originally used of the two natures in Christ and not of relations within the Trinity.

RULE OF FAITH (*REGULA FIDEI*): the authoritative tradition by which the true sense of scripture could be interpreted in line with the beliefs that early Christians professed in their baptismal creeds. In the second century, Ireneaus explained the word "rule" (*kanōn* in Greek) in the same way as Aristotle, who had said the carpenter's rule was used "discern both the straight and the crooked": the baptismal creed provided the rule of faith by which interpretations of scripture were judged straight or crooked.

SABELLIANISM: also known as Modalism (q.v.), this heresy is named for Sabellius, a third-century theologian of whom little is known, but who probably denied the distinctness of the three divine persons and preferred to speak of three "modes" in which God is successively known. Although Newman and his contemporaries drew parallels between this ancient heresy and modern Unitarianism or Socinianism (named for Faustus Socinus, leader of the anti-Trinitarian party among sixteenth-century Reformers), the latter was the product of Reformation and not patristic debates.

SEMI-ARIANISM: a much later name used to describe the position taken by those in the fourth century who rejected the teaching of the Nicene Creed in favour of describing the Son as "of like substance" (*homoiousios*, q.v.) with the Father.

SUBORDINATIONISM: as a result of the teaching of the *monarchia* (q.v.), the Son and Spirit may be understood as somehow inferior—or "subordinate"—to the Father. "Subordinationism" is a later term used to label such an understanding as heretical, employed by Newman when he came to deny the subordination of the Son. By contrast, Anglicans from the seventeenth-century onwards tended to accept both that the Son was subordinate and also that he was coeternal (q.v.) with the Father, thus avoiding the teaching of Arianism (q.v.) that there "was [a time] when he was not".

Index